DON'T STOP THE CARNIVAL

D1388495

KEVIN LE GENDRE

DON'T STOP THE CARNIVAL
BLACK MUSIC IN BRITAIN
VOLUME 1

PEEPAL TREE

First published in Great Britain in 2018
Peepal Tree Press Ltd
17 King's Avenue
Leeds LS6 1QS
UK

Printed & bound by Imprintdigital.com, UK

© Kevin Le Gendre, 2018

ISBN 13: 978-1-84523-361-7

Supported using public funding by
ARTS COUNCIL
ENGLAND

CONTENTS

For Conrad Zeno Le Gendre,
a West Indian ex-serviceman

INTRODUCTION

BLACK BRITAIN, IN SOUND, SIGHT AND DEED.

In early 2018, the UK national press carried the story of the facial reconstruction of one of the earliest known inhabitants of Britain. DNA analysis carried out by researchers from the Natural History Museum of a skeleton that dated back at least 10,000 years produced results that unceremoniously overturned long-held assumptions about the ancestry of the nation. Or at least what it looked like.

"Cheddar Man" was black. Whether this was a quirk of evolution or a reminder that modern science needs to look as far back as it does forward, the discovery raised no end of debate. If the "first Briton" was actually not white, then what does that say about successive generations down to today? Is there a spook haunting the family house rather than just sitting by the door?

National identity remains a concern in societies all over the world, and Britain is no different, especially when some politicians and media are wilfully advancing the notion of a distinct, unexpurgated British Britain, a "Britain first" or, as Eurosceptics trumpet, a Britain that craves and deserves its "independence". Freedom from the fair-skinned technocrats of Europe as well as from the onslaught of dark-skinned migrants from Africa, or even, in the 70th anniversary of the arrival of Empire Windrush, a hunt to find and expel elderly West Indians who have lived and worked in the UK for fifty years, but don't have the requisite papers.

The existence of an ancestor, or an indigenous inhabitant with roots running so deep that it turns racially polarized stereotypes on their heads, cannot but strengthen the case for asking who exactly we are, and from where we might have come. UCL geneticist Mark Thomas was forthright on the value of "Cheddar Man" in the context of education and cultural awareness. "If it becomes a part of our understanding then I think that would be a much better thing. I think it would be good if people lodge it in their heads, and it becomes a little part of their knowledge."

This should force us to ask: how much do we really know about the peoples of Britain and their journey through the ages? Cast against the emblematic backdrop of the Union Jack, the flag that was flown proudly around the world to denote the expansion of England beyond its original borders, the perception of our population as mono-racial, a comforting 'we' before a discomfiting 'they', has long looked absurd.

In keeping with the way historians and scientists continue to bring vital new information to light on the real complexity of the past, *Don't Stop The Carnival* is based on the premise that tracing the lives that black people in, and of, Britain may have led, and the forms of cultural expression they devised, can make a contribution to our understanding of the past as not just multi-faceted, but decisive in its contribution to the present. As a pervasive, dynamic, and often exhilarating artform, music has always been an outlet for the imagination of people of vastly differing circumstance, whether from a privileged elite or from a disenfranchised working class. The goal of this book is to put under the spotlight as large a cross-section as possible of the music makers in British history who have been classified according to a range of terms: Negro, coloured, African, Ethiopian, Black American, West Indian, Caribbean. Of course, the geographical range of musics that have arrived in Britain and taken root here is wider than this. However, because the cut-off point in time for this first volume, of what is intended as a two-part study, is the mid-1960s, it does not deal with the emergence of music whose origins were the South Asian continent, the home-grown phenomenon of bhangra, for instance, in the 1980s.

All of the various epithets noted above reflect the whimsical lexicological shifts through time with regard to the naming and position in society of those who are perceived as the racial "other". To this day, the chess-playing with words continues. BAME – Black And Minority Ethnic – is an official designation of communities in Britain who to all intents and purposes, trace their roots elsewhere and stand connected to another part of the world, which for the most part, means areas of the globe formerly known as the colonies or overseas territories, or even the "dark continent", lands that were once part of a UK plc, constructed on conquest and lucrative dominion.

If the assets of the Caribbean islands and African states included such valuable commodities as sugar, cotton, cocoa and tropical fruits, and oil and minerals, then the export of their human resources has been equally important in the enrichment of the British national heritage. These were people who came to take up arms and fight wars for the "mother country", who served for instance in the NHS, the transport system, on ships, in factories, and – the subject of this book – in the entertainment and cultural "industries". These people brought with them sound as well as word and deed, and my focus is on the immense range of creative output and its roots in the quotidian experiences of these arrivants and settlers, who were recipients, variously, of adulation and disdain, lightning rods for complex, and often contradictory feelings about what actually constituted entertainment, art, culture, decorum, the emotionally and sexually exciting and the socially acceptable. Music played by Blacks asked questions about what it meant to be a human being, to exist in the world, to stand alongside others, to broach questions of freedom, family, friendship and fidelity, to have trouble in mind as well as joy in one's heart. There is a deep repository of stories about black musicians in Britain over time, from the minstrels and trumpeters of Tudor times, the street entertainers of the eighteenth and nineteenth centuries, the skilful practitioners of western classical music, the exponents of gospel and blues, the forerunners and innovators of what became marketed as jazz, and the pioneers of calypso, ska and high life. Then there are the champions of the idioms built on those ground-breaking foundations: rhythm & blues, soul, rock and rocksteady. The constant is change. The sound moves on. The instruments with which the sound is made also evolve.

All this points to the fact that music made by Blacks in Britain has never been one thing, and we can only understand its artistic scope and social ramifications if we embrace its multiplicity. Part of the creative momentum underpinning musical development has always been its proximity to other forms, including dance, cinema, theatre, literature and even the visual arts. This constant interconnectedness and cross-fertilization makes the story of Black music in Britain all the more vital. What and how a musician plays, the gestures they adopt on stage and the language used all connect to this wider cultural milieu.

With voices came instruments – drums, strings, wind instruments of brass and wood. But there were also devices that did not fit into any existing western musical conventions. There were adaptations, if not adulterations, of percussion instruments, the use of sundry objects assembled for the purpose of rhythm that were initially subjected to the long arm of censure before enjoying the embrace of approval. The development of a music of passion, even of an explosive violence of sound, was part of a spirit of invention – the ability to see something mundane as a blueprint for something ingenious – the genius to make music from what, according to the norms of the day, was condemned as anti-musical. For defenders of received ideas about British or European culture, the music of the non-west was often perceived as noise.

Yet, over time, black people holding strange things from which they 'magicked' original music, or invigorating song and dance, have become an integral part of the musical history of Britain. Musicians, lest we forget, are also members of society, and their human story, regardless of any elevated status a small minority enjoyed, is not separate from the stories of their peers who earned their daily bread less glamorously. An immigrant musician is still an immigrant. A black musician is still a black man or woman. They could be visible and esteemed providers of pleasure and invisible outsiders at the same time. Get in, stand under the lights, get out by the servants' door.

There is no way the story of Black music in Britain can be told without recognising its context of racial discrimination, the arc of which stretches over centuries rather than decades. This has provided a bitter undertaste to all the sweetness of Black sounds filling our green and pleasant land. No portrait of a singer or player would be complete without an insight into the litany of prejudice they encountered – the xenophobia of "swampings" and "invasion", fear of miscegenation and job loss, the moral panics over the alleged erosion of civilized values, and the actual occurrence of insult, bodily harm, murder, eviction from the home and dismissal from the workplace. All this inevitably became a part of the musicians' chronicles, not least because they made their music in conscious response to this state of affairs.

To do justice to these histories requires the broadest possible vision of Britain. Not an account of events and life stories in a single location, but a trek from north to south and east to west. In real terms, this means the Black experience in Birmingham, Bristol, Cardiff, Cornwall, Glasgow, Leeds, Liverpool and Manchester, as well as London, all key locations for the growth of Black populations as well as Black artistry. Black music in Britain really is just that: a national rather than a local or even exclusively metropolitan phenomenon, a wellspring of talent that has not been confined to a single place or time. This reflects the fact that Black people have existed in Britain in a variety of circumstances that are not reducible to the cliché of fast living under the neon lights of the sprawling capital.

Although the existence of Black ghettoes in some of the above locations has been a regrettable reality, people of colour have never been entirely isolated from mainstream white communities, and as social relations have crossed racial lines, so have musical collaborations. Music created and developed by black people has been played by whites for at least the past hundred and fifty years, leading to varying degrees of conflict over issues of ownership, copyright, remuneration and authenticity. However, the interaction has been extensive and the prevalence of both racially mixed groups and white ensembles drawing on Black culture to varying degrees forms a vital subtext to the central narrative of Black music performed by black musicians.

Distinctions between black and white bands, certainly in the 19th and early 20th centuries, were often firmly entrenched on either side of the Atlantic, but by the 1930s the racial borders in music were crossed with greater regularity. This was a much more rewarding development than the phenomenon of the repackaging of the work of a black artist by a cynical and bigoted music industry using a white artist, who is perceived as less threatening and more palatable to a majority white audience.

There is, in the case of Britain's record industry, in existence for around one hundred years, an additional and often fascinating strand to the story. There is the actual physical journey of songs through time and space that we can still hear, that sound across the changes in the nation's status from colonial to post-colonial times, music which reflects shifts in language as well as instrumentation, that gradually makes the passage from the exotic to the home-grown. The story of calypso as once only a Trinidadian form that became part of the music of popular British culture in the 1950s is one such instance.

By critiquing and celebrating these odysseys in sound we are able to ask and hopefully answer some questions about the role of music in a society at different stages of cultural transformation. Blues, jazz and calypso have incredibly rich vocabularies, a database of sound and word, that hold up a mirror to the world, and provide insights into human nature shaped by actual lived events, whether that be the euphoria of carnival or the oppressive policing of it.

But this is not just a story of the meeting between black and white, or of music in Britain seen as an isolated country. Part of the story of the post-second World War migrations to the imperial centre was the meeting of musicians from those then colonies: West Indians, Ethiopians, West Africans and South Africans all played together and influenced each others' musical languages. And even before these colonial migrations, the story of Black British music is always one of trans-Atlantic exchange – what Paul Gilroy named the Black Atlantic – as musical birds of passage from the USA sometimes became long-term stayers or even permanent residents, but invariably left their imprint of British musical culture. These encounters are of the greatest interest to me.

Calculating how many sounds fall under the umbrella of Black music made in Britain is a nigh impossible task. Songs and music were being performed long before the birth of the modern music industry and the large-scale manufacture and distribution of commercial recordings. Nevertheless, in the early part of my study, I make what I hope are insightful observations on the basis of available written material on the lives of singers and players who at some level secured their place in history. It was the technology of sound reproduction, the 78 rpm gramophone disc that evolved into the 33 rpm album and 45 rpm single, which brought new convenience for consumers, as well as sizeable profits for producers, that offers a significantly broader database and scope of inquiry. Scores of recordings made from the turn of the 20th century onwards provide us with a wealth of evidence to examine and interpret.

Two horrific world wars formed a bloody background to this period of relentless, frenetic musical experimentation and sustained mutations in the frameworks and agencies that played the role of gatekeepers in recording and distributing music.

The advent of new media such as radio as well as the arrival of television makes the post-1945 period one of the utmost importance and proportionately more of the book is devoted to it. It was a time of recovery, of re-evaluation after the blood-letting of the war and particularly of dealing with the UK's changed status as Empire ended and independence came to former colonies. Mass migration from the Caribbean was only one of a series of fundamental jolts to British society, and the music of black musicians, and sometimes its cross-over into the work of white music-makers, provides some of the most sensitive antennae to pick up these social and cultural changes. It is another reason why, to make this study as illuminating as possible, I have chosen not to look at the work of artists beyond the late 1960s; I did not want to sacrifice analytical depth for the sake of bringing the narrative up to the present. What has happened since the 1960s has been equally noteworthy and, to my mind, deserves an in-depth examination by way of a second instalment. There is, I believe, much in the period I have written about that still informs music today.

We still live in times when people leave one territory to settle in another in precarious circumstances; when attack-dog popular newspaper editors still engage in political scaremongering about the threat to "ways of life", and flash teeth with the kind of pearly-white menace Louis Armstrong evoked in the immortal "Mack The Knife". Party like it's 1918? Or 1948? Or 2018? The choice is yours. Good songs are great time travellers.

Vocal versions of this song by Louis Armstrong and Ella Fitzgerald, to name a couple, are timeless, as is the instrumental rendition by saxophonist Sonny Rollins ("Moritat"). The continuum of Black music, brought to life with and without words, is fundamental to my story. But this is a story that goes back to the British 18th century, because Bertolt Brecht's and Elizabeth Hauptmann's play the *Three Penny Opera* (from which comes "Mack the Knife", the melody written by Brecht's great collaborator, Kurt Weill) was inspired by John Gay's, *The Beggar's Opera*, which premièred in 1728, introducing the characters of Macheath, the Peachums and Vixen, among others. As I have noted in the book, this was a time when enslaved black children were bought as decorations for rich households, but also when black street performers became part of the everyday scenery.

Just recently, the *Three Penny Opera* ran at the National Theatre in 2016, adapted to reflect the Britain of recent times. Its depiction of a world mired in poverty, immorality and corruption resonated with the widespread public contempt for a political and business class besmirched by sleaze and expenses scandals, insider trading and financial market manipulation. This was another instance of old stories coming back home, adorned in new clothing and inflected with new accents and rhythms.

At the time of the NT production, the call for diversity in the arts had reached a fever pitch, with echoes of the "Oscars So White" campaign ringing in the ears of anybody interested in real social equality. It was a sign of the continuities with the period I have written about that the presence of black performers in the cast still had to be noticed. Chief among them was the pivotal figure of the balladeer, played by George Ikediashi, whose rendition of "Mack The Knife" and other songs was exemplary.

Apart from *Three Penny Opera*, Ikediashi has a hugely impressive list of credits that straddles the worlds of opera and theatre, from *La Traviata* to *Porgy and Bess* to *Anxiety Fanfare*, and takes his place in a long lineage of black singer-performers who have trodden the boards in works reaching right back to *Showboat* in the 1920s.

An ex-law student who grew up in Nigeria before moving to Britain, Ikediashi became a national sensation in 2010 when his version of Iggy Pop's "The Passenger", captured by hidden cameras at Heathrow's Terminal 5, was selected by T-Mobile for one of its television adverts. That the performance should have taken place in an airport, a gateway for past, present and future generations of black musicians, was fitting.

Ikediashi embodies a uniqueness that chimes with many artists discussed in *Don't Stop The Carnival*. He has a provocative cabaret alter ego called Le Gateau Chocolat. It is larger than lycra, a nouveau black sweet to the ancient savoury of Cheddar Man.

Seven Sisters,
London,
February, 2018.

1 DRUMMING UP BUSINESS

These blacks – as they were designated on the muster rolls – displayed great ability and agility in the handling of their 'tools', as Wagner would have said.

— Henry George Farmer

Perched on metal stands, thin and straight as a stork's legs, the silver half-circles of the steel drum can sometimes be heard on the concourses of shopping centres from Kent to Yorkshire, Lancashire to Essex, Sussex to Tyneside. People may stop and listen to a lone 'pan man' on a pavement. They might throw a coin into the leather basket which serves as a carrying case for the instrument, which was initially much maligned when its homeland of Trinidad was under British rule.

It is also not uncommon for bigger bands, steel orchestras, to play an afternoon programme of soothing Yuletide themes as shoppers enter Westfield or Bluewater on Christmas eve to secure last minute gifts. Pan is a staple of the urban consumer experience in the UK.

A competent player will play anything from mainstream pop, jazz or calypso. Music by Sparrow, Kitchener, Miles Davis, The Police, Gnarls Berkeley or Billy Ocean may be supplemented by improvisations that highlight the tonal richness of the instrument, which, when played well, can attain the warmth of a church organ or the piercing clarity of a vibraphone.

If not every Briton has seen a pan player on the street, there can be few who have not watched the spectacle of a steel band on TV during the Notting Hill carnival – "Europe's biggest street party". Many children have experienced pan workshops in their schools. There are pan groups of pupils in Seven Sisters, North London and pan groups of pensioners in Gateshead, in Tyneside.

Now a national phenomenon, steel pan is an emblem of something distinctive in the cultural life of the UK that came from outside. Most associate its arrival with mass migration from the Caribbean beginning in the late 1940s, part of our national culture shaped by the arrival of people of colour.

But pan is not the beginning of the story, and this book sets out to answer the question about when, how and with what effects black musicians reached these shores. Even so, the lone pan man who busks on the street is a good place to start. Busking implies entertainment by performers who are generally unknown, rarely documented, and the paving stone on which they stand is anything but spotlit. For the most part, theirs is a hidden history and this book sets out to uncover what can still be found, remembering that much is forever lost to view. Black street musicians are a significant part of the story.

How far back does the story go? Who were the first musicians to be seen and heard on these shores? What instruments did they play? What were the first melodies, harmonies and rhythms brought to life by the hands, feet and breath of earlier black arrivals in Britain?

One thinks of jazz trumpeters in the 1920s and 1930s, gospel singers in the 1890s, or maybe fiddlers in the 18th century, but what of Africans at the time of the Roman Occupation?

There is convincing evidence of a black presence in Britain during the Roman Occupation, quite probably North Africans enlisted in the legions (dispatched to 'civilize' the local unruly tribes), who may well have brought their music with them. Indeed, documentation for this period is much better than for the 'Dark Ages' after the Romans left, when a researcher intent on uncovering the presence of the first black musicians in Britain hits silence rather than sound.

For the earlier period there is written evidence, albeit sketchy, of the lives of the earliest arrivals from Africa, a vast territory, whose cultural and ethnic spectrum is so wide that qualification is required when identifying an individual as an African. The differences between North and South Africa are as marked as those between East and West; Tunisians, Nigerians, Ethiopians and Ghanaians: the diversity is immense.

The Romans in Britain had access to peoples from around the world, and many were co-opted for military service. In *Staying Power, The History of Black People in Britain*, Peter Fryer notes that 'Among the troops defending Hadrian's wall in the third century AD was a "division of Moors" [*numerus Maurorum Aurelianorum*]from North Africa. This unit was stationed at Aballava, now Burgh by Sands, near Carlisle.'[1]

The word 'Moor' has been enshrined in the English language by way of Shakespeare's powerful tragedy, but before we picture Ira Aldridge, the legendary 19th century London-based African-American stage actor (or latterly Chiwetel Ejiofor) in the title role of *Othello,* we should clarify what is meant by the term. It referred to the inhabitants of a vast geographical region rather than a single country, covering Morocco, Western Algeria, Western Sahara, Sicily, Malta and that part of the Iberian Peninsula once known as Al-Andalus. In the popular imagination, the Moors were Muslims against whom valiant Christian crusaders waged war in the Middle Ages. But their existence reached much further back in time. Classical literature tells us that the Romans led military campaigns to Mauritania as early as the second century AD, which is why there could have been Moorish soldiers enlisted in the Roman legions sent to retain control over British territory, whose conquest began in AD 43.

Ethnically, the Moors were Arabic or African. Whilst this is sketchy and imprecise, what mattered in Britain was that the Moors were *not* white. They did not look like the Romans, Celts, Norsemen, Angles, Saxons or other people who inhabited early Europe. Moor, which may be an adaptation of the Latin word *Mauri*, became common currency in Britain over time and the orthographical variation of Mor, More and Moore reflects its passage into the formal written language.

While the presence of Africans in Roman army units appears an historical fact, there are no accounts of how the Moors acquitted themselves in service, what responsibilities they shouldered, or what relationship they may have had with their Roman colleagues, how they were regarded by the native Britons or what became of them after the fall of the empire in 410 AD.

What is known is that the Romans used brass instruments as a means of communication. The straight trumpets and tubas, *cornu* – g-shaped with a supporting bar between the two curves – and *buccina* (a smaller cornu) sounded the orders of charge and retreat, gave signals to adopt a specific battle formation, and featured in grand victory parades and funeral processions. Military historians think that the different units or divisions of the Roman army was each assigned at least two or three drummers or horn players, so it is very likely that a division of Moors – of some 500 persons – would have had musicians.[2]

Between the fifth and eleventh century, there came wave after wave of invasions from Frisians, Saxons, Angles, Jutes, Danes, Norwegians and the Normans who landed in 1066. How many Moors might have remained in Britain during that period is something on which historians cannot agree. Some take the view that there were very few. Others believe there was a residual community from Roman times, perhaps bolstered by the arrival of Moors from parts of Spain, Portugal and France.

Moorish culture, and music in particular, exerted an influence on Spain and Europe that survives to this day. What is considered to be classical Andalusian music has its roots in Arabic music introduced in the 9th century, when Cordoba was a caliphate. There is evidence that by the 11th century a wide variety of string instruments such as the oud, rabab quithara and naquereh were all in fairly regular use. Knights returning from the crusades carried some of these devices back to England, but what also furthered their dissemination were minstrels, itinerant musicians who criss-crossed the land performing for king and queen at court, the lord and lady of the manor as well as the serfs in the public square or the market place.

The term "minstrel", derived from the word *menestrellus*, did not particularly denote a singer or player of an instrument. Originally meaning a minor court servant, the term encompassed entertainers of all kinds – acrobats, dancers, jugglers, actors, conjurers, puppeteers, oral poets and tellers of tales.[3] The Register of Royal and Baronial minstrels in the 13th century mentions Conrad the geige player, Gillot the harper, Bestrude the vieille player as well as numerous players of the tabor, a small hand drum. Minstrelsy was not an exclusively male occupation. Mathilda, a saltatrix – acrobat or tumbler – appeared at a 1306 Pentecostal feast. There was no rigid separation between these different skills; poetry and storytelling were often performed by or with a musician, which was in the lineage of the poets of antiquity who accompanied their stanzas with instruments such as the lyre.[4]

Players could give "the men light hearts by thy pipe and the women light heels by thy tabor", but not everybody viewed minstrels benevolently. There was a sharp divide between religious and secular song and harpers or tumblers were, in the eyes of the church and the pious, to be scorned. The 12th century scholar John of Salisbury lumped together court entertainers with other figures of ill repute: "Concerning actors and mimics, buffoons and harlots, panders other like human monsters, which the prince ought to exterminate entirely than foster."[5]

Even so, because they were in demand for social events, the numbers of minstrels increased to the extent that the state felt it necessary to legislate the conditions of their existence. Minstrel guilds thus formalized what was hitherto informal. There were specializations. Players had to take tests in competence after a minimum of four years training. An officially recognized trumpeter under the patronage of the King or another member of the royal court was a post of prestige, and the principle of high standards was enshrined in the practice of various guilds.

As Henry George Farmer, an authority on early music in Britain, observes: "The minstrel guild system of Medieval and Renaissance times played a notable part in the development of wind music, since the organizations were not only protectors of the artists but also conservatories of the art."[6] This more regulated existence raised musical standards at a time when the arrival of new instruments and musical ideas from abroad led to a growth of particular types of players. Generally speaking, the Middle Ages were marked by the rise of trumpeters and kettle drummers, both in the court and in the battlefield. The trumpeter announced the arrival of a nobleman, signalled meal times or indicated specific hours during his watch, and was an essential cog in the machine that kept order in a royal life.

This is the context for one of the earliest and most iconic images of a black British musician, or at least a black musician in Britain. In 1511, Katherine of Aragon, two years into her marriage to Henry VIII, gave birth to a son, Henry. To mark the occasion a tournament was held at Westminster and a gorgeous hand-painted scroll shows the pomp and circumstance in fine detail. Mounted on horses are three trumpeters adorned by splendid royal livery with ornate fleur de lys banners strung across their golden horns. One of these men is black.

His name was John Blanke[7] and according to the ledgers that contain the salaries of Royal personnel, he was paid 8d a day for his services. Further biography on his life and family is sadly not in existence but his presence on the scroll, where his dark complexion stands in contrast to the almost ghostly pallor of his colleagues, shows that at least one black musician was at the heart of the British establishment. Blanke would have learnt the heraldic fanfares that were performed on state occasions. This was music whose *raison d'etre* was grandiosity. The airs had to imply the characteristics of royalty – munificence and splendour. Depicted on the Westminster roll, his left arm holding the horn, his right the reins of his mount, Blanke could have been playing either a rousing or solemn melody.

Placed in a wider cultural perspective, the image of the black trumpeter also questions our perceptions of musicians of African descent and the instruments with which they have become closely associated over time. His skill on the trumpet may have been passed on by a family member, as was often the case in an age when formal education was nowhere near as widespread as today. It is worth considering that the western device he is playing is part of a larger, far-reaching tradition of non-western wind instruments, which includes horns in Asia and Africa, some of which were made of ivory and wood such as the Mbuti molimo, for example.

Blanke had probably come to Britain with Katherine of Aragon in 1501. In addition to the pictured tournament, he performed at important Court events such as coronations, pageants, banquets and a range of popular entertainment, including jousts. His sense of self-worth is underlined by the fact that he asked for the same salary as one of his fellow musicians, Dominic Justinian upon the latter's death.

The anecdote says much about his degree of wherewithal, but if Blanke was what today might be called an "ethnic minority" in England he was nonetheless just one of many people of colour to be seen and heard at the greatest courts of Britain and Europe, notably those of Spain, Portugal and Italy.

Italian dancers also performed with several "Black Moors" for the Shrove Tuesday celebrations in 1505 at the court of King James IV of Scotland. Miranda Kaufman sheds light on a black drummer among them who discharged important duties.

"This musician, who is known only as the 'More taubronar', not only played the tabor drum but was something of a choreographer. He devised a dance with twelve performers in black and white costumes. This may have been a boisterous event, resulting in some wear and tear to the instrument because the following month he was given 28 shillings to pay for the painting of his taubroun.'[8]

It was not until the 1650s that slaves were shipped from West Africa to the West Indies in substantial numbers, and to Britain in smaller quantities. It was a trade that peaked in the mid 18th century. Consignment registers show that the first ships bound for West Africa to exchange textiles, cutlery and weaponry for slaves set sail from ports such as Bristol and Liverpool. Whilst the major purpose of the trade was providing enslaved labour for the West Indian islands of Barbados, Jamaica, St Kitts and other smaller islands under English control, and the American colonies, it was not only such commodities as sugar, rum, cotton, tobacco and spices that made the return journey to England, but Africans too. The vestiges of the slave trade and sugar production can be seen written into place names up and down the country. There are a multitude of lanes and public houses, containing the generic name Black Boy in London, Banbury, Bristol, Headington, Winchester, Oving and Sevenoaks. Some of these establishments can be traced right back to the sixteenth century as evidence of presence of blacks in Britain.[9]

There was also hysteria. As early as 1601, Elizabeth I ordered the lord mayor of London to expel the small population of slaves who were largely, as Sukhdev Sandhu asserts in *London Calling*, 'employed as servants, prostitutes and court entertainers. Their visibility far exceeded their physical presence.' Nevertheless, the monarch decreed the removal of: "The great numbers of negars and blackamoores which [as she is informed] are crept into the realm... who are fostered and relieved here to the great annoyance of her own liege people."[10] The panic of being "swamped", by the ethnic other, raised by politicians over the years, in racially charged language, has a long history. The epithet "blackamoor" entered the English language around the middle of the 16th century, interchangeably with the terms Ethiopian, negar and Moor. One text states that "a blake Moor" is "borne in Barbary", and this specification is present in Shakespeare's *Othello* (1604). Complex and mercurial as is the eponymous Moor, who as a captain in the Venetian army stands as a distant scion to the "*numerus maurorum*" of Roman Britain, there are nonetheless several manifestations of a casual but spiky racism running through the text. Othello is described as having "thick-lips", a "sooty bosom", and Shakespeare clearly draws on public attitudes when he has Iago describe Othello as an "old black Ram [tupping the white ewe]", and a "Barbary horse."[11]

People of colour were often marked out as villainous in popular culture in subsequent decades. For example, "The Blackamoor in the Wood"[12] is a folk story that has been found in a number of guises around the country, the earliest of which dates from around 1690. A woodcut of the tale was sold at a printing office in Bow churchyard in 1750 and other versions were found in Newcastle Upon Tyne in 1796 and Edinburgh in 1819. The subtitle of the piece describes it as: "A lamentable Ballad of the Tragical End of a gallant lord and a vertuous lady, together with the untimely end of their two children, wickedly performed by a heathenish bloodthirsty villain, their servant. The like of which cruelty was never before heard of."

This is no exaggeration. The story involves a fiendish black servant who when his Lord is away, rapes his wife. The husband rushes back in a vain attempt to save his beloved. The assailant is seen as an animal worthy of only inhuman retribution:

> Hold thy rude hand, thou savage moor
> To hurt her do forbear
> Or else as sure that I live
> Wild horses shall thee tear.

Then, in a bloodcurdling sequel, the black servant dashes the head of the first of the lady's two babes against the wall, while other has his throat cut and "down the brains did fall". If "The Blackamoor in the Wood" was an extreme case of racial stigmatization in popular culture, it was not isolated. The existence of regional variations of the story attest to its national spread, and the longevity of this monstrous caricature was still to be found a century later. In 1776, at the Theatre Royal, Drury Lane, patrons could enjoy "A new comic opera" with the jolly title of *Airs And Ballads In The Blackamoor Wash'd White* by Sir Henry Bate in lame and vapid verse. Its racist premise is flagged up in its prologue in the opposition of "Christians and Negars". There is little plot except dandyish gentlemen singing of the fun to be had from asserting the superiority of whiteness. The foreigner in their midst has to be bleached to respectability:

> No never mind little Jerry
> Let your heart be merry
> British boys will still be right
> Till they prove that black is white.

The final part of the play has a more stark tone.

> Mayhap the nabob that brought the poor creature
> From his father, and mother, and all,
> Is himself of a blackamoor nature
> Dark within as the tribe of Bengal.[13]

Almost a century separates "The Blackamoor in the Wood" and *The Blackamoor Wash'd White*, but they are connected by form and content; the racist metaphor of washing the black white continuing in satirical prints and a Pears soap advert of as late of 1901 in which a black child is washed white. However, such representations do not necessarily tell us everything about the relationships between the white majority and black minority of the time. Without documentary evidence, it is hard to reconstruct attitudes at any given point in time with certainty, and one of the failings of the discussion of race in history is precisely the tendency to look for absolutes rather than nuance and elements of contradiction. Relationships between races are never simple.

According to reliable records, the black population of London had reached 20,000 by 1787,[14] so it is likely, given what is know about the presence of black communities in other urban centres, that the black population nationally was around 50,000. Describing the relationships between black and white is not straightforward because records of the lives of people involved in contact are scarce, which is why the testimonies of ex-slaves Olaudah Equiano (1745-1797), Ignatius Sancho (1729-1780) and Ottobah Cugoano (1757-1791) are so valuable. All of the above became published authors – Equiano's 1789 autobiography, *The Interesting Narrative of the Life of Olaudah Equiano* was a best seller that ran to nine editions – evidence of widespread interest.

As for Ignatius Sancho[15] he is notable for the great breadth of his activities. Like Equiano he was an indefatigable campaigner against the slave trade but if the pressing matter of social justice greatly exercised him then that did not distract him from artistic pursuits that gave lie to the notion that the Negro lacked the same intellectual faculties and emotional sensibilities as the white man. Sancho was a composer as well as a man of letters. Luckily scores of his music have survived and are still performed to this day, revealing an impressive command of the vocabulary of European classical music, particularly the minuet, the delicate skipping dance music of noblemen whose light, dainty rhythmic patterns required precise choreography.

Dance played a prominent role in Sancho's composing, and it's interesting to note that in one of the four collections of music he published in his lifetime, "Les Contes Des Fees", circa 1767, he also set themes to other popular steps of the day such as the cotillion. Also worthy of attention is the fact that Sancho wrote melodies for lyrics, such as "Sweetest Bard", an adaptation of "Mr Garrick's ode". What stands out from these examples, with their flighty allegro pulse, is Sancho's complete embrace of highbrow European culture.[16]

A Negro who penned musical works of the kind that had charmed the French and English courts flew in the face of a racial hierarchy that placed people of colour on a very low rung. Enjoying the patronage of the wealthy Montagu family, and the friendship of the novelist and clergyman Laurence Sterne, Sancho had been able to receive an excellent education that stood him in good stead in British society, and the magnitude of his cultural output, his writings and compositions, presented an image of an ethnic minority that was anything but morally contemptible.

But if there were "Moors" who endeared themselves to liberal sentiments, then there is still plenty of evidence to suggest that such approval
went against the general grain of perception. When Shakespeare describes
Othello as a *"noble* Moor", is he responding to a more general assumption
that a moor must be ignoble?

Critics were still uncomfortable with the interracial romance at the heart
of the play two centuries after it was written. In *Notes and Lectures Upon
Shakespeare and Other Dramatists* (1808), Samuel Taylor Coleridge contended:
"As we are constituted, and most surely as an English audience was dis-
posed in the beginning of the seventeenth century, it would be something
monstrous to conceive this beautiful Venetian girl falling in love with a
veritable Negro."[17] This was a writer who, as a younger man, had risked
injury preaching against slavery in Bristol. A similar objection came earlier. In *Absurdities in the structure of Othello* (1692), Thomas Rymer criticises
a lack of verisimilitude: "The character of the state is to employ strangers
in their Wars, but shall a Poet thence fancy that they will set a Negro to be
their General or trust a Moor to defend them against the Turk? With us
a black-a-moor might rise to be a trumpeter but Shakespeare would not
have him less than a Lieutenant-General.'[18]

This is the prejudice of its time, but Rhymer's statement makes an
interesting and early connection between race and music, with music as
the vessel in which white Britain felt able to accommodate black people.
It suggests that Rymer had actually seen Blacks as musicians in the military. Even if admired, at this point in history, generally musicians had an
anomalous standing in society, so fitting in other people who were also on
the margins because of their race involves no contradiction. Our search
for players of instruments of African descent thus appears to continue with
the ranks of the armed forces. These were not necessarily musicians who
earned a living through music, but soldiers who played music.

There is evidence to support this view such as the mezzotint engraving
of a 'Negro Tambourinist' of the Coldstream Guards that dates from the
late eighteenth century. He is wearing a large white turban with black
beads running right over the fabric and holding a very large tambourine
with small bells clasped on the rim. Next to the bells are large, broad pins
with flared heads. This elaborate paraphernalia looks designed to create a
high-pitched clanging sound when struck by the musician. This instrument could be what was known as "the Jingling Johnnie", which was an
anglicized corruption of the Turkish word *chaghana*.[19]

The adoption of this tambourine in the British army was a sign of the
considerable influence exerted by what was known as Janissary music.
This referred to percussion such as the above and the low sounding bass
drum. Poland, Russia and Austria all hosted Turkish bands in the early 18th
century, but eventually musicians from the Ottoman empire were replaced

by Africans whose skills on the above instruments did not go unnoticed. Henry George Farmer notes: "These blacks – as they were designated on the muster rolls – displayed great ability and agility in the handling of their 'tools', as Wagner would have said."[20]

For us today, that picture of the 'Negro tambourinist' in the Coldstream Guards in the 18th Century is a priceless historical document, as is the one of the black trumpeter, John Blanke on the Westminster painted roll in 1511.[21] They make black people visible.

More to the point, they outline a hidden history in which three key components interlock – Africans, music and the military. When the most popular acts of modern day pageantry – the trooping of the colour and the changing of the guard – appear in primary colours on television screens, it may leave many incredulous to think that centuries ago similar events unveiled some of the earliest known Blacks in Britain.

John Blanke and the Negro tambourinist may not have been harbingers of mass migration, but they were real people who either travelled here, or may even have been born here. They denote the tiniest of shifts in the demographics of the United Kingdom, but other black musicians followed them, some of whom moved in circles that were more rarefied than army barracks.

Notes

1. Peter Fryer, *Staying Power* (London: Pluto, 1984), p.1.
2. Henry George Farmer, *Military Music* (Parrish, 1950), pp. 8-9.
3. Farmer, op. cit., p. 10.
4. John Southworth points out that in *Beowulf*, the Old English Anglo-Saxon epic of the 10th century, there is a description of the synthesis of the two artforms – when the lord's harper rises in his accustomed place: "A fellow of the King's/ Whose head was a storehouse of the storied verse/ Whose tongue gave gold to language/ Of the treasured repertory."
5. Farmer, op. cit., p. 11.
6. Quoted from Salisbury's *Policraticus* in Paul Dalton, "John of Salisbury and Courtiers Trifles" in *The English Medieval Minstrel*, ed. David Luscombe and Paul Dalton (D.S. Brewer, 1989).
7. This account of Blanke is indebted to Miranda Kauffman, *Black Tudors* (London: One World, 2017), p. 11.
8. Kauffman, op. cit.
9. https://www. ordinancesurvey.co.uk/getoutside/guides/the-history-of-pub-names/
10. Sukhdev Sandhu *London Calling* (Harper Collins, 2003) xv.

11. William Shakespeare, *Othello* (Penguin, 1980).

12. British Library, National Library of Scotland, LC 2838 (17).

13. Sir Henry Bate, *Airs and Ballads* (including "The Blackamoor wash'd white"), (London: Cox & Bigg, 1776)

14. Mayerlene Frow, *Roots of the Future: Ethnic Diversity in the Making of Britain* (CRE, 1996)

15. For Ignatius Sancho see Reyahn King and Sukhdev Sandhu, *Ignatius Sancho: An African Man of Letters* (London: National Portrait Gallery Publications, 1997).

16. To hear some of Sancho's music and for further information go to http://sanchomusic.synthasite.com/.

17. Samuel Taylor Coleridge *Notes And Lectures Upon Shakespeare And Other Dramatists*, 1808. (Quoted in *Othello* [Bantam Classic, 1962]).

18. Thomas Rymer *Absurdities in the structure of Othello*. Quoted in the Bantam Classics edition of *Othello*.

19. The term was also sometimes shortened to 'jingler'.

20. See Farmer *Military Music* (Parrish, 1950) p. 35. The man was called John Fraser.

21. Blanke was also known as 'the blacke trumpet'; see Peter Fryer, *Staying Power* (Pluto, 1984) p. 4.

2 FROM STREET SONG TO SONATA

Master Bridgetower, son of the African Prince, who had lately figured so much at Bath on the violin, performed a concerto with great taste and execution.

— *The Times*, 20 Feb, 1790.

The late eighteenth century was an important period for the articulation of the ideas of democracy, the rights of the individual and the injustices of inequalities of wealth and power. But if in the early nineteenth century Lord Palmerston is reputed to have said that "there is no such thing as permanent friends only permanent interests", he might also have added there is such a thing as a permanent, self-serving flexibility in ethics.

It was not merely that the old landed interests across Britain and Europe held onto power and defended it mercilessly, but when those who overthrew that power in America and France had power themselves, they behaved no better, particularly towards Black people.

Settlers in America waged the War of Independence in 1775 over unfair taxes levied by the colonial power, Great Britain, but showed little concern over the existence and condition of the slaves on the tobacco and cotton plantations. As the French fought for 'liberté, égalité et fraternité, and aristocratic heads rolled, other bodies remained bound and chained for export from West Africa. Nine years after the French revolution, the 1798 slave uprising in San Domingo, otherwise known as the Haitian revolution, shared the same revolutionary objectives, but the new French government was not prepared to end slavery; the maritime bourgeoisie had too much to lose by recognizing the human rights of Africans. Frequently otherwise at odds with France, Britain supported France in putting down the insurrection. Revenues would decline and spheres of influence shrink if "the black Napoleon", Toussaint L'Ouverture, were to prevail. The triangular trade of manufactured goods, enslaved human labour and raw colonial produce had been too important to capitalist accumulation in Western Europe.[1]

Even as a Frenchman, Victor Schoelcher and an Englishman, Thomas Clarkson, were winning popular support for the moral case for abolition, they struggled to be heard above the demands of the West Indian interests for the protection of their investments.

If the creation of the West Indies as plantation societies with imported populations (after the original Amerindian inhabitants had been largely exterminated) was the main legacy of the enterprise of sugar and slavery, there were also lasting impacts on British society and culture. Fortunes were made (and lost) and a good many "noble" families and stately country houses such as the Lascelles and Harewood House outside Leeds in Yorkshire have their origins in the profits of slave-grown sugar and the slave trade.[2] Along with these architectural displays of landed wealth, one of the most striking fashion statements for the well-to-do lord or lady was the little black boy who would be in attendance at social functions. In a good many paintings of the landed gentry from the late seventeenth to the late eighteenth century they appear as mascots or pets. Mostly (but not always) shown in deferential poses, these black children reflect a duality in eighteenth century attitudes to race, namely that the African was lauded for his appearance in youth but mistrusted for the threat that he might pose in adulthood. The benign presence of the Negro boy emphasises of the absence of the Negro man.

Young black boys and girls were part of a vogue for exotica that also included the use of fabrics from the Far East as well as perfumes and spices from Asia and the Middle East. Dressing the servant in finery reflected the ample means of the household in which he appeared.

Among the most notable paintings in this manner is *Captain Graham in His Cabin* by William Hogarth. Painted in 1745, the canvas was intended to celebrate the capture of valuable cargo after Graham had launched a raid on a squadron of French ships outside Ostend in Belgium. The conquering hero is the central focus of the image and his imperious pose – back straight, leg outstretched and gaze firmly trained on the viewer – denotes a man of stature, self-confident in his privileged place in society. Clad in a gold brocade waistcoat, breeches, stockings, white cravat and a red fur-lined cape, Graham is puffing on a long tapered pipe and he affects something of a dandyish demeanour in the way his head is cocked slightly to the side. On a chair in front of him is a small dog, rearing up on its hind legs, head practically drowning in Graham's cascading white wig, and standing right behind the animal is a Negro boy. He is holding a small naker (kettledrum) under his arched left arm and is beating it with a straight wooden stick.[3] The young black is an elegantly attired music-maker. Both the dog and the servant are presented as subservient references to the master, who dominates the picture. The pet, by dint of the wig, is made lordly in a ridiculous way. The boy is decked out in a yellow waistcoat and a blue velvet jacket studded with large gold buttons, a brilliant red cravat round his neck, a beige cap upon his head. Like the Captain, he also has a long pipe hanging from the side of his mouth. Negro boy and dog appear as playthings fashioned in the image of the master and, as much as the painting tells us about hierarchy and the place of blacks among those with power, it also connects to other images of black musicians in British society. Indeed, Graham's servant vividly recalls the mezzotint engraving of the Negro tambouriner in the Coldstream guards discussed in the previous chapter. It is tempting to think that the difference is that Graham's player is now outside the military environment, but the location for Hogarth's painting is a ship, possibly part of the fleet used for raids on the French, which suggests that black drummers were used on British war vessels as much as they were in infantry units.

Another common denominator in these images is the headgear of the two black figures. The Coldstream Guards drummer wears an elaborately designed wrap modelled on a turban and the Graham drummer sports a puffed, voluminous, rounded hat whose provenance is not easy to pinpoint. It may be European. It may be Middle Eastern. Both look *exotic*. The sophistication of their clothing reveals the convention of adorning slaves in ways which would have enhanced their function either as musicians performing practical duties in the armed forces or entertaining polite society in the drawing room or parlour.

Consider the case of David Marat. He was a servant who absconded from his 'Master', one Edward Talbot, known to reside in King Street near Soho in central London. From a broadsheet advertisement issued in early 18th century we learn this:

> A black about seventeen years of age, with short wooly hair. He had on a
> whitish Cloath livery, lin'd with Blew, and Princes-mettal Buttons, with
> a turbant on his head. He sounds a trumpet.[4]

Again the contiguity of the exotic and a black musician. Whatever his musical ability, David Marat also reflects the trend of dressing Negroes, or more precisely young Negro boys, in non-western headgear that creates a kind of Ottoman-African continuum in eighteenth century Britain.

If such figures existed on the fringes of cultural history, they nonetheless make the point that black people were playing instruments in various circumstances in the eighteenth century. They were both seen and heard.

Apart from the battlefield and the parade ground, the other setting in which black musicians were present was the street. The picture that emerges of life for Africans in Britain, if they did not have the security of an army or household post, was of a hand-to-mouth existence. For the most part, apprenticeships do not seem to have been offered by distrustful masters, so hawking and entertaining were prevalent trades.

One of the most popular outlets was bare-knuckle fighting. Tom 'The Moor' Molineaux, Bill Richmond and James Wharton were among the celebrated black prizefighters who plied their trade in the capital, but for those who were not blessed with the constitution and stamina of a success-ful pugilist (who had to endure bouts that could last well over an hour), there was the chance of amassing pennies by finding a 'pitch', throwing a hat on the pavement and singing songs or 'scraping the catgut' i.e. fiddling.

These street musicians should not be seen in the same context as modern day buskers, whose performances have a degree of novelty because they take place in an age when music is widely available by way of recorded media and broadcast communications. As noted in the previous chapter, news and song were much more closely aligned in the days when minstrels and itinerant players wandered the land.[5]

For sheer visual panache, it seems that few black street players could match Joseph Johnson, who worked in rural villages and market towns such as Romford or St. Albans. He sported a model of a ship, the *HMS Nelson* on his head and cut a striking figure as he performed a number of patriotic songs such as "The Wooden Walls of Old England", a song that references a naval ship.[6] A drawing of Johnson (1817) gives him something of a circus performer's curiosity by virtue of the ship on his head, as if he was a mythical giant sea dweller who had risen from the depths of the ocean, a dark Neptune carrying mast, sail and hull onto dry land.[7]

There was a more prosaic reason for the elaborate prop. Johnson was a former merchant sailor who had sustained injury during his working days, as indicated by the wooden crutch under his left shoulder and a walking stick in his right hand. Because his injuries were suffered in peace-time, he was given no pension. Johnson, facing destitution, had no choice but to take to the streets. The existence of black beggars in Britain in the eight-eenth century reflected the precarious nature of life for people of colour. Johnson displayed a pragmatic resourcefulness. Whilst the picture with a ship on his head may have freak-show connotations, it was actually part of the tradition of Jonkunnu masquerading in the West Indies, and it becomes a memento of ingenuity when the eye is directed towards the crutch that is holding him up.

Disability is the common denominator shared by Johnson and another musician who was well known on the streets of London. Billy Waters was an American-born Black, a peg-leg fiddler who plied his trade on the streets around Covent Garden. According to a broadsheet from the 1800s, he was maimed while in "His majesty's service", for which he did receive, unlike Johnson, a modest pension. Pictures of Waters show a flamboyant character who, like Johnson, had an eye for millinery. His broad-brimmed cocked hat, its central peak rising high into the air, streamed with ribbons and feathers, the gaiety of which was enhanced by an act that would see the fiddler discard his wooden peg and dance on one leg.[8]

Waters would sing as well as "scrape the catgut" and from his pitch just outside the Adelphi on the Strand, near Charing Cross in central London,

JOSEPH JOHNSON, DRAWN FROM THE LIFE BY JOHN THOMAS SMITH, DECEMBER 31ST, 1815.

From *Vagabondiana, or Anecdotes of Mendicant Wanderers through the Streets of London* (New Edition, 1874)

he won the hearts of many passers-by. Whilst he fiddled and sang outside of theatres for most of his life, he actually crossed the threshold of the Adelphi, one of the most modish theatres in the capital, when he appeared as himself in the stage adaptation of Pierce Egan's *Life In London* (1821). This was a book that over the next hundred years sold 300,000 copies.

His standing among the lower social orders was cemented by his election as "King of the Beggars" before his death. When he passed away in 1823 there was a funeral procession in Covent Garden that drew large crowds. His sending off, as depicted in the press, acknowledged him as part of the traditions of popular entertainment that reflected the seamier side of life in Georgian Britain. Broadsheet illustrations of the event show that there was dignity if not grandeur bestowed upon the deceased, whose casket was covered in a large velvet drape upon which were placed his fiddle and hat. Sewn to the drape over Waters' coffin was the legend "Poor Black Billy", and whilst this signals the affection in which he was held, it reminds that he was predominantly defined by his race. Behind the coffin there is a man with no legs who is being carried in what appears to be a sedan chair. Ahead of the pallbearers is a group of seven, most of whom sport black hats with long trailing fabrics. Right in the middle of that group there is a black man with flowing, striped trousers. He is barefoot and wears a turban. The Eastern or Moorish style of the mourner is a reminder that Waters was still living in a time when Africans in Britain were elided with the exotic.

In the background there stands a row of buildings, one of which bears the sign *Beggar's Opera*,[9] the popular stage show that satirised the upper-classes by casting them in the clothes and culture of the demi-monde of the London poor, "pickpockets, prostitutes and lawyers", indicating that criminality existed at all levels of society, high and low. It was one of the earliest comic operas, staged in 1728 with a libretto by John Gay and music by the German-born Johann Christoph Pepusch. Its music drew on "already familiar street ballads." The reference to this opera in the engraving of Billy Waters' funeral signals his place in the lineage of British entertainment.

Despite the daily hardships it endured, the working class Black community in 18th century Britain was well known for its lively social life, and it is likely that the fiddlers and horn players who took part in the "Black hops" or "Black balls" in city backstreets, were a mixture of civilians and ex-military personnel. Here Negroes "drank, supped and entertained themselves with dancing and music." Indeed, entertainers such as Waters attained such popularity that they influenced their white peers. Because of the crowds that black musicians attracted they prompted others who were not from Africa or the West Indies to black up in order to grab the *browne*.[10]

★

There were also black musicians who moved in very different circles.

Whilst Billy Waters and Joseph Emidy (1775-1835) played the same instrument, it was not appropriate to say that the latter was a fiddler. He was in fact a virtuoso violinist, composer and tutor who became the toast of classical music audiences in the South West, in Truro, Cornwall.

There had been a black presence on the South-west coast since the middle of the eighteenth century, primarily through the arrival of people of colour in the military, including some who were musicians. There were black drummers in the 29th Worcestershire Foot, which was stationed in Plymouth, Barnstaple and Bideford between 1759 and 1843, and also in the 46th South Devonshire Regiment of Foot. Devon was a focus for military recruiters keen to sign up ex-slaves who came to Britain from America after fighting for the motherland in the War of Independence in 1775, for which they were promised freedom. There were precursors even before this. In 1688, the Dutch Prince, William of Orange, landed at Brixham, South Devon before he set off on a march to London to claim the English throne from James II. To bolster his army he travelled with 200 African slaves, former labourers on Dutch plantations in America. Some may have absconded en route.[11]

In any case, the growth of a black community in Cornwall and Devon coincided with an increased naval presence in Falmouth and the continuing but declining trade links with New World territories such as the West Indies and South America and Old World states like Portugal. Lisbon was the home of the man who would become the most renowned black musician in Cornwall. Born in Guinea but sold to Portuguese traders who took him to their country after he had been a slave in Brazil, Joseph Emidy showed such talent on the violin as a boy that he made a name for himself in Lisbon's very fashionable opera house by the time he was a teenager. He caught the ear of a British naval commander, Sir Edward Pellew, who instructed his men to kidnap Emidy for use as a fiddler aboard his vessel, The Indefatigable, in 1795. For several years he was forced to "climb down" musically, playing jigs and reels for the entertainment of a raucous crew rather than Haydn and Mozart for Portuguese polite society.[12] To the trauma of violent removal from his home was added the indignity of artistic degradation. "Scraping the catgut" was the lot of many Africans who found employment on ships in the eighteenth and nineteenth centuries, either as fiddlers or drummers, whose purpose was to entertain crew members with ditties or keep time with percussion instruments during the singing of shanties. This was intended as a distraction for crew members who had to contend with boredom and homesickness as well as the lack, on occasion, of exercise. Herman Melville's Moby Dick (1851) shows such a scene. On board the Pequod, French, Maltese, Sicilian and Icelandic sailors are just some of an international crew that pitches in with verses, but it is Pip, the young Negro cabin boy, the 'blackling', who is given the task of setting the beat for the uproarious jig that is danced by the men.

Pip! Little Pip! Hurrah with your tambourine.
   Go it, Pip! Bang it, bell-boy! Rig it, dig it, stig it, quig it, bell-boy!
Make fireflies; break the jinglers![13]

Note how closely Melville's language chimes with the lexicon developed for the British military musicians of African descent mentioned in Chapter 1. The name for Pip's tambourine is the "jingler"; the Turkish percussion played by 18th Century Negro drummers was known as the "jingling Johnnie".

This was the kind of life Emidy had to live when he was forced to sea. However, after Pellew left *The Indefatigable* in 1799, Emidy was allowed to go on shore where he settled in Falmouth. It didn't take long for him to make an impression, since Falmouth and neighbouring Truro were becoming fashionable areas for socialites. Emidy was appointed leader of the Falmouth Harmonic Society, with whom he performed a wide variety of symphonic and chamber music, and also began teaching and composing.

One of his pupils, James Silk Buckingham, took some of Emidy's original music to an impresario in London and there was talk of the violinist coming to the capital to play. Nothing ever came of this; there were apparently misgivings over the suitability of a black musician in the drawing rooms of the country's elite. It may also have been because Emidy was described as "the ugliest Negro I have ever seen", so he did not fulfil the criteria of being ornamental, like the Negro boy in the painting referred to above.

Emidy died in Truro in 1835 at the age of 60, survived by a wife and several children. His gravestone in the town's Kenwyn churchyard bears a moving epitaph:

Devoted to thy soul inspiring strains, Sweet Music! Thee he hail'd his chief delight. And with fond zeal that shunn'd nor toil nor pain his talent sear'd and genius mark'd its flight in harmony he liv'd, in peace. Took his departure from this world of woe. Here his rest til the last trumpet's call, shall 'wake mankind to joys that endless flow'.

Emidy's story may have ended somewhat sadly, given that his talent was not given the chance to shine on a national scale, but the mere fact that he managed to overcome the adversity of his early years, surviving the trauma of a kidnap to rise to a level of considerable prestige in Cornwall, is a sign of admirable resilience. His place in the pantheon of South West cultural figures is an important one. Had he been able to establish a permanent base in London and enjoy the favour of more of the key powerbrokers in music, he may have gone even further in his career. He nonetheless remains a black Cornishman of note.

George Augustus Polgreen Bridgetower (1779-1860) did attract patronage and move in the right metropolitan circles. His story was one of an artist who rubbed shoulders with the aristocracy, enjoyed Royal patronage, and, most significantly for the history of black music in Britain, showed himself worthy of a seat at the high table of European composers such as Haydn, Viotti and Beethoven. Yet what linked Bridgetower, a child prodigy who showed aptitude for the violin as a nine-year-old, to the black mourner at Billy Waters' funeral was the attire of his father, John Augustus Frederick Bridgetower. The association of people of colour with exotica in the era was widespread:

> Appeals to the curious were made by parading minorities of all kinds [ethnic, young, old, handicapped]. Thus the young mulatto violinist George Polgreen Bridgetower was marketed as the 'son of the African Prince'; his father dressed in extravagant Turkish robes.[14]

Known as an "Abyssinian from the West Indies", Bridgetower senior married a Polish woman, while living in Barbados in the early 1770s. It is likely that he was taken to the British colony as a free man serving on a merchant ship, and whether of his own canny devising or not, the sobriquet of "African Prince" was attached to him as he made his way to Europe. He was helped by the law passed in 1772 that decreed that slaves would be free as soon as they set foot in England, even though they could be reclaimed in the West Indies. It was thus in Bridgetower senior's interest to make his way to the Old World, to reach which he crossed many national borders. George was born in Biala in Poland in 1778 or 1780, and accompanied his father to Austria where he became a page to Prince Nicholas Esterházy, and it was during this time that George first displayed a natural talent on the violin that was quickly identified by music teachers who gave the boy formal lessons. It may have been, though it is not proven, that one of his earliest tutors was Franz Joseph Haydn.

By the age of nine, Bridgetower was playing at a sufficiently high standard to make his debut in Paris. He was presented as a "jeune negre des colonies" when he performed at the *Concert Spirituel* on 13 April 1789. The consensus was that this was a precocious, prodigious talent. Thereafter, he lived in the other major hubs of European classical music – London, where he was taken under the wing of the Prince of Wales and accommodated at Carlton house, and in Vienna, a key turning point in his musical education. It was there that Bridgetower developed a close friendship with Beethoven who tutored the young violinist and wrote a sonata for him, a notoriously demanding piece that, as a mark of respect, initially bore his name. But the two men fell out, apparently over the affections of the same girl, and Beethoven crossed out Bridgetower's name on the original manuscript and replaced it with that of Kreutzer.

However, Bridgetower was more than a footnote to Beethoven, since his rise coincided with major developments in the work of the "serious" composers of the day. The resources of the orchestra – strings, woodwind, brass, horns, percussion – are taken for granted as the tools with which all manner of pieces have been written for the past two hundred years, but concertos and sonatas for solo instruments gained greater currency from the 1750s onwards. In particular, Bridgetower's career dovetailed with the rise of the violin as the most important orchestral instrument in classical music. As a solo instrument capable of producing a quite vocal-like beauty, the development of the sonata form gave skilled players of the violin new prominence, bringing to the fore the role of the virtuoso who could play lines that were more and more demanding. Beethoven was inspired by musicians who could play their instruments to an exceptionally high standard, which is why the violin sonata was written for Bridgetower, *because* of his ability, or rather as a challenge to it.

Falling out with Beethoven did not halt the success that Bridgetower enjoyed. There were a string of stellar performances in Bath, Bristol and London, where he took part in recitals organized by George III's court musician, Christopher Papendiek. His most triumphant appearance was a concerto by Feliks Giornovic performed between the opening and second act of Handel's *Messiah* at the Drury Lane theatre on 19 February, 1790. A very favourable review was published in *The Times* the following day;

> Master Bridgetower, son of the African Prince, who had lately figured so much at Bath on the violin, performed a concerto with great taste and execution.[15]

Bridgetower held a number of very notable positions such as first violin for the Prince of Wales Band, the Covent Garden Lenten Oratorios and the Italian Opera at Haymarket. He was also a member of the Royal Society of Musicians.

The prestige of these appointments underlines the fact that the "servant boy groomed in Turkish attire" became a major fixture on the European classical music scene. As a nine-year-old violin prodigy who, in the common parlance of the day, was a "mulatto", Bridgetower was an artist who performed at a turning point in the history of classical music, playing pieces that stretched the sight-reading ability of the most highly trained musicians.

As well as his achievements as a soloist, Bridgetower was also a composer, and although there is no comprehensive record of his output, manuscripts of some pieces he wrote have been preserved. One ballad that was penned in 1812 for voice and piano was called "Henry". The piece was sung by Miss Feron and was eternally dedicated "with permission" to the Princess of Wales – a reminder that patronage was paramount during Bridgetower's career.

A year before "Henry" was written, Bridgetower was awarded his Bachelor of Music degree at the University of Cambridge and for the next three decades he continued to accept engagements in European capitals such as Rome, where he stayed in 1825 and Vienna (where he had previously studied) and to which he returned in 1845. Things evidently became more difficult for him when he seems to have lost royal support after the death of George IV, and the final years of his life remain shrouded in mystery. He died of synochal fever in Peckham, south London in 1860.

Although the story of Bridgetower is largely defined by his precocious talent, the issue of race is impossible to ignore, primarily because as a violinist and composer he entered a social milieu where people of colour were conspicuously absent. His youth was passed in a world where slavery still existed and where racism began to adopt a distinctively pseudo-scientific mode of discourse about the inferiority of Africans. Such twisted rationales made complete sense to those who sought reasons to justify slavery and colonial rule. If blacks were lesser beings than whites, then they should not enjoy the same rights.

There was even a school of polygenesis in the seventeenth century that argued that blacks were a kind of organic link between whites and primates in the evolutionary chain, while Sir William Lawrence, a proponent of phrenology, would, over a century later, earnestly compare "the Negro structure" to a monkey's.[16] Edward Long's *The History of Jamaica* (1774), drew similar conclusions on the basis of black physiognomy:

> There are extremely potent reasons for believing that the White and Negro are two distinct species. Instead of hair, black people have a covering of wool, like the bestial fleece.[17]

The image of the bestial fleece reinforced the idea of the proximity, if not common identity of Negro and animal – an image that chimes with Iago's description of Othello as "an old black ram". Hence when an African in Britain was described in a broadsheet advertising an absconded "black about seventeen years of age" with "short wooly hair"[18], common parlance coincided with academic writing. When a black man was described as sporting a "Turbant on his head" it was really due to the fashion for Turkish attire, but for anybody who followed Long's form of "science" it may have been a proper accoutrement for a Negro because it kept the unseemly "bestial fleece" from view.

Such imagery continued into the twentieth century. If the term "fuzzy", used liberally by writers such as Rudyard Kipling, echoed the earlier "woolly", then it is interesting to see how a great black artist, Nina Simone, references the roots of such language in the opening verse of her 1965 masterpiece "Four Women", where she has the matriarch Aunt Sarah wearily declare: "My hair is woolly."[19]

Edward Long to Nina Simone is not an incongruous leap when one notes that the issue of "good" hair is still contentious today, and that the psychological scars inflicted by the text of the former and displayed in the music of the latter are by no means fully healed.

A Van Dyck or Hogarth painting in which a Negro boy or servant girl is cast in an ancillary role, under the command of a white mistress or master, conveys a vivid image of powerlessness. Combine that with the kind of overt self-denigration that is recorded in the bible by the Queen of Sheba – "I am black but comely" – and it is not surprising that the Negro has had to struggle to assert his or her aesthetic value in white society.

This is why Bridgetower's entry into and deft negotiation of the upper classes of 18th century Europe, among those for whom bodily attractiveness, sartorial finesse and proper manners were of the utmost importance, was particularly impressive. A good command of several of the major European languages was also a considerable asset and both Bridgetower and his father were known for their multi-lingual skills. Perhaps even more tellingly, both were noted for their "beauty of person".

That Bridgetower was a handsome mulatto and not a one-legged black man like Billy Waters, was an advantage, and no doubt made him easier to accept because he was not seen to embody any threat. Even so, Bridgewater's position brought a level of attention to his colour that could not be played down. He was talked about in an era when few other black men managed to capture such attention. One such was Julius Soubise, born in 1754 in St. Kitts, one of the oldest British colonies in the West Indies, who was brought to England as a ten-year-old in the care of Kitty, the wealthy Duchess of Queensberry. Under her tutelage, he became a fencer and equestrian, but above all a man-about-town famed for his dandyish ostentation – he was known to use the most overpowering perfumes. Although he enjoyed the enduring favour of the Duchess, he had to flee to India to evade the law when he was accused of the rape of one of her maids.

Bridgetower, by contrast, was respectable and respected as an artist rather than known for his narcissism and stylistic excess. No greater symbol of the success of the "young African Prince" can be found than his appearance at the Theatre Royal, Drury Lane in 1790. He played a concerto by Giorno-vic which won favourable notices in national newspapers and magazines. This was only fourteen years after the performance of *Airs and Ballads in The Blackamoor Wash'd White* or *A New Comic Opera*. This was a transition from blacks as passive objects of ridicule to active performers in one of the most iconic theatre spaces to be found in Britain. After his debut in Paris, a review appeared that did not skirt around the issue of prejudice and presented his performance as a rebuttal of those who would not have considered his kind worthy of playing such refined music. *Le Mercure De France* stated unequivocally:

> It is one of the best answers that can be made to the philosophers who want to deprive those of his nation and his colour of the opportunity to distinguish themselves in the arts.[20]

While the positive nature of the statement is clear enough, the detail warrants further discussion. What exactly was Bridgetower's nation, or indeed his nationality? Here was the son of an "Abyssinian from

Barbados" and a Polish woman. He was born in Poland and went on to reside in Paris, London, Vienna and Dresden. To talk of Bridgetower as a representative of a nation clearly references a nebulous Africanness, rather than any specific country of origin. What was important was whether one was a freeman or a slave, or whether the economic constituency in which one moved, either in liberty or in bondage, was the West Indies, America or Britain.

Ignatius Sancho, Billy Waters, Joseph Emidy and George Bridgetower form a quadrumvirate of black musicians in 18th century Britain and are notable for the wide stylistic and social spectrum they covered. Between them they played street music among lowlifes and classical concerts for royalty. Emidy and Bridgetower travelled widely, performing in London, Bath and Cornwall, as well as in many major European cities bringing something substantial to European and British concert music. They made the point that people from Africa or the Americas could do more than scrape catgut on street corners. Perhaps of the three, Bridgetower has had the greatest legacy, as film-makers, musicians and poets have been drawn to his story. There is the film, *Immortal Beloved* (1994) which portrays him with Beethoven, the film, *Mulatto Song* (1996), directed by Topher Campbell, Rita Dove's narrative poem, *Sonata Mulattica* (2009) and a jazz opera, *Bridgetower – A Fable of 1807*, by Mike Phillips and Julian Joseph.[21]

Joseph Emidy has more recently been the subject of a multi-media collaboration between composer Tunde Jegede, film-maker, Sunara Begum and dancer-choreographer Ishimwa Muhimanyi in *He Who Dared to Dream* (2014).

Notes

1. Madison Smartt Bell, *Toussaint L'Ouverture: A Biography* (Vintage, 2008).
2. Simon Smith, *Slavery and Harewood House*, BBC Leeds 24.09.2014
3. Naker is derived from the Arabic *naquara*.
4. The advert for David Marat was reprinted in *Roots of the Future, Ethnic Diversity in the Making of Modern Britain* (CRE, 1996).
5. Mayerlene Frow, *Roots of the Future*.
6. The Wooden Walls of Old England is also a common name for many pubs up and down the country.
7. The source of the image of Joseph Johnson is *Vagabondiana, or, Anecdotes of mendicant wanderers through the streets of London* (1817).
8. Frow, op. cit.
9. *The Beggar's Opera* ran for 62 performances, the longest run in theatre at the time, after premièring at Lincoln's Inn Fields on 29 January, 1728.
10. Frow, op. cit., p. 21.

11. Black Cultural Archives, Ephemera 271, Cornwall, 1800s.
12. Black Cultural Archives, 5/1/72 Joseph Emidy.
13. Herman Melville, *Moby Dick* (1851, Penguin ed.) p. 174-175.
14. Clifford D. Panton, *George Augustus Polgreen Bridgetower, Violin Virtuoso And Composer Of Colour In Late 18th Century Europe* (Edwin Mellen, 2005) p. 31. Much of the information here is courtesy of Panton's biography.
15. Panton, *George Augustus Polgreen Bridgetower...*, p. 39.
16. William Lawrence, *Lectures on Physiology, Zoology and the Natural History of Man* (J. Callow, 1819) p. 363.
17. Edward Long, *The History of Jamaica: Or General Survey of the Ancient and Modern State of That Island; with reflections on its situation, settlements, inhabitants, climate, products, commerce, laws and governments* (T. Lowndes, 1774).
18. The advert for David Marat was reprinted in *Roots of the Future, Ethnic Diversity in the Making of Modern Britain* (CRE, 1996).
19. Nina Simone "Four Women" featured on the LP, *Wild Is The Wind*, Phillips, 1966.
20. Panton, op. cit., p. 17.
21. Wikepedia.

3 AFRICA, AMERICA, VICTORIA.

Instantly the fiddler grins and goes at it tooth and nail; there is new
energy in the tambourine; new laughter in the dancers.
— Charles Dickens, *American Notes.*

A stout, ruddy-faced lady, simply dressed in black.
— Ella Sheppard of the Fisk Jubilee Singers on Queen Victoria.

In 1837, when Bridgetower was fifty-nine years old, and entering the
twilight of his career, William IV died and Victoria of Kent became queen.
In the British psyche, the daughter of the Princess of Saxe-Coburg has
a place of monumental importance, as much for the longevity of her
reign as for the social and environmental transformations that we are
still witness to.

The age of steam brought irreversible modernity; 5,000 miles of railway
had been laid in Britain by the end of 1848. At the queen's coronation, the
"horse bus" was a common sight. By the time of her death in 1901, the
honk of the motorcar could be heard. The falling cost of private transport
in the decades following Victoria's death was a revolution as far reaching
as that in public transport during her reign.

The iconic images of the Victorian era evoke hardship and suffering, as
well as progress and possibility in commerce, society and politics. Imagine
sewer-hunters, tourists to the Lakes, rows of bony, ragged beings in the
workhouse, countless hoops on a lady's lace petticoat sewn by Thomas
Hood's seamstress "with fingers weary and worn/ with eyelids heavy and
red", pallid chimney sweeps with soot-stained cheeks, white entertainers
smeared in burnt cork, queues at standpipes, match-factory girls, crin-
oline-clad duchesses enjoying croquet, rural labourers in loose smocks
and tight neckerchiefs, gentlemen with whiskers and top hats, the rise of
cricket as a national sport, the village parson issuing sound advice, a baby
being put to sleep with a drop of laudanum at the Blackamoor Inn, slender
moving fingers at the first typing pool, blocks of "planned housing" and
"model dwellings" funded by wealthy philanthropists such as the American
merchant George Peabody.

Such images underline one defining characteristic of Victorian England – the growth of towns and cities to accommodate the population that
was drawn out of the countryside following the enclosure of the common

land to work in the mills of Lancashire and Yorkshire and the factories of Birmingham, Sheffield and the East End of London, and the ribbon development of suburban housing for a growing middle class when the railways made daily commuting possible.

The rapid industrial growth of Britain in the early nineteenth century (from capital accumulation built on the profits of the slave trade) and its accompanying ideology of Free Trade were amongst the factors that eventually tilted the balance against the old landed lobby (still powerful in Parliament) with vested interests in the slave trade and slave-grown sugar.[1]

The crusade against slavery led eventually to the Slave Trade Act 1807[2] and then to the Abolition of Slavery in 1833, but the situation of blacks in the Caribbean did not change for the better. Abolition left power in the hands of the old slave owners and they ensured that freed African-Caribbeans had little access to land. In Trinidad, British Guiana and elsewhere the sugar planters imported labour from India and China to reduce the bargaining power of black workers. Parallel to this, cane sugar declined in importance as European-grown beet sugar took over. Even before that time, the Caribbean, once the source of imperial grandeur, was becoming a neglected backwater as the centre of empire moved to India, with Africa in the rear. From the 1840s onward, all parts of the British West Indies had large labour surpluses and high un- and underemployment that could only be addressed through emigration. People chased work from island to island, and some found a brutal economic salvation in the labour demanded by the building of the Panama canal. These were the conditions that lay behind the story of migration to Britain that follows in later chapters. What added insult to injury was the fact that slave owners c. 1840 were compensated with £20m (worth £16.5 billion in current values) for their loss of their human property. The ex-enslaved are still awaiting reparations.

By 1820 Britain ruled over 26% of the world population and controlled one third of international trade by controlling an efficient network of sea routes to India, Africa, Australasia and the Caribbean. But imperial outposts had costs. Overseas territories brought profit to some and prestige to the nation state, but the Empire also had to be *sold* to the taxpayers of metropolitan Britain. One major marketing exercise was the "Great Exhibition"[3] at Crystal Palace, south London, in 1851. This was a large scale show that was equal parts trade fair, political propaganda and exercise in nation building. Visitors, estimated to number 43,000 a day, could see "the world for a shilling". Stands from the colonies presented wondrous products and curiosities: cod liver oil (Newfoundland), exotic fruits and flowers (the West Indies), the skins and meat of the kangaroo, the possum, the duck-billed platypus, the teeth of the sperm whale and the feathers of the sooty petrel (Australia), ostrich eggs and a mighty elephant's tusk weighing 103 pounds (South Africa). But if the Great Exhibition was a show of Britain's industrial strength and colonial muscle, it was also a display of shameless plunder. Along with technological feats such as the prototypes of fax machines and state-of-the-art weaponry came the ostentatious parading of the Koh-i-Noor, the dazzling diamond that had been "confiscated" from Duleep Singh by the East India Company in the days of the Raj. The appropriation was just. Victoria was Empress of India.

Even before the Great Exhibition, Londoners in particular were entertained with exotic spectacle from India and Africa. What came from the remote outposts of the Empire was the unknown, the unheard and the unseen, harbouring wonder and danger in equal measure, as surely as Othello the Moor in his conversation with Desdemona's father evoked "rocks, hills whose heads touch heaven", and "cannibals that each other eat" (Act 1, Scene 3).

Visitors to the Vauxhall Pleasure Gardens in central London – a venue for fireworks displays and grand concerts – could also have seen two men playing percussion, one with a round tambourine, the other with two straight twelve-inch-long horse bones. This was in 1848, three years before the Great Exhibition.

One of the performers was a black man, William Henry Lane;[4] the other was a white man whose face was smeared in burnt cork. Both were members of the Ethiopian Serenaders, a "blackface" minstrel troupe hailing from New Orleans, which had enjoyed enormous success in the New World, including a concert at the White House. By now, the word "minstrel", once generic to the court entertainers and itinerant performers during the Middle Ages, had acquired a specific racial dimension with the birth and growth of slave songs and dances in America. The characters of Jim Crow, the plantation slave, and Zip Coon, the city dandy, became black archetypes and eventually white performers started to copy what they saw slaves doing, giving rise to the practise of "blackface", whereby burnt cork would enable a whitey to become a darkey. For much of the 19th century, Black music in Britain came from across the Atlantic in such racialised forms.

The first African-American blackface troupe was the Georgia Minstrels in the 1860s, and they are largely credited as the act that opened the door for other forms of "authentic" Black performance of plantation melodies. They were followed by blackface troupes such as the Virginia Minstrels who played to packed houses in America. Such was America's convoluted racial power structure that Whites copying Blacks became a norm to which Blacks had to submit, essentially copying those who were originally copying them.

That William Henry Lane and the Ethiopian Serenaders were drawing crowds in London two decades prior to this is important. Lane was a performer whom both Whites and Blacks wanted to imitate. He was also known as Master Juba, which for Victorians was a byword for darkest Africa. Juba was the capital of modern day Southern Sudan, from whence the explorer Samuel White Baker launched a number of expeditions that took him into Uganda. Juba was sign of all things exotic and dangerous. In *Moby Dick*, the narrator, Ishmael, evoking the unknown shores that a hardy sailor might discover on his lengthy voyages, talks dramatically of the remote land of Ptolemy and the kingdom of Juba.

Born in Providence, Rhode Island, possibly in 1825, Lane grew up in New York and was a musician as well as a "hoofer". He played banjo and tambourine, which is why he could also fill the role of the "Tambo" in the "Tambo and Bones"[5] duo that supplied rhythms for singers and dancers in the minstrel troupes, supporting the high-energy choreography and spirit-raising tunes. Juba was a virtuoso performer who is regarded as one of the inventors of contemporary tap dance. One of his early admirers was Charles Dickens, who visited New York to write the investigative chronicles that were published as *American Notes* (1842). Dickens describes a performance by Juba at the fabled Five Points, a melting pot of black and Irish immigrant communities, painting a picture of the interaction of music and dance that practically jumps off the page.

> ... suddenly the lively hero dashes into the rescue. Instantly the fiddler grins and goes at it tooth and nail; there is new energy in the tambourine; new laughter in the dancers...
>
> Single shuffle, double shuffle, cut and cross-cut, snapping his fingers, rolling his eyes, turning in his knees, presenting the backs of his legs in front, spinning about on his toes and heels like nothing but the man's fingers on the tambourine.[6]

These are significant observations because they pinpoint the interaction of both physical and musical expression in slave culture that would resonate down through the ages. Sounds and steps elide and blend into one integrated surge of creativity, galvanized by a rhythmic drive that unites the dancer's body and the player's deployment of the instrument. Tellingly, choreographic terms are also musical ones: a shuffle is a rhythm as well as a movement, and the shift from single to double pinpoints a key strategy in what would eventually become known as jazz, namely generating interest through alterations of tempo and accent. Time is fluid rather than rigid. Changing a count of beats engaged a dancer's improvisatory prowess, pushing them to raise energy and creativity in the moment. All of which maps a clear path to the future – the 19th century shuffle will give way to swing, boogie and groove in the 20th century, and way beyond. This foundation is fundamental.[7]

The dance at which Juba excelled was called "The Breakdown". This is yet another example of Black dance tied at the hip, so to speak, to Black music. Two or three dancers would gather and one by one they would improvise hops, taps, shuffles and jumps as inventively as possible, the point being to highlight the soloist. New Orleans jazz musicians would later perform solos during the "breaks" of an arrangement where some players dropped out in a mirror image of the convention in black dance, and many decades down the line funk musicians would make an art of "the breakdown" where drums and percussion took prominence as the horns and vocals momentarily stop playing in an arrangement.

Research into the precise origins of Black music in the African Diaspora is ongoing, and essential questions remain on how song and dance evolved and interacted over time so as to precisely determine the convergence between them. One historical fact that might explain why dance is so integral to African-American and African-Caribbean expression is the practise adopted by captains of slave ships in the Middle Passage of regularly encouraging the captured Negroes to dance in order to keep them healthy.

Negroes were thus made to dance to remain viable units of production in a slave economy. Negroes later danced to entertain. Negroes who danced could also be seen by arbiters of good taste as a corruption or adulteration of European styles, or atavistically holding on to savage African movements.

Whether they were allowed to sing on slave ships is unclear, but rhythmic movement took the form of "ring dances" and impromptu solos to the sound of fiddles played by the sailors as well as hand-clapping from the slaves. Dancers like Juba thus provided a conspicuous link to a past in which dance was part of a system of survival as well as a glimpse of a future in which black musicians brought a strong rhythmic sensibility to the fore, and it is no surprise that magic occurred when dancer and singer coalesced, as exemplified by James Brown, Prince and Michael Jackson.

Reviews of the 1848 European tour echo the excitement of Dickens' description. *The Theatrical Times* described Juba's movements as "grotesque and poetical", which resonates with other perceptions of blacks at the time as excitable and wild compared to the propriety that was supposedly native to European behaviour. And though Juba became something of a sensation in Britain, and though his talent was feted, there is no escaping his status as an exotic, an otherworldly being who gave performances in an age when people of colour were largely seen as a source of wild mystery.

As one can tell from Dickens' description, the dancers and musicians in the minstrel shows performed with verve and theatricality, but their exaggerated gestures such as rolling the eyes and strutting with the hips or backside reinforced the stereotype of Blacks as funny, lazy, backward, childish folk.

Minstrelsy is an extremely complex subject because it is borne of division *within* white America as well as *between* white and Black America. The first whites to black up were Northerners who imposed their vision of Southern Negroes on the world of entertainment, exposing the myth of progressive Yankee thinking and the ease with which stereotypes could cross the Mason-Dixon line. Blackface performances ritualized a form of control over African Americans, who were already living with enormous restrictions on their lives. What Northerners *thought* Blacks were like obfuscated how Blacks actually lived, and impacted on their worldviews, aspirations and sense of self. The place of the Negro in a dis-United States of America, with its regional, social and political conflicts, could only be problematic, and minstrel entertainment added to the confusion over the real identity of human beings introduced to the New World in dehumanizing circumstances.

Most perniciously, the defining traits of the minstrel archetype – frizzy hair, bulging eyes, rubber lips – transposed from literature to the packaging of household consumer items, the most obvious manifestation being golliwog dolls on the labels of marmalade, entrenched forms of offensive racial iconography. As such, blackface brought into play a set of crude audio-visual tropes that made invisible the individual trapped behind the painted mask. Touching on the replacement of the real by the constructed image, Ellen Gallagher, the African-American artist who has produced some of the most startling works of visual art of the 21st century, called minstrelsy the "first great American abstraction".[8]

Yet minstrelsy was embraced by Blacks primarily because it afforded them economic opportunities, even in circumstances that set great store by buffoonery. The Georgia Minstrels won plaudits in America for its exacting standards of musicianship, which were so high that some members later joined prestigious string groups and opera companies.

In his fascinating history of Black Gospel music, *People Get Ready*,[9] Robert Darden collates a number of alternative views on minstrelsy and quotes the scholar Dale Cockrell who argues that there was a degree of subversion on the part of the practitioners, who behind the masks passed comment on an unjust society. Speaking in the midst of constraints, finding a voice by way of codes, living a double life, has long been a part of the Afro-Diasporan condition.

Ultimately, Minstrel shows were a sign that White America, and by extension, White Europe, was unable to ignore Black America. The immense popularity of this form of entertainment in New York and London, and the numerous appearances of both white blackface and Negro blackface troupes makes it clear that plantation melodies and "Ethiopian dances" had captured the public imagination. The minstrel became one of the first influential cultural commodities that the New World exported to the Old.

It is worth noting that whilst there were parallel forms of plantation music and dance in the British West Indies – survivals of African song, parodies of European forms and satiric precursors of the calypso – none of these took on the dominance that minstrelsy and the "Negro Spiritual" had in the USA and were rarely exported in the 19th century. There are probably quite straightforward explanations. Black forms of music and dance in the USA were largely shaped by their minority status and majority white audiences always had significantly more spending power. In the British West Indies, Blacks were always a majority, but their cultural expressions remained within the group in communal, non-commercial forms, regarded as primitive and subversive of social order by the tiny white elite and the small culturally Eurocentric, brown middle class.

Besides, except for the moment of alarm over the 1865 Morant Bay rebellion in Jamaica, there was scarcely any interest in Britain over what was happening in the West Indies. Over Morant Bay there was a national quarrel amongst British intellectuals and writers over whether the savage repression (over 500 Blacks executed) directed by Governor Eyre could be justified. Charles Dickens, Thomas Carlyle, Alfred Tennyson and John Ruskin were on the negrophobic side backing Eyre, whilst Charles Darwin, John Stuart Mill and T.H. Huxley called for Eyre to be tried for mass murder.[10] But in general the West Indies was fading from national consciousness. What was coming from the USA, whether cotton or minstrelsy, was much more interesting.

From any perspective, the emergence of African Americans as the drivers of what became a cross-Atlantic musical culture was a surprising turn of events. Africans had been efficient beasts of burden on plantations, and they had not been brought to the Americas to sing songs, but their ability to make instruments from animal carcasses and execute invigorating dance steps showed that they could serve a purpose beyond the purely industrial. In the nineteenth century this was a circumscribed role. For the most part minstrels were figures only of fun, valued for their ability to "elicit shouts of laughter and applause",[11] and because the bulk of Negroes lacked access to other forms of expression regarded as more elevated, such as playing classical music in concert rooms, it was inevitable that many audiences came to believe that the *only* type of activity Blacks were fit for was this kind of clownery. This had uncomfortable resonances with the kind of "freakshow" of Georgian England, gawping at the disproportionate derrière – to the European eye – of a South African woman, Saartje, aka the Hottentot Venus, who become a sensation in 1810. Master Juba's appearance with the Ethiopian Serenaders at the Vauxhall Pleasure Gardens in 1848 was not quite in that category of display; it was in a popular setting, and therefore much more in line with the lively, boisterous street entertainment provided by Black Billy Waters rather than the noble salon concerts of George Bridgetower.

By mid century, large-scale fairs and pleasure gardens were giving way to a new kind of venue for entertainment. The music hall grew from the noisy saloon bars of public houses where, for a small fee, punters were entertained by singers, players and dancers, although bills also included "specialty" acts, including jugglers, plate-spinners, knife-throwers, magicians, acrobats, strong men, puppeteers, mime artists and mind-readers, also known as mentalists. This cross-over with the world of the circus did not alter the fact that the core element of music hall entertainment was popular song, above all tunes in which the audience was encouraged to participate, mainly by repeating a chorus that followed the verses sung by the performer. Music hall thrived on songs that struck a chord with an largely working-class audience, which could be lively if not unruly. Lyrics and melodies had to have an immediate appeal and tap into the sentiments and concerns of the day. Traditional English songs such as "Pop Goes the Weasel" went down a storm, but so too did pieces by American songwriters, in particular those of Stephen Foster. Born in Pittsburgh and of Irish parentage, Foster was hugely influenced by Negro culture and he penned several minstrel tunes that became immensely popular around the world. British music hall patrons were known to enjoy numbers such as "Old Folks At Home", "Oh! Susanna" and "Massa's in the Cold Ground". Being able to raise one's voice in a convivial atmosphere with a tankard of ale and smoking tobacco in a clay pipe suited the needs of the new urbanites who were earning a living as machine-minders in factories.[12]

Such conviviality was regarded with distaste by the respectable middle classes. There were organisations such as the National Temperance League, whose moralist policy of zero tolerance of alcohol consumption was one of the most forceful attempts of the middle classes to "civilize" the workers. Evangelicals preached that if "the eyes of the Lord were everywhere", so the bottom of a gin glass would be no less likely to be spared his scrutiny than the inhumanity of man against man – or heathens in need of conversion.[13]

For such middle-class Victorians, faith was a kind of empowering, multi-purpose energy that could improve material as well as spiritual health. A god-fearing working man would have the discipline and moral fibre to serve the cause of free trade and industrial expansion. Godliness, cleanliness, respectability and the saving of souls were the watchwords of Evangelism. Christian Missionary organizations existed on both sides of the Atlantic and it was one of the pioneering organizations in the New World, the American Missionary Association, that decisively broadened the experience and understanding that Britain had of Black music and musicians. Heavily involved in the Christian Reconstruction of the South following the ravages of the American Civil War in the 1860s, the AMA worked closely with the Freedman's Bureau to increase educational opportunities for people of colour. Its membership was open to "any person of evangelical sentiments who professes faith in the Lord Jesus Christ, who is not a slaveholder or in the practise of other immoralities." So said General Clinton B. Fisk, one of the Bureau's assistant commissioners and it was his name that was given to one of the first major institution for Blacks in the Southern States – Fisk

School, which was established on 9 January 1866, just three years after Abraham Lincoln made his historic Emancipation Proclamation.

The students were the sons and daughters of slaves who had to abide by a strict code of conduct, drawn up to foster their growth as individuals in what was a psychologically disorientating point in American history: the moment when those who had hitherto been seen as chattel would take their first steps to autonomy. The AMA insisted on imposing strict discipline on all aspects of the daily life of Blacks in order to achieve this goal.

George Leonard White was a music lover and he formed a chorus of AMA students under the direction of a talented black music teacher and pianist, Ella Sheppard, who joined the school in 1868. They made their debut in 1871 with a well-received performance of William Bradbury's *Cantata of Esther* at the nearby Nashville Masonic Hall.[14]

By that time Fisk School had run into financial difficulties, and the premises needed maintenance; White had the idea of a tour with the choir to raise money. From this desire to sing in the name of Jesus, a blessed "symmetry of Evangelicalism and Utilitarianism", was born the Fisk Jubilee Singers. With between five and nine members, the ensemble became the foremost international black artists of the Victorian Age. Among the vocalists in the first incarnation of the group were granddaughters of slaves such as Jennie Jackson as well as Maggie Porter (soprano) and bass singers Greene Evans and Isaac Dickerson as well as 8-year-old George 'Little Georgie' Wells who did short, light-hearted skits before the performance of the singers began in earnest.

They embarked upon their successful debut tour of cities in the American North in the autumn of 1871. It was clear that their voices were outstanding and that in Ella Sheppard the Fisk Jubilee Singers had a musical director with the skill and rigour to ensure that they performed effectively.

They had to overcome the cultural and political legacy of minstrelsy and its role in lowering the expectations of the artistic capabilities of people of colour. The prevalence of minstrelsy meant that groups of black singers would be perceived as minstrels, whether or not they were doing Jim Crow and Zip Coon. Toni P. Anderson points out in *Tell Them We are Singing for Jesus* (2010), her account of the early years of the Fisk Jubilee Singers, that ministers were reluctant to countenance them as a worthwhile Christian enterprise because of the connotations of burnt cork. Anderson uncovered an early advertisement for the group that tells its own story: "A band of Negro minstrels will sing in the Vine Street Congregational church this morning." On several other occasions the group was unceremoniously referred to as "nigger minstrels". Early visitors from England to the American South, such as the actress Fannie Anne Kemble, had written of the "wild and unaccountable" music of slaves[15] while other commentators, like the 19th century Louisiana historian Grace King, wrote of their "incoherent, unintelligible words". For such reasons, the Fisk group attempted to distance itself from slave associations. George Leonard White's decision to call them the Jubilee singers shrewdly circumnavigated the issue of racial identity. The name did not signify that the singers were black.

For the same reason, it is not surprising that the group was reluctant to develop a repertoire that featured any kind of piece that could be readily identified as a slave song or plantation melody. According to Maggie Porter, the Fisk soprano, there were many free blacks who were keen to bury such music in "the grave of slavery". This meant turning their backs on some forms of vocal expression that had been crucial to the psychological survival and self-expression of African Americans, such as the rhythmic chanting used to sustain morale during the backbreaking task of picking cotton – the work song or field holler, the most "African" forms of Black American music. These offered a vital form of emotional release because the slaves were hearing something that they themselves created outside of the instructions of a foreman.

Where the Fisk did draw on Black cultural traditions was in their repertoire of Negro Spirituals, where African voices drew on a range of European hymns to make something of their own. The question of how much "blackness" the Fisk were allowed to impart to their performances, in terms of their demeanour and gesture, was vexed. Early critics may have praised the beauty of their voices, but they also noted what was missing from their behaviour: they were not being *too* black. After seeing a performance, John Sullivan Dwight, a Boston critic wrote:

> They do not attempt to imitate the grotesque bodily motions or the drawling intonations that often characterize the singing of great congregations of colored people in their excited religious meetings.[16]

Whether it took place in a wooden church or a tent revival, it is clear that the coming together of Blacks in excited, joyful voice clearly alarmed many whites; it was too close to "wildness", too close to a loss of control that could upset the established social order. "Excitable" was the term applied to Negroes by colonial governors in Jamaica, while colonial administrators in Australia noted, when observing Aborigines, "the savage yells", "diabolic whoops", "contortions" and "shifting of their bodies" that could not refrain from movement. The context of racial prejudice that the Fisk Jubilee Singers had to operate within was thus all too real. Proximity to what could be seen as slave expression – any exuberant gesture or demonstrative behaviour – had to be avoided. Jubilee was not Master Juba so any double shuffle was off limits.

Regardless of these misgivings, Spirituals did enter the Fisk Jubilee repertoire. The string of concerts that the singers performed in packed churches in New York, netting close to $4,000 in the space of a week, marked their arrival as a national phenomenon. The highpoint of this tour was a performance for President Ulysses S. Grant at the White House. Even so, despite the recognition of their talent and the decorum of their performance, epithets such as "purely natural", "rude" and "uncultivated", "quaint", "strange" and "wild" were all applied in reviews, indicating that there was still uncertainty over exactly what to make of these "dusky" singers.

The tour was sufficiently successful for George Leonard White to think about sending his charges to Europe. Newly formed competitors such as the Canaan Singers and Hampton Singers were threatening the success of the fundraising campaign, so it made good sense for White to arrange for a tour of England, because this was virgin and potentially lucrative territory.

Hence, in April 1873, the company sailed to Liverpool on the *Batavia*, on a voyage that took eleven days and resulted in several bouts of sea-sickness for some of the less hardy members of the ensemble.

Here was a ship that was carrying the sons and daughters of slaves to the hub of the slave trade, but they now had the status of passengers, unlike earlier black musicians for whom the sea had more uncomfortable meanings, such as Joseph Emidy, who as noted above, was kidnapped and forced to play jigs and reels on his violin for the sailors, after having performed opera in Lisbon. Fisk's transatlantic crossing was, therefore, a powerful statement of progress for artists of colour.

The great and the good of England greeted the Fisk Jubilee Singers warmly. Among their most fervent supporters was Anthony Ashley Cooper, the Earl of Shaftesbury, the philanthropist who had worked tirelessly for social justice in many areas of national life, including to improve working conditions in factories, mines and, famously, the notoriously dangerous lives of juvenile chimney sweeps. Shaftesbury also headed the Freedmen's Aid Society of Great Britain, which was an auxiliary organization to the American Missionary Association. Like his transatlantic counterparts, Shaftesbury was a committed evangelical who believed that the world could only be made a better place by following the word of God. Artists such as Fisk could not fail to move a man of such deep emotional sensibilities and progressive political convictions.

Shaftesbury arranged a private concert at the Willis Rooms in St. James, London, in the presence of several high-ranking personalities on 6 May, 1873. The Duke and Duchess of Argyll attended and it was they who subsequently convened an audience for Fisk with Queen Victoria. Royalty was to meet the scions of slavery.

The press did not refrain from attaching political importance to the encounter. *The Times* declared: "It is remarkable that the company of Negro singers should have vaulted to the highest circles in the land." But Ella Sheppard, musical director of the group, was not, according to the journal she kept on the tour, overwhelmed by the famously imposing British monarch. Her descriptions were far from fawning. Victoria was: "A stout, ruddy-faced lady, simply dressed in black." She could not contain her great surprise at the monarch's plain appearance, adding that the queen was a "matronly looking lady, dressed like ordinary mortals."[17]

With Shaftesbury as a patron, many doors in British society opened for Fisk, and appearances followed at the Union Chapel in London as well as at venues in Scotland and northern England where, according to reports by the group members, they were granted good receptions at hotels – which was not always the case on their first tours in America.

In a short space of time, Fisk became sufficiently fashionable to receive afternoon tea or breakfast invitations from prominent Londoners, including Prime Minister William Gladstone. He hosted them at Carlton House Terrace, specifically so that they could make the acquaintance of the Prince and Princess of Wales. The meeting had a historical resonance. This was the same venue at which the then Prince of Wales had met the young mulatto violin prodigy, George Bridgetower, around seventy years before.

The remarkable success of the Fisk Jubilee Singers, which included a performance in front of a crowd of 7,000 at Hengler's circus in Liverpool, would appear to lend credence to the idea that British society was willing to accept people of colour on their own artistic merits. But there are important caveats to that statement. Amid all the good press, the adulation and the attention from nobility, there is no escaping references to the otherness, if not the oddity of these artists. On a later visit to the UK in 1875, Mable Lewis, a recently recruited singer, recalled how the "dark complexion" of one of the founding members of the troupe, Jennie Jackson, fascinated the public. Lewis's own thoughts on the way the singers were perceived was abundantly clear: "We were great curiosities."[18]

Although the first phonograph recordings were made in the 1860s, the earliest incarnation of Fisk Jubilee Singers was not captured for posterity, though many sessions were recorded in the early part of the 20th century. A 1915 disc of the Fisk Jubilee Male Quartet – John Work II and James A. Myers (tenor), Everett Harris (baritone) and Lemuel Foster (bass) – is striking. The music sounds as if it has been made by many more than four people such is the depth of the low register lines and the rich, at times creamy, character of the harmonies. The 1870s' description of voices of "superior power and sweetness" is borne out even by this greatly reduced version of the original group. What also contributes to this richness is the prevalence of long tones in arrangements, and the absolute clarity with which many notes are held, sometimes to the extent that the music acquires a slow pace that borders on a kind of suspended animation. Sounds are clearly enunciated by a group, who want to be anything but "wild" or "unintelligible".

Call and response, one of the central tenets of black Diasporan music, defines a piece such as "Little David Play on Your Harp", where the contrast between solo and ensemble vocal parts is superb, the effect of which is enhanced by the use of lengthy pauses between lines. Other pieces such as "Oh, Mary, Don't You Weep" stand out for the way that a soloist starts a line and the whole ensemble deftly completes it. Aside from its vocal richness, the quartet makes much creative capital from its changing configuration from one composition to the next.

Although the songs are performed *a cappella*, what stands out on several tracks, none more so than the gripping rendition of "Oh, Mary", is the quartet's sure mastery of rhythm. Here the beat, a steady insistent 4/4, upholds the arrangement and the pulse is so strong and regular that one can feel, or at least imagine, the time tapped out by hands or a percussion instrument.

One wonders: did the Fisk Jubilee Singers rehearse with a tambourine or handclaps to act as a metronome? Did they stomp their feet on the floor, or make movements of some kind in order to set a song's pulse? History tells us that in the earliest known "prayer shouts", in which slaves assembled in a ring, there was great emphasis on time-keeping by shuffling and sliding steps, and that the incidence of hand-clapping to the beat passed into the earliest Black Baptist churches.

Awareness of those critics who decried "grotesque bodily movement" may well have discouraged the Fisk singers from behaving in too expressive a way during concerts. However in 1876, Theodore F. Seward, editor of the *New York Musical Gazette*, addressed the issue of rhythm and speculated on what the singers may have been doing while lifting their voices to heaven:

> The first peculiarity that strikes the attention is the rhythm. This is often complicated, and sometimes strikingly original. But although it is new and strange, it is most remarkable that these effects are so extremely satisfactory.
>
> Another noticeable feature of the songs is the rare occurrence of triple time or three-part measure among them. The reason for this is doubtless to be found in the beating of the foot and the swaying of the body which are such frequent accompaniments of the singing. These motions are in even measure, and in perfect time; so it will be found that, however broken and seemingly irregular the movement of the music, it is always capable of the most exact measurement.[19]

According to gospel music scholar Robert Darden, it was Seward himself who was responsible for arrangements for the group that actually "smoothed out" some of the rough edges that he evokes in the above quotation, which highlights a lack of understanding of the fact that the original Negro spiritual was an improvised form, because nothing was transcribed, and singers in a congregation often added lyrics and exclamations at will. Fisk took the spiritual towards a form that was more sanitized. It became known as the Jubilee song. It was by no means a total loss, and one suspects that for the Victorian ear, the Jubilee's rhythmic sensation would have been heightened by arrangements where, by careful phrasing, the singers created powerful momentum with their voices.

For example, on "Everybody's Talk About Heaven" the singers raise the energy of their performance by executing a crisp jump in tempo in the last two beats of the final bar of the chorus, squeezing a volley of extra notes into the line without losing the sense of the "one" of the new bar. Energetic delivery was one of the most salient features of Fisk's work and their form of phrasal punctuation has verve.

Their phenomenal popular and critical success in England would have been inconceivable had they not had the reassuring stamp of religion on their credentials. It is thus hard to escape the sense that "the colored singers" fulfilled a range of expectations amongst their white audiences. On the one hand, there was no denying that their talent and the power of their performances lent a degree of dignity to Black entertainment in comparison to minstrelsy. On the other hand, the Fisk Jubilee Singers were living proof of how "civilisable" the descendants of slaves could be, especially as one of the goals of the age was that the souls of savages and heathens would be saved.

The triumph of the Fisk Jubilee Singers remains one of the great building blocks in the internationalization of African Diasporic culture. It was Black America inviting Britain to embrace, if not confront, music often regarded as strange, weird or grotesque, but by no means lacking in appeal. And when one listens to both Negro spirituals, and its outgrowth, gospel, the overriding impression is the supreme self-possession and stout conviction of the performers. The wholehearted and incontrovertible sense of emotional anchoring; the safe haven of solidarity within an ensemble; the united front in the face of adversity; the common desire to "fit the battle of Jericho": these are central tenets of music that is empowering, and by extension, political in a time of inequality. The spiritual's aesthetic is "we're gonna" not "we might". I may only have "this little light of mine" but "I'm gonna let it shine"'. The onus is on affirmation rather than interrogation, a summoning of faith by way of earthly sounds.[20]

Fisk's successful national tour did not go unnoticed in America, and it should come as no surprise that there were others who crossed the water in later years. Gospel music was one of the most vital forms of Black self-expression in Victorian times, primarily because the church was one of the few places of congregation where Blacks could enjoy a degree of autonomy denied to them elsewhere. And if the Fisk adapted their music for white audiences, there were other composers who came from the African-American church who were more forthright in their political statements. There was James A Bland, the son of a former slave who had found employment as a government clerk in Washington D.C. He has a claim to the title of being America's first successful Black songwriter. Prominent in his 1860s' repertoire was a song that overtly addressed the post-emancipation world: "De Slavery Chains Am Broke At Last". That piece captured the wave of optimism amongst Black Americans at the end of the civil war, and there were several other songs that conveyed the sense that a new day was dawning for those who had lived in bondage.

Indeed, the idea of emerging from darkness into light defined some of Bland's other enduring pieces. One was "In The Morning by the Bright Light". Another was "Keep Dem Golden Gates Wide Open". Perhaps the most celebrated was "Oh Dem Golden Slippers". If the title sounds familiar it was because it was an irreverent variation of "Golden Slumbers", a staple in the Fisk Jubilee repertoire.

Bland also followed the Fisk on a similar international path. Within a few years of enjoying success and making a name for himself in America, he travelled to Europe in the 1880s with the repertoire of songs he had written and secured bookings at major venues all over the Old World. He was reported as having performed for the great and the good in both England and Germany. The troupe of performers he led was clearly identified along racial lines, and made a no nonsense claim to being "the real thing", as were Haverly's Genuine Colored Minstrels, brought by the impresario Jack H. Haverly (1837-1901).

Notes

1. Prominent British and American abolitionists included Olaudah Equiano, Harriet Jacobs, John Brown, Henry Ward Beecher, Zachary Macaulay, Granville Sharpe and William Wilberforce.
2. The Slave Trade Act of 1807 led to fines of up to £100 if ships were found with slaves on board by Royal Navy patrols. This enforcement sometimes led slave traders to throw their human cargo overboard if they were about to fall foul of the law.
3. See Michael Leapman, *The World for a Shilling* (Headline, 2001), p. 8.
4. Derek B. Scott, *Sounds of the Metropolis* (Oxford Scholarship, online).
5. The Tambo 'n' Bones routine was a major contributor to the success of minstrelsy due to its visual novelty as well as rhythmic ingenuity.
6. Charles Dickens, *American Notes* (London: Chapman & Hall, 1842).
7. Edward Thorpe, *Black Dance* (Chatto & Windus, 1989), p. 13.
8. The comment featured in a text Gallagher wrote to accompany her retrospective at Tate Modern, London, 2013.
9. Robert Darden, *People Get Ready* (Continuum, 2004).
10. See Bernard Semmel, *The Governor Eyre Controversy* (London, 1962).

3: AFRICA, AMERICA, VICTORIA

11. An 1847 advertisement for the Ethiopian Serenaders at the Princess's Theatre, London has the strapline "Whose performances elicit shouts of laughter and applause."
12. See Donald Clarke, *Rise and Fall of Popular Music* (Viking, 1995).
13. Brian Harrison, *Drink and the Victorians: The Temperance Question in England, 1815-1872* (Faber and Faber, 1971).
14. Toni P. Anderson, *Tell Them We are Singing for Jesus* (Mercer, 2009), p. 28
15. Fanny Anne Kemble, *Journal of a Residence on a Georgia Plantation 1838-1839* (Harper & Bros, 1863).
16. Quoted in Toni P. Anderson, *Tell Them We are Singing for Jesus*, p. 131.
17. Quoted in Anderson, op. cit., p. 54.
18. Anderson, op. cit.
19. Robert Darden, *People Get Ready* (Bloomsbury, 2005).
20. Donald Clarke, *Rise and Fall of Popular Music*.

4 WAR SONGS AND HIAWATHA

The first thing that these black troops do when they get into camp is strike up some of their unearthly tunes. They have been known to fashion old tin biscuit boxes into a species of wind instrument.
— War correspondent on Sudanese soldiers serving in the British army, 1890s

A well dressed, curly-headed, dark little boy, holding a small violin in one hand and his marbles in the other.
— Early description of the composer Samuel Coleridge-Taylor, 1882

As outlined in Chapter 1, the British state had been ready to use black musicians in its armies, with black drummers famed for their pageantry and time-keeping on the parade ground and marching to battle. By the mid-nineteenth century, when the focus of empire had moved to India – and at its peak the British maintained an army of close to one million soldiers – the ruling class cannot have been pleased to discover that British music was being used in a revolt against empire. This occurred in 1857 when the sepoys recruited to the British army in India mutinied over what they believed was disrespect for their religious and cultural practices – the greasing of cartridges with beef and pork fat – and joined battle with British units in Uttar Pradesh. Song was used as a weapon of war by the sepoys, whose command of British culture was shown in their assimilation of the anthems of the day. The reports of war correspondents provide fascinating details:

It is ironic to find them persistently playing British marches 'as if in defiance'. At Lucknow 10,000 sepoys besieged British troops. They gave a regular morning performance plus an occasional evening encore that included The Standard Bearer's March, The Girl I Left Behind Me, See the Conquering Hero Come and concluded with God Save The Queen. The bands played the besiegers into action and it must have been a bizarre and fearsome nightmare to see the sepoys, ragged badmarshes and the picturesque retainers of the thalukadars [barons] sweeping in, like so many demons in human form, to some well loved English air.[1]

As Lewis Winstock has shown in his revealing study, *Songs and Music of the Redcoats*, this was a potent sign of the psychological and cultural complications that flowed from the expansion of England and the growth of its colonial dominions. Here were former subjects of the realm, whose task had been to combat local resistance to exploitative commercial activity, claiming a British heritage and its romantic and patriotic songs on their own terms. In the context of the mutiny, the songs became bitter mockery. If brown "demons in human form" really wanted to wage psychological warfare against white soldiers, then a verse or two of "See the Conquering Hero" would have unnerved even the most battle-hardened infantry, as the sepoys presented a "bizarre and fearsome nightmare".

Insurgent sepoys playing "Send Her Victorious, long to reign over us" was an early example of writing back to the Empire, but it also indicates how song was an important part of the British military tradition. British regiments chronicled events in songs that often aired their feelings about their adversaries. For example the "Ceylon Ballad" evoked "the black rebels" of the Indian Mutiny, but granted them a certain respect for their valour in battle.

However, British imperial songs often articulated crudely racist sentiments, employing derogatory terms to describe the natives in various territories. A popular song at garrison concerts and officers' parties was "Paddy Among The Kaffirs", yoking the Irish and Black South Africans in common insult. South Africa, which produced fine black choirs, several of which visited Britain in the 1890s, was the site of a protracted and bloody conflict at the end of the nineteenth century, because it was hotly contested by the British, the Dutch and the Zulu nation. To achieve imperial control, the British army fought first against the Zulu Kingship in 1879, and against the Boers of the South African Republic in 1880-81 and again in 1899-1902. Prior to battle, British soldiers sung racially abusive songs such as "Razors in the Air" against their Zulu adversaries:

> Don't you hear de niggers now?
> All dem nigs is cut to death
> Soon we'll make us darkeys one[2]

Chants such as these are shocking for many reasons. The alignment of racial taunt and graphic threat of violence remain familiar to anybody who has either stood on a football terrace or been confronted by skinheads or fascist boot-boys on the streets of postwar Great Britain. There is a clear parallel between political hooliganism and the tradition of insults and intimidation in the history of the British army. There are reports of some white British troops assaulting native recruits in colonial Africa and India for having the audacity to lend their voices to patriotic British tunes.

Racism notwithstanding, music was also a vital part of military recreation and entertainment. Tours of duty, especially in India, were often very lengthy, and the music played by regimental bands was intended to lift the spirits of troops and counter boredom and indiscipline. Inevitably, elements of local music were picked up by British bandsmen, although they were often dismissed for their "crudity". Even so, the Queen's Regiment, stationed in Calcutta in 1885, had a composer called J. McKenzie Rogan who based several marches on Indian themes. Another popular song was "Zachmi Dil, The Wounded Heart", which came from the Pashtuns of Afghanistan. It was a very candid homoerotic lament.

> There's a boy across the river
> With a bottom like a peach
> But alas – I cannot swim.[3]

This tune was later adapted as an unofficial march by the North Staffordshire and Liverpool regiments. Global cultural history is nothing if not complex, but to think that hard-as-nails squaddies in the British army, an institution that once punished homosexuality with a court-martial, were playing an Indian ode to a fruity fundament, underlines how the Empire could be subverted in the most surprising ways.

Tempting as it is to dismiss the phenomenon of "Zachmi Dil", it is nonetheless a sign of how Britain was affected by its engagement with foreign cultures, and not always being able to control the direction of the flow as tightly as it would have liked. What observers called "Native Music" was never segregated from British ears abroad, though the first instinct was to disparage. Of particular offence to European ears was the apparent problem afflicting Sikh brass bands, whose style sometimes deviated from those of Albion. According to a German officer called Sauer, these bands produced "the most discordant... vile music I had ever heard." British officers explained this as the result of the physical inferiority of the Sepoy musicians. It was both a matter of style and puff. As one officer explained: "The natives are generally slow in adapting their ears to European strains. They seem not to possess that strength of lungs necessary for filling our wind instruments."[4] In the dispatches of war correspondents of the period it is evident that the Indians and Africans who played music in the British colonial army were viewed with a mixture of passing curiosity and be-grudging admiration. It was noted by observers that Sudanese who were recruited by the British army in the 1890s had a desire to make music at all available opportunities, but what they played still seemed strange and disconcerting to European ears:

> The first thing that these black troops do when they get into camp is strike up some of their unearthly tunes, and in the absence of normal appliances they have been known to fashion old tin biscuit boxes into a species of wind instrument.[5]

Improvisation such as this, making music without conventional musical instruments, resonates with developments in the West Indies in the 20th century. The precursor to the steel band in Trinidad was the percussion group in which household implements and labourer's tools were all deployed to create rhythms for carnival parades. The biscuit tin was a much-favoured item in these groups.

But it was not just in the making of unconventional instruments out of serendipitous materials that African and European cultures intersected. The lyre is one of the oldest instruments found in both Sudan and Egypt, with origins as far back as 3000 BC. In Victorian times there were versions of it that provided a fascinating reflection on the way material objects coursed through channels opened up by imperialism and invasion. Some lyres had a circular sounding board with a horizontal bar to which were tied various charms that ensured that the musician could be heard and recognised as he made his way from one recital, mostly at religious ceremonies, to another. Among the charms were beads, bells, amulets and cowrie shells sourced locally, as well as metal levers and cogs culled from steam trains, and ha'penny coins from England. The industrial items and currency most probably denote the interaction of British workers and soldiers with Africans, either employed in civilian or military life.

Among the most musically active of the many "native" musicians con-scripted to British colonial regiments were Egyptians and Sudanese, who saw action in Khartoum in the 1890s. Their bands featured a wide range of horns and percussion instruments, though the soldiers were also known to chant heartily on marches, including popular music hall songs taught by their colleagues from England. There was also the 15-piece Sierra Leone Frontier Police Band which, in 1897, greatly impressed at Queen Victoria's Diamond Jubilee celebrations in London. In its ranks was a soldier known as "Little Tom" who was awarded a prize for his bugling. What all these bands demonstrated, with their eclectic repertoires, was how cultures around the world were intermingling in the Empire. Here were units of Africans, enlisted by the British, playing a range of songs that included Arab tunes that had sometimes been arranged by Italian bandmasters. Another piece the Sierra Leoneans had taken to their hearts was "Oh Dem Golden Slippers", which, as noted in the previous chapter, was the parody that James A. Bland wrote of "Golden Slumbers", one of the Negro spirituals performed by the Fisk Jubilee Singers. A slave song, born in the realm of the sacred and dragged into the secular world, now linked outposts of the British Empire and Africans to their descendants in the New World.[6]

The idea of African-American music travelling to Africa via Britain's armed forces makes the point that even the military apparatus that under-pinned Empire was by no means detached from culture. The songs played by British regiments are thus a vital if somewhat overlooked part of the bigger story of Black music in Britain, and their existence underlines the growing complexity that comes with the expansion of a country beyond its natural borders. Just as words from Indian languages became an integral part of standard English – curry, pyjama, bungalow – it is evident too that melodies and rhythms heard in India and other parts of the Empire must have caught the ear of any bandleader with a modicum of curiosity. If "Zachmi Dil" could end up as a march, then it is likely that other compositions, or at least fragments of them, may have been adopted by units who returned to Britain after a tour of duty. Sounds travel.

★

While the Fisk Jubilee singers, with their sober garments and serious demeanour, presented a wholesome image of the black artist, the raucous drumming of Sudanese soldiers and "half-caste" bandsmen enlisted in the British army in Africa and India were at the other end of the spectrum. Between them they show the vastly differing circumstances in which black musicians operated during the time of Empire.

A marker of a significant change in the artistic scope of those who followed is to be found in a dramatic encounter that occurred in 1905, four years after the death of Queen Victoria. The meeting took place between two men who symbolized a confluence of the worlds of letters and music. One was black, the other white. They sat in an elegant drawing room and drank tea.

The fair-skinned Englishman was Ernest Hartley Coleridge, the grand nephew of the poet Samuel Taylor Coleridge. His "dark complexioned" acquaintance was Samuel Coleridge-Taylor, the first black British composer to achieve both national and international fame. The twinning of the two names was not coincidental, but reflected the fact that the father of the latter, Daniel Hughes Taylor, a West African, was an avid reader of the poetry of Coleridge, and had paid tribute to him by using his surname as the middle name of his first-born son. The musician was intended to carry something of the spirit of the poet.[7]

Hence the meeting between Coleridge-Taylor, the composer, and the poet's descendant both brought personal and wider cultural history into focus. It was not small talk that the two made, either. Ernest Hartley Coleridge read his famous antecedent's poem "Kubla Khan"[8] and the composer subsequently agreed to set the words to music, which was completed and performed on several occasions in 1906. The poem became a rhapsody for soloist, chorus and orchestra and was heard at the Handel Society in London and the Scarborough festival.

It is easy to see why the poem captured the imagination of Coleridge-Taylor, given that it told of a mythical, fantastical palace in strong, bold, rhymes – "it was a miracle of rare device/A sunny pleasure dome with caves of ice" – and the poem made reference to music in the "dancing rocks" and "the damsel with a dulcimer". The line "Could I revive within me/The symphony and song" is an invitation for any musician minded to use image or metaphor as a launching pad for an overture or a cadenza. But of all the lines that

COLERIDGE TAYLOR

may have struck a chord with the composer, it was quite possibly: "It was an Abyssinian maid/And on a dulcimer she played". This explicitly African reference would not have gone unnoticed by Coleridge-Taylor, for evocations of Africa and its diasporas were defining features of his substantial body of work.

His composition titles tell their own story: *Variations on an African Theme*; *Bamboula Suite,* named after a popular West Indian dance; *Toussaint L'Ouverture,* inspired by the legendary leader of the Haitian slave revolt; *I'm Troubled in Mind,* based on the Negro spiritual "Nobody Knows the Trouble I See". These sources were not European, but the last piece was first heard by the composer in Britain, where it had been performed by the Fisk Jubilee Singers. Here then was the beginning of a transatlantic exchange of ideas that developed between musicians of colour throughout the 20th century.

Coleridge-Taylor, of whom Elgar, the leading British composer of the day, said, "he is by far the cleverest fellow going among the young men", exhibited an interest in African and African-American culture from early in his life. He had studied the work of the leading figures of the European classical canon, specifically Antonin Dvorak,[9] but his relationship with Black artists was even more important. In 1896, he met Paul Laurence Dunbar[10], one of the most accomplished of the post-slavery writers who was pioneering the use of the African American dialects of the South in his poetry. When the latter visited London, they performed joint recitals. The musician wrote scores for several of the writer's poems such as "The Corn Song", "At Candle Lightin' Time" and "The African Romances".

Born in Holborn, London, in 1875 and raised in Croydon, Surrey, to an English mother and a Sierra Leonean surgeon father, who returned to Africa because of the failure of his progress in the medical profession, Samuel Coleridge-Taylor was discovered by a local conductor, Joseph Beckwith. "A well dressed, curly headed, dark little boy, holding a small violin in one hand and his marbles in the other," was what Beckwith said of the precocious child after happening upon him in the street.[11]

By the age of seven, Coleridge-Taylor showed ability on the violin, revealed an excellent singing voice and a keen interest in composition – an early indication of which was an arrangement of "God Save the Queen". Among his first pieces for the Royal College of Music (to which he was admitted in 1890), performed with his fellow students were a clarinet sonata in F minor and *Nonet*, a piece scored for violin viola, cello, double bass, clarinet, horn, bassoon and piano, an instrument on which he had become proficient in just a few years. It made sense for him to gravitate towards the keyboard, with its rich harmonic and melodic possibilities, because his compositional gifts had been there for all to see from the outset.

Although the RCM was founded in 1883, with the philanthropic aim of making advanced training in music theory and performance available to winners of scholarships, it was, perhaps inevitably, not immune to racial prejudice. George Grove, who became the first director of the college, did not immediately endorse Coleridge-Taylor's admission. There were concerns at objections from the other students over a 'nigger' crossing the threshold of the institution.

Even so, Coleridge-Taylor soon began to fulfil his potential. He found that composition rather than violin was where his heart really lay and, hopefully to the delight of Grove, he availed himself of the performance of his pieces by the RCM orchestra, set up by Grove to develop original work. Little is known of his very earliest compositions, but it is likely that he would have made a start with compositions for small ensembles within RCM rehearsal rooms. And if he was the only black person in the establishment, he may never have been happier than in that setting, surrounded by instruments, manuscripts and music stands.

In spite of, or maybe because of his isolation, Coleridge-Taylor had a marked sense of his blackness and took an explicit pride in it. He referred to himself as a black man rather than the more commonly used term of "coloured", which would have been addressed to him as a man of mixed race with a light skin tone, and up until the very end of his life, he emphatically insisted on being called a Negro musician, noting on his death bed with a barely concealed degree of distaste: "When I die the critics will call me a Creole." He was probably using "Creole" in the West African rather than the Caribbean sense, referring to the Westernised, often mixed-race elite in Sierre Leone who regarded themselves as superior to those who were culturally African.

It is probable that his racial pride was fostered by his experiences of racial discrimination. There were the "high jinks" he endured at school when other boys set fire to his "woolly" hair to see if it would burn. And whilst his work achieved great critical acclaim, he was not spared the indignities that stemmed from prevalent assumptions about the African continent. "Do you actually drink tea and eat bread and butter like the rest of us?" one clergyman asked. One can only wonder what the incredulous man of god would have made of the sight of the musician holding a bone china cup in the company of Ernest Hartley Coleridge years later as they discussed music and poetry instead of the pressing need to subject Africans to evangelisation.

He did not allow such indignities to hamper his progress as a composer. Surveying Coleridge-Taylor's vast output, it is clear that his primary strength was the use of contour and contrast – tonally, metrically, rhythmically – to create music that had a wide spectrum of colours and movement that sometimes creates a carefully wrought mosaic effect.

Of his very early works, *Fantasiestucke*, five fantasia pieces for string quartets, stands out for its shifting time signatures, with the second movement's serenade moving quite stealthily between 5/4 and 6/4. Commentators have evoked the "spirited melodies" of other parts of the piece such as "Minuet Trio", where the volleys of short, curt notes, mostly eighths and sixteenths, have a galvanizing effect on the themes. There was a lively, hearty side to the composer's character, and it surfaced in the dynamism of his scores.

In 1898, Coleridge-Taylor wrote a work that met with instant success when it was premièred at the Tin Tabernacle Room at the RCM and it still remains his signature piece: *Hiawatha's Wedding Feast*. This is the "little oratorio" that captured the imagination of the British public and launched "the coloured composer" internationally. Two sequels, *The Death Of Minnehaha* and *Hiawatha's Departure* were composed in the two years that followed and the complete trilogy was performed at the Royal Albert Hall in 1900.

Based on Henry Wadsworth Longfellow's narrative poem, the original score has passages of soaring lyricism, tonal contrasts and richness of timbres and the general grandeur of sound that characterizes the late Romantic in classical music. This was the period when Strauss and Mahler created music in which both a yearning sensuality and an evocation of the natural world was able to touch listeners. Coleridge-Taylor caught some of this feeling, though the overt imagery in the succession of tableaux in his composition had something of a "light", populist touch without being at all vulgar. Listeners may also have been attracted by the exoticism of the "red Indian story" with its array of characters whose names alone – Hiawatha, Minnehaha, Pau-Puk-Keewis, Yenadizze – evoked a "strange adventure" that was far removed from familiar English musical tropes.

Although the movements for orchestra and chorus have moments of majesty, it is the feature for solo voice, "Onaway Awake Beloved", that represents Coleridge-Taylor at his most engaging. This has become a staple of the repertoire of tenor singers since its first airing at the RCM, and several recent recordings of this song can be found. The piece is a love song in which Hiawatha's friend Chibiabos, beholding the maidens Minnehaha and Laughing Water, celebrates their beauty by evoking the "wildflower of the forest, lilies of the prairie, wildflowers in the morning." While the natural imagery of Longfellow's lyric provides the singer with rich raw material, it is the ingenuity of the composer's score that catches the ear and conveys the essence of Chibiabos' performance "in accents sweet and tender" and "in tones of deep emotion". This is what vocal line and orchestration achieve, particularly in the way that the strings go through myriad shifts from slender and light to dark and thick timbres which convey if not a hint of foreboding, the implication that the blissful nature of the moment is tied to a certain undercurrent of seriousness. Throughout the piece there are many juxtapositions of legato and presto phrases, the effect of which is to have the voice floating bird-like over a forest of activity rustling in the strings and woodwinds. Several vocal lines are punctuated by discreet melodies comprising three to five notes. Coleridge-Taylor also uses the common classical composer's method of having the same phrase played by several different instruments in the orchestra in turn, so as to anchor the character of the line in the mind of the listener, all the while emphasizing the distinct identity of the components of the ensemble.

Above all, "Onaway Awake Beloved" shows that the young Anglo-African, as he was referred to by many reviewers, understood one of the great maxims of orchestral music – the whole is greater than the sum of the parts. The most conspicuous elements of the score – the infusion of brightness wrought by some of the key changes; the descending spiral of short, truncated string phrases that capture the delicacy of images such as "wildflower in the morning"; the chirpy, busy glissando effects that mark a contrast with the tranquil, relaxed glide of the central melody – catch the ear without jumping out too ostentatiously. And upon repeat listening, one hears shifts in the roles assigned to the instruments, such as the growing strength of the piccolos that pierce through the canopy of strings in quite aggressive fortissimo motifs towards the end of the piece, which contrasts with the relative subtlety of earlier lines.

Previous compositions had revealed Coleridge-Taylor's desire to play with meter, realizing that alternations of an even six beats to the bar to an odd five could lend to a score the kind of wavering pulse that enables music to toy with perceptions of a regular and irregular unfolding of time. Yet with "Onaway Awake Beloved" the composer used a 4/4 rhythm to anchor the long, languorous notes that suggest his professed admiration for the "open air sound" and "the genuine simplicity" of Dvorak, one of his great idols. No doubt, one of the attractions of Dvorak was that the Czech composer had made his own discoveries of African American music in his Symphony No. 9 (the *New World Symphony*). In the 28 May, 1893 edition of the *Boston Herald*, Dvorak, who was then the head of the National Conservatory of Music in New York, had stated: "I am now satisfied that the future music of this country must be founded upon what are called the Negro melodies. This must be the foundation of any serious and original school of composition to be developed in the United States."[13]

From the time he left the Royal College of Music in 1906, up until his death in 1912, Coleridge-Taylor continued to compose and travelled widely to perform his work. Apart from many concerts in London, there were recitals in Leeds, Brighton, Middlesbrough, Gloucester and, most significantly, in America. There his reputation spread rapidly to the black intelligentsia. He was one of their own. So the collaboration between Coleridge-Taylor and Paul Laurence Dunbar noted above was not serendipitous. Dunbar knew of Coleridge-Taylor. He *wanted* to meet him. Here, nationality was second to race. This was borne out by Coleridge-Taylor's meeting with the Fisk Jubilee singers in Britain in the 1890s, when he was greatly inspired by them. The admiration was not one-sided. The group's manager, Frederick

Loudin, sang the young composer's praises to all who would listen. He took Mamie E. Hilyer, the founder of The Treble Clef club, a group of women music lovers from Washington D.C, to visit Coleridge-Taylor and his wife at their home in Croydon. Such was their mutual empathy that the Treble Clef club became the Samuel Coleridge-Taylor Chorale Society upon Hilyer's return to America. The composer's work soon crossed the Atlantic. *Hiawatha* was performed at the Metropolitan Methodist Episcopal Church in Washington on 23 April 1901.

The following year Coleridge-Taylor made the first of three visits to America at the behest of Hilyer. From the moment he stepped off the boat at Boston there were half a dozen eager newspaper reporters waiting to "devour" him and thereafter his schedule took him to major cities such as Washington and New York.

The pleasure that he took in attending an African American church service and having the opportunity to conduct an orchestra with a Black chorus was uppermost in his mind as he explained in a letter to Hilyer: "I don't think anybody else would have induced me to visit America, excepting the fact of an established society of coloured singers. It is for that first and foremost that I am coming."

Press reports of the performances were entirely favourable, but what came to the fore very quickly was the socio-cultural significance of the appearance of a black composer in highbrow theatres and concert halls. The regional African-American newspaper, *The Georgia Baptist*, did not hold back in expressing pride at the achievements of the artist who was less a Briton and more a Black. He was *their* man from across the water who was made to feel very much at home.

> When Samuel Coleridge-Taylor of London walked upon the platform of Convention Hall last Wednesday night, and made his bow to four thousand people, the event marked an epoch in the history of the Negro race of the world. It was the first time that a man with African blood in his veins ever held a baton over the heads of the members of the great Marine Band, and it appeared to me that the orchestra did its best to respond to every movement of the dark-skinned conductor.[14]

Plans were made for Coleridge-Taylor to be introduced to President Theodore Roosevelt, but he was unavailable when the meeting was supposed to take place. Nonetheless, the fact that such an encounter was proposed indicates how far his star had risen. He was courted by the ruling elite as well as by the Black community.

A sign of his elevation was the name given him by the prestigious New York Philharmonic, with whom he worked on his third trip to America in 1910. They dubbed him the "African Mahler" because Mahler was regarded as the greatest living composer to have ever visited the New World. The fact that Coleridge-Taylor was not referred to as British, or even Black

British, underlines the lack of recognition of a black British identity. Elgar was white. He was authentically British. Coleridge-Taylor was seen as an African before anything else, though he was really a South Londoner.

Given the appalling racism Coleridge-Taylor had received from some of the classical music establishment – the renowned conductor Hans Richter expressed disdain for his scores on the grounds that they were the work of a "nigger" – and because he was well aware that his father had returned to Africa because of the difficulties of being a black doctor in London, it is not surprising that Coleridge-Taylor related his achievements to his race, rather than to his geographic location: "I am a great believer in my race."

He had read *The Souls of Black Folk*, W.E.B. Dubois' seminal 1903 treatise on the condition of the Negro in America, and was very much aware of the political resonances that his work acquired. Musical development was not the sole issue. What was at stake was the wider perception of Blacks and their place in society. Any Black music that was able to win the favour of a monarch or moneyed patrons, because it was thought to be on a par with the sophistication of European classical music, would thus gain the greatest accolade. It would show that a supposedly inferior race could reach the level of the superior one. Describing Negro songs as American or British was problematic because Negroes were seen as neither American nor British – an issue that has resonated into the 21st century. Inevitably, Black music was perceived as a phenomenon that fell outside well-established European norms, which is exactly why Coleridge-Taylor was not so much a British composer as an "African" Mahler.

Coleridge-Taylor's commitment to his blackness led him to materials that emphasised his race. The use of more explicitly African and West Indian elements in the music first emerged between 1904 and 1905 when he wrote *Four African Dances* and *Twenty Four Negro Melodies*. Of the latter, Coleridge-Taylor said: "What Brahms has done for the Hungarian folk music, Dvorak for the Bohemian, and Grieg for the Norwegian, I have tried to do for the Negro melodies."[15]

The sources of the *24 Negro Melodies* were found far and wide: east, west and South Africa, the West Indies, and Black America. For the latter, Coleridge-Taylor turned, perhaps inevitably, to a book of songs used by the Fisk Jubilee Singers as well as to an extensive collection of Jubilee and Plantation Songs and Afro-American folk songs. One might expect the result to be a kind of Afro-classical music, but judging from the analysis of excerpts of available scores, as well as from the insights provided by Coleridge-Taylor himself, the aim was not necessarily a blend or fusion of "ethnic folk" and concert music, but rather an attempt to stay true to his identity as a symphonic composer whilst using a range of materials that was not exclusively European.

Recurrent in the American themes is the emphasis on intervals such as minor thirds, which has the effect of imparting some of the emotional warmth that pervades idioms such as the Negro spiritual. Yet Coleridge-Taylor's training and education as a European classical composer is what dominates. Ultimately, it can be said that the work is really classical music with mild African and African-American resonances rather than Afro-classical music per se. The title of one of his other works, *Symphonic Variations on an African Air*, makes his position clear. It is also fair to describe Coleridge-Taylor's work as accessible and appealing rather than esoteric or dense, and that may well explain why he was able to catch the ear of the general public in the way that he did. In Britain, he was, after all, writing for a white audience.

In 1912, just seven years after the completion of *24 Negro Melodies*, Coleridge-Taylor died, at the tragically young age of 37. Although the official cause of death was pneumonia, the sheer weight of his workload was a contributory factor, and that may have been tied to the paltry income he received for his compositions and conducting engagements during his lifetime. *Hiawatha's Wedding Feast* was immensely popular, but was sold to a publisher for just three guineas.

A cursory glance through his substantial oeuvre is sufficient to remind us that Samuel Coleridge-Taylor was a serious classical composer, but the immense appeal of some of his works reveals his openness to qualities that were not necessarily taught in the practise rooms of a venerable institution such as the Royal College of Music. Among the letters that Coleridge-Taylor wrote to a friend is one that clarifies his thoughts on the question of musical nature versus nurture. The friend had travelled in Eastern Europe and its border with Asia and was surprised at how *good* the local gypsy musicians were. To which Coleridge-Taylor replied:

> Were they to study such things as harmony, would they be better off?
>
> But I warn you not to allow harmony to cramp your artistic development, because it should be remembered that these things must always be subservient to the beauty of sound. Imagination should be far more thought of than it is in the playing of music.
>
> Technique is not everything and everyone has some small amount of imagination. We must look upon music from a more impersonal standpoint. It is becoming too much admiration for the man, and too little love for his music.

Those words are ironic, because Samuel Coleridge-Taylor's works did not die with him at all. In later years there would be grand revivals of his work, and in the West Indies classical music societies bearing his name were established.

Notes

1. Lewis Winstock, *Songs and Music of the Redcoats: A History of the War Music of the British Army 1647-1902* (Leo Cooper, 1970) p. 173
2. *Songs and Music of the Redcoats,* p. 246
3. Ibid., p. 205
4. Ibid., p. 295
5. Ibid,. p. 197
6. Paul Oliver, *Black Music in Britain* (Open University Press, 1990), p. 88.
7. The account of Coleridge-Taylor's life is drawn from Jewel Taylor Thompson, *Samuel Coleridge-Taylor: The Development of His Compositional Style* (Scarecrow Press, 1994). The descriptions of the music come from my own listening.
8. Samuel Taylor Coleridge, "Kubla Khan Or A Vision In A Dream" (1816) in *The Complete Poems* (Penguin, 1997).
9. Dvorak, with his admiration for African American music, was a great source of inspiration to Samuel Coleridge-Taylor, so there was a certain symmetry in the declaration.
10. Paul Laurence Dunbar continues to be relevant to black musicians long after his death. In the early 1960s, American jazz vocalists Abbey Lincoln and Oscar Brown Jnr both recorded outstanding versions of his poem "When Malindy Sings".
11. Jewel Taylor Thompson, *Samuel Coleridge-Taylor: The Development of His Compositional Style*, p. 14
12. Jewel Taylor Thompson, op. cit. p. 116.
13. Jewel Taylor Thompson, op. cit.
14. Jewel Taylor Thompson, op. cit.
15. Jewel Taylor Thompson, op. cit.
16. Quoted in Jewel Taylor Thompson.

5 DAHOMEY DANCE

He used to do exhibitions during galas and he enjoyed making the kids
laugh by sitting on the bottom of the baths with a bucket on his head
singing songs like Oh My Darling Clementine and Jerusalem.
— Description of James Clarke, swimmer and vocalist, who arrived
in Liverpool from Jamaica in 1900.

When dey hear dem ragtime tunes
White fo'ks try to pass fo' coons
— Will Marion Cook's *In Dahomey*, Shaftesbury Theatre, London, 1903.

The rise of Liverpool from 18th century port whose consignments were
mainly domestic to a lucrative 19th century international thoroughfare
was a pivotal development in British mercantile history. No greater
sign of the status of the city could be found than at the prestigious
Great Exhibition of Crystal Palace in 1851. On display to visitors
was a scale model of Albert Dock, Liverpool. Its five miles of wharfs
were squeezed into a pen of 40 feet and its 1,600 ships replicated with
meticulous accuracy in order to convey the grand sweep of commerce
through that city, then known as "the New York of Europe".[1]

Changed too was the complexion of its population. Liverpool, which had
played a leading role in the slave trade, launching ships to Africa since 1699,
also saw the growth of a black population. This included the descendants
of freed slaves, African students, some the sons of wealthy traders who
were sent to Europe to further their education, and a large number of
black sailors, a good many of whom put down roots, often marrying white
women. This gave rise to a substantial black and mixed-race community
centred on the inner city area of Toxteth.

Blacks were highly valued in the British merchant navy because they
were thought to be better equipped to stand the blistering heat of the engine
room on the latest steamships, and West Africans, particularly the Kru, were
in demand as "stokers". There were also Arabs, East Indians, commonly
known as lascars, and West Indians, for whom life in the colonies had not
become any less arduous following abolition in 1838. As noted earlier,
the British government's free trade policy exacerbated the financial crisis
that engulfed the colonies as the plantation system collapsed, but without
freeing land for the independent settlement of ex-slaves. This created a

free, impoverished and disenfranchised black working class that jumped at labour opportunities abroad, primarily to Cuba and Panama. Others emigrated to America and Europe, though these were difficult territories to reach for those of limited financial means. Signing on as a seaman was one way to get to Britain; a few took the risk to travel illegally as stowaways.[2]

What we gather from the life stories of early black Liverpudlians is that they were resourceful and talented individuals. As Ray Costello, the great Liverpool historian, has pointed out, they also knew how to spring surprises, none more so than James Clarke (1886-1946), who arrived as a 14 year-old stowaway from British Guiana in 1900. An exceptionally strong swimmer, he represented the Everton Swimming club which won the North Lancashire League cup several times. More impressive was Clarke's feats as a lifesaver. He became known locally for rescuing people from the canal that connected Athol Street to Burlington Street in the city. He also taught many children to swim at Burrough Gardens swimming baths, which involved some showmanship, which can only be described as novel, as his son Vincent later recalled.

> He used to do exhibitions during galas and he enjoyed making the kids laugh by sitting on the bottom of the baths with a bucket on his head singing songs like Oh My Darling, Clementine and Jerusalem.[3]

The repertoire was completely in step with the times. "Oh My Darling, Clementine", a country and western folk ballad attributed to Percy Montrose, was one of the great popular songs of the 19th century, with its references to the gold rush and America as the land of opportunity, and with the kind of rousing chorus that suited audience participation in the music hall or family gatherings around a piano. The sight of a black swimmer belting out a tune for school children at the local baths is the kind of novel spectacle that enriched Liverpool's folklore.

Clarke was thus an immigrant singing a song that framed a movement of mass migration triggered by the desire to escape economic hardship. The involvement of a West Indian singer, who was also an accomplished sportsman, in popular culture, was a forerunner of what was to come.

Little is known about James Clarke's personal circumstances in British Guiana prior to his arrival in England, but chances are that he was from an impoverished background. As a stowaway he ran the kind of risks that are taken by people with very little to lose; the punishment for those who were caught could be a lengthy jail term, if not immediate repatriation

Liverpool further enhanced its national and international status by hosting the Colonial Products Exhibition of 1906. This grand fête put the spotlight on the luxurious output of the overseas territories, such as New Zealand kauri gum, African fabrics and West Indian fruits, but it also made the point that maintaining this rich harvest left no room for complacency in a competitive world. At the opening ceremony, Sir Alfred Jones warned

UK merchants, such as the powerful British Cotton Growing Association, that if it did not "look after" production in the colonies, then it would find the high yields of America hard to match. The colonies, exciting as they might be in "the eyes and imagination", to be a worthwhile enterprise had to be prosperous too.

The other dynamic was the "sentimental, the patriotic", the putative sense of kinship and belonging, of ties that bound the Mother Country to the children of the dominions, something encapsulated by Empire Day in schools where pupils donned the national dresses of the dominions and gathered around a little girl dressed as Britannia, all shiny helmet and sharpened trident. Hence the idea of presenting colonial people alongside colonial products struck a chord with Sir Alfred. He invited the Kingston Choral Union from Jamaica. Singing subjects would reflect well on the Crown and to make that colonial position clear, Jones renamed the choir the "Native Choir from Jamaica".[4]

After arriving in England in late January, the group made its debut at St. George's Hall for a short run of performances from the 30th of that month until February 8. The company was ten strong, one of whom Harry Nation, the pianist, accompanied the singers on pieces such as "Motherland" and "Climb Up Ye Little Children", as well as the British national anthem. Over the next two years the group went on to enjoy considerable success, appearing in Whitby, Bridlington, Wrexham, Tynemouth, Plymouth, Dundee, Waterford, Londonderry, Kilkenny, Ennis and Dublin. The press reports noted the "good English" and "quaint enunciation" of the vocalists. It is evident that many Britons, in an era before mass tourism, did not realize that West Indians spoke English.

The other aspect of the choir that deserves attention was the reported ability of one of the singers, Carlton Bryan, to make people laugh. He was described in several newspaper reports as an "amusing comedian" and a "humorist" who would launch into rib-tickling skits before the much more serious business of singing got underway. The humour appears incongruous in the context of the dress of the choir, as revealed in the surviving photographs. Clad in severely pressed tuxedos, bow-ties and evening dresses, T. Ellis Jackson, Connie Coverley, J. Packer Ramsay, Evelyn Gordon, Louis George Drysdale, J.T Loncke, Adeline McDermott, Marie Lawrence and Bryan look far too much like symphony hall artists for them to indulge in anything that could be regarded as trifling. Yet the fact that there was an element of humour in the performances underlines both the eclectic nature of many black stage presentations of the period and the proximity between accomplished artistry and "lighter" entertainment. Tomfoolery did not preclude technical excellence in the worlds of minstrelsy and music hall, and this duality seems to have been part of the Jamaican performances, where a concert delivered with great gravitas might have an interlude that had a distinct touch of levity. Indeed, Bryan's antics connected to the Fisk Jubilee Singers. They too initially had a young singer who was known for his comic verve: 8 year-old George 'Little Georgie' Wells who "often amused audiences with improvised songs, dances and humorous recitations."[5]

For the most part, it appears the Jamaican singers enjoyed their time in England, and their positive impressions may have prompted some of them to wonder whether they might be better off actually taking up permanent residence in a country that had been sufficiently liberal to pass a law that made primary school education compulsory.

Thomas Rutling,[6] a Fisk Jubilee singer, did indeed decide to make England his home. He took part in the group's last tour of Europe in 1878, after which he stayed on the continent before moving to England in 1890. It is not clear what he did upon arrival but it is known that he lived and taught singing in Manchester in 1901 before settling in Harrogate, north Yorkshire in 1905. In the same year he performed solo at Crystal Palace in London but struggled for concert work in the period that followed. He fell back on voice tuition and also wrote his autobiography, *Tom*, which was published in 1907. Rutling started to tour again, singing a repertoire of classic spirituals, no doubt to the delight of Fisk fans. However, in 1909 he suffered a stroke in Morecambe, was admitted to a nursing home in his adopted Harrogate and died in 1915. Although largely a footnote in British history, Rutling is nonetheless a no-table name in the history of black music in Britain, not only as a member of a pioneering group, but because he published an autobiographical record of his experiences. If he ever felt like a lone Christian soldier, he could have taken heart from the knowledge that his arrival in England coincided with the establishment of the first black Pentecostal church in England. It was set up in Peckham, south London by a Ghanaian, T. Brem Wilson.[7]

Other late nineteenth century Black arrivals in London from North America were the Bohee brothers, James (1844-1897) and George (1857-c1905). In 1891, at 7a Coventry Street, London W1 they started a school for students of the banjo, the instrument that the Canadian-born brothers had played when they formed the Bohee Minstrels in 1876. Thereafter they joined two other popular minstrel troupes, Callender's Georgia and Haverly's Genuine Colored Minstrels whose founder was James Bland, parodic composer of "Oh Dem Golden Slippers". In 1881 the Bohee brothers travelled to England with Haverly's and toured extensively, with George singing tenor as well as dancing, before they opted to make Lon-don their home. With its "frying pan" body, broom-handle neck and steel strings, the banjo caused quite a stir when it was handled with dexterity and technical flourish by the Bohees, and the Coventry Street studio that they founded soon became something of a focal point for aspiring banjo players, and the instrument's standing was given a significant boost among high society types when the Bohee brothers took on the most privileged kind of celebrity imaginable – the Prince of Wales. Now, playing the banjo became eminently fashionable. As Catherine Parsonage points out, its attraction maintained stereotypes: "The continued appeal of the banjo as representative of a sentimental, exotic, primitive alternative to 'official' culture, led to banjo music becoming an important musical craze in Britain in the 1880s."[8]

Articles that appeared in the British press reveal the fascination the banjo exerted as well as the persistence of the overarching notion of what constituted music in a polite society. *The Bristol Times and Mirror* of 20th November 1888 reported:

> Readers of newspapers, and particularly society journals, will remember that some time ago there was much discussion about the merits of the banjo as a drawing room instrument, and many illustrations were given in the comic serials of the effect its introduction into society could, would and should produce. Well, with such performers as the Bohee brothers [from whose entertainment there is an entire absence of everything unseemly] the banjo would not be out of place at social gatherings at the West-End, and indeed so long as the novelty lasted it would be a welcome change at those assemblies where the difficulty is to find something new. Their playing of the instrument which they have made their study was the most perfect ever. There was a considerable amount of artistic excellence about their manipulation.

Between 1890 and 1892, the Bohee brothers made wax cylinder recordings of duets in London, and George went on to cut at least 11 banjo solos without his brother. Although this music is not widely available today it was made at the cutting edge of Victorian technology and marked the transition of the Bohees from performers to recording artists which, at the time, was something of a rarefied status.

The Bohees undoubtedly brought an enrichment of the sounds available to Victorian Britain and it is clear from the *Bristol Times and Mirror* review that its writer did not take for granted the general public's familiarity with the instrument, speculating on "the effect its introduction into society could, would and should produce." The banjo was a new thing.

★

By the 1890s, a new and most significant strand in the development of African American music began to emerge – ragtime. Most significant because it led to jazz, the music that changed popular culture on both sides of the Atlantic. The key instrument here was the piano, made possible by the growth of substantial Black urban communities and the social venues that went with them – from the bordellos of New Orleans to the drinking clubs whose clientele was black. Black pianists were developing ragtime's percussive, propulsive way of playing. Between the 1890s and 1920s, it enjoyed enormous popularity throughout America and thereafter in Europe.

SOUTHERN SYNCOPATED ORCHESTRA

The term was a diminutive of "raggedy time", an approach to the metre of a song characterized by punchy, vigorous syncopation. Instead of the accents falling squarely on the strong or "on" beat, they would also fall on the weak or "off" beat, the effect of which was to evoke a flitting, wavering sense of time that suited dancers doing the cakewalk who shuffled, strutted and bent, instead of moving in a "straight", stiff manner. The whole point was to create irregular and far less predictable notes over a regular under-lying pulse. It was the resulting tension that captured the imagination of new listeners.

Ragtime's great composers such as Tom Turpin and Scott Joplin showed that when rich melodic and rhythmic lines were imbued with a playful, see-saw-like character they could be deeply engaging. The beat acted as an infectious energy. It made people want to move. Although often overlooked, the other significant thing about ragtime is its linguistic reach. The word became a generic term, a suffix that could be joined to any subject, from an animal – *Tiger* – to a city – *Harlem* – to nature – *Maple Leaf* – and this meant that composers could apply their syncopation to whatever inspired them. But whatever the range of the music, it was invariably seen through a racial prism.

In *A New History Of Jazz*, Alyn Shipton quotes the view expressed in *The New York Age* that, in 1912, "Syncopation is truly a native product – a style of music of which the Negro is the originator, but which is generally popular with all Americans."[9] Perhaps inevitably, there was also a white moral panic around ragtime, as reports in papers like *The Musical Courier* decried a "primitive morality" and "lack of sexual restraint" that attended the music, or more pertinently, "the Negro type".[10]

Although ragtime's original exponents were pianists such as Scott Joplin and Louis Chauvin, who became immensely popular, the music was also played by different kinds of bands, such as string and brass ensembles. These laid the foundation for the trend of the "Syncopated Orchestra" around 1910, which was a prototype for the jazz big band that would achieve commercial success in the decades to come.

Will Marion Cook, one of Dvorak's several African-American students, emerged as a significant composer of the ragtime era, and he went on to bring his own Southern Syncopated Orchestra to Britain in 1919. Long before this, in 1903, Cook's production *In Dahomey*, a collaboration with writer Jesse A. Shipp and poet Paul Laurence Dunbar had been a remarkable success; it was the first all-Black show to open on New York's Broadway and it enjoyed a lengthy run at London's Shaftesbury theatre after its American première. As such it was a landmark, "black Atlantic" phenomenon, which highlighted the paradox of being an artistically ambitious African-American composer in the early 20th century. Driven by the desire to create a "Negro opera", in part under the influence of what Samuel Coleridge-Taylor had achieved in the late 19th century, Cook incorporated classical elements into the production alongside not only passages of ragtime, but elements of blackface entertainment, in particular "coon songs" and cakewalks. It is not clear whether Cook regarded these as "authentic" Negro forms; certainly, the cakewalk had to be danced because of the prevailing expectations of white audiences.

The plot of *In Dahomey* was picaresque, focusing on the misadventures of two African-American detectives whose sleuthing leads them to West Africa where they seek to outwit colonisers. While the character of the ruler they encounter, King Eat-Em-All, displays the stereotypes of the uncivilised buffoonery associated with Africans, the show also presented African-Americans as people who had a degree of self-respect and aspiration. This gap between African American racial pride and negative views of Africa was by no means uncommon, and it was not until the emergence of Marcus Garvey in the 1920s that this dichotomy was addressed – and even Garvey was not immune to the idea that the New World Negro would bring civilisation to continental Africa.

In Dahomey was written primarily for the black comedian-dancers George Walker and Bert Williams, and was performed by a fifty strong troupe that had other dancers and musicians on horns, strings and percussion. If the music in the production was striking, the libretto was remarkable for moments of audacity in its references to social and political issues. For example, the following couplet, from the song "On Emancipation Day", identifies one of the key socio-cultural phenomena of the 20th century that continues into the 21st: the shaping impact of black culture on the mainstream: "When dey hear dem ragtime tunes/ White fo'ks try to pass fo' coons."[11] For black artists of the 1900s to recognize their own worth in so forthright a manner, asserting their position as leaders and not followers, innovators not imitators, was remarkable. Given the phenomenon of light-skinned Blacks being able to "pass" for white, here were the tables being turned through the allocation of that same verb "pass" to *white* people. They have no choice but to go in the opposite direction and "pass" for black because of the irresistible nature of Negro culture. Ragtime will make them do it. *In Dahomey* thus celebrates the empowerment of African-Americans, even as it has to make artistic compromises for its white audience. The simple yet important "when" adds weight to the claim; it is not *if* white fo'ks hear dem ragtime tunes. This degree of confidence is all the more remarkable given the lack of status that Negroes had in a segregated society where the careful avoidance of direct eye contact with the white man was in counterpoint to the wild dilation of minstrels' pupils on stage, where, as *In Dahomey* states, "darkies eyes look jes like moons."

These lyrics are significant because they introduce several currents that become more pronounced in black popular culture in the decades to come: confidence, conviction, challenge, humour and irony. Explicit in the championing of ragtime is the notion that Negro music can affect change, and, more impressively, cut across racial lines in terms of audience appeal, hence the phrase is really a call to arms that can be heard in a wide range of future tropes. It is the blues artist who dares to say "what I got is what you need", and his successors in soul, funk and hip-hop who warn "let the beat hit 'em", which basically means that there can be no resistance to the all-conquering energy in black music.

Whether white audiences, comfortable with coon songs and comedy, picked any of this up is moot. For the most part UK audiences probably still viewed black composers like Cook, regardless of their ambition, through the reductive prism of minstrelsy. There is no evidence of a different response to that made to earlier acts such as the Ethiopian Serenaders and Master Juba in the 1850s, but the success of the production gave further credence to the notion that African-Americans had sufficient verve in the field of popular entertainment to enjoy mass appeal. After the run in the Shaftesbury theatre in London, the musical toured the provinces before a performance for the Prince of Wales at Buckingham Palace.

In Dahomey stands as a milestone in the history of early black music in Britain because of the scale and ambition of the production as well as the impact that it made on audiences who were charmed by song and dance in a story set in distant, exotic lands from a vibrant all-coloured cast. Its success in Britain was partly due to the fact that it was presented at a time when musical theatre was beginning to replace music hall as the dominant popular entertainment, though *In Dahomey* is also a reminder that several of the precursors of what would become known as jazz were very active on the theatre circuit.

The other importance of *In Dahomey* was the fact that some cast members chose to settle here permanently, just as Thomas Rutling of the Fisk Jubilee singers had done several years before. As will be discussed in the next chapter, these settlers fed into the emergence in 1921 of a versatile, hugely talented band that played a range of music that included an early manifestation of jazz, the Southern Syncopated Orchestra, another brain-child of Will Marion Cook.

Chief among the *In Dahomey* émigrés was Pete George Hampton. He had been a member of a banjo playing, singing group that toured with various minstrel troupes in America before coming to the attention of Bert Williams and George Walker, the show's two star comedian-dancers who, in turn, introduced him to the composer Will Marion Cook.[12]

Despite its association with country & western, the banjo is one of the oldest African-musical instruments, and its origins can be traced back to West African precursors such as the n'goni.[13] Relatively easy to make and transport, the banjo was a vital musical device for slaves on plantations and subsequently took its place alongside the violin, tambourine and bones in minstrel shows. The African-American banjo player who loudly "tapped" his foot to set a steady pulse for his vigorous rhythmic strumming became a key element of blackface entertainment. Hampton played an "authentically Negro" instrument. The banjo was not the only weapon in the black musician's armoury. There was also the smaller, more transportable but no less potent device called the harmonica or mouth organ. Like the banjo, this was an instrument that had non-western origins. It is widely acknowledged that the Chinese sheng, a semi-circular construction of bamboo pipes, was its precursor (and early blues musicians such as Henry Thomas played a version of the panpipes), but the western mouth organ was invented by Christian Buchmann in 1821, before another version, offering chromatic possibilities, was manufactured by the German instrument maker Hohner in 1857. Hence the "pocket piano" was in its infancy when Hampton brought it to British audiences.

After settling in London, Hampton became a prolific recording artist, cutting dozens of plantation melodies on wax cylinders, the new means of capturing audio. What we recognize today as the modern format of vinyl albums (returning to favour in the digital download age), had its forerunner in shellac, a bio-adhesive polymer used to manufacture 78 rpm discs in the 1890s. These pioneering devices, although crude and cumbersome by today's standards, pointed the way towards the mass production of audio and the real possibility of reaching consumers in their homes. (In addition, Marconi's first radio in 1897, pointed to a future in which recordings of Hampton's songs could reach audiences around the whole world.) The scholar Rainer E Lotz, fortunate enough to have heard Hampton's wax cylinder recordings, such as "Dat Mouth Organ Coon", describes him thus:

> Hampton's specialty was playing the organ through his nose, but on this cylinder, after stating the melody, he performs at such breakneck speed that it is hard to believe. He bends the melody, adds blue notes, produces all sorts of strange sounds that must have made Ireland's national poet Thomas Moore – who wrote *The Last Rose of Summer* – turn in his grave, and composer Friedrich von Flotow as well.[14]

There were other black performers active in Edwardian Britain. During the First World War, musicians like Dan Kildare brought banjo ensembles to London. There was an eager audience and a vast network of theatres as well as assembly rooms and civic halls staging shows in which the boundaries between music, dance, comedy and spectacle in the general sense, although not as ghastly as the Victorian freak show, was blurred.

At the dawn of the 20th century, black entertainers plying their trade in Britain were industrious and energetic individuals who made a living on a circuit that involved multiple performances on a nightly basis, all over

Britain. Jeffrey Green, author of *Black Edwardians*, sets the scene with a description of the realities of the world in which they operated:

> Urban theatres throughout the United Kingdom had two – sometimes three – shows, each of two hours, six days a week. Acts toured from town to town, appearing in these new and grand halls seating over one thousand, providing glamour, thrills, music, humour and song. In cities some acts rushed, by cab, to another theatre and thus could make four appearances nightly.[13]

To make the most of professional opportunities, performers had to travel. Brighton, Bristol, Hastings, Leeds, Leicester, Manchester, Glasgow and Swansea were just a few of the cities in which performers, largely African-Americans and occasionally Africans, were known to appear and the billing of a show as "all coloured", "creole" or "all black" was a common occurrence. Among other explicit racial terms in newspaper pieces were nigger, ebony, picaninny and dusky. There were lots of ways of identifying non-whites. Green argues that the terms Negro, coloured, black or African when they appeared in press coverage of events did not necessarily mean that these were black performers because of the phenomenon of whites in "blackface". Even so, there is ample documented evidence, especially photographic, to confirm the substantial activity of people of colour on stage.

Those whose lives were defined by the rigours of tough touring schedules included Billy McClain who led a "smart, colored sextette" and Smith and Johnson, a lively song-and-dance act that worked extensively between 1902 and 1905. Their appearance at the Royal Hippodrome in Salford made the pages of the leading entertainment trade paper of the day, *Era*. Perhaps the black doyenne of the circuit was Belle Davis. After arriving from America in June 1901, she sang at various venues in London accompanied by two "Senegambian picaninnies" who were reported to dance in a very acrobatic style. Regional gigs in Bradford, Sheffield, Hull, Edinburgh, Glasgow and South Shields followed, before returning to London – and then Dublin. According to Green they also "made gramophone records" and "in June 1903 Belle Davis was still performing in British theatres; the following year she married, in London, Henry Troy – another American entertainer of African descent."[16]

The description of Davis' two young accompanists as "Senegambian" relates to the ferocious competition between Britain and France for dominance in West Africa, the outcome of which was that the formerly British controlled Senegambia was divided between British Gambia and French Senegal, with destructive consequences for families divided by colonial boundaries.[17]

It is not hard to account for the increasing flow of African American musicians and entertainers settling in Britain given the continuing inhumanity of life in America for Blacks. Emancipation may have come in 1863, but the period of so-called Reconstruction saw segregation enshrined in law and backed by lynch-mob violence when whole white families attended the ritual slaughter of black men and sometimes women – and were later invited to purchase souvenir-photographs of the event. Britain was no racial utopia, but despite occasions of mob violence, despite the underlying prejudice, there was undoubtedly more civil space for black talents.[18]

Even so, alongside the acceptance of African American performers was the existence of the kind of human zoos featured at various Imperial Exhibitions. Content included anything from the re-enactment of battles, to reconstructions of African villages complete with genuine natives, so that the daily routines of a black family, from eating to washing, socializing to working, could be observed at close quarters. But while reporters were busy describing the ebony skin and long slender limbs of Senegalese natives in their transplanted dwellings, few sought to enquire what imperial competition was doing to their lives.

The most remarkable of these Imperial Exhibits was the group of Congolese pygmies who spent two years in Britain (1905-07), touring up and down the country appearing at numerous garden fêtes, halls, hippodromes, Empires and the obligatory stop at Buckingham Palace. The most significant legacy of the "Pygmies", who were in the charge of a Yorkshire landowner, James Jonathan Harrison,[19] with an interest in globetrotting and big game hunting, was a recording that they made for the Gramophone Company in 1905. This was the first commercially available disc made by Africans in Britain. The recording features a member of the group called Matuka and the chief Bokani singing while others play drums and two women talk in Swahili. For fans of "anthropological entertainment" the recording was designed to meet the growing interest that had been shown in the tribe of "dwarf savages". The record label identifies the content as: *Conversation Between Bokani the Chief of the Pygmies, and Mongongo With Interpreter.* How is this classified by the record label? As *Oriental Talking.* In other words, Africans were seen as part of a wider world that stood in opposition to the western world. In the Edwardian mindset, this was synonymous with degeneracy and a lack of moral rectitude. The "tricky Chinaman" was as marked a stereotype as the "noble savage", so it is no surprise that the two were somehow confused by dint of the fact that they both spoke languages that the British, a few missionaries apart, could not understand.

Notes

1. Michael Leapman, *The World For a Shilling: How the Great Exhibition of 1851 Shaped a Nation* (Faber & Faber, 2011) p. 18
2. Liberal estimates of those who sneaked on to ships bound for Europe from the West Indies in the late 19th century run into thousands. It was an extremely hazardous undertaking with the threat of imprisonment and deportation hanging over those who were caught, not to mention a serious risk of ill health during the voyage.
3. Ray Costello, *Black Liverpool: The Early History of Britain's Oldest Black Community 1730-1918* (Picton, 2001) p. 33
4. Online, <u>Famousjamaicachoirweebly.com</u>
5. Ibid.
6. Jeffrey Green, *Black Edwardians, Black People in Britain 1901-1914* (Cass, 1998), p. 83.
7. Steve Smith, *British Black Gospel* (Monarch, 2009) p. 46.
8. Catherine Parsonage, *The Evolution of Jazz In Britain*, 1880-1935 (Ashgate, 2005) p. 111.
9. Alyn Shipton, *A New History of Jazz* (Continuum) p. 32.
10. Ibid. p. 37
11. Rainer E. Lotz, "Cross-Cultural Links, Black Minstrels, Cakewalks and Ragtime" in *Eurojazzland* (Northwestern University Press, 2012), pp. 147-167.
12. Ibid.
13. The roots of the banjo in the African n'goni were well established, and by credible ethnomusicologists such as Paul Oliver.
14. Lotz, op. cit.
15. Jeffrey Green, *Black Edwardians, Black People In Britain 1901-1914* (Frank Cass, 1998) p. 50.
16. Green, op. cit., pp. 81-82, 138.
17. See James M. Campbell and Rebecca J. Fraser, *Reconstruction: People and Perspectives* (ABC-Clio, 2008).
18. The tragedy of the division of Senegal and Gambia was brought home to me when I taught English in Dakar in the early 90s. Senegalese students sneered at the "strange Wolof" of the Gambians but recognized they "came from the same family".
19. Green, op. cit., pp. 81-82, 138

6 CLUBS IN THE CITY, PARTIES IN THE VALLEYS

The presence of Colonial seamen is socially undesirable. The police are
anxious to get rid of them. It would be safer and better to place all the
men in concentration camps.
— Chief Immigration Officer's statement on black males in Tiger Bay,
Wales, 1919.

When I myself have appeared on a concert platform in Wales, the Welsh
people have appeared to be the most responsive, there appeared to be a
real link between us.
— Paul Robeson.

Following the success of *In Dahomey*, there was an increased presence
of African-American musicians in London. This was partly the result of
the formation of the Clef Club, one of the earliest known black artist
collectives, which was set up in 1910 in New York by the composer,
arranger and bandleader James Reese Europe. As a meeting place, forum
for ideas and an informal labour exchange, the organization yielded a
number of progressive ensembles that made their mark on the European
continent during the First World War. Reese Europe formed the High
Society Orchestra, which played imaginatively scored ragtime that met
with critical acclaim, and then led the Hellfighters, an all-black military
band of the 369th US Infantry that enjoyed enormous success when it
played in French cities. Reese Europe's ability to compose and arrange
rags, marches and cakewalks to high orchestral standards did much to
enhance the reputation of black music as a burgeoning force abroad.
Europe's legacy was also the existence of satellite ensembles that were
affiliated to the original Clef Club organisation and went some way
to fulfilling its stated ideal of greater opportunity for black musicians.
Unlike Europe, who died in tragic circumstances upon his return to
America after the war, some of these bands travelled to Britain.[1]

In London, the Jamaican-born Dan Kildare (1879-1920) led a banjo
group under the name of the Clef Club Orchestra, which had a residency
at Ciro's in the West End. As a bow to the lingering presence of minstrel
vocabulary in popular consciousness, the band, one of the earliest Black string
bands, whose recordings can still be found, was renamed Ciro's Club Coon
Orchestra and proved a successful draw with several remarkable musicians.
One such, the drummer Louis Mitchell, known for his technical skill and

charisma, later took his own group, the Syncopating Sextette, to Glasgow.

Dan Kildare was in London between 1915-1920. When the Ciro club was shut down for selling liquor without a licence, Kildare performed in a duo with a drummer called Harvey White. He married a pub-owner called Mrs Fitch, but then succumbed to drug addiction and alcoholism. His life in Britain ended tragically when he murdered his wife and her sister and then shot himself. [2]

Ensembles like Kildare's can be seen as part of a wider trend of African-Americans experimenting with instrumentation and personnel, as strings, horns and percussion were all used by black bandleaders. Another inventive combo that visited Britain was Joe Jordan's Syncopated Orchestra. A brilliant arranger and composer, who had worked with James Reese Europe in New York and in minstrel shows in theatres all over America, Jordan (1882-1971) made his earliest appearances in the UK in 1905, and in the years that followed he returned many times. In 1915 he led his Syncopated Orchestra for the revue, *Push And Go* at London's Hippodrome, bringing together singers, dancers and musicians. The ensemble included piano, banjo, cornet, trombone and drums, a bold choice of instrumentation that yielded rich timbres from upper to lower register. In other ensembles Jordan had used saxophones, trumpet, guitar and mandolin, evidence of his willingness to stretch his textural palette.

Following the London engagement, the Syncopated Orchestra embarked upon a tour of the regional network of grand Empire theatres before some of its members returned to America and others, pianist W.H. Dorsey and drummer Hughes Pollard settled in Britain. Jordan began working with the Clef Club drummer Louis Mitchell as "the Comedy Entertainers & Syncopators". The return in 1919 of Will Marion Cook further expanded the African American London fraternity. Cook was already known to London audiences from the success he had enjoyed with the show, *In Dahomey*, in 1903. Joe Jordan had been both the assistant director and business manager of the New York Syncopated Orchestra Cook formed in 1918. [3]

Perhaps the most influential of the visitors was the Southern Syncopated Orchestra, what the New York Syncopated Orchestra became (via being the American Syncopated Orchestra). In their earliest days the ensemble was booked for a six-month residency at the Philharmonic Hall in Great Portland Street, central London, playing two shows a day. They had a revolving door in terms of membership. The departures and arrivals of singers, players and dancers were sufficiently frequent to make it possible for audiences to see and hear new approaches. With soloists and vocalists who were set to become stars in their own right, the Orchestra became a prototype of the ensemble-as-institution that would nurture and launch new talent and develop new performance ideas.

The array of instruments SSO featured greatly widened the harmonic

range of the bands led by Jordan, Mitchell and Kildare – violins, mando-
lins, banjos, guitars, saxophones, trumpets, trombones, bass horn, timpani,
pianos and drums. Cook was evidently drawn to a sound that was both
symphonic and rhythmic. This band also had a prestigious engagement
from the Prince of Wales who requested its presence to perform at a specially drained lake in the grounds of Buckingham Palace. Although associated mainly with ragtime and syncopated music, the SSO developed an
eclectic repertoire that reflected Cook's concerns to dignify black culture.
Hence, in addition to ragtime, Negro spirituals and plantation songs, there
were European classical pieces by composers such as Brahms, Dvorak and
Grieg. The latter's *Peer Gynt* was given a syncopated arrangement. This
was "blacking up" of a different kind to that of the Minstrel age. The fact
that the SSO straddled many forms of music and dance, from the cakewalk
and plantation melodies to banjo tunes and light classical music, made it a
vital representation of the flexibility and versatility of black performers in
the immediate First World War period, located as they were between high
and low-brow worlds, the supposed dignity of European aesthetics and
the energy of Black music. As much as the SSO can be seen as a forerunner of what would be termed the jazz big band or swing orchestra, all the
available documentation on their repertoire, engagements and personnel,
above all else flags up their eclecticism. Such diversity was paramount to
the orchestra's economic survival as well as a sign of the ongoing ambiguity
over where black musicians should be located on the cultural exchequer,
clear as it was that they were doing something that was capable of striking
a chord with mainstream audiences in both North America and in Europe.

Of no less significance was the fact that the SSO was a truly Black diasporic phenomenon, as members were drawn from America, Africa, and
the West Indies, as well as Black Britain, such as the vocalist Evelyn Dove.
Of Ghanaian – or as it was known in Edwardian times – The Gold Coast
– and English heritage, Dove, who studied pianoforte and singing at the
Royal Academy of Music, became a highly successful artist whose career
spanned early jazz and musical theatre. SSO was one of the first major gigs
that she had in 1921, appearing with the orchestra in Glasgow.

The SSO had an impressive personnel and a wide-ranging songbook.
There were some 24 players and 19 singers, and after its first three-year
sojourn in Britain, the original American personnel changed extensively.
To members from New Orleans, New York and Philadelphia were added
players from Guyana, Barbados, Antigua, Sierra Leone and Ghana, giving
the ensemble an international identity that was a precursor to the transcon-
tinental collaborations that were a feature of the jazz scene in the 1950s.

The SSO was a touring band that also played in the regions. While the
response to Cook's musicians was largely positive, his aim of elevating the
Negro race through music that eschewed the staples of minstrelsy still proved

difficult to achieve seventeen years after he had encountered the same problems with the audiences of *In Dahomey*. A look at the publicity for a 1920
SSO show at the Albert Hall in Nottingham shows the continuing depth
of racist sentiment of those engaged in the promotion of the ensemble:

> To hear this Orchestra with it singers is to experience an entirely new
> sensation in Music, and in these days when a love of novelty is one of
> the most striking features of the human character, they should prove
> immensely popular wherever they go.
>   The Negroes are a race comparatively young to the complexities of
> modern civilization, and therefore nearer to nature than we are, and to
> this fact is probably due the spontaneity of their art.[4]

In spite of these assumptions, African-American musicians were
proving to be a good deal more than naively spontaneous when it
came to exploring the possibilities of their instruments and bringing
new verve to American music. This was as Cook's former teacher,
Antonin Dvorak, had predicted in the 1890s. There was no greater
symbol of innovative artistry than the young New Orleans trumpeter-
vocalist Louis Armstrong, who was producing anything from tunes in
"raggedy" time to the raucous polyphony of the New Orleans style,
also known as Dixieland. With its frantic tempos, throbbing two-beat
pulse, spiralling phrases and tightly meshed counterpoint, drawn from
the overlap of clarinet, trombone and sometimes two cornets, his music
crackled with an effervescence that was hard to ignore.

At this point, to understand later developments in Black British music,
it is necessary to cross the Atlantic to look at a period of intense musical
innovation in the USA.

Black music in America has always been marked by the diversity and
complex relationships between its sub-genres. There was the sacred of
the spiritual, the profane of the blues, but both feature the use of call and
response and pitch-bending and emotional intensity in vocal delivery. Musicians drew on all these materials, and it was out of the ragtime groups,
solo pianists, banjo ensembles, blues singers, marching-band brass players
and the syncopated orchestras of the early 20th century that grew that grand
African-American musical fermentation that became jazz, a singular word
for a plurality of ideas.

Originally, a music of collective improvisation in the bands of New
Orleans, one of the distinguishing features of the development of jazz was
the extension of the solo break into longer passages of improvisation. This
was the space that allowed and encouraged someone like Louis Armstrong,
a prodigious soloist able to create an array of rich tones and potent, danceable
rhythms, really to come into his own. Whether they used brass to evoke
the joy of laughing or reeds to express the despair of weeping, or made the
singing voice imitate a horn, African Americans showed that their music

had a spirit of invention that rendered it "the sound of surprise". It was this quality that led to its lionization, especially in Europe, where some critics were ready to give fulsome praise.[5]

However, the first real arrival of jazz in Britain came not from an African American group but from a white band, the Original Dixieland Jazz Band, from New Orleans. This had a series of engagements in Britain at roughly the same time as the Southern Syncopated Orchestra. This all-white ensemble stayed for just one year rather than the SSO's three, yet the synchronicity of the two groups together paved the way for the future growth of jazz culture in Britain. What was problematic were the alleged claims made by the ODJB's leader, Nick La Rocca, that the "real" origins of jazz were actually white and *not* black. When the ODJB quintet (cornet, trombone, clarinet, piano and drums), appeared at the Palladium, the impresario Albert De Courville presented it grandiloquently as: "For the first time in England. The creation of jazz. The sensation of America."[6]

Due to a lack of accurate documentation, the origins of jazz are anything but clear, but if these musicians called themselves Original Dixieland Jazz Band, then they were laying claim to a title that was undoubtedly not theirs, muddying the waters on who was really the first person to make the crucial innovations – which in all probability was Freddie Keppard's Original Creole Band, operating a good decade before the ODJB. And then there was Buddy Bolden, going back to the turn of the century, but sadly never recorded.

To the question of "who" was added the "what". The advent of this new form of black music was also shrouded in semantic confusion, for it was "jazz" to some, "jass" to others (possibly derived from jism – spunk or sperm, but with an undoubted sexual connotation), and also the lesser known jaz, which, according to an article published in the *San Francisco Bulletin* in 1913, meant "anything that takes manliness or effort or energy or activity or strength of soul." This range of definitions reflected the birth of something maddeningly elusive, teetering on the cusp of invigoration, disorientation and adulteration.[7] There was also debate on the need to plane down the rough edges of whatever jazz was and elevate it to fit European symphonic norms. Inevitably, so-called jazz bands were often programmed on variety bills, often to the dismay of some of the other acts – as well as certain audiences.

Pathé newsreels presented jazz as very much a form of novelty in which zany humour is foregrounded. In one clip, a group of saxophonists attempt to charm animals at a zoo and have the converse effect – "A little jazz has a very restless effect on Mr. Bear" – while in another, musicians are seen hanging off a plane in mid air like circus performers as they hit the "high notes". Tellingly, all the musicians in these scenes are white.

Regardless of the legitimacy of their claim or name, the ODJB residency at the Palladium exposed the cultural fissures in British society at the time. Just below the band's billing is an advert for Maud Gibson's Academy, 20 West Kensington Gardens, W.14, which offered "classical dancing, rhythmic exercises, ballroom dancing and 'grace culture'." A tutor called May Vincent took singing and elocution classes. The entire advert suggests decorum and deportment, which chimes with one of the house rules right at the start of the programme: "Ladies are respectfully requested to remove their hats so as to afford greater comfort to those seated behind." Sightlines are important and standards of behaviour must be maintained. At the end of the evening, which also included "comedy creations", jugglers and a "grand orchestral selection", the audience was expected to rise to lift their voices for a rendition of "God Save The King". Whilst ladies were requested to remove their headgear and maintain a respectable stance, antics such as "shimmying" were not encouraged at all. How concert-goers behaved at a public performance, the extent to which they engaged, physically as well emotionally, their freedom of movement, was a vexed issue. Evidently, for some, the Victorian ideals of buttoned-up, if not strait-jacketed behavioural norms still held sway in the 1920s.

By contrast, the ODJB performed with "a jazz dancer", Johnnie Dale, who according to one report "came in and wiggled himself about like a filleted eel about to enter the stewing pot", which the reviewer dismissed as "the most discordant and uninteresting entertainments I have ever seen."

The phenomenon of jazz dancing was seen as a threat to the moral order, because of its association with wildness and blackness. Thus members of the clergy in the south London suburbs felt that they had to take a stand against the frightful degradation creeping in through dance. An article published in *The Times* in March, 1919 recounted tales of racial bacchanalia in darkest Berkshire.

> Presiding at the annual meeting of the Maidenhead Preventive And Rescue Association at Maidenhead, Canon Drummond strongly denounced Jazz dancing... a dance so low, so demoralizing and of such low origin – the dance of low niggers in America, and with every conceivable crude instrument, not to make music, but to make noise.[8]

Such racism both dogged black music – and provoked it. Levels of volume in jazz were perceived as cacophonous; bands were happy to endorse that perception – from the altitude of the notes reached by the brass and reeds, the theatrical stance of musicians who tilted their horns skyward, to the thunderous low thuds and sharp crashes issuing from the drum kit.[9]

It was the drum that perhaps became the key signifier of jazz, a source of consternation to jazz's detractors precisely because of the amount of noise the instrument could produce and the violence of the action required to make it. In the 21st century, we are so used to the sight of a drum kit that it is hard to imagine how strange it might have appeared to an early 20th century audience, but it was indeed an unusual and, more to the point, a new mechanical invention. The earliest models were nothing more than one cymbal, a snare and a bass drum, but the latter was a huge dome that dwarfed the musician seated behind it. A foot pedal was needed to play the bass drum and later the high-hat, and these two contraptions underlined the fact that the drum kit engages the whole body of the musician, all four limbs providing the opportunity for an individual to exercise polyrhythmic creativity. This made the jazz drum kit revolutionary, a small orchestra within the larger orchestra of horns and piano. Players also added components to the drum kit as they saw fit, from tom toms to cowbells to timpani and, in some cases, gongs and Chinese temple blocks. So an instrument, which was really an aggregation of several instruments, could be set up and modified according to the vision of the individual drummer, enabling a degree of personal expression that was of enormous benefit to any band that was attempting to create a palette of original timbres. Early pioneers such as Warren "Baby" Dodds showed that the "traps set" could greatly enhance the narrative of an arrangement, and prove central to the jazz aesthetic, which in turn hugely shaped twentieth-century popular music.

Inevitably the sight of musicians moving, either crouching down, bending knees, or thrusting shoulders upwards as they produced new sounds, was troubling to a society that, just a few decades previously, had not looked kindly on gospel groups who stomped their feet during performances. What jumps out in early footage of Louis Armstrong is how much he shuffles when he listens to other musicians playing, as if he is absorbing the notes into every muscle of his body, like an additional source of energy that will ignite his own imagination as a soloist.

As compositions such as "Tiger Rag" (first recorded by the ODJB in 1919) and "Dippermouth Blues" (first recorded by King Oliver in 1923) became standards, pieces that were played so frequently that their appreciation assumed the status of core values for a growing audience in America and Europe, the arbiters of taste and self-appointed moral custodians found themselves in an invidious position, because this "extraordinary noise", "crazy rhythm", or whatever it was, this otherness and outlandishness, also carried great exhilaration. The net result was a bi-polarity of attraction-repulsion, embrace-censure, fascination-fear, to quote the scholar Catherine Parsonage, which led to a wide spectrum of behavioural and attitudinal responses to the so-called "Jazz Age". On one hand, men of the cloth felt compelled to take a stand against the scourge of jazz dancing. On the other, moneyed men about town with a taste for fine tailoring were minded to take lessons in that same devilish new trend in swish apartments in Mayfair.

With the advent of the Parisian "vogue negre", epitomised by the sensational success of Josephine Baker, the identification of black expression with modernity and freedom from social constraints had widespread currency. References, either implicit or explicit, to jazz in other artforms such as painting, dramaturgy and literature showed the extent to which the phenomenon was affecting all cultural discourse. In Britain, the debate around jazz showed clearly that social and behavioural norms were in a state of flux.

This is evident in D.H. Lawrence's *Lady Chatterley's Lover* (1928). The book broaches the subjects of class, education, social standing and the metropolitan-regional divide, as much as it does sexuality. In its latter stages, the story of Constance Chatterley's affair with the gamekeeper Mellors in the "utter, soulless ugliness of the coal-and-iron Midlands" is broadened to chart her tentative, stuttering liberation in the exotic settings of Paris and Venice. In Paris, the new Black music is seen as something both risqué and outré, a "drug" aligned with "hot sun, slow water… cigarettes, cocktails, ices, vermouth", as well as a potent, cosmopolitan eroticism that divides the modest Constance from her more openly hedonistic, if not "animalistic" sister Hilda.

> Hilda liked jazz because she could plaster her stomach against the stomach of some so-called man, and let him control her movement from the visceral centre, here and there across the floor, and then she could break loose and ignore 'the creature.' He had been made use of. Poor Connie was rather unhappy. She wouldn't jazz because she simply couldn't plaster her stomach against some creature's stomach.[10]

This evocation of "creatures" rubbing up, or rather "grinding" against one another would have outraged proponents of more chaste ballroom dancing, but the passage is also striking for its inversion of gender power. The men are casually objectified by Hilda, discarded after serving their purpose, and this is linked to the role that jazz dancing played in providing more freedom of movement for women. The post-war period was notable for imported Black dances from America and these tended to be centred on the individual rather than the couple (in which the man led the woman). Jazz and jazz dancing in *Lady Chatterley's Lover* is portrayed as raw, unfiltered and unprecedented.

This appeal did not escape the record companies, so that new record releases were invariably associated with all of the latest "steps". So a 1920 Columbia records list, featuring both jazz and Hawaiian titles, promised "joyous, sparkling up to the minute music" for the "newest and liveliest dances." The Charleston, the jitterbug and the rubber legs were a must for anybody in tune with the times. A quick glance at the original sheet music of a landmark piece such as Jelly Roll Morton's "Jelly Roll Blues" highlights this. Above the title is the slogan "Full of Originality". Below it is the word "Fox-Trot".[11]

However, the record companies were also guilty of presenting jazz in a way that trivialized and demeaned rather than legitimized its progenitors. For example, a promotional poster by the Victor label for the ODJB dramatically stated: "They say the first instrument for the first Jass band was an empty lard can, by humming into which sounds were produced resembling those of a saxophone with the croup." This framing of the music chimed with complaints about "crude" noise, which had so exercised the conscience of some Home Counties religious leaders.

If promotional posters for the Southern Syncopated Orchestra could hail the band as an "entirely new sensation in music", with the caveat that Negroes are a "race comparatively young to the complexities of modern civilization", it was clear that the British musical establishment did not see Black artists as equals.

Trying to determine the exact social and cultural valuation of new black music around the 1920s is problematic, precisely because of the duality of thrill and threat it carried: the recognition of the power of African-American bands to affect white audiences countered by the projection of anything from outright suspicion to deep prejudice; from exoticisation to wilful racialised fantasy. What jazz meant as a form of musical expression was confused with the question marks that were still hanging over white evaluations of the "Negro type". White they may have been, but the Original Dixieland Jazz Band were still playing Black music and, along with the Southern Synco-pated Orchestra, were viewed by their detractors as distasteful, even if the smart set in Mayfair and various playboy royals were somewhat "gassed" by what they heard.

Beyond the social clamour, it's important not to lose sight of the fact that these jazz groups had members who were exceptional musicians, none more so than the SSO's clarinettist, Sidney Bechet. His talent was too great to ignore and the endorsement given to him by the European classical establishment – such as the renowned Swiss conductor Ernest Ansermet dubbing him a "genius" – was significant in moving jazz towards a greater legitimacy. As noted, the SSO not only played jazz, but classical music and music hall songs, and Bechet stood out as a player adept at handling such an eclectic repertoire.

His background was significant. Bechet's grandfather, known as Omar, had been a slave who was both a dancer and drummer, who played an im-portant part in the musical gatherings in Congo Square in New Orleans, and it was he that Bechet credited as a major source of inspiration. Sidney Bechet took up the clarinet as a boy and as a teenager he played in bands led by legends such as Bunk Johnson before eventually coming to the attention of the Southern Syncopated Orchestra's leader, Will Marion Cook, joining the group on its visit to Britain. Along with Armstrong, Bechet embodied the ideal of the jazz soloist, showing the ability to operate within a dynamic that involved individual-collective interaction and improvisation. Reading scores did not suffice, as Bechet himself explained. "When you're really playing ragtime, you're feeling it out, you're playing to the other parts, you're waiting to understand what the other man's doing, and then you're going with his feeling, adding what you have of your feeling."[12]

Other musicians recognised the creative avenues that Bechet and others were opening up in spontaneous improvisation, and the impression he made on them was increased by his willingness to teach others. He had several pupils to whom he passed on invaluable knowledge of his striking use of vibrato and his intensely lyrical, melodic approach to the art of soloing, thus joining the linage of expatriate African-Americans, such as the Fisk Jubilee singer Thomas Rutland, who also gave lessons in addition to their own activities as professional musicians.

An innovative thinker who purchased an instrument in London that proved to be a considerable asset to the players of his generation and beyond – the "straight" horn, the soprano saxophone – Bechet was also something of a hellraiser. His erratic behaviour eventually caused his departure from SSO, after which he joined another group called The Jazz Kings, who replaced the ODJB at the Hammersmith Palais and thereafter he played at a central London club called Rector's whose clientele leaned towards the city's seamier side. Arrested and charged with affray in 1922, Bechet was imprisoned and then deported, eventually settling in Paris where he became a national icon.[13]

In the Valleys

From the earliest days of minstrelsy and blackface, the language of New World Blacks, enslaved or free, was subject to caricature. Plantation life in America and the Caribbean did not provide formal education, so newly imported Africans had to learn the rudiments of English in an improvised way, which led to the creation of a Creole with a limited vocabulary and a grammar and syntax based on African rather than European models. This developing language was seen as corrupted or broken English, rather than a distinctive language growing from two parents, as English itself had developed as a Creole based on its Anglo-Saxon and Norman French parents. Black speech, like other "dialectal" speeches such as Irish English or Indian English became a target for ridicule. One example is the representation of the character of Cook, "the old black" in Melville's *Moby Dick* as the speaker of an infantile, bastardized language:

> "When dis old brack man dies," said the negro slowly, changing his whole air and demeanour, "He hisself won't go nowhere; some bressed angel will come and fetch him."[14]

In the creation of language, the Black was seen as an imperfect imitator. The philosopher David Hume wrote of the eighteenth century Black

Jamaican poet Francis Williams (who wrote learnedly in Latin): "In Jamaica, indeed, they talk of one negroe as a man of parts and learning; but it is likely he is admired for slender accomplishments, like a parrot, who speaks a few words plainly."[15] The emergence of accomplished black writers such as Olaudah Equiano and others in the late 18th and early 19th century was one important counter to such prejudice.

On a lighter note, there is the story of J. Alexander, a St. Vincentian on a trip to England, who learnt Welsh from the ship's captain. As well as reading prose, he learned a number of popular ballads, and as Ray Costello explains, when he arrived in Liverpool and settled there:

> This was to stand him in good stead during the 1870s, enabling him to earn a living as a street-singer in the absence of other employment, literally singing for his supper.[16]

A West Indian singing Welsh songs in Liverpool in the late 19th century may seem unusual, but it is not wholly incongruous. Wales is an integral part of the story of Blacks in Britain. Cardiff, like Liverpool, is home to one of the oldest African-Caribbean and mixed communities in the United Kingdom.

With industrial growth, in the 1850s Cardiff exported large quantities of coal, iron and steel to Europe and subsequently became a thoroughfare for trade. Lord Bute, a wealthy landholder, invested heavily in the port and the dockland area was rechristened Butetown in his honour. This became the home of black colonial seamen who decided to stay in Cardiff after service around the world. 'Black' Butetown eventually became known as Tiger Bay, a name implying both danger and the exotic, and not entirely original, since it was also the name of the docklands settlement in Limehouse, in the east end of London. Scandinavian, African, Chinese and East Indian (or lascar) seamen settled there. As was often the case in Victorian England, street singers and fiddlers, very often African-Americans, and prostitutes were on hand to entertain deep into the night.

The inhabitants of Tiger Bay in Cardiff included Somalis, Arabs, Indians, West Africans and African-Caribbeans. In 1935, 2,179 black sailors were listed amongst its population, all in the British merchant navy.

Another source of black settlement in Wales was the African Institute at Colwyn Bay, on the north coast, long a popular seaside resort. This had been founded by a Christian missionary, William Hughes, who, after working in the Congo in the early 1880s, brought young boys and girls from all over the Africa to receive vocational training with a view to them returning to their homeland to assist in missionary work. Some, instead, settled in Wales.[17]

Wales was also on the vaudeville circuit, with venues in Wrexham and Cardiff. Many of the Black acts that criss-crossed England also visited hose places. The Fisk Jubilee Singers performed at Clydach, Aberavon and Ystalyfera, while Charles Johnson and Dora Dean, dubbed "A Merry Pair Who Make Things Hustle" brought their lively act to the Swansea Empire in 1905.

Some black musicians opted to make the land of "green valleys" their home and as early as the 1850s a handful of West Indian players were scattered around the country, making a living through performances in local theatres as well as making occasional tours.

Nonetheless, the biggest concentration of black people in Wales was in Tiger Bay, and this presence was not welcome to some. Whilst racial harmony was noted among the children of African and West Indian seamen and their white schoolmates who were waving Union Jacks to celebrate Empire Day in 1913, in the aftermath of the First World War, a period of economic decline and unemployment, creeping paranoia over miscegenation came to the boil. "Half-caste" children were seen as a sign of the eroding moral fibre of the nation, the result of white women being corrupted by black men, or as the *Western Mail* of 17 January 1918 delicately put it, "A Cardiff problem/White Women In Alien Boarding Houses." The aliens were Somalis and Arabs, whose alleged sexual prowess so alarmed the local police chiefs that when a black cricket team was formed, white flannels were not deemed appropriate for the players because they were too revealing.

Tensions came to a head in a race riot in 1919, during which black Butetown suffered sustained assaults from the neighbouring white community. White attackers made it clear that Blacks should stay in their own quarter, or violent retribution would be visited upon them. The investigating Chief Immigration Officer reported:

> The presence of Colonial seamen is socially undesirable. The police are anxious to get rid of them. It would be safer and better to place all the men in concentration camps.[18]

Things didn't go that far, though repressive measures were taken against black sailors, including the 1925 Special Restriction Order of the revealingly named "Colonial Alien Seamen Act". Black sailors had to register with the police and carry an ID card bearing their photo and a thumbprint. Their movements could now be tracked. Though born and bred in Cardiff, these seamen were to be treated as foreigners, and as Neal Evans eloquently put it in his article "Regulating The Reserve Army: Arabs, Blacks And The Local State In Cardiff 1914-15": "Being black and British became almost impossible."[19]

Having lost their citizenship, the black seamen of Tiger Bay found it increasingly difficult to find work on government-subsidized ships. In response, they formed the Coloured Seamen's Union, which was an effective and constructive means of channelling the energy of the community. Desperate times called for solidarity and Neal Evans argues that these oppressive days for black Butetown fostered a great sense of togetherness. The union was less a labour organisation than the organiser of recreational activities. More than ever, song was a form of solace. Among the social activities was the house or "rent party", where musicians would play for dances in exchange for food and drink. Sometimes a small fee would be charged at the door but for those wishing to socialize and to meet the opposite sex the levy was evidently worthwhile.

The phenomenon of rent parties had been established in African-American communities in Harlem at the turn of the century, where stories of musicians hopping from one engagement to the next, on increasingly full stomachs, were legion. Meeting in the homes of other black people offered a safe environment when the world outside their doorstep was hostile, and although the rent party had existed in Butetown prior to the riots and control orders, afterwards they assumed a greater importance. The strengthening of community also brought musicians together. Playing the part of the artistic patriarch in Butetown was Antonio Deniz (1878-1931), a black Cape Verdean seaman who had married a Cardiff woman of mixed race, Gertrude Boston. She was a pianist and he a guitarist and violinist and they taught these instruments to others, including their two sons Joe and Frank and another youngster, Don Johnson. Interviewed by the author/photographer Valerie Wilmer, Johnson recalled:

> I used to go to the Deniz house regularly. Their father played the quatro and was teaching Frank, and Joe could play the ukulele so I started to bring the mandolin over. All we could play at first were calypsos, Sly Mongoose, The Bargee. After about twelve months in the front room of Mrs Deniz's house we became quite good. It was like a music shop in there, we were collecting all these instruments.[20]

Indeed, the Deniz household became the source of important developments in British jazz in the 1930s and 1940s, the sons playing in such bands as the Blue Hawaiians, The Spirits of Rhythm and the Hermanos Diaz Cuban Rhythm Band – discussed in a later chapter.

Given the large numbers of West Indian seamen who were living in Butetown it is inevitable that they should have been playing calypsos but the use of the ukulele and mandolin as well as the quatro lends the scene an wider cultural currency.

The quatro, used in the early calypso bands, was a small 4-string guitar introduced to Trinidad by Venezuelan bands in the 1850s, so when Don Johnson sat down to learn to play with Frank Deniz he was exposed to one of the earliest instruments in West Indian folk music, and a surviving Spanish element in Trinidadian music. The quatro also came out at Christmas when bands toured the villages playing and singing a very specific musical form known as parang, which had arrived with migrants from Venezuela. Moving from house to house in rural communities, the parang singers used instruments such as quatro, flute, maracas, toc-toc, scratcher and box bass and sang nativity songs and tunes on daily life. The families whom they entertained greeted them with food and drink such as pastilles, arepas, sorrel and ginger beer. Johnson recalls how his musical development unfolded in rather similar circumstances:

> After a year or so we got a reputation as a calypso group. We would play at house dances for when the seamen came back. We'd play from ten at night 'til five or six in the morning non-stop. There'd be a long table with West Indian food, a lot of the men were good cooks or they'd teach their wives. The dances would be attended by all the local ladies of the night and all the West Indians, and, after a while we'd be playing three times a week. Calypso was mainly the music that we heard, these guys would get hold of as many West Indian records as they could.[21]

Eventually a coterie of very gifted black Welsh musicians emerged from these gatherings. In addition to Johnson and the Deniz brother there was George Glossop who, picking up the vogue for the Hawaiian guitar that swept the world in the 1920s, specialized in the languorous tremolo phrases of that instrument. There was also a talented double bassist, Victor Parker. These musicians formed a band that could play both Hawaiian music and calypso, though after a time the Deniz brothers left Wales to further their careers in London. Even so, the development of Black music in Britain was as much a regional as a metropolitan story.

For all the laurels heaped on artists in high society, Black communities on the frontline of working-class Britain were facing a worsening situation as "colonial" subjects at the end of the First World War. Soldiers had been recruited from all over the Empire to form units like the Gold Coast Regiment, the King's African Rifles or the West Indian Regiment, and once military engagement came to an end, some were demobbed in Britain, pushing up the numbers of Blacks resident in Britain to unprecedented levels. Their valour on the battlefield was eclipsed by their presence in the high street, the dance hall or the labour exchange, and they became scapegoats for the difficulties faced by all demobbed soldiers who had to adapt to civvy street.

Racial tension was an inevitable consequence. The Cardiff riot in 1919 was not an isolated case. Disturbances also occurred in other cities with sizeable concentrations of people of colour – Glasgow, Liverpool, South Shields, Hull, Salford and London.

Notes

1. Mervyn Cooke, *Chronicles of Jazz* (Thames and Hudson, 1997), pp. 40–41
2. Catherine Parsonage, *Evolution of Jazz in Britain* (Ashgate, 2005).

3. Parsonage, op. cit.
4. Supplied by Nottinghamshire Country Library Service and reprinted in *Black Music In Britain, Essays on the Afro-Asian Contribution to Popular Music*, edited by Paul Oliver (Oxford University Press, 1990).
5. Whitney Balliett, *The Sound of Surprise* (JBC, 1961).
6. Words from the programme for the ODJB.
7. See Mervyn Cooke, op. cit.
8. Quoted in Cooke, op. cit.
9. What follows regarding the development of the drum comes from conversations the author held, particularly with older African American jazz artists, over a number of years.
10. D.H. Lawrence, *Lady Chatterley's Lover* (Penguin 1997), p. 271.
11. From a 78 rpm Victor record label, 1915.
12. See Fairweather, Carr & Priestley, *The Rough Guide to Jazz* (Rough Guides, 2000).
13. On Bechet, see Daniel Sidney Bechet, *Sidney Bechet My Father* (Books of Africa, 2014), p. 14 and Sidney Bechet, *Treat It Gentle* (Da Capo, 2002).
14. Herman Melville, *Moby Dick* ([1851]Penguin Ed.) p. 290.
15. David Hume, footnote to "Of National Character" (1748), in *The Philosophical Works of David Hume*, Volume III.
16. Ray Costello, *Black Liverpool: The Early History of Britain's Oldest Black Community* (Picton, 2001).
17. For more information on the black heritage of Colwyn Bay see Jeffrey Green's excellent website, Jeffreygreen.co.uk
18. Quoted in Colin Prescod's film *Tiger Bay Is My Home* (IRR, 2008).
19. Published on-line, 21 June 2010, as part of *Immigrants and Minorities: Historical Studies in Ethnicity, Migration And Diaspora*.
20. Interview with Val Wilmer, "The Oral History of Jazz in Britain", British Library Sound Archive, 1988,
21. Ibid.

7 ATLANTIC CROSSINGS

"London was the center of the British Empire and it was there that I discovered Africa. Like most of Africa's children in America I had known little about the land of our fathers, but in England I came to know many Africans."

— Paul Robeson

The collapse of the New York stock exchange in 1929 sent shockwaves around America and the world, which led to The Great Depression, the period of mass unemployment, grinding poverty and, above all, a sense of hopelessness encapsulated in the photographs of mothers with a bunch of grime-faced children clinging to their skirts, or men in flat caps and dungarees staring blankly into the middle distance or marching with placards demanding jobs and dignity. Stock values in America fell by as much as 40% while the country's industrial production, along with that of its debtor nations, Germany and Great Britain, also plummeted.

Austerity was not the destiny of all, though. Some still had money and needed ways to show it. If there were folk songs about the Depression there were also jazz-related dance crazes such as the Charleston that captured the imagination of decadent, cocktail-sipping flapper-wearing "Bright young things."[1]

America in the 1930s, particularly New York, was still in a state of artistic ferment despite the hand-to-mouth existence to which many working-class folk had been condemned. The "Harlem Renaissance", the creative explosion of which Paul Robeson (the main subject of this chapter) was a part, alongside others such as Langston Hughes, Duke Ellington and Zora Neale Hurston, brought together a cornucopia of Black talent in literature, theatre, music and dance. For the liberal white elite, there was further evidence of the inventive eclecticism of African-American artists. For those who took a closer interest, it was evident that the movement included a strong West Indian presence amongst its intelligentsia, political firebrands, theorists, writers and musicians. Chief among them was the brilliant Jamaican writer, Claude McKay, who wrote a number of landmark works, the most impressive of which was the critically acclaimed and award-winning novel *Home To Harlem* (1928).[2]

The figure who eclipsed all of these in world impact – in notoriety to some, immense popularity to others – was the radical Jamaican leader Marcus Garvey, a champion of the notion of blackness as a positive rather than negative attribute, an articulate advocate of the rights of the descendants of slaves and, above all, the originator and populariser of the Back to Africa movement. Garvey's time in New York was controversial, and the support that he drew from many American Blacks (his United Negro Improvement Association was reputed to have four million followers at its peak) was offset by a long running campaign of ridicule from African-American intellectuals, many of whom were notably lighter in skin shade, who saw him as a "Jamaican jackass".[3] Politics was not the only engagement of Garvey or his wife Amy. Readers of the New York *Amsterdam News*, the Black community's paper, would, in August 1927, have seen the advert for the musical revue *Brown Sugar*, noted in the previous chapter at the Lafayette Theatre in 7th Avenue at 132nd Street.

But New York and Harlem were not the only places where musical innovation and political ferment went hand-in-hand. Because it was at the centre of a world empire, London (and later Manchester) was a magnet that attracted both musicians and migrants with political objectives in mind. Unquestionably the greatest of these figures was the singer, actor and political activist Paul Robeson, and his story is one that brings together both the African American struggle for civil rights and respect and the anti-colonial struggle which Africans, West Indians and Indians, amongst others, took to the heart of empire.

In those days (indeed right up until 1962), colonial subjects within the empire did not require a passport to board a ship. New World Africans had been crossing the Atlantic since the days of the War of Independence, and England became a meeting place for the many different peoples from around the colonial empire. Among them were preachers, thinkers, philosophers, rabble-rousers – individuals who were aware of the challenges facing "the Negro" and attempting to devise strategies to meet them. There were some who just wanted to make a living, but others who were prepared to fight for their constitutional rights and racial dignity. This credo, later to be termed Pan-Africanism, advocated universal solidarity for people of colour. Pan-Africanist sentiments had first been expressed in the late 18th century when the first Black writers to be published in Britain – Ottobah Cugoano, Ignatius Sancho and Olaudah Equiano – had anticipated the dominant themes of the years to come: pride in ethnic origins and the refusal to accept white supremacy in any form.

From the mid 19th century onwards, a number of Black intellectuals settled in Britain, such as the African-American physician Martin Robinson Delany and the Dominican labourer Samuel Jules Celestine Edwards. In 1900, a Trinidadian teacher and lecturer, Henry Sylvester Williams[4] staged the inaugural Pan-African conference between July 23rd and 25th at West-minster Town Hall in London. Thereafter came organizations such as the African Progress Union founded by John Archer (1863-1932), born in Liverpool to Barbadian parents, who became mayor of Battersea in south London, and subsequently a key figure in local affairs, as well as a great international champion of the rights of people of colour.

Britain became the centre for the Pan-Africanist movement because it was here that Africans, West Indians, African-Americans and mixed race Anglo-Africans could assemble, exchange ideas and create networks. Because London was the hub of the British Empire, people from all over the world met and interacted in places ranging from the raucous public houses of the East End to the refectories and common rooms of the city's institutes of higher education.

There were times when it was possible to hear Marcus Garvey preach his message of black self-empowerment at Speaker's Corner in Hyde Park. There were the activities of pioneering civil rights organizations such as the League of Coloured Peoples, which was founded by the Jamaican doctor and social campaigner, Harold Moody in 1931. The League of Coloured Peoples drew together intellectuals from the West Indies and Africa and set out clear objectives in its charter. While its overarching mission was "To interest members in the Welfare of Coloured Peoples in all parts of the world", the League also proposed: "To render such financial assistance to Coloured People in distress as lies within our capacity."

The organisation was criticized by more militant activists. The Marxist publication *The Negro Worker* branded Moody a typical "Uncle Tom", possibly the worst insult that could be thrown at a politicised person of colour. But the League's efforts to help the colonial seamen of Cardiff who had seen their lives become increasingly difficult in the wake of the Special Restriction Order were admirable.[5]

Another significant Black organisation was the West African Students Union. Founded in 1925 by 21 African law students, and subsequently provided with premises by none other than Marcus Garvey, the organisation was vocal in its denunciation of western imperialism and had an inevitably difficult relationship with the Colonial Office. Its London headquarters in Camden Square was "not only a social centre but a hive of intellectual and political activity and a market place for ideas."

> London was the center of the British Empire and it was there that I discovered Africa. Like most of Africa's children in America I had known little about the land of our fathers, but in England I came to know many Africans. Many of the Africans were students and I spent long hours talking with them and taking part in their activities at the West African Students Union building.[6]

So wrote Paul Robeson (1898-1976) in the opening chapter of his autobiography, *Here I Stand*. For a highly intelligent man like Robeson, this meeting fostered the growth of his thinking on the themes of ancestry, fraternity, solidarity, unity, history and cultural heritage. Some of the African students he met, such as Kwame Nkrumah and Jomo Kenyatta, subsequently went on to lead their countries, Ghana and Kenya respectively, to independence. Robeson became one of the key patrons of the West African Students Union, a characteristic gesture of an indefatigable champions of civil rights, a man who was intent on seeing the Negro obtain full enfranchisement as well as recognition for the great richness of his culture. This bond epitomised Robeson's embrace of his African roots in the period when London was his home. He liked nothing better than to spend time in the library of the School of Oriental and African Studies where he researched the languages of Africa. He was convinced that the continent had much more to offer than the "barbarous dialects" commonly evoked by scholars during his youth.

Actor, singer, political activist, and polyglot, Robeson was an African-American who had a sizeable impact not just on British but on global culture during his lifetime. He grew into an emblem for those who refused the constraints and restrictions placed upon them because of their race. In his approach, Robeson was an internationalist, never provincial or ghettoised. He was erudite and curious, and never afraid to be thought subversive. He fully exercised his right to think, move, sojourn, speak and create in as many different fields as he saw fit. Freedom was the passion of his mind.

Born in Princeton, New Jersey, in 1898, Robeson was the son of a runaway slave who became a minister, who graduated from Lincoln University. Paul himself went to Columbia Law School and proved himself a brilliant sportsman, but it became clear at this stage that Robeson had assets that predestined him for a life in the performing arts. His physique was striking. Tall, broad-shouldered and barrel-chested, he had an imposing presence that came through equally on stage and screen. If Robeson looked extraordinary, he sounded more so. He had a deeply sonorous bass voice that could seduce and entice just as easily as it could intimidate and threaten. Besides stage and screen, his talents were seized on by the developing recording industry. But whatever rewards came to him, he remained a committed civil rights activist.

He won plaudits in the lead role of *The Emperor Jones* at the Provincetown playhouse in Greenwich Village, New York in 1924, but also received death threats for his part in the interracial drama *All God's Chillun Got Wings*. Just a year later, accompanied by pianist and arranger Lawrence Brown, he performed a repertoire of Negro spirituals at the Greenwich Village theatre. He went on to act and sing for over three decades, and Brown remained Robeson's trusted collaborator for most of that time, providing a strong thread of continuity as the singer's fame steadily grew.

Arriving in London in 1927, Robeson wasted little time in making inroads into the world of theatre and by the end of the decade he performed a series of iconic Shakespearean title roles as Hamlet, King Lear and Othello. The latter was a part for which he prepared with the help of Amanda Aldridge, the daughter of the African-American actor, Ira Aldridge, who had toured Europe in the early 19th century, to great acclaim. Robeson's work in West End theatres such as Drury Lane was met with consistently good press and he became a courted figure among London's cultural elite.

One of the defining entries in his extensive list of theatre and film credits was the character of Joe in the musical *Showboat*, a production that premièred in New York in 1927 and transferred to London to open at the Theatre Royal, Drury Lane on 3rd May, a year later. Although he had been unavailable for the original American shows, Robeson was a star attraction in the very strong British presentation that included two other renowned figures in African-American music: singers Alberta Hunter and Mabel Mercer.

Showboat, by Jerome Kern and Oscar Hammerstein II, remains powerful on the subject of colour prejudice, and the prohibition of sexual relations between the races in late 19th century America. The title refers to the steamers that sailed up and down the Mississippi with their rooms for music and gambling, a phenomenon crucial to the history of Black music because it was the setting for early gigs by Louis Armstrong. Robeson's character, Joe, is a black dockworker who is the eyes and ears of the action, advising other characters, such as the naïve young actress Magnolia, on the ways of debonair cardsharps. Whilst Joe submits to the permanence of the great Mississippi, recognizing that the mighty river "jes keeps rolling along", his songs do not sidestep the black man's oppression at this point in American history.

It is the song, "Ol' Man River", featured in the opening act of the play and reprised in the second, which became the anthem with which Robeson is indelibly associated. He recorded the song as a 78 rpm single for Victor records in 1928, and performed it many times during his career. Over the years the lyrics of the song were altered several times, and a precise chronicle of the changes would be an essay in its own right, but the essential amendment to note is that the original Hammerstein lyric, which used the word "niggers" who sweat and strain, later became "darkies". Robeson himself objected to "nigger", but the concrete image of black labour/white leisure – "darkies all work while the white folks play" – was a potent contrast to the abstract idea of the river as a person of advancing years who is a silent witness to the inequality that exists on land:

There's an old man called the Mississippi
That's the old man that I'd like to be
What does he care if the world's got troubles
What does he care if the land ain't free?

Old man river that old man river

He must know something but don't say nothing
He just keeps rolling, he keeps on rolling along.

This grand metaphor of the river as an irresistible force that is also a
backdrop to oppression and exploitation is vividly served by Robeson's
commanding voice, and in the 1928 version, the depth of his tone and
the authoritative but measured nature of his delivery packs a considerable
emotional punch. In the song's chorus there is a more explicit reference
to the condition of blacks consigned to plantation life, to which Robeson
responds by hardening his timbre just a little, underlining the political
undercurrent in the haunting second line of the couplet:

He don't plant taters, he don't plant cotton
Them that plants 'em is soon forgotten.

The river is a hard taskmaster. For Blacks at least, it is exertion and
exhaustion, rather than the pleasure taken by the showboat's idle white
gamblers. In the midst of registering the suffering, Robeson's voice,
on all the recorded versions, is intensely moving in making a cry for
help. The text becomes overtly biblical, and as the singer's emotional
pitch rises, he builds a bridge between the material and spiritual world,
making a direct plea for freedom from racial oppression. He does this
by invoking one of the most potent images in the vocabulary of Negro
spirituals: the river Jordan.

Let me go away from the Mississippi
Let me go away from the white man boss
Show me that stream called the River Jordan
that's the old stream that I long to cross.

The Jordan is salvation, redemption and deliverance for people of colour,
both a secular and spiritual image. Wade across its water, scramble to
the other bank, and one might reach a land free of iniquity. Its place
in the sermons and songs of the African-American church gives the
allusion in this song a deep rooting in black culture, acknowledging and
drawing on the wellspring of Black church music, making a connection
with Robeson's forerunners, The Fisk Jubilee Singers. Whether it is
set to creamy, lush orchestration or just as a voice-piano duet, the
steady, insistent pulse of the verse and the grand, sweeping nature of
the choruses, marked by their sustained notes and repeated phrases,
are redolent of Negro spirituals.

Whilst the word "darkies" evokes the era of minstrelsy, "Ol' Man River" still stands as a bedrock of Black musical culture, making the point
that American song has evolved with the input of African-American
elements. What the moneyed patrons of the Theatre Royal Drury Lane
thought about the relevance of *Showboat* to black Britain is a moot point.

Although the hardships evoked in "Ol' Man River" are very much rooted in the African-American experience, it had obvious parallels in Britain for colonial seamen in Liverpool and Cardiff, who no doubt had similar experiences to those of the character of Joe the stevedore. There is no evidence of how much Robeson knew about these communities and their marginalization, but since the 1919 race riots in Wales made the British national press, he might well have been aware of them. In any case, as he pointed out in his autobiography, the plight of the common man was always his priority. Songs espousing the rights of Black people and songs expressing support for the struggles of oppressed workers anywhere in the world were always central to his repertoire.

An incident that occurred one day in 1929 became a defining moment in his life. On his way to a gala dinner in central London, he heard the sound of miners singing to sustain themselves after a long, weary march from South Wales. They had walked all the way to the capital to petition the government for help in the face of spiralling unemployment in the coal industry that had devastated whole villages. Spontaneously, Robeson joined them and when they reached government offices in Whitehall, he gave a rousing rendition of spirituals and popular ballads, one of which was inevitably "Ol' Man River".[7]

This was the beginning of a love affair with the people of Wales that lasted for the rest of his life. Robeson went out of his way to help this group of miners, raising money so that they could catch the freight train home, and thereafter he gave fees from some of his concerts to the Welsh Miners Relief fund and visited Cardiff, Neath and Swansea to sing for those who spent long hours underground. Accounts of Paul Robeson as an individual inevitably – and correctly – draw attention to his common touch, his affinity with workers of the world, regardless of whether their toil was in the cotton fields of Georgia or the mines of the Rhonda Valley. The great coherence of his life was that as a man of the people he sang the songs of the people – "the eternal music of common humanity." This was an expression of his socialist ideals and his vision of the possibility of empathy and solidarity across racial and cultural divides, which is why he went on to make the following statement after living in Britain for many years:

> When I myself have appeared on a concert platform in Wales, the Welsh people have appeared to be the most responsive, there appeared to be a real link between us.[8]

If the struggles of common humanity were always uppermost in his mind, Robeson was nonetheless always focused on the inescapable reality of his blackness. In his autobiography, *Here I Stand*, the definition "I am a Negro" preceded the classification "I am an American". Yet this pro-black stance of Robeson must be seen in the wider context of a commitment to the rights of working people regardless of race. The farthest reaches of Eastern Europe were also of interest to him.

Indeed his greatness lies precisely in his espousal of the ideal of empow-erment for all of those who were on the lowest rung of the social ladder. His frames of reference were wide. As he said, when accepting an honorary degree from Morehouse College of Atlanta: "The tremendous strides of the various peoples in the Soviet Union have given greatest proof of the latent abilities, not only of so-called agricultural peoples presumably unfitted for intricate industrial techniques, but also of so-called backward peoples who have clearly demonstrated that they function like all others."[9]

Empathy was something that Robeson had in great supply. His support for humanitarian causes in Wales was a given. On 25 March 1934, Robeson performed a gala concert organized by the Wrexham FC Supporters club in aid of the local St. John's ambulance association, which attracted some 2,000 people. Such local initiatives were supplemented by events that had far-reaching international ramifications, such as the commemoration held at the Pavilion, Mount Ash, in 1938 in order to pay tribute to the 33 men from Wales who died supporting anti-fascist forces in Spain in 1936 when the civil war unleashed by General Franco's reign of terror reached a bloody climax. Robeson was named the guest of honour at the event that was attended by a crowd of a staggering 7,000 people. Arthur Horner, of the South Wales Miners Federation, introduced Robeson as "a great champion of the rights of the oppressed people to whom he belongs."[10]

Notes

1. The name given to the set of rich socialites, as satirized in Evelyn Waugh's *Vile Bodies*.
2. See Arnold Rampersad, *The New Negro Voices of the Harlem Renaissance* (Simon & Schuster, 1997).
3. See Tony Martin, *Marcus Garvey Hero: A First Biography* (Majority Press, 1984). For an excellent insight into Garvey's life see also Colin Grant's *The Negro With A Hat* (Vintage, 2009).
4. See Owen Mathurin, *Henry Sylvester Williams and the Origin of the Pan African Movement 1869-1911* (Greenwood Publishing, 1976).
5. See Blackpast.org: The Pan African Congresses 1900-1945.
6. Paul Robeson, *Here I Stand* (Dennis Dobson, 1958).
7. See Paul Robeson Jr., *The Undiscovered Paul Robeson: An Artist's Journey, 1898-1939* (John Wiley and Sons, 2001).
8. *Here I Stand*.
9. Ibid.
10. Peoplescollection.wales / casgliadyweincymru.co.uk

8 CALYPSONIAN MANNING, TRUMPETER THOMPSON, HITMAN HUTCH AND THE RECORDING INDUSTRY

> At the end of the biscuit section, where you had your biscuits weighed [There weren't any packets then] there was a tin where they put the broken biscuits. You could buy a pound [450 gm] for 3d. And that's what I ate.
> — Leslie Thompson

Fanciful as it may seem, there was a serious concern in the British High command in the First World War that the Germans would invade Jamaica and other British colonies in the West Indies. To the already deep-seated patriotism that drove many in the islands to join up and support the war effort was the added urgency of manning defences against the spectre of one of the Kaiser's gunships cruising into the Caribbean, possibly altering the course of history, so that a black man from Kingston might have greeted his neighbour with "Wie gehts?" instead of "Wa' gwan?"

While soldiers in the British West India Regiment were deployed in Europe, the Middle East and Africa, mostly to perform labour duties, such as trench-digging and stretcher-bearing, other personnel had to secure Britain's tropical territories against the enemies of the King.

It is estimated that some 16,000 Caribbean soldiers, as well as a million Indians and a million Africans, were prepared to sacrifice their lives for King and country during the Great War, though their service was still defined by their second-class status as 'Colonials'. The army high command was evidently very conscious of the need to control the natives, so the Manual of Military Law stated that the number of "aliens" in any corps was not to exceed the proportion of one to every "fifty natural-born subjects." The British West India Regiment was formed to take black soldiers out of white units and concentrate them in "coloured" ones – though invariably officered by Whites.

Discrimination was brazen, the most shocking instance of which was the refusal of the British authorities to allow coloured battalions to participate in victory parades at the end of the war. News of these insults circulated throughout the West Indies in newspapers such as the New York-based *Negro World*, the organ of Garvey's UNIA. The discontents fostered by this experience contributed to the growing militancy of black workers in Trinidad in the 1920s, whose numbers included demobbed soldiers.

Nevertheless, the West Indian musical presence in the British army continued. The military offered a high standard of training, the chance of studying in Britain, and the opportunity to perform at public events. For example, twenty members of the West India Regiment band, which was based in Kingston, Jamaica, travelled to England in 1924 to take part in the British Empire Exhibition at Wembley.

The career of one significant Trinidadian musician, Sam Manning, illustrates not only the connection between the military and music, but also the pressures that drove West Indian musicians to emigrate in the interwar years. His is another narrative that shows how Black British music is a Black Atlantic phenomenon. In Manning's case this linked Trinidad, New York and London. He was also the precursor of a flow of West Indian musicians, principally Leslie Thompson, Leslie Hutchinson and Ken Johnson whose stories follow.

Little is known about his origins, other than that he was born in Cuva, Trinidad in 1898. On finishing his secondary education in Trinidad, Manning tried his hand at a variety of jobs: chauffeur, mechanic and jockey. In 1914, he joined the British army, initially as a member of the Middlesex Regiment. However, Manning's longest commission was in the British West India Regiment, a unit comprising men who were recruited from all over the Caribbean. Serving in France, Egypt and Palestine, Manning gave expression to his musical talent when he took part in "concert party work under the colours", entertaining the troops. This suggests that Manning already had some experience of playing music in Trinidad prior to joining the army, but the experience that he gained in the army was important because it gave him the opportunity to perform regularly. Information on some of Manning's peers suggest that there may have been many other black musicians serving in the British army in the first world war whose instrumental skills were duly recognised in nicknames. For example, another Trinidadian who served in the 25th battalion was George Roberts, also known as "Drummer", though it is not known whether he performed in concerts for his fellow soldiers as Manning did, or played informally when he and his unit enjoyed time away from action.

Manning first came to public attention when he featured as a calypsonian in a 1926 review, *Brown Sugar*, produced by Mrs Marcus Garvey, of whom more later. Topping the bill was the legendary jazz pianist, Fats Waller. Manning had made his way to New York in the 1920s, where he performed in vaudeville shows, in which he was billed as a comedian as much as a singer. When he headlined in *Keep Scuffling*, at the Lafayette, "America's leading colored theatre" in 1928, Manning was sold as "the laughing sensation of the year"[1] on adverts that appeared in the *New York Age*.

Another of the West India Regiment's first battalion recruits, registered in 1917 as 6868: Leslie Anthony Joseph Thompson (1901-1987)[1] and he was part of a rich crop of servicemen who were also excellent musicians. As well as Manning, these included saxophonist Joe Appleton (1900-1991), clarinettist and saxophonist Louis Stephenson, and cornet player Leslie 'Jiver' Hutchinson (1906-1959). Although originally a double bass player, Thompson was also a trumpeter and he made his name on the London music scene with both instruments. Born in Kingston, he attended the Alpha Cottage School, a catholic orphanage which later passed into musical folklore as the training ground for a large number of the island's legendary ska and reggae players, several of whom changed the nature of Jamaican music. Thompson initially played the euphonium in Alpha's brass band and he also received tuition from the West India Regiment band, which was talent-scouting for its own purposes. In 1917 Thompson joined W.I.R's first battalion, which was assigned to guard Jamaica in case of German invasion.

In the 1920s, before Thompson settled permanently in London, he travelled back and forth between Jamaica and the mother country both for training and for performances, such as at the Wembley exhibition. In Kingston he played in theatres and cinemas at a time when silent movies had a live soundtrack performed by an orchestra using cue sheets. By 1929, Thompson was the band director at the Palace, Jamaica's leading venue, recruiting artists from abroad, including "a song and dance act" from New York: Sam Manning. The presence of these two musicians in Jamaica is significant for it shows the extent of movement of Black performers within a diasporic framework.

In the summer of that year, Thompson moved permanently to London to find work as a freelance player. He made use of contacts from his youth, and got a tip from one of his old army buddies, Joe Appleton, who was already in Britain. He pointed Thompson in the direction of the charmingly named Jewish violinist, Muzikant, who led a 16-piece orchestra that appeared at "kosher" weddings and dances. He hired Thompson to play, but the work eventually dried up. As Thompson wrote in his autobiography, *Swing From A Small Island,* freelance black musicians in Britain in the late 1920s were not in the greatest of demand, and no anecdote is more poignant about those desperate times than his recollection of how he kept his stomach quiet when there was no money in music. He would go to a branch of Woolworths where foodstuffs were put on scales before being wrapped in brown paper bags. "At the end of the biscuit section, where you had your biscuits weighed there was a tin where they put the broken biscuits. You could buy a pound [450 gm] for 3d. And that's what I ate."[2]

Things did pick up, though. Thompson eventually toured and recorded with leading American exponents of the new music some called jazz, as well as gigging with British bands over the decades, to enable him to sustain a long-term career. What is endearing in Thompson's life story is the great resolve and determination he showed in making his way in the inter-war music scene, despite the lean times described above. Furthermore, he was a source of pride for Jamaica. In the popular imagination, the phenomenon of "our man abroad" is an important one. West Indian islands did not yet have their own governments, but they did have local newspapers that monitored the fortunes of their expatriates. On 18th March, 1932, Jamaica's *Daily Gleaner* ran the following triumphant piece:

> Information received in the island recently states that Mr. Leslie Thompson, who was formerly of the West India Regiment and a member of the West India Regiment band, is making steady progress in his musical career in England. He is now playing in Spike Hughes' band at the Theatre Royal at the Drury Lane Theatre London.

The other area where he looked for employment was in the musical theatre of London's West End. Most jazz musicians hunting for work in London would congregate in Archer Street in Soho, in the heart of theatre land, which acted as an informal labour exchange where news of opportunities were openly traded. A stage production with actors, comedians and chorus girls also needed a pit orchestra, which meant the chance of work for a trumpet player like Thompson. He was a player who was developing his range by taking a close interest in jazz, which he considered to have the most advanced players.

The presence of jazz bands on a "variety programme", which could include dancers and comedians, was, as noted in the previous chapter, well established – a pattern that continued well into the 1960s. Indeed, the close alignment of these types of expression, particularly dance, can be seen in the interest of many Black musicians in choreography, particularly in the work of the great masters of rhythmic styles such as tap.

Thompson made good use of such opportunities. The first show that he worked on was *Brown Birds,* which featured a largely coloured cast, and he went on to appear in the musicals of the man who was fast becoming the giant of West End shows: Noel Coward. Playwright, singer, actor, director, composer and diamanté wit, Coward had been active since the 1920s and had become successful by tapping into something quintessentially British in the texts and characterization of his shows, and by his ability to write snappy urbane sketches and songs for his energetic revues. *Words and Music* was one of the Coward creations that Thompson worked on, and he may have found it ironic to be involved in a show that featured the song "Mad Dogs And Englishmen", a piece that trumpeted white superiority – "Every native [is] a simple creature" – though within the context of imperialist self-mockery – "it seems such a shame that when the English claim the earth, they give rise to such hilarity and mirth."

Leslie Thompson was not the only West Indian to appear in Coward's prolific output.[3] In 1928, Coward's *This Year of Grace* featured in its orchestra a pianist by the name of Leslie Hutchinson.[4] The fact that he was also a colonial subject was one of the few things that he had in common with Leslie Thompson, for when he arrived in London in 1926 he did not have to stomach a diet of broken biscuits to sustain him through lean spells.

Hot lobster and champagne cups were more to Hutchinson's taste. Born in Gouyave, Grenada in 1900, Hutchinson was a gifted pianist and vocalist who took an interest in ragtime and syncopated music. He moved firstly to New York to develop as a musician and later to Paris, where he became the protégé and allegedly the lover of Cole Porter. In addition to performing regularly at clubs in the "ville lumière", Hutchinson was also asked to play at the private functions of the wealthy and this trend continued when he crossed the Channel. His life was colourful to say the least and alleged trysts with socialites and aristocrats summed up the high society decadence of the era. Handsome, charismatic and talented, Hutchinson became a star who attracted a large female following in the lucrative dinner-dance market called cabaret. In the publicity shots of Hutchinson in his prime, the image is dazzling. He is immaculately turned out in a crisp white bowtie and tails, his jet-black hair is neatly pomaded, his expression sultry. It is clear that he was styled in much the same way as a matinee idol or movie star, whose picture would be pored over by adoring fans. His nickname "Hutch" created the image of informality, if not intimacy, between artist and fan, the illusion that every performance involved a personal relationship with every single member of the audience.

But Hutch did not have to depend on live performances. He was (with Paul Robeson) one of the first Black stars of the British recording industry which gained momentum during the inter-war years. To understand his status one has only to look at an advertisement for the Parlophone recording label of the time. Established in Germany in 1896, its British arm started operating in 1923 and in 1929 it was issuing the cutting-edge of American jazz, the work of pioneers such as Louis Armstrong, Bix Beiderbecke, Duke Ellington and Joe Venuti. A photograph of the perfectly groomed Hutch, clad in mandatory evening wear, and framed by the outline of a star, is shown next to a list of his recordings, starting with R1126 "Guilty"/ "If I Didn't Have You" and ending with R871 "Memories of You"/ "Overnight". These were the days of just one song on each side of a 78, and there are 16 compositions listed, and if the size of the artist's' catalogue is intended to impress fans (who, it doesn't need to be spelled out, should have been thinking about purchasing *all* of their idol's offerings), then what is no less important is the way the label presents its prize asset. He is *theirs*. "Hutch records only for Parlophone." The underlining is as bold and clear as the artist's demeanour is suave and sophisticated with the right blend of elegance and excitement required by a fast-growing audience.

Advertising copy such as this says a lot about Hutchinson, but there is no better way of understanding him as an artist than by viewing priceless Pathé newsreel footage shot at London's Malmaison café in 1931. Again, the way that he is presented is telling. The first caption reads: "Millions have heard Leslie Hutchinson ['Hutch'] on the air, stage and or record." The second caption brings up the curtain: "Here he is on screen." The camera pans around the venue to show couples on a dance floor, while white-jacketed waiters weave between tables to serve the patrons, most of whom sport full evening wear. Finally the focus lands on Hutch, in his trademark white tie and tails, sitting at a grand piano, accompanied by an acoustic guitarist and clarinettist. They launch into "Close Your Eyes", and the music swings gently, as the pianist negotiates the jaunty chords with relaxed precision. His tenor voice delivers the chorus with a considerable amount of power and the clarinettist soloing behind him, adding a number of emphatic high-pitched phrases, becomes something of a peripheral figure. As for the guitarist, he is simply drowned out. Halfway through, the band jumps into double time. Hutch stops singing, leans into the piano and launches into a vigorous burst of "stride", the school of jazz piano that evolved from ragtime, where his right-hand lines are rapid sparkles while his left-hand bass figures are full of robust leaping movement. In that passage he instantly conjures up the "hot" quality for which jazz had become known, which makes his voice all the more conspicuous when he sings again on the coda. His enunciation is ultra polished. He sounds so terribly, terribly English.

Applause erupts as the performance finishes. Hutch quickly stands up, takes a bow and leaves. His deportment and bearing are those of a showman who is professional, classy and self-possessed, and, as the cheers ring out, he seems perfectly at home in this gilded setting. At that point in time Hutch was at the height of his commercial powers, and was reputedly one of the highest paid entertainers in Britain. In addition to his numerous recordings, he was heard regularly on the BBC, whose broadcasts of concerts were instrumental in giving an artist exposure and building a fan base. With this kind of exposure in show business, it followed that Hutch's presence at the lavish parties of the "in crowd" in Mayfair was mandatory.

From the mid 1940s his career went into decline, and while the fact that he fell out of fashion musically has to be taken into account, the scandal that engulfed him following a dangerous liaison with Lady Edwina Mountbatten, to the disgust of her royal-in-laws, seems to have made him a *persona non grata* among the upper crust of British society.

His life stands as parable for the complex relationship between the mainstream and black culture in the 1920s and 30s. While Hutch was a star who purveyed a version of Black entertainment that, due to its astute calibration of energy and sophistication, was wholly palatable, he was still a colonial subject and was by no means immune to the prevailing prejudices, particularly the fear of the appeal of the black male to white women. As noted above, in the previous decade legal orders had been enacted to restrict the movement of West African seamen in industrial ports such as Cardiff.

Tales of Hutch having to use the servant's entrance to appear at high class engagements also chime with the experience of blacks in America,[5] but if there is one image that vividly symbolizes the paradoxes of his life, it can be found in the Pathé newsreel. As he makes his exit at the Malmaison, his silhouette is cast against a white wall streaked by the flopping fronds of a palm tree. Exotica proves inescapable. Cabaret star or not, Hutch is still an "island boy". A native. An artist on stage, a Negro off it.

Issue of race aside, the phenomenon of Hutch also displays the changing face of culture in Britain in the interwar years. Victorian music hall had evolved into variety theatre, taking performers into bigger and mostly better appointed venues, but the underlying principle of the mixed bill remained firmly intact as promoters and entrepreneurs were convinced of the compatibility of song, dance, comedy and "novelty" acts. The other related form of presentation was cabaret, the circuit in which Hutch plied his trade, where patrons were similarly used to the idea of a show in which one kind of performer followed another, however different in character, serious or not so serious. For example, on the bill for one of Hutch's London cabaret shows (in which "tea and coffee is served in the auditorium on request") are Miss Dorrie Dene, comedienne, The Macelle trio, Adagio dancers, the Condos brothers, the world's greatest tap dancers, and "Hutch". He is also described as "an Entertainer".

Over time, the nature of programming began to change, with a greater separation between the different genres. Yet several decades into the future, both in America and Britain, it was still possible to see a trumpeter or saxophonist lead a modern jazz ensemble on the same bill as a stand-up comedian, magician or a muscleman. Indeed, some patrons who remembered the interwar years with fondness were minded to complain that their nights out, whether they were deemed art or entertainment, became less enjoyable with the rise of popular music and the precedence taken by the singer or band over the comedian. The popularity of "Tonight at the London Palladium" from 1955-1969 (with a couple of revivals) and, in our own day, the widely heterogeneous mix of acts on a popular show such as "Britain's Got Talent", indicates that for some audiences the old style of variety remains popular.

In the 1930s and after, key developments in the material of recording media conspired to maintain this variety culture. As the shellac and vinyl EP and LP album gained greater currency, recordings were made by comedians – in fact the popular vaudeville stand-up, Cal Stewart, did so as early as 1898 – as well as by musicians and singers, making the point that what was, until the present, the music industry's defining unit of reproduction, was never confined to music. The stock-in-trade was sound in the widest possible sense, and that could mean the human voice telling stories as much as the human voice singing a song or a musician playing the piano or horn. A recording afforded consumers the magical opportunity to enjoy words, spoken or sung, again and again in their own homes. Recorded music became a highly lucrative product in western capitalism and, somewhat inevitably, this development lead to targetting specific audiences. Whilst a performer like Hutch had an international, sophisticated image, discs began to appear made by West Indians, Africans and African-Americans in which more specific cultural resonances became an a unique selling point.

Black music and the Recording Industry

Segmental marketing had been an integral part of the American music industry from its earliest years. The advent of the "Race record", black music for black consumers, underlined the deep social divisions in the USA, but the great interest in syncopated music that went beyond Black audiences prompted labels to broaden their strategies. Parlophone presented sides by the likes of Armstrong and Ellington in a series that was entitled "Rhythm". There was thus no ambiguity on the nature of the product, and the use of such terminology effectively captured the changes that Black musicians were bringing to popular music. Whether it was a pianist enriching a chorus with a flurry of tricky accents or blues and gospel singers using tambourines or handclaps to set a strong pulse in a song that was shot through with a righteous, unalloyed emotion, the "beat", the galvanising current, was paramount.

By the 1920s, record sales jumped by a significant 15%. Records became objects of desire and listening to shellac and discussing the merits of artists became an element of social intercourse. Documentation of the works of the "Jazz Age" began to capture the imagination of a British public that became increasingly eager to hear those who could not be heard performing live. "Rhythm" clubs came into existence, small groups of record enthusiasts who congregated to spin the latest 78 rpm releases, many of which had to be specially ordered because the record shop was not yet a common feature in the high street. The phenomenon increased the popularity of certain artists, such as Duke Ellington, and also fostered the sharing of information on *how* to actually replicate the music on the discs, because many rhythm club members were musicians themselves and some would take instruments to sessions in order to demonstrate the techniques that were deployed by recorded bands. Shellac discs were essential educational tools for aspiring players.

Pictures of the standard living room the interwar years indicate that there was a technological revolution underway. A set of photographs taken in New

York in the 1930s makes this clear. The scene takes place in the Harlem apartment of Mary Lou Williams, a prodigiously gifted pianist who made a vital contribution to the development of jazz in the inter-war years, writing arrangements for stars such as Louis Armstrong and Andy Kirk as well as developing as a formidable soloist and band-leader in her own right. In one picture Williams and other musicians are gathered at her upright piano, studiously watching Hank Jones as he plays. In another picture, the same musicians are huddled around a record player with a look of utter glee as they enjoy what were presumably the latest "sides" of music made by their peers. Both images are bound by the sense of the musicians engaged in a learning process. Like the audience member, the musician is also a consumer, regardless of his ability, who sees the necessity of listening to the work of his peers, both for pleasure and to keep abreast of stylistic developments. This is another rhythm club, then, hosted informally by African-American artists themselves, the people whose recordings would cross the Atlantic.[6]

Hence, the gatherings of musicians and record buyers to source music that was not widely available was a cultural phenomenon whose importance cannot be overstated, primarily because it offered such a clear prelude to the future. Quaint as they may seem, the rhythm club is a precursor to modern day DJ culture, in which the dissemination of audio, captured and stored on ever evolving formats, from vinyl to CD to digital files, becomes a central dynamic of social intercourse.

Together, the rhythm club and Parlophone's "Rhythm" series reveal a growing audience for African-American music in Britain. Yet if labels such as Parlophone recognized as much in their promotional strategy, there were other fields waiting to be ploughed.

There is a general consensus that the advent of "World Music", largely a byword for African music, can be located at some point in the early or mid 1980s, but long before that music from the Africa was actively documented and sold by European and American labels. Parlophone had a "West African" series in the mid 1930s. It took its lead from Odeon, the label founded by Max Strauss and Heinrich Zuntz in Berlin in 1903. And preceding both of them by several years was Zonophone, established in Camden, New Jersey in 1899, and later acquired by Columbia, Victor and Gramophone, which then became the Electrical & Musical Industries, better known by the acronym, EMI. Zonophone made substantial inroads into the West African market, recording a number of Ghanaian and Nigerian musicians in the second half of the 1920s.[7]

Thankfully, these sides have survived, and a superb anthology issued by the Honest Jon's record label in 2008, *Living Is Hard*, provides a priceless overview of the original catalogue. Although there is scant biographical information about the artists, it is likely that several were students drawn from Black communities around Britain, such as Cardiff and Liverpool.

Music by Oni Johnson, John Mugat, Domingo Justus, George Williams Aingo and the Kumasi trio is of enormous historical interest because it shows some of the primary African elements of the Black music from America that had greatly attracted audiences in Europe: strong, percussive rhythms, pitch bending, and call and response vocal choruses.

There is an emotional charge in the music that at times is overwhelming, no more so than an extraordinary solo vocal performance by Ben Simmons. The fact that the piece is untitled suggests that it may have been improvised in the studio, and it's hard to imagine that something so mercurial was rehearsed. Simmons delivers a barrage of phrases of continually shifting length and emphasis in meter that is not so much "raggedy" as dragged over the beat in every which way imaginable, and at several junctures he uses a series of almost frenzied exhalations to further displace the rhythm of his vocal. This is as much avant-garde as it is folk music. If some Victorians objected to the "wildness" of certain black minstrels, then they would have been scared out of their wits by Simmons' sheer intensity.

However, it is likely that very few Britons ever heard the Zonophone recordings. The label's adverts for the series indicate that these were recordings intended for the West African market, as the strapline shows. "Zonophone records are available in the following West African Dialects." Then 18 languages are listed, including Fanti, Ashanti, Ga, Sobom, Yoruba, Hausa, Anecho and Duala. The final entry in the list of dialects on the Zonophone advert is "Coast English", which is presumably a euphemism for the Creole that was spoken on what was known at the time as the Gold Coast, before it became the state of Ghana. Here then is a key effect of colonialism, namely an imposed but then heavily subverted European language, refracted through the prism of new music. This phenomenon was not confined to the African territories of the Empire. The birth and growth of creolised English was well underway in the West Indies, which imparted to the music of calypso a distinct character and flavour that could not emanate from Standard English.

Production of calypso music was initially based in New York because there was no local recording industry in Trinidad, and because the colonial government objected to "native music" whose satire and ribaldry flouted elite proprieties in a crown colony. Roughly at the same time, the first recordings of mento, a form of Jamaican folk music with parallels to calypso, were made. The word actually derives from the French *menteur*, meaning liar or trickster, which is an essential archetype in the West Indian imagination. Thus, Okeh records sub-titled Trinidadian singer Sam Manning's "Lignum Vitae" single as "Mento" when they issued it in 1927, as part of a Race series, though there had been a West Indian batch issued previously, and the use of the word is noteworthy because it identifies a new genre of music.[8]

The West Indian market was small, but it was just as valid a proposition as a West African one, and its particularities were highlighted in a parallel to the treatment of its West African counterpart. What is intriguing is the precision with which the record companies described their wares. Some Manning songs are simply termed "West Indian" but others are "West Indian Vocal Accomp. by Jazz Trio", while one song, "Jamaica Blues" is "Mento with Incidental Singing". The African releases are even more detailed. Ben Simmons' "Mu Kun Sebor Wa Wu" is a "Song in Fanti" with "Chorus, Castanets and Clapping". These are descriptions for highly segmented markets and for retailers who could not sample on-line. What is also clear is that whilst such records, though produced in Britain may have had only a tiny domestic market of West African students, they were not intended for a more general British market, but only for export. The taste for African and World music was some years ahead, though there seems to have been more space for West Indian sounds. But even here, such was the ignorance over the artistic output of Trinidad that sometimes marketing departments felt the need to spell out *what* language was spoken. For example, the colourfully designed sleeve of Manning's EP, *African Blues*, has the caption "West Indian tunes with English lyrics". One could argue that this was stated because some of the singer's songs, such as "Femme Martinique", were sung in French Creole, but that does not disguise the disconnection between public perceptions of West Indians and their administrative status in the Empire. They were British subjects, so why would a record company feel the need to point out that they performed in the Queen's English? Because they were still seen as curiosities. Their otherness took precedence. Put Manning's case within a wider historical context and a more subtle racial overtone can be discerned. Confusion persisted over what was the black man's language. "African Blues" was issued in 1924; just 18 years earlier, reviews in the British press of the Native Choir of Jamaica, touring the UK at the behest of the Colonial Products Exhibition, noted that the Kingston singers impressed with "quaint enunciation" and "good English".

As much as they were part of the entertainment and recording industry, the lack of status of most black musicians was still apparent. Having a contract with Okeh or a tour of concert halls in Britain could not disguise the fact that there was little understanding of the culture that underpinned calypso. Manning's were Race records, or Specialty discs. On the sleeve of "African Blues" there is a photograph of the white quintet that accompanied Manning – Fred Hall's Royal Terrace Orchestra, immaculately dressed and posing with banjo, bass drum and saxophone. There is no image of the black singer himself. However, there is a sketch of a palm tree.

Records such as these, complete with their ethnically airbrushed packaging, were available on order in Britain and Europe as well as America, and they stand as priceless artefacts that reveal how Black artists and, by extension people of colour, were assigned to a lower rung of the social ladder in the inter-war years. Understanding the "other" is not easy in any society built on hierarchies of class and cultural values, but that task is rendered impossible if the other is taken out of the frame and made invisible.

We don't know whether he was emotionally wounded by episodes such as this – and one can only imagine that he was – but Sam Manning proved to be one of the most industrious and adventurous of the calypsonians who came to prominence in the 1920s and '30s. His substantial body of recordings, numerous theatre shows and articles for the *Trinidad Guardian* marked him out as a social commentator as well as a musician. He evidently understood that New York was only one part of a network of international cities in which black artists could further their development. In 1934 he crossed the Atlantic to settle in London.

Notes

1. For the material on Leslie Thompson, see his autobiography, with Jeffrey Green, *Swing From a Small Island* (Northway, 2009) p. 60.
2. *Swing from a Small Island*, p. 60.
3. *Swing from a Small Island*, pp. 74-76.
4. For the material on Leslie Hutchinson, see Charlotte Breese, *Hutch* (Bloomsbury, 1999).
5. I'm thinking of black artists having to use the side entrance of the Cotton Club in the 1920s.
6. Located at the National Jazz Museum in Harlem, 58 West 129th Street, Ground Floor, New York, NY 10027.
7. Paul Vernon, "Savannaphone", Folk Roots, No. 122.
8. Details drawn from the two cd's that offer Sam Manning's work: Sam Manning Recorded in New York, Vol 1, 1924-1927; and vol 2. 1927-1930, both on the Jazz Oracle label.

9 CHARING CROSS LONDON AND
CHARING CROSS GLASGOW

For a Jamaican, the Glasgow accent and idiom were very hard to understand.
– Coleridge Goode

And now for another new one, "The Lambeth Walk", an honest to
goodness cockney number with a rollicking tune.
— Pathé newsreel of the Locarno dance hall, Streatham

While there is a traditional divide between the club owner and artist,
which in the worst-case scenario sees the former as the unscrupulous
exploiter of the latter, history throws up many examples of one person
who combines both roles. In fact, an establishment run by a respected
musician can become a considerable draw for an audience because of
the added credibility and kudos of the person in charge.

Trinidadian Sam Manning (1899-1960), who first came to Britain as
a soldier in 1924, was also one of the most industrious and adventurous
of the calypsonians who came to prominence in the 1920s and '30s. His
substantial body of recordings, numerous theatre shows and articles for
the *Trinidad Guardian* marked him out as a social commentator as well as
a musician. He evidently understood that New York was only one part of
a network of international cities in which Black artists could further their
development. In 1934 he returned to Britain, this time settling in London.
He had exactly the right credentials to run a "hip joint".[1]

In 1934, a few months after arriving in London, Manning set up the
Florence Mills Social Club in Carnaby Street in Soho, central London,
with the help of his companion Amy Ashwood Garvey, former wife of
Marcus Garvey. This was a different kind of rhythm club, a restaurant
with a stage for live performances, which became a meeting place for Black
intellectuals and artists who were either resident in or passing through
the city. The presence of such notable figures from the world of politics
and the arts as Paul Robeson helped to establish the club's reputation, and
naming it in honour of Florence Mills (1896-1927), a major figure of the
Harlem Renaissance, a singer and dancer who appeared in the successful
1921 Broadway musical *Shuffle Along*, who also recorded many times with

Duke Ellington's orchestra, was a significant choice. Mills was lionized by the Black press as a role model, so Manning and Garvey were paying tribute to a figure who was seen as uplifting the "race".

A sense of self-empowerment underscored the creation of the Florence Mills Social Club and its gatherings should be seen the context of the popular struggle taking place in Black America and the West Indies. The mid 1920s and '30s saw the growth of trade unionism in Trinidad as well as the founding of the League of Struggle For Negro Rights. Manning's musical activism was preceded, as Chapter 6 indicated, by James Reese Europe's founding of the black musicians collective, the Clef Club, in New York and the activities of members such as Dan Kildare and Louis Mitchell in Britain and the continent. Reese Europe had led the Hellfighters, an all-black military band of the 369th US Infantry that made a number of successful appearances in France during the First World War. Mitchell had a long term residency in Paris in the early 1920s, which helped open the door for other black musicians in the coming decades. Duke Ellington, Fats Waller, Noble Sissle, Valaida Snow, Florence Mills, Leslie Hutchinson and Sidney Bechet all made the journey from London to Paris. The *Revue Negre* of 1925, featuring the star dancer-actress-singer Josephine Baker, was a key event. As noted earlier, the crossing paths of musicians from the USA, the West Indies, and those settled in Britain and Europe was a feature of those times. A noteworthy example was the 1934 tour of France by the Jamaican trumpeter Leslie Thompson at the same time as Louis Armstrong.[2]

This was a chance to learn first-hand from someone whom musicians in London regarded as at the cutting edge of jazz. The shows that Armstrong had performed in Britain in the early 1930s were must-hear events for players trying to keep up-to-date, while Armstrong's recordings such as "Heebie Jeebies", "West End Blues" and "Memories of You" were assiduously studied prior to his arrival. Leslie Thompson recalls falling under Armstrong's spell in the most vivid terms. "The style was new to me, and that swing, that beat, was tremendous. That beat and punch, and swing."[3] The words were well chosen. Swing reflected the ongoing relationship that African-American musicians had with the idea of energy in sound, how to convey a rhythmic vigour and thrust by the way a note was executed. How a phrase was attacked, how certain notes were shortened or lengthened in the most subtle ways without the underlying pulse being disrupted, how a feeling of tension crept into the momentum: all these elements conjured up the sense that the music had "punch". If this was an appropriate epithet, so too was "hot", which stood as one of the central shibboleths of jazz as it evolved from ragtime towards swing. With his groups, the Hot Five and Hot Seven, Armstrong significantly developed the role of the improviser, taking solos that lasted much longer than the 'break' of two bars that had been the been the case in earlier styles of jazz.

"Swing" really meant a vigorous 4/4 rhythm, steady but infectious, and defined another stage in the evolution of jazz, as the syncopated orchestras of the 1910s turned into the swing big band, of the later 1920s, showing that African-American music was invariably dynamic. Its pace of change was relentlessly rapid, sparked by the imagination and curiosity of composers and bandleaders, who showed their willingness to tap into an extremely wide range of musical sources.

Swing, especially in the hands of a visionary such as bandleader-composer-pianist Duke Ellington, appeared as an astute consolidation of multiple forms. He drew on the jauntiness of ragtime, the raucousness of New Orleans marching bands, the stirring call and response of gospel, the deeply emotive pitch-bending of the blues and the range of harmonic nuance of European classical music.

Equally significant was his experimentation with different instruments. The greater rhythmic propulsion brought by the double bass, which began to "walk", as well as the effects created on brass by the use of hats and cups enriched the sounds and sensations for the audiences of the day. Applied to a 12-piece big band with a four-piece rhythm section, 2 trombones, 3 trumpets and 3 saxophones, these new ideas delivered "that beat and punch, and swing" as well as inventive textures that startled audiences in the 1930s, especially when the soloists proceeded to growl and "wa wa" their way through scores that could move from driving momentum to passages of immense sensitivity.

Although Ellington made recordings with small groups, he was the definitive exponent of orchestral music in which rhythmic ingenuity was matched by a rich timbral palette. The talents of fellow composer and arranger Billy Strayhorn, as well as those of horn players Johnny Hodges, Harry Carney and Cootie Williams, to name but a few, combined to create a body of work that is outstanding in the way it conveys such a wide range of human emotions with a complex tonal palette, from the primary colours of joy and pain to the more subtle shades of introspection and pathos, a recognition of life's complexities and contradictions. The kaleidoscopic nature of Ellington's oeuvre reflected a man who understood the need for showmanship and entertainment, such as he had presented at the Cotton Club in the 1920s where his music was essentially for dancers, yet who also pursued the ambition to reach high standards of artistry through the development of socio-political suites and works that flowed from his interest in theatre. On the one hand Ellington's music has the primal power of the blues, the ability to get everybody rockin' in rhythm, on the other hand it reaches poetic grandeur, through its evocation of humanity in a state of grace, its artful portraiture of a sophisticated lady.

The visit of Ellington's orchestra to Britain in 1933 was a sensation, and he drew an audience of 4,000 to the London Trocadero in July of that year, reflecting a popularity of which the artist himself was unaware. In his autobiography *Music Is My Mistress* he reminisced:

> We were absolutely amazed at how well informed people were in Britain about us and our records. They had magazines and reviews far ahead of what we had here and everywhere we went we were confronted with facts we had forgotten and questions we couldn't always answer. A broadcast we did for the BBC provoked a lot of comment, most of it favourable. Constant Lambert, the most distinguished British composer of the period, had written an appreciation of our early records years before.[3]

The last point was an important one as it highlighted the persistent debate over exactly what jazz was and where it should be ranked in a musical hierarchy. The endorsement of Ellington from a respected exponent of classical music was significant given the fact that some critics contended that jazz could gain its *lettres de noblesse* as "serious" music only if it acquired more European elements.[5] This is not surprising when one considers the great divide between "respectable" classical music and "light entertainment", a state of affairs enshrined in the programming policy of the highly influential BBC.

A strain of jazz of a more symphonic and smoother, softer, more "tame" character had been the desired goal for some artists and critics who felt the music could not have dignity otherwise. The term "dance music", employed as it was in the 1930s, was definitely perceived as a lesser form of artistic endeavour than a grand work by a European composer. And it is true that bands that played dance music drew on a wide repertoire of popular tunes that included everything from "Teddy Bear's Picnic" and "I've Got A Lovely Bunch of Coconuts" to "Pennies from Heaven" and "St. Louis Blues".

Dance bands thus had varying degrees of "jazziness", some groups being "hotter" than others, some having strong soloists, though, for the most part they were not afforded opportunities to improvise. This was perhaps inevitable when some bandleaders were still unclear about what constituted a reasonable quotient of "hot playing" or "crazy rhythm" for a White audience. Listen to the successful British dance orchestras of the day, such as those led by Jack Payne, Jack Hylton and Ambrose, and you hear musicians who are competent, but the ensembles really lack the hard-edged propulsion of their American counterparts. Moreover, generally speaking, such popular dance bands eschewed the timbral flourish or skilled flirtations with dissonance so beloved of more progressive bands and players. The real dividing line, though, was in the use of vocals in dance music. Whilst the singers Ellington used are variable, and sometimes the least jazz-inflected parts of his recordings, the English singers who worked with Ambrose, such as Phyllis Robins, were resoundingly devoid of the blues.

Interestingly, the rise of dance bands provoked divergent responses to the shellac 78 rpm recording. The new technology aroused suspicion as well as enthusiasm and while certain American jazz musicians refused to enter studios and have their work captured for posterity for fear of being imitated, some members of musicians unions thought that the playing of records in public could threaten the livelihood of bands. The BBC launched its own dance band, directed by Henry Hall, and schedules from the 1930s reveal it was given airtime alongside the BBC military band and string quartets, while recorded music was restricted to "gramophone interludes". It was not until much later that the network programmed entire shows in which a "disc jockey" played "hits".

At this period, then, popular culture was still mainly dependent on live music. Just as the Victorian music hall had given way to the variety theatre so variety theatre was rivalled by the rise of the dance hall, a good many of which opened in the mid 1920s. The recurrent use of names – there was a Locarno in both Glasgow and London (Streatham), and a Palais in Nottingham and London (Hammersmith) – reflected the strength of branding. The appeal of a whole evening of dancing to a band was strong and what is striking today is just how big these establishments were. Accounts of the successful bandleaders of the day – for example Harry Roy, Jan Ralfini and Maurice Winnick – emphasize the large audiences they had stepping through the door. When Billy Cotton opened the Locarno in Streatham in 1929, no fewer than 1,500 revellers pitched up at the venue that promised "London's Finest Dance Bands". As an astute piece of marketing, the Locarno had also offered to pay their rail fares. Promotional posters show a couple decked in tails and evening frocks dancing in hold, and Pathé newsreels of the mid and late 30s, make it clear that the ritual of learning the latest steps had captured the public's imagination.

> New dances for everybody! Now we're taking you over to the Locarno, Streatham to learn something of the latest dances. Here's one you can all dance and it's sweeping the country; the Palais Glide! What better than the Palais Glide for making everyone... pally! Where the Palais Glide originated we don't known, some say the Midlands but its popularity is tremendous. And now for another new one, the Lambeth Walk, an honest to goodness cockney number with a rollicking tune.[6]

All this points to what could be called a fundamentally British strain of cultural expression, and the rise of dance music in the UK in the interwar years is an intriguing, multi-faceted phenomenon precisely because of the way that exuberance and restraint are in contention, as if social grace is a vice that could tighten around impulses that are too unbecoming. Lest we forget, patrons had been told to refrain from "shimmying" at jazz gigs in the 1910s, but the Palais glide, where three couples stood shoulder to shoulder and dipped back and forth, and

The Lambeth Walk, with its jaunty carefree sway, were deemed to be acceptable. It is no great surprise that the dance bands playing at these venues tended to be on the sedate side. There is no overt sexuality at play here, not like jazz dancing, such as depicted in *Lady Chatterley's Lover*, and the infusion of hotter steps came later as the "rollicking tunes" of the American bands, which really did swing, started to exert their influence around the world.

Though lacking the vitality of the jitterbug or lindy hop, English dances like the Palais glide were nonetheless democratically "for everybody", and this bolstered the way dance crazes that were reshaping social mores. In a quirky twist in the tale of transatlantic musical call and response, Duke Ellington had a hit in America with a version of the tune that accompanied the Lambeth Walk. With its growling brass and its short, pithy improvisations, it was altogether hotter than Billy Cotton's take.

Some of the leading British bandleaders of the time saw that Ellington was able to transcend conflicting paradigms and make music that appealed to dancers at the same time as displaying an admirable degree of artistry. Spike Hughes, who led an immensely popular orchestra and also recorded with several American stars in New York, wrote in the programme notes for the 1933 tour: "Duke Ellington was the first essentially American composer, the first composer to produce music that was really American in its idiom; not just European music watered down, or jazzed up with fancy titles."

As for Jack Hylton (1892-1965), the band-leader and impresario who set up the tour in the first place, he hailed the "provocative style and methods, their peculiarly individual compositions, their undoubted genius as instrumentalists and the spontaneous joy and feeling of their playing". [7]

The key word was "provocative", which stresses the intellectual quotient of Ellington's work, its ability to surprise. This countered the view of the Oxford academic R.W.S. Mendl who said of jazz: "So far from giving us furiously to think, it hardly seems to carry any thought at all for its complete appreciation." His likening of jazz to something "pleasingly sentimental" obliquely referenced the days of plantation revues and minstrels minded to flash a watermelon smile and do the cakewalk. [8]

Brunswick records, which issued classic Ellington sides such as "It Don't Mean a Thing", "Creole Rhapsody" and "Mood Indigo", endeavoured to frame him as a composer of music of great artistic merit to capitalize on the increased interest raised by the British residency. The somewhat unwieldy strap line that was drawn up for Duke and the Orchestra – "exponents of the new theory in modern rhythmic interpretation" – bestows a florid compliment whilst betraying a difficulty in defining their aesthetic. Were the players theorists or practitioners? Moderns or modernisers? Interpreters or transformers? Clearly, Ellington's image, from the immaculate tailoring, as in the famous promotional poster of him in top hat and tails, was one of gentility rather than vulgarity, and his refined deportment probably increased his appeal to royals such as Prince George, the Duke of Kent, who sat in on drums when the Orchestra attended a party after the Palladium concert.

The concerts by Ellington and Armstrong were key events in the dissemination of jazz in Britain during the interwar years, but for all the ensuing Duke-a-mania and Louis-philia among the general public, some critics still expressed racist attitudes that rested on the perception of Black vulgarity. Ellington's suave appearance and good looks worked in his favour, but Armstrong's tendency to sweat profusely when he was under the house lights of a theatre raised the spectre of the "low nigger" who was lacking in decorum. *The Daily Herald* had no compunction in likening him to "an untrained gorilla".[9]

Understanding what these innovators were doing musically, and how their works related to their ethnic identities remained beyond the grasp of many, for the place of the Negro in society was still a source of confusion. Ellington's music reflected black life in New York as he experienced it, so that what appears a prosaic title might hold a poetic truth. For example "Harlem Air Shaft" was a gateway to daily experience, as he explained: "So much goes on in a Harlem air shaft. You hear fights, you smell dinner, you hear people making love. You hear the radio, an airshaft is one great loudspeaker. One guy is cooking dried fish and rice and another's got a great big turkey."[10] The food-stuff references in the last line evoke the co-existence of West Indian and African-American populations, as Ellington observes the daily existence of these communities for their universal stories. According to the pianist Randy Weston, who knew Ellington well, Ellington would spend time in Harlem watching the way black people walked and gestured in the street and these observations permeated his compositions, so that his music offered portraits of the "Negro race" that drew on empirical data, an uncommon imagination and advanced musical ability. Here, "Rockin' in Rhythm" is a landmark title because the African American vernacular of its linguistic and semantic content is given such a vivid musical parallel. These are the sensual dance rhythms expressed through the tightly gripped agitation of the brass triplets, hopscotching ends of phrases, dynamic improvisations, swinging beat and sharp hisses of high-hat – an important recent addition to the evolving drum set, which is like a raised shoulder or an eyebrow arched suggestively. From one chorus to the next, the shape and character of the parts become strikingly vivid, the fast eighth-note whirls full of zest and humour, the slower, whole-note swoons deeply sensual.

Spike Hughes said that Ellington's work was not "just jazzed up with fancy titles", but the very choice of name for this song was an integral part of jazz as defined by Ellington. It is also the future language in youth culture, a trope that prefigures the coining of rock 'n' roll in the 1950s and continues in the phenomenon of rockin' the house in hip-hop in the 80s. "Rocking" would not have been the same as "rockin'", for the swing is emphatically in the colloquialism well as in the music.[11]

The mainstream cultural agenda often failed to recognise the richness of this conceptual verve. The narrowness of purist frameworks was shown in the way some critics responded to an exuberant showman such as Armstrong. They objected to the fact that he sang. There were in fact some audience members who walked out of Armstrong's Palladium shows while others cheered rapturously. Opinion was split on whether the scatting that accompanied his choruses was artistically valid. The fact that there was generally more acceptance of his trumpet playing than his singing, no doubt rested on such English critics' views of what constituted good taste.

The fact that Ellington's work had also been defined as "Jungle music" added to the ambiguity. But then finding an appropriate term, a really meaningful description of the work of Black musicians was (and still is) problematic, so much so that one artist could easily be taken as an exponent of a style stereotypically seen as "Black". Early perceptions of jazz were saddled with such misconceptions, so that some people still expected Duke Ellington to play Negro spirituals rather than swing.

This was a period of extremes of opinion when perceptions of Black artists could shift according to views on their "blackness" as well as the music they were making. What further muddied the waters was the existence of racial stereotyping among some of the musicians intent on developing and disseminating Black music in Britain. The expressed belief that African-Americans had certain innate artistic gifts made it harder to establish that the artistic advances they were making were achieved through imagination, technique and hard work. Playing "hot" was seen as a "natural" thing to do rather than a difficult, demanding technique that required rigorous application, both intellectually and physically. Jamaican trumpeter Leslie Thompson, who toured France with Armstrong, saw how much he worked on his sound. He recalled the words of Nigel Hill, one of the first white English bandleaders he worked with on his arrival in London. "He wanted to set up a jazz band, and, having heard Louis Armstrong's recordings, thought that you had to be coloured to play like that." Thus was Thompson recruited.[12]

Thompson had the talent to cut it, but the anecdote reveals the expectations that were placed on West Indian musicians arriving in Britain. A "Coloured" big band, which was West Indian rather than African-American, could "pass" as the genuine article. Jamaican, Guyanese or Trinidadian accents would not be heard on instrumental tunes. Attired in the appropriately sharp suits or tails, they *looked* the part.

Hiring musicians from the islands was a more practical business proposition, because the 1930s was a period when the Ministry of Labour and the Musicians Union imposed bans on American musicians for fear that they would deprive their British counterparts of work. Home Office applications and tiresome rounds of form-filling to obtain special permits was a burden many promoters were unwilling to spend time on, particularly when good musicians could be found from Britain's Caribbean colonies.

Thompson's Jamaican colleague from the West India Regiment, Leslie 'Jiver' Hutchinson, formed the Colored Orchestra; Guyanese Rudolph Dunbar[13] started the All British Coloured Band and his compatriot Ken 'Snakehips' Johnson led the West Indian Dance band. The names tell their own story: the groups were identified as black, continuing the Victorian convention of calling musical groups "Negro". The term "British Coloured", in particular, indicated clearly that these musicians were blacks under the jurisdiction of the Empire.

Such racial signifiers in the music industry were part of a wider taxonomy in the world of entertainment that encompassed cinema and dance. Cast an eye over the work of the pioneering African-American filmmaker Oscar Micheaux in the 1920s and 1930s and you'll see the acronyms A.C.C, A.S.C.C or A.G.C.C, as in "All Colored Cast", "All Star Colored Cast" or "A Great Colored Cast" that characterise the promotional posters for features such as *The Flying Ace*, *God's Step Children*, and *Temptation*. While the marketing proudly trumpets the quality of the product, it nonetheless distinguishes between these movies and those of the mainstream, where the whiteness of the performers is not deemed worthy of notice.[14]

This reflected the realities of a segregated America. This was not just a simple division between black and white, because the polarisation of racial values also produced a hierarchy of skin tones. Nowhere was this more apparent than in the dancers at the Cotton Club in Harlem, New York, a venue made legendary by the performances of Armstrong, Duke Ellington and Cab Calloway. Look at the photographs of the female dancers who accompanied these bands. All of them are light skinned. They are not allowed to be dark, unlike the male musicians. Black entertainment at a whites-only venue had specific obligations to fulfil. Negro women who looked more European were deemed much more comely than those who looked more African.[15]

Sadly, this value system of skin-shade prejudice was internalised at the heart of the black community itself.

Blacks were not allowed to patronise the Cotton Club so they frequented other venues, and also organised "Rent parties" in which live music and food would be provided at a person's home for a small fee. These gatherings proved immensely popular, so much so that hosts had to compete for custom. The calling cards printed to this effect ironically repeat the Cotton Club's anti-dark skin policy in the vernacular of the times. Many of the adverts hail beautiful "yellow" girls. Some talk of "brown". Others "café au lait". Or black and tan, as Ellington described the fantasy.

Thus, it is inane to say that a term such as "All Colored Cast", objectionable to the present, is somehow excusable as "the language of the day." The discrepancy between the degrees of blackness acceptable for Negro women and men sometimes took a grotesque twist. If Black women in the entertainment industry had to be light-skinned to meet the white gaze, Black musicians had to be black, a requirement in dance music that reached back to the days of the Ethiopian Serenaders. A sad reflection of this state of affairs can be seen in the fact that one of Ken 'Snakehips' Johnson's all-black bands occasionally had whites who were darkened by the infamous burnt cork. This was evidently what the public wanted. The culture of minstrelsy and blackface entertainment was far from dead. A big band from the West Indies had to fulfil the expectation of appearing as an all coloured cast. Blacking up, was thus entirely logical. Presenting a band that was *mostly* black would have jarred.

Even so, Ken 'Snakehips' Johnson's orchestra (originally formed by trumpeter Leslie Thompson) emerged as the iconic West Indian swing combo of the interwar years. This black band was one of the most accomplished on the British scene at the time, and had a rhythmic ingenuity that compared favourably to their American role models. Thompson had correctly identified that the Duke's musicians played with a vigour and drive that "kept you tapping your feet whether you wanted to or not",[9] and he himself had greatly benefited from working with Louis Armstrong. Thompson's and then Johnson's bands certainly showed their understanding that self-confidence and intensity were pre-requisites to swing, along with technical proficiency and discipline.

The stage names Johnson and Hutchinson adopted both had an American origin. "Jiver" reflects the alignment of 1930's jazz and dance, where people went to swing concerts to "jive" – one of countless African-American terms to designate joyful, limb-loosening activities. The fact that "Snakehips" was a "hoofer" simply increased the draw of his orchestra at a time when dance music had captured the imagination of the British public. He had taken his name from Earl "Snakehips" Tucker, the Harlem-born dancer who was credited with inventing the shimmy. Johnson had come to London to study law, but instead took tap-dancing lessons with the African-American choreographer, Buddy Bradley, who had made a great impact on West End shows. Dancing in the lithe and liquid way suggested by his nickname, Johnson had charisma, and his 12-piece ensemble emerged as one of the best in Britain.[17] It had excellent soloists such as the Trinidadian clarinettist Carl Barriteau, Jamaican alto saxophonist Bertie King and the Tiger Bay guitarist Joe Deniz.

For the most part it was clubs in London's West End (seen as dens of vice by the more conservative members of society), that provided employment for black British swing musicians. However, as war clouds loomed over Europe, opportunities for work dwindled.

Hence gigs had to be picked up from bookings on the variety circuit, performances for cinema audiences, appearances on the BBC and occasional sessions for a record industry. Johnson's band was lucky enough to secure residencies at The Old Florida Club and then Willerby's. The band's fortunes took a decisive upturn when it moved to the Café de Paris in Leicester Square in late 1939. The unfolding events of world history proved to be serendipitous, as Andy Simons, jazz curator at the British Library's National Sound Archive explains:

> It was while at this location that the British entry into the Second World War was declared in September. During the initial 'phoney war', so termed because almost the first year it was free from mass aerial bombardment, no one knew what to expect. But nightlife continued to be just the right remedy for an uncertain time, when people at the very least expected to lose friends or relatives in the war.[18]

As well as being an upmarket venue, the Café De Paris was also used by the BBC for live broadcasts, several of which featured Johnson's band and would have had helped to widen its audience. The orchestra also made recordings at the West Hampstead studios of the Decca label in the autumn of 1938, a prime example being the self-referential "Snakehips Swing", a song which stands out for the cohesion of its written parts and the *joie de vivre* created by the rhythmic-melodic axis of the arrangement.

Played at mid tempo, the song is a classic piece of swing. The defining element of the music is the emphatic role of the horns, often played with a liberal vibrato that increases the sensual, purring quality of the sound. The rhythmic base, which is a rolling tom tom beat, embellished by cowbell fills – à la Ellington in "jungle" mode – pushes the band along with energy.

Section playing was an art in itself, and every musician had to be precise with his reading in order to impart the required tonal colour and rhythmic attack to his "family" (the trumpet, clarinet, saxophone and trombone) which would, with the right timing and feel for the beat, blend with the other families to create an ensemble sound that was as cohesive as it was detailed.

Johnson's rhythm, brass and reed sections, bolstered by drummer Tommy Wilson, trumpeter Dave Wilkins, and King and Barriteau on alto saxophone and clarinet, do just that. The energy ebbs and flows with the constantly changing shapes and colours of the numerous horn parts, with climaxes of intensely dramatic rises in pitch. The phrasal richness of the piece is outstanding. From a bright, buoyant opening melody spins a whole web of related statements of varying degrees of complexity that provide stimulus without disrupting the steady flow of the music. Only a few bluesy chord changes are used in the piece. It is the stealthy movement of the horns that provide much of the interest, as they slalom around vigorously, the length of the lines fluctuating, the attack changing the levels of intensity.

A perky four-note run gives way to a slick five-note flurry; more legato languid harmonies neatly cushion some of the concise solos, and in the latter stage of the piece a high-pitched, curling 12-note phrase rings out to increase the tension, which is subsequently released by jolting, staccato three-note figures. It is like a game of push and pull between riffs of shifting character. The entire horn section is constantly busy, but not frantic or cluttered. Mention must also be made of the precision with which the solo improvisations, some of which last no more than eight bars, alternate with the unison lines, enhancing the light and shade of the entire performance. Whether the music is called orchestral or big band, the magic achieved by Johnson's men rises from the co-ordination of the many elements at play, the well-oiled functioning of a machine that does not lack for emotional power. "Snakehips Swing" lasts just 2:38 minutes but does not want for action.

The reason why this swing music is important is because it announces so much of what was to come in popular music in the subsequent decades. The energy of the horn statements, their focused punch, would define R&B, rock & roll, soul, and finally funk, because a swing riff is really a rough blueprint for a funk groove waiting to be repeated over a snare with an offbeat attitude. James Brown initially led a band that was inspired by Ray Charles, who was inspired by Basie and Ellington. Swing denoted a genre of music, but it was also a verb – to swing, to create momentum, drive, thrust, make things happen. Apply that principle to an ensemble comprising instruments drawn from the western brass band traditions and classical music, all pumping around the subversive engine of a new thing called a drum kit, and you have music whose seductive push in four beats to the bar far exceeds the erotic sway of a waltz set to three.

Listening to the recordings of Johnson and 'Jiver' Hutchinson that, thankfully, have survived, it is clear that these West Indian dance bands and Coloured Orchestras played well enough to compare favourably with the Americans, above all the revered Duke Ellington, who had served as their templates.

Swing Bands of this kind live or die on their ensemble playing, and generally speaking the solos taken by band members were relatively short, primarily because the overall goal was to keep dancers moving. There was nonetheless an occasional extended improvisation that gave a player an opportunity to "stretch out" for several choruses. The scintillating 32 bar clarinet solo that Carl Barriteau takes on "Washington Squabble", which he performed for a 1938 BBC broadcast, is a case in point. The whole improvisation has a vaulting, skipping quality that is given several peaks of energy by Barriteau, increasing the strength of his attack amid relatively short, pithy lines, fragments of which are repeated or reharmonised at just the right juncture. These create contrasts amid his sustained rhythmic drive. The technical gifts are evident, but Barriteau also does what some soloists fail to – he builds and paces like a good storyteller.

Several other recordings by Johnson, Hutchinson and Thompson, thankfully preserved in the British Library's National Sound Archive, make it clear that the London-based West Indian musicians of the 1930s played to an impressively high standard. But what is noticeable is the absence of any discernible Caribbean influence in the music. Rhythmically, there is little of the ambling, swaying character of the calypso beat that marked the songs cut by Sam Manning just a few years earlier – recordings of which Johnson and his peers would have been aware. However, this was the era of the cult of the bandleader, swing orchestra and dance, whereas calypso was centred first and foremost on the singer, the master of wit and wisdom.

Because the African-American influence was so strong, the cultural impact of someone like Sam Manning simply couldn't compete. Even so, the Caribbean was sufficiently strong as a cultural touchstone for another pioneering American player, the hugely talented pianist-vocalist, Fats Waller, to name one of his bands The Jamaican Jazzers, which indicated something of the place that "the small island" had in the African-American consciousness. There was a vogue for "tropical" flavourings that crystallised in the popularity of Cuban rhumba music, a hypnotic percussive style that also designated a form of dance.[19]

Indeed, one of the popular London clubs of the time was called The Cuba and it traded on an image of Latin exotica, where Black players could play non-European music that they knew from recordings. Jamaican, Bajan, Guyanese or Trinidadians musician could easily *pass* for imports from Havana or Rio De Janeiro – a throwback to an earlier century when Negro tambourinists in the army were sometimes presented as Janissary or Turkish bands. The point is that they were *not* white.

The evidence is, though, that these Latin and West Indian idioms did not have the same standing as American swing, and were largely regarded as novelty music, or music that could be played in smaller venues after hours when musicians sought to relax and loosen up.

The perception that some Caribbean musicians had of music from their region was probably a factor. For those who desired to reach a musical standard that was on a par with the Americans, the Trinidadian calypso or Jamaican mento was seen as undeveloped, and the schooled Caribbean musician might well have wanted to set himself apart from the unschooled musicians who used folk instruments such as the quatro to strum out catchy tunes.

Leslie Thompson, for instance, evoking his childhood in Jamaica, spoke of the "few keys" and "limited technical skills" of practitioners of "native music" who in turn referred to him, a player versed in theory, as "the professor".[20] If he looked down, then they apparently looked up. However Thompson also recognized that mento musicians "played right from the heart" so there is not a comprehensive dismissal of their activities. The tension between emotion and technique is a fundamental issue in music, and the fact that some West Indian players identified their homegrown sounds as unsophisticated, and satisfying neither to their ambition nor education is a reminder not to make assumptions about what the music of origins may mean to musicians. What they'd heard at home and what they aspired to play may be very different. It was an issue of complex cultural attitudes. With an "official" culture that related to Britain and a folk culture that was despised by those who aspired to higher status, because its roots could be seen as uncomfortably African, many West Indians had ambivalent feelings about what was theirs. Whether Trinidadians, Guyanese and Jamaicans could play calypso was not the point. Whether they *wanted* to, and how they saw the genre in the greater scheme of things, varied from one individual to the next, just as there were some African-Americans who took pride in the advent of both ragtime and swing and others who saw them as cheap degradations of the race. Blacks who subscribed to the notion that European classical music was at the top of a cultural hierarchy would have agreed with the assertion that jazz, and jazz dancing, was the preserve of 'low niggers'. In the same way, some trained West Indian musicians did not consider calypso as serious music because it was not scored or orchestral and the lack of recognition of indigenous culture hardened their stance. With education systems closely modelled on that of the mother country, no West Indian history was taught in West Indian schools in the 1930s, so the creole heritage and current events in the local arts never became part of the curriculum. Calypso and its Jamaican affiliates such as mento or the fife and drum music that accompanied junkanoo[21] were perceived by some as folk forms that lacked the legitimacy of the music of the composers, or at least musicians who wrote and read detailed scores. Steelband was still in the future.

It is no surprise, then, that the Black British composer, Samuel Coleridge-Taylor, was lionized in progressive middle-class circles in Jamaica. For them he was a role model because he fulfilled the criteria of the colonial establishment, proving that a person of colour could effectively play the Europeans at their own game.

In September 1913, Jamaica organized a festival in honour of Coleridge-Taylor. The Kingston Glee Singers marked the composer's passing the year before by what was an ambitious large-scale event that brought together no fewer than one hundred singers and a thirty-piece orchestra. This occasion was master-minded by George Davis Goode. He was trying to raise musical standards in Jamaica.

For young local musicians such as Leslie Thompson, Goode was a man of considerable stature. His massive choirs were regarded as being on a par with what you could hear in choral events in Worcester or Birmingham – again the yardstick was Britain – and he was credited with laying the groundwork for the birth of the Jamaica Philharmonic Symphony Orchestra in 1940.

George Davis Goode's other contribution was to be the father of Coleridge Goode, the future double bassist, named in honour of Samuel Coleridge-Taylor; not surprisingly the father was bitterly disappointed by the musical direction of the son. But what symbolism: a Jamaican musician who made his mark on jazz in Britain in the mid 20th century bearing the name of a black British classical composer whose fame had spread to America and the West Indies in the early 19th century. Black culture was echoing through time and space, crossing the water in one form and coming back in another. As a side-note, the connection was also echoed in the presence of the Jamaican trumpeter, Leslie Thompson, at one of the many revivals of Samuel Coleridge-Taylor's most famous piece in London. Between 1928 and 1939 the English conductor Malcolm Sargent conducted ten seasons of a costumed ballet version of *The Song of Hiawatha* at the Royal Albert Hall with the Royal Choral Society (600 to 800 singers) and 200 dancers. This became something of a cult event among classical music-lovers who were minded to don native American dress to attend the performance. White people pretending to be "Red Indians", coming to listen to music that was written by a black man. Leslie Thompson noted that he did not see any other people of colour at the performance he attended.[22]

Coleridge Goode was not supposed to have become a musician, let alone a jazz musician – an outrage to his parents' belief in the superiority of classical music. Coleridge had studied the violin as a boy, and also excelled at sport. Yet he also, as he himself noted, had an aptitude for mechanics and technology, and decided to study electrical engineering. After a year's preparatory course at Cornwall College in Montego Bay he travelled to Britain to complete his higher education, where he enrolled at Glasgow University in 1934. Over the next eight years Coleridge Goode became part of that city's music scene.

Seduced by the sounds of Count Basie, whose gramophone records he collected, Goode gradually drifted away from electrical engineering and, after acquiring a double bass from a local musician, he entered the world of big band music that was centred around venues such as Green's Playhouse with "its huge dance floor that could accommodate about 4,000 people."[23]

Glasgow had been an important destination for Black vaudeville entertainers in Edwardian Britain and in the 1930s, a steady stream of top artists came to the city, enabling Coleridge Goode to see the likes of the Oscar Rabin Orchestra as well as excellent locals such as the drummer Bobby Foley. These were formative experiences and he soon started to play around town with small groups, his debut gig being at the Charing Cross ballroom.

For Goode, the main problem of cultural adaptation seems to have been language. West Indians were used to hearing the received pronunciation of colonial administrators or BBC announcers on the World Service. The Scottish didn't talk like that.

"For a Jamaican, the Glasgow accent and idiom were very hard to understand," Goode recalls in his autobiography, *Bass Lines*. Given that culture clash is invariably seen from the point of view of the indigenous population rather than the migrants, this is a nice reminder that the outsider status can easily fall one side or the other.

As Goode tells it, there were precious few other "darkies" to be seen on the streets of Glasgow in the war years. However, Scotland's Black history was not insubstantial. Records show that there were Moors at the court of King James IV at the end of the 15th and early 16th century, and, as was the case all over Europe at the time, some were musicians as well as servants. More significantly, Scotland was very active in the slave trade in the period that followed, and many merchants crossed the Atlantic to become wealthy plantation owners throughout the West Indies, a lasting vestige of the enterprise being found in the names of Glasgow thoroughfares such as Kingston Bridge, Jamaica Street and Tobago Street.

Scottish slave owners also had children with African women and a descendant of one of the so-called West Indian "mulattoes", whom Goode would have been aware of, was Edmundo Ros. Although he was usually described as a Trinidadian, or of Venezuelan ancestry, Ros was actually part Scottish. Greatly inspired by Cuban and Latin music, he became a very successful big band leader in the war years, attracting a high society crowd when he appeared at upmarket clubs in London's West End.

By the end of the 1930s, Goode had reached the point where he held down regular gigs in Glasgow, but felt that he had to move to London to further his career as a professional jazz musician, so he made the switch from Charing Cross Dance hall to clubs around the Charing Cross Road in London.

In the coming decades, Goode became a key player in British and European jazz, working with stars such as George Shearing, Django Reinhardt and Stéphane Grappelli, but his initial sessions on the London scene were with lesser-known bandleaders such as Johnny Claes – but in those days any job that a young jazz musician could secure was priceless. Jazz tuition was not institutionalized as it is today and the dissemination of essential knowledge was much more informal, learned in the club or at after hours jam sessions.

The band, especially the larger bands, offered both education and occupation. Hence the presence in Britain at this time of African-Caribbean and African-American artists who could provide a form of education for developing young Black musicians was instrumental in furthering the development of Black music in Britain.

★

As outlined in Chapter 5, the phenomenon of African-American musicians moving to London and becoming highly valued teachers went back to the late 19th century, when the banjo virtuosi, James and George Bohee, established a school for the instrument in the heart of the West End.

A few decades later, there came the brilliant New Orleans clarinettist Sidney Bechet, who took on several students when he was working in ensembles in London, but the musician who shared his knowledge in a more formal institutional setting was Rudolph Dunbar, a Guyanese, who like Bechet was a clarinet player. In December 1931, he founded the Rudolph Dunbar School of Clarinet Playing in London, where he taught on a regular basis. He also wrote influential essays on advanced techniques for the instrument.[24]

In fact, Dunbar's life illustrates several key points about the evolving relationship between British colonial citizens and cultural expression within a transatlantic and trans-European perspective. Like other West Indian musicians, Dunbar left his country as a young man, having trained with a colonial institution, the Guiana Military band. Then he went to New York where he worked and studied, before doing the same thing in Paris, Rome and Vienna.

Significantly, he straddled the jazz and classical worlds. He worked in both symphonic and plantation orchestras, the two forms of expression often placed in a dichotomy of high art and popular culture. Dunbar's career provided evidence that musicians of colour could exist in these two apparently opposed spheres, that there did not have to be an absolute choice as to which path to take. Dunbar lead his Coloured Band and also conducted philharmonic orchestras in London and Berlin, a Black British musician who was simultaneously international and eclectic in his professional scope. He crossed borders and musical boundaries, learning from the best in each world, and in turn he passed on knowledge in a formal educational setting of his own making.

Here he had learnt from the example of the African American alto saxophonist-clarinettist, Benny Carter, who had a significant impact on local musicians during his sojourn in London between 1936 and 1938. A native New Yorker, Carter spent his formative years with swing music pioneers such as Duke Ellington, Fletcher Henderson and Chick Webb and had become a brilliant arranger. It was in this capacity that he was employed by the BBC Dance Orchestra. For the members of the band, Carter's presence was invaluable as he would guide them through the charts that he had written and give explicit instruction on the phrasing of parts – which is one of the greatest challenges that any jazz musician has to face.[25]

Important as this process was, more spontaneous but no less valuable lessons were learnt when Carter, and another feted American resident, tenor saxophone giant Coleman Hawkins, sat in at after-hours sessions in clubs such as the Bag O' Nails, the Shim-Sham and the Nest. This reflected the fact that whilst the musicians tended to play a more audience-friendly swing for their living, they then stretched out and experimented in the smaller clubs that were dotted around central London. These were places such as the Panama which offered a blend of vaudeville and hardcore playing as the American dancer-comic Freddie Crump would perform before the music, and there was a similar scenario at the Caribbean Club where Rudy Evans performed cabaret as a warm-up act for the main bands.

Prominent among the venues frequented by West Indian musicians was Jigs in Wardour Street, Soho. Owned by Jamaican drummer Happy Blake, the brother of trumpeter Cyril Blake, the club had a predominantly West Indian clientele. Recordings of the band at the club, featuring Lauderic Caton on guitar and Freddie Grant on clarinet, show that the prime source of material was swing, often reprises of Ellington songs. An original piece written by Blake, "Cyril's Blues" is a further recognition of the primacy of African-American music. This sweet song illustrates both the musicianship and the great strength of feeling that this small group (sextet), was capable of producing.

While the Jigs Club Band was a West Indian combo, there were several mixed ensembles operating at the time, and some of the significant early gigs that black musicians had were with white groups – such as Leslie Thompson in Nigel Finch-Hill's Rhythm Fish. In this respect, it could be argued that the racial divisions in music in Britain were less marked than was the case in America, but there is documented evidence of discrimination, as the historian Andy Simons has uncovered in his invaluable research on the period. Joe Deniz, who along with his brother Frank, both guitarists, had moved to London from Cardiff in the early 1930s, was not allowed to dep for a white counterpart in the Ambrose band at the classy Ciro's club. That was down to a bigoted white American owner who was intent on importing segregation.[26]

The Deniz brothers did, though, go on to find work with numerous bands, the most high-profile being "Snakehips" Johnson's, where Joe sometimes offered a unique cultural melange: a black Welshman playing Hawaiian guitar with a West Indian dance band. This came about because Deniz had picked up on the vogue for "aloha" music and played it to enthusiastic house parties when he was a boy in Tiger Bay. However, there were also long periods when these Black musicians got no work. The opportunities for securing a gig on a lucrative British or European tour with a top American star were rare and competition was intense.

Notes

1. Information drawn from the *Sam Manning Recorded in New York* cds.
2. Mervyn Cooke, *Chronicles of Jazz* (Thames and Hudson, 1997).
3. *Swing from a Small Island*, p. 71.

4. Ellington, *Music is My Mistress* (New York, 1973), p. 84.
5. British Pathé promotional material "New Dances for Everybody".
6. Catherine Parsonage, *Evolution of Jazz in Britain*.
7. Programme notes for Duke Ellington's British tour, 1933.
8. Quoted in Parsonage's *Evolution of Jazz in Britain*, from Mendl's book, *The Appeal of Jazz* (1927).
9. Quoted in Garth Cartwright, "Fascination and Fear: Rhythm and Reaction", *New Statesman*, Feb. 2011, which shows how Edwardian Britain responded to jazz.
10. *Music is My Mistress*.
11. Programme notes for Duke Ellington's British tour, 1933.
12. Leslie Thompson, with Jeffrey Green, *Swing from a Small Island*, (Northway, 2009) p. 71.
13. Ibid., p. 63, 67.
14. See Patrick McGilligan, *Oscar Micheaux: The Great and Only: The Life of America's First Great Black Film-maker* (HarperCollins, 2007).
15. Located in the National Jazz Archive, Traps Hill, Loughton IG10 1HD.
16. *Swing from a Small Island*.
17. Edward Thorpe, *Black Dance* (Chatto & Windus, 1989).
18. Andy Simons, *Black British Swing, The African Diaspora's Contribution to Britain's Own Jazz of the 1930s and 40s* (Topic/NSA).
19. Simons, op. cit.
20. Thompson and Green, *Swing from a Small Island*, p. 25.
21. Junkanoo is a form of Jamaican masking performance analogous to the more African elements of Trinidad carnival, but usually performed at Christmas.
22. *Swing From A Small Island*, p. 32.
23. See for material on Coleridge Goode, with Roger Cotterrell, *Bass Lines: A Life in Jazz* (Northway, 2002).
24. Rudolph Dunbar became the first black man to conduct the London Philharmonic Orchestra (1942). See Miranda Kaufmann, "Rudolph Dunbar (1899-1988) in *Oxford Companion to Black British History* (Oxford UP, 2007), pp. 135-136.
25. Alyn Shipton, *A New History of Jazz*, p. 369-370.
26. Andy Simons, *Black British Swing*.

10 FROM RADIO DAYS TO MOVIE NIGHTS

Folk songs are the music of basic realities, the spontaneous expression
of the people for the people of elemental emotions
— *Paul Robeson*

Tobacco had smouldering glamour in the 1930s. Virtually, all the major
Hollywood film stars, literati and recording artists wielded a cool
cigarette as they struck their most iconic poses, with the femme fatale
opting for a sleek enamel holder, colour coordinated with her string of
pearls, gloves and gown. To smoke was to be sophisticated. The idea
that the habit might eventually induce a slow and painful death did
not have the currency that it does today.

Aware of the link between cigarette and star status, cigarette brands
started to launch their products in a way that encouraged smokers to feel
closer to figures in the world of entertainment. Associate the nicotine fix
with a honeyed voice rather than yellowed teeth.

Wills, a popular British brand of the 1930s, launched a series of portraits
of "Radio Celebrities" printed on cards given away in cigarette packs, which
consumers were encouraged to collect and place in an album where each
artist had its allocated place complete with a potted biography. With space
for 44 cards on 17 pages, the album cost one penny. This product placement
appeared innocently juvenile because it bore a close resemblance to similar
promotional initiatives in the world of sport, where football players and
cricketers were "carded" and given away with anything from magazines
to packets of cereal.

As a sign of the overlap between the worlds of mass-market commerce
and large-scale public entertainment, the 1935 Wills Radio Celebrities album
is an invaluable historical document. The cover features an open-mouthed
vocalist in front of a tall bulb microphone, while the inside cover depicts
a family of four huddled around a wireless the size of a fridge from which
lightning shafts of broadcast crackle fly out, presumably because the virtual
presence of the celebrity is immeasurably exciting.

Flick through the pages and behold immaculately turned-out stars whose
hair glows in Brylcreemed splendour. Among those in the hall of fame are
Ronald Gourley, known for improvising humorous interludes at the piano;
George Baker, the baritone from Birkenhead, Harry S. Pepper, composer
and BBC producer; Will Hay, "one of the most versatile of entertainers, a

character comedian of the first rank, but also an astronomer"; Eve Becke, "the girl with 'It' in her voice"; Stanley Holloway, "actor, singer and jester", Beryl Orde, impressionist.

Several things stand out. A large percentage of the celebrities are from the north of England, reminding us how much that part of the country has contributed to entertainment. Many of those chosen are engaged in popular culture as well as classical music. They remind us that this was a time when some cinemas had orchestras, the most feted of which was that led by organist Reginald Dixon, whose portrait shows a man with a pencil-line Errol Flynn moustache. Above all, the album makes it clear that an appearance on the BBC gave prestige, which was why radio announcers and compères, people with the right accent and gravitas, are also in the album. So while the biography of the monocled J.H Squire, the man who apparently "introduced jazz to England in 1919", trumpets the fact that he was at one time the musical director of six West End theatres, the final line of his entry is that: "he has broadcast over 300 times."

Look again at that totemic family leaning towards the wireless, and after thumbing the pages, you gain a strong impression of how they may have regulated their listening to the BBC. They could tune into "light" music, dance music, organ recitals, string quartets, "gramophone interludes", and to a BBC military band or a BBC orchestra.

So it made perfect sense for W.H. Wills to insert themselves into the fabric of popular culture, just as other brands had done in earlier years. Programmes for the 1922 musical, *Shuffle Along*, written by ragtime legends Eubie Blake and Noble Sissle (which ran for 504 performances on Broadway), advised patrons to purchase Mild Havana Blend Little Cigars, because "They are short smokes of real cigar quality". Perfect for a theatre interval. Shuffle, incidentally was a word with a long history in African-American entertainment that reached back to the days of minstrelsy and was part of the range of dances such as the heel and toe, turkey trot, buzzard lope and cakewalk. In everyday speech, as in "Time to shuffle off", shuffle meant to move off the sidewalk, especially if under the threat of a policeman's nightstick for the crime of being black.

One might imagine that traces of Zip coonery would not show up on something as supposedly urbane as the Radio Celebrities album of 1935. One would be wrong. The most striking card in the album is that of Scott and Whaley. The former has ebony skin and bright pink lips. He is a "black-face clown", These were two highly successful African-American entertainers who lived in Britain in the 1930s. Harry Clifford Scott hailed from Cleveland, Ohio and was a tinsmith prior to embarking on a career as a minstrel, while Eddie Peter Whaley was a dentist from Montgomery, Alabama. They arrived in Britain in 1909 to work in vaudeville and debuted on the BBC in 1926 with the show *Kentucky Minstrels*. In this, Whaley played the golf-loving character, Cuthbert, and Scott the pianist, Pussyfoot. Little documentation of the lives of Scott and Whaley survives, but it is known that the latter moved to Brighton in the late 1930s, and moved into a house next door to the great stand-up comic, Max Miller.

Discomfiting as the thought of a minstrel show being broadcast on the BBC in the 1930s is, the success that Scott and Whaley enjoyed points to the mixed fortunes of Black performers on the road to more enlightened and empowering creative possibilities. For if blackface clownery persisted, the Radio Celebrities album also tells another story. One of the other Black performers given the honour of a Wills cigarette card was, perhaps inevitably, Paul Robeson. If Robeson's performance in Kern and Hammerstein's *Showboat* at the Theatre Royal in 1928 had made him a household name, then his role in the film version in 1936 cemented his position in the show business firmament. Directed by James Whale[1], the film was a commercial and critical success and is still considered to be one of the most faithful and powerful stage-to-screen adaptations. Joining a cast that included Oscar nominee Irene Dunne, vaudeville stalwart Charles Winninger, as well as Hattie McDaniel[2], the first African-American to win an Academy award, Robeson became indelibly associated with the role of Joe, such was the power of his performance. His rendition of his signature tune, "Ol' Man River", was given an additional edge by Whale's direction. This cleverly montaged scene shows the plight of "darkies" consigned to a life of planting cotton and longing to cross the Jordan.

Film, as a conjunction of sound and image, was a natural fit for Black music given the charisma of African-American performers such as Duke Ellington, Louis Armstrong and Bessie Smith, all of whom appeared on screen, in performances that both consolidated their status as artists and located them in technological modernity. In fact, the coincidence of jazz and talkies as new forms of expression is one of the great subplots of modern art. Parallels between these forms in the use of tempo, editing-arranging techniques and narrative make a fascinating study, as does the role that jazz played in defining the film soundtrack.

The capture of Black musicians on film goes back to the beginnings of cinema, and Britain was a significant rendezvous for African-American players and European filmmakers. In 1896, French cinema pioneers, the Lumière Brothers, shot historic footage of black minstrels in Leicester Square in London. Lasting just 45 seconds *The Wandering Negro Minstrels* is one of the earliest cinematic records of black musicians in action, dancing, playing banjos, "tambo and bones".[3] The historical value of the footage is enormous. These players provided an echo of the previous century when the fiddler Black Billy Waters played for passers-by in nearby Covent Garden.

The tragedy is the survival in film of doggedly enduring racist stereotypes. Almost four decades on from the Lumière brothers' film, minstrels were still to be found shucking and jiving on celluloid. After their success on BBC radio with the series *Kentucky Minstrels*, the British-based African-American duo of Scott and Whaley transferred the series to film in 1934. It was anything but a progressive presentation of Blacks on screen as the lead characters, Pussyfoot and Cuthbert, guffawed their way through a series of misadventures with their landlady and Massa Johnson.

This is why *Showboat* is such an important film. It came just two years after Scott and Whaley's movie but, as the discussions above indicate, it is very different in tone. Although Robeson was not the star per se, he was one of the heavyweights of the cast, worthy of having his name on promotional posters above those of Kern and Hammerstein. He may have had to sing about "darkies" on the river but he did not act like one on screen.

His presence as Joe in the film version of *Showboat* is magnetic, from the nonchalance with which he leans back on the harbour jetty to the back-breaking strain of his lifting of bales while the white folks play. But the peak of Robeson's rendition of "Ol' Man River" is the chorus where his voice harmonizes with those of others as he is joined by dozens of other workers. We see a Black American song as an expression of community solidarity, for Robeson is not singing to, but *with* his fellow sufferers. Even though *Showboat*'s story centres on romantic entanglements amongst well-to-do white folk, the black characters are nonetheless afforded a framework for their artistic performance that carries political weight.

By this point, Robeson had made Britain his home, because it offered him liberal values that were not to be found in America. "My reasons were quite the same as those which over the years have brought millions of Negroes out of the Deep South to settle in other parts of the country. It must be said, however, that for me London was infinitely better than Chicago has been for Negroes from Mississippi."[4] Robeson was still officially resident in Britain when he made *Showboat* and given his extensive travelling in Europe he really had the status of an international Black man who exercised the right to unrestricted travel. In this respect, Robeson was a kindred spirit to the Harlem Renaissance writer, Langston Hughes, who also wandered, and wondered as he did so, extensively in Europe.[5]

Four years after the success of *Showboat,* Robeson made a film that went much further in bringing dignity to the image of the Negro at the same time as championing the cause of the working man across the racial divide. It is a film that makes a case for the brotherhood of man without succumbing to queasy sentimentality. Set in Robeson's beloved Wales and produced by Ealing studios, Pen Tennyson's 1940 feature *The Proud Valley*[6] dramatized the lives of members of a small mining village, the pride of which is a male voice choir.

Robeson plays the part of David Goliath, an African-American who arrives seeking work and joins the choir, run by Parry (Simon Lack). While the subplot of a national singing competition gives Robeson and fellow cast members a chance to display their fine voices, the central theme of the film is the unbreakable spirit of a tightly-knit community in the face of tragedy, and the need for central government to recognize that industry must be run for people rather than profit.

Robeson presents an empowering image of the black man. Goliath has talent and integrity but above all he has the intelligence to understand what the mine and the choir mean to people in this Welsh village, and how that resonates with his own background as an itinerant Negro worker in search of stability.

The film also had significant resonances for Black Welsh history. Goliath was a ship's stoker, one of the primary jobs done by colonial seamen from Africa and the West Indies, and if there was an authenticity in his portrayal, then it was because Robeson had engaged personally with the subject matter. "I also came to know another class of Africans – the seamen in the ports of London, Liverpool and Cardiff. They too had their organizations, and had much to teach me about their lives and their various peoples."[7]

The political activism portrayed in *The Proud Valley*, when the miners walk to London to lobby against the pit closure, must have struck a chord with Robeson, who, as noted above had joined a group of Welsh miners and sung with them after a march to London in 1928 to demand emergency funds for villages hit by unemployment. However, it is the scenes involving the choir that are the most memorable in *The Proud Valley*, particularly "Deep River", a beautiful spiritual whose melody is embellished by the glorious harmonies of the voices. Compelling as his vocal performances are in the film, Robeson also impresses in the scenes of straight dialogue, because he brings subtleties to a character who is ultimately defined by his heroism. In an age where stereotypes of Blacks were common, Robeson unveiled a man with a wholly credible dignity and self-respect.

Negro spirituals are what Robeson remains indelibly associated with, and although his voice could easily stand out against the full accompaniment of a choir or rhythm section, it is really when he was backed by nothing more than a piano that he comes into his own. A marvellous example of this is the version of "Sometimes I Feel Like A Motherless Child" that Robeson recorded on March 1937 at the BBC premises: No3 studio, 37 Abbey Road, London. The pianist, Lawrence Brown, who accompanied the singer for much of his career, had a measured, sensitive touch on the keyboard, and the delicacy with which he brings chords to life provides an effective contrast to Robeson's deeper strains and gives space to his lighter ascents. It is the voice, though, that attracts our attention, not just for its tonal richness but the transformations that it undergoes as the song unfolds, giving the performance a distinctly choral feel, as if there were other singers present.

The changes occur at very specific words of the lyric. On the "feel" of the title, Robeson has a levity and brightness, but elsewhere all is gravity and sombre colours. A single syllable, such as the very symbolic "way" is stretched into "wa-ay-ay" to highlight a rounder quality of basso, suggesting that the singer liked to shift at will between baritone and bass, but he also hits a low pitch close to the area known as sub-bass in contemporary electronic music.

Given the fact that this range is enhanced by adjustments in Robeson's volume and attack, it is reasonable to assume that he must have had a good microphone technique, such as using changing distances from the recording device to heighten the impact of his voice. This was at a time when even the latest microphones, of which the iconic chrome bulb of the Shure was then the state of the art, were nowhere near as responsive as they are today to the slightest breath or murmur, so the way singers positioned themselves, leaning back or leaning in to vary the sound of the voice, was important.

Striking as Robeson is, the accompanist, Brown, plays a key role in the performance, by leaving liberal amounts of space between some of his chords, which he brings right down to sotto voce as the piece reaches its conclusion. For most of the arrangement, he introduces discreet shades to the canvas against which Robeson is cast, but his rhythmic push in the second verse lends necessary momentum to the piano part as the singer intensifies his emotion. The artistic empathy between the two men is very evident.

"Motherless Child" makes the case that the Negro spiritual may indeed be the genre in which Robeson excelled, despite the fact that he also included pieces by European classical composers in his repertoire. But to hear him on this song, as well as "Joshua Fit De Battle of Jericho" or "Deep River", is to hear a man accomplish the ultimate goal for a singer, and that is to make the story of the song the story of his life.

Whilst rhythm is an integral part of the musical vocabulary of the Negro spiritual, another essential is the very precise control that is exerted over languorous, legato phrases by singer and choir. Holding notes, sustaining them over the pulse of a song suggests that the singer is calling on, if not supplicating, God, giving the call an added sense of passion and sincerity. It is as if the long tone in gospel music is a kind of material offering.

"Swing Low Sweet Chariot"[8] is a vital link in Black British musical history. It was sung by the Fisk Jubilee singers in the Victorian age and by thousands of British soldiers during the imperial campaigns in India. On his rendition of the piece, again recorded at Abbey Road with Lawrence Brown on piano, Robeson sounds majestic.

Although he was a contemporary of artists such as Duke Ellington, jazz was less apposite for his approach. In the same year that he recorded "Motherless Child", Robeson also cut a version of Duke's "Solitude", also in a London studio, and the result was by no means satisfactory. He is not aided by an orchestral arrangement that lacks both dynamics and textural invention, but Robeson himself is far too rigid in his delivery, and he won't play with the pulse of the music, even in the most understated way, to introduce a degree of the structural flexibility, the easy trickery with time, that is such a key part of the imagination that lies at the root of the jazz aesthetic. Ultimately, Robeson was a master of folk song. Beyond the great gift of his voice, he understood why the genre existed and retained an essential place in society: "Folk songs are the music of basic realities, the spontaneous expression of the people for the people of elemental emotions."

That declaration was made to the *Wrexham Leader* in 1934. Over the next six years Robeson was artistically prolific, making five feature films that included *Song of Freedom, My Song Goes Forth* and *Big Fella* as well as *Showboat* and *The Proud Valley*. The last movie was an entirely positive presentation of race relations in Britain, and shows a degree of liberalism missing in the States. Yet the world was in a dark place by the time Ealing Studios produced *The Proud Valley* in 1940. World War II was underway in earnest and the threat of Nazism engulfing Europe was all too real.

Unthinkably abhorrent as the proposed annihilation of Jews and other so-called 'untermensch' was to almost all in Britain, Hitler (who also denounced jazz as 'Entartete Musik' [Degenerate music]) had sympathizers in many reaches of British society, notably the aristocracy. Oswald Mosley and his British Union of Fascists was the most visibly loathsome, and the forthright kicking they got when he tried to preach hatred in the East End – the 1936 battle of Cable Street – is an example of social cohesion in the midst of the most repugnant of politics. The anti-fascists comprised communist, socialist, Anarchist, Irish and Jewish groups.

Yet while events such as this provided an uplifting example of one kind of anti-racism, the understanding of and sensitivity to people of colour was by no means as developed. Discriminatory and demeaning attitudes to people of colour were still woven into the fabric of society, in many areas of mass entertainment, and the image of the Negro as a wide-eyed minstrel was matched by the deep permeation of racist epithets in popular consciousness. A "nigger brown" coat was a winter essential. A black band was a "nigger" band. Language that imparted to people of colour the status of outsiders or lesser beings, who could be treated with condescension or outright contempt, was still prevalent, and crucially among the opinion formers in the arts. Talk of "nigger opera"[9] may have appeared a kind of twisted progress from the days of mentioning nigger minstrels, but the sad reality was that Blacks were still referred to disparagingly.

On the eve of the Second World War, the BBC was the benign auntie to whose bosom the nation huddled, and amongst what it heard were blackface performers. The cover of a book by Britain's most cherished author, Fontana's issue of Agatha Christie's *Ten Little Niggers*, featured a small golliwog doll clad in a bow-tie, white gloves and spats, the garb of the 19th century banjo-playing minstrel. There was also a noose around its neck.

Notes

1. Among James Whale's other acclaimed movies are *The Invisible Man* (1933) and *Bride of Frankenstein* (1935).
2. Hattie McDaniel won the Oscar for playing the part of Mammy in *Gone With The Wind* in 1939.
3. As in tambourine and bones (dried horse-bones used as drum sticks or castanets).
4. Paul Robeson, *Here I Stand* (London: Dennis Dobson,1958) p. 40
5. See Langston Hughes, *I Wonder As I Wander* (New York: Hill & Wang, 1993).
6. *The Proud Valley* was filmed on location in South Wales; this would have lent an additional emotional charge to Paul Robeson's performance, given his strong ties with the country.
7. Paul Robeson, *Here I Stand* (London: Dennis Dobson, 1958), p. 42.
8. Today, "Swing Low, Sweet Chariot" is the unofficial anthem of English rugby fans – not something that the Fisk Jubilee Singers could have foreseen in the 1890s.
9. The phrase has often been attributed to George Gershwin.

1 1 OCEAN 'N MIDLANDS

'Jiver' Hutchinson asked the audience at the end of concert: did you enjoy the music? And they all said 'Yes.' Then he said 'Well, these musicians, they haven't got anywhere to stay. Would you be kind enough to give them a room for the night? And everybody got a place to stay. This was in the provinces, either in the north or the Midlands.
— Frank Holder, singer/percussionist/dancer, born Guyana, arrived in London, England, 1944.

I hired the Digbeth Hall for the night when the Basie band finished playing, we had a good session 'til six in the morning.
— Andy Hamilton, born Port Maria, Jamaica, 1918, arrived in Birmingham, England, 1949.

Enter the Music Press

By the outbreak of the Second World War, the weekly music magazine *Melody Maker* could look back on a substantial history. It was founded in 1926, the year that John Logie Baird switched on the first television set, and the year of the British general strike. *Melody Maker* covered frontline events in popular music. Jazz dominated. It featured reviews of the latest recordings as well as news stories and profiles of those who made them. As such it was a significant contributor to what is now known as "pop culture", primarily because it acknowledged that the work of musicians, both in the studio and on stage, fed into a body of opinion. The magazine later had a supplement called "Rhythm", the name of the clubs formed by record buyers, or "gramophone enthusiasts" who shared knowledge of must-have discs.

If people not only danced to but discussed the latest sides cut by Louis Armstrong or Duke Ellington, then editorials and reviews, praising or denouncing them, recognised that this public interest constituted a target market. Listeners were consumers. The purchase of a shellac disc that was written about in *Melody Maker* connected with the purchase of music-playing equipment advertised in the *Radio Times*. The Western Electric Company announced that it "made over half the world's telephones"[1] while it advertised "loud speakers" with a scene of neatly-attired dancing couples.

Late 1920's editions of *Melody Maker* give an invaluable insight into the way that the music industry was being shaped by its conjunction with mass media. The magazine was a platform for debate and a source of practical information for anybody interested in new sounds.

Over the following two decades *Melody Maker* included longer features and news items as well as columns dedicated to current events in jazz and dance music in both Britain and America. Such reports fuelled consumer desire for the products of named musicians, and the use of terms such as "famous", perhaps not yet as tiresomely trivial as it has become in the internet age, evidently carried some weight. The death of a celebrity in the dance world was bound to make the front page.

Costing three pence, the 15 March 1941 edition of *Melody Maker* carried one of its most dramatic headlines ever: "The Profession mourns... Ken Johnson killed in Blitz: Ace Tenor Dies: M. Poulsen a Victim: Dancemen Injured." Startling as this headline is, the bolded line of the first paragraph vividly captures both the indignation and tendency of any nation at war to view events through the lens of potential propaganda. In highly emotive language, the editorial denounces "The Nazi murder raids on civilians." Citizens living in terraced streets in Liverpool, Birmingham, Bristol or London who had to seek refuge in bunkers while the Luftwaffe's bombs laid waste to residential and business areas would have been able to relate.

How people felt about music at the time of a world war involving such large-scale losses of life is a complex subject. Whilst songs might be seen as frivolous and superficial when the prospect of the street where you live being reduced to rubble was very real, the news of the death of a bandleader who provided solace when the night skies were being lit up by enemy fighter planes was poignant. The image chimes with one the most beguiling photographs of the Blitz: people huddled around the curled horn of a gramophone in an air raid shelter, looking at the bulky machine as if it were a blessed altar.

Habitués of West End nightclubs would have felt the news as an emotional blow. Ken 'Snakehips' Johnson was the leader of what *Melody Maker* described as "one of the smartest swing outfits" in London. His West Indian Orchestra was something of a hot ticket. The lethal bomb that reduced the suave upmarket setting of the Café De Paris to rubble and buried such a dapper artist as Johnson brought the war too close to home.

The *Melody Maker* report makes for thought-provoking reading. Also killed in the air raid was a West End promoter called Martinus Poulsen who had instigated the policy of paying well for top talent and was part of the management of five-star haunts such as the Paris as well as the Cafe Anglais, the Embassy and the London Casino. He was a naturalised Dane. Another victim of the bomb, the Trinidadian saxophonist Dave Williams was described as a "coloured boy".[2]

Interestingly, there is no mention of the race of the other injured band members, guitarist Joe Deniz and Yorke De Souza, in the report, but the editorial presents Carl Barriteau as "the coloured sax star". At a time when terms such as West Indian Band and All Coloured Orchestra were interchangeable, it is not surprising that such epithets as "coloured boy" were used, with its deeply patronizing refusal of adult status to black males. Indeed, the tone of the reporting highlights a central contradiction in the life of black British musicians in the 40s, namely the way the genuine respect for talent merged with the language of racism. "Coloured boy" was part of a range of epithets that appeared in the *Melody Maker*. The respected editor, Edgar Jackson, described some artists as "darkies" and referred to "nigger bands".

Black Music in War Time

Parallel to the death of Johnson and Williams were the deaths and injuries suffered by numerous West Indians who saw active service during the war. Driven by patriotism and loyalty to the Queen, men and women from right across the region rushed to sign up. The War Department contains no official records of recruitment, but a reliable estimate places the figure of those who enlisted from the West Indies at somewhere between 16,000 and 18,000. How many died is disputed by military historians.

Musicians associated with Ken 'Snakehips' Johnson could have been amongst the number who served. The trumpeters Leslie Thompson and Leslie 'Jiver' Hutchinson had formerly been in the armed services, but were civilians before the outbreak of the war in 1939. Johnson's band, in any case, did entertain the troops when it was sent on morale-boosting tours of territory held by the Allies. If the popular memory of the power of wartime songs is occupied by voices welling with emotion, singing along to Vera Lynn, then the thought of troops tapping their feet to the sparky horns of a West Indian orchestra full of "coloured boys" is really no less meaningful. Recently there have been documentaries and books on the lives of these soldiers, but whether they genuinely form part of mainstream British historical consciousness is doubtful.[3]

The fate of Colonial servicemen in the postwar period is important in understanding how the Black British community was developing from the 1940s onwards. Although many servicemen returned to the West Indies, some elected to remain in England and Wales in the belief that they would have better employment opportunities. Furthermore, the Army and Air Force operated a scheme offering college courses to prepare demobbed servicemen for the challenges of life during peacetime, though it turned out that those who ran this scheme had specific jobs for Black ex-servicemen in mind. Whilst many of these men aspired to become accountants, bookkeepers or engineers, numerous veterans have recalled that they were instead offered places on training courses for manual work such as cab-inet-making or machine operating. Evidently, black ex-servicemen were not suited to any form of white-collar employment.

With Army and Airforce bases located throughout the country, the Black presence was nationwide because many men sought work in the areas where they had been stationed, though they would also go to places where they heard on the grapevine that employment might be had: to cities such as Birmingham, Nottingham, Derby, Liverpool, Leeds and Manchester. Swelling the ranks of the demobbed black soldiers in Britain were former military colleagues who had gone back to the Caribbean, but found they were joining the already swollen ranks of the unemployed. A good many came back to England in the hope of reviving their fortunes.

Significantly, the 492 West Indians (predominantly Jamaicans, but also from Trinidad and the Eastern Caribbean) who sailed to Tilbury, South-ampton on the SS *Empire Windrush* on 22nd June 1948 included many such ex-servicemen. Although that event is held up as a watershed moment in Black British and indeed British history, it has an equally notable resonance as part of an extensive West Indian "military" presence in British music. West Indian musicians who were former servicemen, such as Leslie Thompson, Joe Appleton and Leslie 'Jiver' Hutchinson were joined by other younger musicians who were taking a similar path.[4]

One was Frank Holder, a young Guyanese with aspirations to be a singer, an all-round showman who was just as happy dancing or "hoofing" a whole range of steps that included the splits, as he was crooning a slow ballad or a higher tempo swing number. Hailing from Georgetown, Holder joined up in 1944, and after training, or "square bashing" at the Royal Air Force base in Cranwell, he was later stationed at in Melksham, a very pretty spa town in Wiltshire. Holder went on to work with several significant names in British jazz and at the age of 88 was still gigging at the time of writing. When I visited him at his home in Wallington, in the south London sub-urbs, I found a sprightly, energetic man who looked fondly on his days in the RAF and had no trouble recalling that much of his time was spent on stage in the mess hall.

> In this way we were able to keep everybody happy. Those of us who could do something did and everybody who could get into the billet would see us get up and do our thing.
> The troops liked different types of things. Because there were a lot of West Indians there I did calypsos, but I was mainly singing swing, all the ballads and so forth because that was the way I was brought up.
> I combined that with calypsos and my dancing, so I was trying to become a complete entertainer. I just took this as my opportunity.[5]

For the most part, the band had a piano, bass and drums and occasionally horns and, as Holder recalls, the opportunity to perform was there for people with a mind to take it. "You just got up and sang standards. The musicians – some of them were trained to a degree, and being in the RAF it did give us an opportunity to develop more and more. For that matter it helped us not to have to drill so much. We were entertaining."[6]

Holder's popularity in the RAF was high, and post-demob, he was represented by the Mecca agency, which had a large national network of dance halls, the most prestigious of which was London's Paramount, and he also worked on the Northern club circuit. In 1948 he was asked by Leslie 'Jiver' Hutchinson to join his band after impressing him at a gig where, on Holder's insistence, the Jamaican trumpeter allowed him to sing. As a permanent member of the 12-piece orchestra, which also had three other vocalists, Holder went on regular tours, though some nights on the road were memorable for the wrong reasons. The band members found that many hotels refused to accommodate them. Holder lamented:

> Many a time I turned up in a town and it was difficult to get a place to stay. The reason being that everybody in those days was afraid at what people were gonna say, and that kind of thing. They saw the stereotypes, so people were a bit... "*slow*". 'Jiver' Hutchinson asked the audience at the end of concert: Did you enjoy the music? And they all said, 'Yes.' Then he said, 'Well, these musicians, they haven't got anywhere to stay. Would you be kind enough to give them a room for the night? And *everybody* got a place to stay. This was in the provinces, either in the north or the Midlands."[7]

Holder also had the chance to meet other people of colour who were living outside of London, several of whom were musicians. He told me that, "When I toured regionally, I was rather surprised because I didn't realize that there were so many black musicians in and around these cities, all playing in bands. It was strange at first, but then you found things were changing. It became easier to get a place to stay."

Holder's recollections are important in tracing how in the late 1940s and early 1950s "Black quarters" developed in British cities where musicians were both playing regularly and laying down roots. Butetown in Cardiff and Toxteth in Liverpool had been well established since the early 19th century, but other cities should also be noted. Birmingham had been an important part of the war effort with its munitions factories. These attracted Caribbean workers who turned their hands to packing cartridge cases.

Birmingham, Jazz and Andy Hamilton

Postwar Birmingham, like other parts of the country, underwent reconstruction and gradually a black community grew up in the area of Handsworth, which had been a bustling township with extensive accommodation for factory workers since the mid 19th century. By the early 1960s, the West Indian population in Birmingham numbered around 17,000, with the vast majority employed in public transport, construction and heavy industry.

Pianist Ron Daley, a Jamaican ex-serviceman who was also known as Sam Brown, was part of a coterie of West Indian musicians who came to Birmingham either during the war or in the immediate postwar period. With others he developed a local jazz scene. The most significant amongst these others was the tenor saxophonist, Andy Hamilton. Born in Port Maria, Jamaica in 1918, Hamilton learned his trade during long residencies at hotels in the 1930s, as was the norm at the time. Much of the island's socializing was centred around establishments like the Tichfield where orchestras with horns and rhythm section played swing for moneyed patrons in evening wear.

Inspired by legendary American saxophone players, Hamilton made his way to Buffalo, New York State, during the Second World War, where he was able to develop as a player after landing a residency with a trio in a small club in the city. Furthermore, many of the leading big bands of the day passed through and Hamilton took part in their lengthy after-hours jam sessions. This gave him the priceless experience of playing with and learning from some of the dazzling soloists and section players in orchestras such as Count Basie's, who made a particularly big impression on the young Jamaican saxophonist.[8]

Basie wore his aristocratic name well, gracing the covers of many magazines the world over, one of the most quaintly named being *Jazzology*, a British title which cost one shilling, and was billed as "the monthly magazine for the jazz enthusiast". This publication was another sign of the depth of interest in African-American music in the UK. It was largely feature-led with the bulk of the articles being devoted to the biggest names of the era. Thus while Basie graced the cover of the July 1946 edition, there were several pieces on other legendary musicians like pianist-vocalist, Nat 'King' Cole,[9] who was a major influence on British-based West Indian singers like Frank Holder and a favourite of Hamilton himself.

Following his return to Jamaica from Buffalo, Hamilton landed the kind of gig that cemented the image of Jamaica as a rich man's playground to which the likes of British cultural icons such as Noel Coward and Ian Fleming were irresistibly drawn. After hearing the saxophonist play at the Tichfield hotel, screen idol Errol Flynn asked Hamilton to be the on-board entertainer for his yacht *Zaka* and for the next two years they sailed the Caribbean docking at various islands and hosting social gatherings of the great but not necessarily the good. During this engagement Hamilton wrote a calypso for Flynn, "Silvershine", which became his signature tune. But when the economy declined and unemployment soared in post-war Jamaica, and after work on the *Zaka* dried up, times were tough. Short of money, Hamilton came to England in 1949, stowing away to Southampton where he was detained, before he subsequently made his way to London.

ANDY HAMILTON

COURTESY BIRMINGHAM MUSIC ARCHIVE

Post-war Britain could not have been reconstructed if labour had been solely concentrated on the capital. Major regional cities such as Liverpool had large swathes of both their centre and suburbs reduced to rubble at the height of the Blitzkrieg.

In addition to looking for work, West Indians went to cities other than London for emotional and psychological reasons. There are town and country and social class divides on every island in the Caribbean, just as marked as they are in England, and there are Jamaicans, Trinidadians and Bajans borne in a wide range of environments, both sociocultural and geographical, who do not feel at home in certain places. According to those who knew him well, Andy Hamilton simply did not *like* London. It is sometimes assumed that all immigrants dream of a new life in a bustling capital. This is a misconception. Immigrants have as wide a range of desires as any group of people. The other emotional factor was finding security amongst people from their island of origin. In a real sense, people from Jamaica, Trinidad, Barbados or any of the other islands (and Guyana) did not become West Indians *until* they arrived in Britain, and even then, those island roots often meant more than any regional identity. One can be as Jamaican in Leeds as one can be in London.

Accompanied by a Jamaican friend, Hamilton travelled to Manchester, but on hearing that other musicians from his homeland were living in Birmingham, he headed to the Midlands. Eager to secure a gig at the earliest opportunity, he sat in at a popular venue in the Handsworth area of the city, Club 60, and was said to have blown down the house, galvanized no doubt by both his desire to make an impression and his artistic talent and maturity. Hamilton was already thirty-one, and could draw on his experience of playing countless hotel engagements in Jamaica and having jammed with leading jazz musicians in America, something few British musicians had done. He was anything but a novice.

Sadly, Hamilton found the door closed to him when he returned the following week and he soon realised that he would have to be self-sufficient, put his own band together and stage his own gigs. He formed a group, The Blue Notes, featuring the pianist Ron Daley aka Sam Brown, and they appeared in school halls, at the Odeon in Birmingham city centre and at the Digbeth Civic Hall, and also made inroads into the West Indian community's lively functions circuit, which could encompass anything from a wedding reception at the Methodist Church in Handsworth to a birthday party in a pub in Aston. During leans spells, Hamilton supported himself and his growing family by working as a machine operator in a factory.

Musicians survived by promoting their own gigs, by talking them up or handing out flyers in public places such as the central post office. It was on one of these bouts of direct marketing that Hamilton met his wife. What also anchored the band firmly in the affections of Birmingham's Black community were the many dances that they played for the West Indian cricket team at St. John's restaurant in the 1950s. Legend has it that some of the sessions went on so deep into the night that they affected the fitness of the players the morning after.

A historic photograph of Andy Hamilton's group in the 1950s gives an idea of what audiences were offered. Members of his sextet – trumpet, piano, bass, drums, vocals and the leader on tenor saxophone – are immaculately turned out in matching evening wear, with band-name placards in front of them, as was the case with the classic swing big bands of the 1940s. Resting on the floor next to Hamilton is a clarinet, an instrument associated with big bands and New Orleans jazz. The image suggests how deeply rooted the Jamaican was in these older forms of African-American music.

Yet, firmly committed as he was to calypso and the swing style of his idol Count Basie, Hamilton was aware that jazz was undergoing significant changes. Bebop, the new music of young players such as drummer Max Roach,[10] trumpeter Dizzy Gillespie and alto saxophonist Charlie Parker came to represent something altogether more idiosyncratic than swing, fashioning an aesthetic in which intricate music that set formidable technical challenges. This was paralleled by a recondite "insider" language and unconventional modes of dress, like Dizzy's beret. Some saw this as studied pretentiousness, others as the peak of "hip" individuality. These musicians saw jazz as an art in its own right, not just a background to dancing. This was a generation of highly urbanised African Americans in the cities of the north, determined to break all connections with minstrel entertainment for Whites.

Bebop had a different sound to swing. While the latter was big band music, the former was mostly played by small groups, usually quartets or quintets in which players wrote new, circuitous themes, often over the chord sequences of known Broadway show tunes, and launched into extended, challenging solos. Swing had a straight, steady, leisurely, mostly mid-tempo beat with smooth vibrato-laden timbres, whereas bebop had a fragmented, nervy, faster pulse, and more dissonant, spikier textures. Some older musicians described Parker's music as "harsh".

Bebop musicians had to be very alert to play the long, exploratory variations over a greater number of chords, which almost seemed to be the result of deliberate puzzle-setting, to catch out those who could not keep up once Diz 'n' Bird started to shuttle through the changes. Musicians had to think laterally and play explosively. The dot-dash introduction of Parker's "Bebop"[11] epitomizes this. The horns punch out two stuttering staccato phrases that then give way to sharply ascending, swirling lines that push the energy towards frenzy. The music somersaults into life. It is a remarkably aggressive, confrontational, way to start a piece. Even so, swing and bebop are both connected by the blues, which was a touchstone, above all, for Parker, a player whose soaring improvisations were always matched by an immense depth of feeling.

Bebop was resisted by some but not all older jazz musicians. As a man who had worshipped at the altar of big bands, Hamilton belonged to the school of thought that still viewed jazz through the prism of the dance hall where players had a responsibility to entertain as well as impress audiences. He could not relate to the new music. "Bebop was very strong, some people were doing well," he once said. "Some were playing too technical. You can't swing." That statement distils a key debate that has framed jazz for decades: in short, had the music become so complex and esoteric that it is now impenetrable and forbidding?

For Hamilton's appraisal of "too technical" one can read "too difficult", abstract and anti-melodic, though Bebop as bedevilment and alienation and swing as engagement and inclusion is too crude a polarization. Many of the iconic bebop performances such as "Now's The Time", "Hothouse" and "Ornithology" have survived because audiences were able to hum the themes, regardless of their tantalizingly mazy nature.

However, Hamilton did not embrace bebop but kept faith in swing style saxophone, as patented by one of his idols, Coleman Hawkins (though Hawkins himself later updated his style). Throughout the 1950s and beyond, Hamilton remained something of an unknown quantity outside Birmingham, playing local gigs, but not gaining the profile of the rising stars of the British school of bebop who were featured in publications such as *Melody Maker* and playing a form of music that could be presented as new and exciting. Hamilton, committed to swing, was effectively sidelined from this world and had to struggle on as best as he could.

It wasn't until 1988 that Hamilton made his studio debut (*Silvershine*) but the time was not wasted, because he went about developing a highly personal composite of calypso and jazz that remained true to his core principle of making songs to which people could dance and romance. On *Silvershine* and the follow-up (1994's *Jamaica By Night*) Hamilton sounds wonderfully self-possessed, even when he is attacking a theme with vigour. He has poise, if not a languid stance, that leads him to slip behind the beat on occasion, and this can be engrossingly seductive. As clichéd as it may be, the epithet "lilting" nonetheless captures something essential about the folk music of Trinidad, Jamaica and other Caribbean islands. Or as the singer as Frank Holder put it, "It was that kind of *pushing* thing in calypso that got people." Rhythm was a striking feature of calypso, and the constant drive of the cowbell, often constructed as a ringing 2 or 3-beat, acting as a metronome, caught the ear of alert musicians who realized that pulse strongly implied a form of dance.

Hamilton's passion for American jazz legends was matched by his love of Jamaican and Trinidadian calypso singers. Although jazz standards were a key part of his repertoire, he also played calypso songs and, inevitably, his compositions reflected an intermingling of forms. Here, when he blended calypso with swing jazz, he was building on developments in calypso in Trinidad itself, particularly the increasing sophistication of the accompaniments to the vocals. The earliest kaisos tended to use makeshift percussion instruments in accompaniment; later this grew to small group backings, but it was still essentially a folk music because many of these early players had no formal training. As the excellent Jamaican trumpeter Leslie Thompson argued, they had "limited technical skills", though that didn't mean that calypso could not be an interesting raw material for competent arrangers, and by the 1940s, in Trinidad, clarinettist Freddie Grant was writing adventurous scores for calypso songs while in Jamaica there were players, such as the revered Sonny Bradshaw, a trumpeter and early mentor to Andy Hamilton, who were also bringing more sophistication to the genre. Some arrangers not only used brass but also European string instruments.

Giving Hamilton his due as an effective blender of styles who achieved a distinctively individual sound tells one side of his story. He was more than just a first rate musician, and his case points to how little attention is paid to the non-performance work that many artists have done over the years. Players who have started their own record labels and run their own clubs are important because they provide opportunities for other musicians as well as themselves, and the existence of the self-starter or "facilitator" has been an absolutely integral part of jazz history.[12]

In Birmingham, Hamilton became something of an after-hours "fixer" for visiting Americans. In his own words he would "put on a bit of recreation" which invariably meant providing food and drink in a venue other than the concert hall where they had been booked to play. At these events Hamilton's band would perform, and inevitably end up jamming with its illustrious guests. Of all the gigs that stuck in Hamilton's mind it was the night that the great Count Basie Orchestra came to town. "I hired the Digbeth hall for the night when the Basie band finished playing, we had a good session 'til six in the morning."

Musicians, so holds received wisdom, don't just play at night, but *through* it, until the sharp whiteness of natural light replaces the glow of a yellow filament. The image of Hamilton and the Basie band blowing until Birmingham stirred into morning life is something that connects the Jamaican saxophonist to blues and jazz history in America, from New Orleans to Memphis, Chicago to Detroit, Los Angeles to Florida, Kansas to New York.

Hamilton became, during the 1950s and beyond, an essential element in Birmingham's jazz scene, though at that time a commercial breakthrough on a national level eluded him. It was in the latter stages of his life (he died in 2012) that his profile rose and there came some belated appreciation of what a unique stylist in jazz he was.

Silvershine was born on the ocean, but it stayed in the Midlands. Sailing on the choppy seas of the music industry was hardly a pleasure cruise.

Notes

1. Catherine Parsonage, *The Evolution of Jazz In Britain*, 1880-1935 (London: Ashgate, 2005) p. 70.
2. These papers are located in the National Jazz Archive, Traps Hill, Loughton.
3. British military sources have little definitive information on the subject. Books which deal with Black involvement in war service include: Stephen Bourne, *The Motherland Calls: Britain's Black Service Men and Women* (The History Press, 2012) and Marika Sherwood, *Many Struggles: West Indian Workers and Service Personnel in Britain, 1939-1945* (Karia Press, 2009).
4. See Mike Phillips and Trevor Phillips, *Windrush: The Irresistible Rise of Multi-Racial Britain* (HarperCollins, 1998).
5. Interview with the author, Wallington, south London, 2013.
6. Ibid.
7. Ibid.
8. The material on Andy Hamilton is derived from an interview conducted by Carl Chinn in 2012. Some of this can be found on https://www.birminghammail.co.uk/news/local-news/the-amazing-life-of-brum-jazzman-andy-182403.
9. Nat 'King Cole' is perhaps known as a great pop "crooner" but his ability as a jazz pianist was quite phenomenal. See a fine compilation *Just Call Him King* (Chant Du Monde), 2014.
10. Max Roach was a committed and outspoken Civil Rights activist as well as an innovative musician. See *We Insist! Freedom Now Suite* (Candid, 1960).
11. Charlie Parker, *Bebop* (Verve, 1946)
12. I'm thinking of the legendary Gil Evans' flat in New York in the 40s.

12 CLAMBERING ON A 9

"We used to play for anthropology students, and all that."
— Ambrose Campbell, West African Rhythm Brothers.

I have no knowledge of their qualifications or capacities and can give no assurance that they can be found suitable work. I hope no encouragement will be given to others to follow their example.
— Labour Minister George Isaacs on the arrival of West Indian immigrants in Britain, June, 1948.

He was born of a black father and Jewish mother, which had him screwed up for a lifetime.
— Spike Milligan on Ray Ellington.

Thus far the narrative has been about the largely individual migrations of musicians from the USA, Africa and the Caribbean. The arrival of the Windrush in 1948 signalled something different, different not only in beginning the establishment of sizeable Caribbean communities, but also as being part of a much larger pattern of post-war immigration. The story includes the long history of Jewish migration, accelerated by those who came to escape existential annihilation from 1939 onwards. There were some 100,000 Poles who had fought under British command and elected not to return to a newly installed communist regime in their homeland, who settled in Lancashire, Yorkshire and London; others included 85,000 Ukrainians, Yugoslavs, Latvians, Lithuanians and Estonians, who had been displaced or were casualties of war; they emigrated to Britain under the European Volunteer Workers Scheme. There was continuing migration from Ireland, so that by the 1960s there were approximately 900,000 Irish citizens living in Britain. They remain the largest formerly immigrant group found in Britain to this day. The media rarely makes this point.[1]

But if Jewish people came as refugees to Britain, they have also been the subject of persecution *in* Britain, with the most heinous manifestations of anti-Semitism being the 1189 massacres and the parliamentary resistance to the 1753 Jewish Naturalisation Bill. Cities such as London, Manchester and Liverpool provided sanctuary to thousands of European Jews to Britain throughout the 19th and 20th century.

Jewish settlement, in London in particular, impacted significantly on many sectors of British economic and cultural life, but what has been less recognised is its impact on the jazz scene of the 1940s and 1950s. Among the Jewish players who made a mark were the pianists Dick Katz and Victor Feldman and the saxophonists Ronnie Scott and John Dankworth, all of whom were the descendants of immigrants from various parts of Europe. They played with West Indian musicians, such as Frank Holder, Dizzy Reece and Coleridge Goode, and the phenomenon of the British ensemble that was multi-faith, multi-cultural and multiracial became part of the jazz scene. Blacks and Jews loved the blues.

The strongest symbol of the Black-Jewish musical union was a player with roots in both communities. Born the son of an African-American entertainer and a Russian orthodox Jew, Henry Pitts Brown became one of the great British drummers of the war and postwar period, playing and singing in a big band led by Harry Roy, before going on to form his own group. Pitts was better known by his stage name, Ray Ellington, a nod to his American idol, the Duke.

Ellington, who served in the RAF during World War II, straddled artistic as well as racial lines. An excellent musician, he gravitated towards the advanced harmonic structures of bebop, but still retained a love for musical humour, surely an inheritance from his tenure with Harry Roy. With his group called The Three Bears, which featured Jamaica double bassist Coleridge Goode, Trinidadian guitarist Lauderic Caton and pianist Dick Katz, whose German family had fled Nazi persecution during the war, Ellington blended skits and swing to good effect.

In 1952, the band was asked by the BBC to appear regularly on a radical new radio programme, *The Goon Show*, alongside the comedians, Peter Sellers, Harry Secombe, Michael Bentine and Spike Milligan. Using the new technology of the day to edit the programme so as to include special effects and incidental music, the programme became very popular and Milligan, in particular, proved a sardonically perceptive social commentator. British culture and society took the full force of his acidly forensic wit, complete with all of the contorted, contradictory behavioural idiosyncrasies, to which he, as a Briton of Irish heritage, born in the Raj, was attuned. Milligan's mordant summary of Ray Ellington's identity pulled no punches on the lives of those who had the dubious privilege of "double minority" status:

> He was born of a black father and Jewish mother, which had him screwed up for a lifetime.
> I once asked him what it was like to be black, and he said "it's terrible, it won't go away."[2]

Such is the shock value of the quip it is easy to underestimate its pertinence. Whether Ellington actually said this, or it was a Milligan invention, the quip fingered the dominant strand of the Black condition in post-war Britain: the permanence of hostility to the likelihood of the permanence of Black residence. 'It', the colour black, won't wash off, and 'it', the black person, might be here longer than any ministers of labour imagined.

The combination of the British Nationality Act of 1948, which gave colonial citizens the legal right to enter Britain and tougher immigration laws in America, formerly the preferred destination, increased the number of arrivals from the West Indies in the coming decade. By the mid 1950s Caribbean immigration had peaked at 46,800, though numbers levelled off thereafter. But of no less importance than the quantity, were the identities of some of those who crossed the Atlantic and their impact on British culture.

Taking the 1948 Windrush contingent as an example, it is clear that West Indian migrants were not homogeneous; the passengers included many kinds of skilled workers and professionals, men trained in anything from journalism and mechanics to electrical engineering and masonry. Also paying the £28 passage were students and 160 ex-servicemen. Most notably, the boat carried the jazz musician Dizzy Reece and calypso singers Lord Kitchener and Lord Beginner, and Mona Baptiste, the singer and later actress.

Recollections by West Indian migrants, who either arrived on the *Windrush* or shortly after, point to the general ignorance of the British population with regard to the lives and countries they had left behind. In turn, arriving West Indians were shocked by postwar poverty, not to mention the low temperatures, which occasioned stories of hastily purchased jumpers and cardigans coming apart at the seams because the new owners had precious little experience of washing wool.

If many were ill-equipped for the change of climate, as well as the culinary peculiarities of the restricted postwar British diet, West Indian staples such as yam, plantain and dasheen were soon imported by enterprising businessmen, though Jamaicans, Trinidadians and Bajans would have felt at home with bottles of Guinness, tins of Nestlé condensed milk and Milo drinking chocolate, which were popular throughout the Caribbean. Also arriving from "home" were discs of calypso, which, along with American rhythm and blues, country music and jazz, formed the standard West Indian record collection.

Calypso had achieved international recognition by the mid 1940s, primarily because artists in the mainstream had recorded songs that were not restricted to the "Specialty" or West Indian market, the most famous being the Andrews Sisters' "Rum and Coca Cola", which became a worldwide hit in 1945 and was released again in 1956. This was also a brazen case of plagiarism, the song having been stolen from its Trinidadian composers, the bandleader Lionel Belasco and the calypsonian, Lord Invader.[2] What "Rum and Coca Cola" showed was calypso's commercial potential, and subsequent recordings in the genre made by American artists can be seen as part of a longstanding American passion for exotica which included

Polynesian, Hawaiian, Asian and Latin music. There was Nat "King" Cole's "Calypso Blues", released in 1947, for instance.

Undoubtedly the commercial highpoint of the "US calypso craze" was actor-singer Harry Belafonte's 1956 sensation "Banana Boat Song" (*Day-Oh*). Tempting as it is to malign Belafonte as a Yankee interloper surfing on island music, his performance on the song is very engaging, and equally significant is the fact that it came from the pen of a brilliant Bajan singer, Lord Burgess.[4] In any case, an emphatic endorsement of the phenomenon of "Day-Oh" came from members of the wider calypso community in the Caribbean who saw the internationalization of the genre as a sign of artistic opportunity. According to George Browne, aka Young Tiger, a Trinidadian who settled and worked extensively in London throughout the 1950s, Belafonte deserved his place in the pantheon of exponents of a genre that stood to gain from overseas exposure, rather than being corralled into limited domestic markets:

> Men like the great Lord Kitchener, Growler, Invader, Lord Executor
> The Roaring Lion, Beginner, not forgetting the Growling Tiger
> A word of praise for I'm bound to say
> And thanks to Harry Belafonte
> His fame is made where he may go through publicizing calypso.

Burgess' melody and Belafonte's voice made for a million selling, chart topping combination. In addition to "Day-Oh", Burgess wrote calypso standards such as "Jamaica Farewell" and in other songs he combines metaphorical ingenuity with references that are anything but parochial.

> Sometimes ago I read she was in A Cabin in the Sky,
> So I ran down to the airport just to learn how I could fly.

A eulogy to a woman as talented as she was beautiful, the piece is called "Lena Horne". Here is a West Indian artist hailing one of the leading African-American singer-actor-dancers of the 1940s (1917-2010), known as much for her role in the musical *Stormy Weather* as *A Cabin in the Sky* (both 1943), which Burgess uses as a launching pad for his memorable pun. The piece reflects the diasporic engagement of West Indians with African-American culture, in which icons of stage and screen from one geographical area resonate with a listener from another.

Another enduring entry in the diasporic calypso canon came from the saxophonist Sonny Rollins with his "St. Thomas", also released in 1957. Besides being beautiful, Rollins' piece displays a thorough understanding of the rhythmic-melodic nuances that define calypso, perhaps not surprisingly given that his parents hailed from the Virgin islands and he spent his formative years playing at dances in New York's West Indian community. Though mainly known as a Mecca for jazz, New York also played a key role in the history of calypso, as it was the location for recordings that were initially earmarked for Caribbean and Latin American markets (such as Attila The Hun's recordings for the American Record Company in 1934), but went on to enjoy international distribution as time passed. With the popularity of the music growing, the legendary folk archivist Alan Lomax presented Lord Invader, the Duke of Iron and MacBeth the Great in a show called *Calypso At Midnight* in 1946 at New York's Town Hall. This was a significant event insofar as it widened the context for the music, placing it in the series of concerts called *Peoples Songs Midnight Special*. West Indian calypso was thus presented alongside American folk music.[5]

All this lay behind the reasons why "Rum and Coca Cola" was appropriated and had such a runaway success. It was the combination of languid melody, carrying traces of the folk songs that Spanish colonisers brought to Trinidad in the 18th century, and the underlying African rhythmic current, hinged on rippling cowbell patterns that provided a constant, hypnotizing pulse, which was deeply enticing.

The presence of many accomplished West Indian musicians in London had already made a British calypso industry a distinct possibility; what was needed was a record label and a forward thinking A&R director sufficiently astute to see that the cultural shift epitomized by the Windrush arrivals could foster a new market.

Emil Shallit (1909-1983), an Austrian entrepreneur who, legend has it, performed duties for the Allied secret service during World War II, stepped into the breach, launching Melodisc and hiring first Denis Preston, a London-based BBC presenter and jazz editor of the *Musical Express*, and later multi-instrumentalist, Rupert Nurse (1910-2001), as producer in chief for sessions. From its inception in 1949 to its closure in 1966, Melodisc became a flagship label for calypso music in Britain, harnessing the abundance of rhythm sections and horn players present at the time and creating a memorable synergy with the calypso singers who arrived on the *Windrush* – Lord Kitchener and Lord Beginner – as well others, who had preceded them such as Young Tiger, and those who followed such as Mighty Terror.[6]

Besides Melodisc, other labels that purveyed British-made calypso in the same period were the major, Parlophone, and another independent, Lyragon, set up by Shallit's former business partner Jack Chilkes, which issued a number of several excellent 78s by the Trinidadian singer Marie Bryant as well as by Kitchener and Al Timothy (1915-2000), who recorded as King Timothy (he wrote the song "Kiss Me Honey, Honey, Kiss Me" which Shirley Bassey had a hit with in 1958).

The catalogues of all three labels are an embarrassment of riches. The sheer verve and quality of the lyrics of those mentioned above is an emphatic reminder that calypso is one of the great vehicles for storytelling available to anybody with strong powers of observation and an inventive turn of phrase. Examined collectively – a sample might include Kitchener's

"The Underground Train", Beginner's "Housewives" and Young Tiger's "I Was There (At the Coronation)" – the songs form a fascinating journey through the mind of the West Indian migrant who was coming to terms with ordinary and extraordinary events in postwar Britain. But this music is more than a soundtrack to a nascent Black Britain, it is a portrait of Britain drawn from a black vantage point. A white Briton in those times could not legitimately utter the key trope of Kitch's "London is the Place for Me": "my mother country". All of these songs are an affirmation of what the essence of calypso is: a folk form borne of the desire for self-expression of African slaves and their descendants in Trinidad, aware of the disapproval and sometimes actual prohibition of their masters, which impelled the performer to pass insightful commentary on *any* given subject, be it cultural, political, social, sexual, local or international in an artful, sometimes oblique way. Beginner's "The Dollar and the Pound" is a memorable example of the calypso speaking internationally. The song addresses the subject of fluctuations in the value of American and British currencies. It touched eloquently on the position of the colonial subject whose ability to put bread on the table at home and to travel abroad, a key theme for West Indians at a time of Empire, was governed by the moment that "the dollar jump up" and the "pound go down."

Carnival, key manifestation of the humanity of the people of Trinidad, in all its irreverence, resistance, passion and wit, is the great stage for calypso. Any true calypso singer, whether accompanying themselves on guitar or backed by a percussionist or band, has to be able to prove their worth in the heat of that cauldron of knowing and opinionated listeners.

The whole point of calypso, and what it shares with the blues in America, is that it is a form of discourse as applicable to the ravages of a hurricane or the wreckage of infidelity as it is the brutality of the police or the beauty of a sporting event. If there is a Kung Fu blues it is logical there is also a Ju Jitsu calypso. A Black American says, "Every day I have the blues" and a Trinidadian declares "You need more calypso",[7] and they are not simply talking about music. They are hailing an empowering attitude to life, a right to engage in debate and adopt a range of emotional and intellectual nuances, from irony and flattery to celebration and confrontation.

Kitchener had as fertile an imagination and as florid a storyteller's gift as anybody. Born Aldwyn Roberts in Arima, north Trinidad, Kitch (1922-2000), the son of a blacksmith, had been a calypsonian since his teenage years, and became the "Chantwell"[8], the designated vocalist of the Sheriff band. He achieved immense popularity with provocative songs like "Green Fig". After successful tours of Jamaica with Beginner, the two men came to Britain on the *Windrush*, with Kitch consolidating his status by appearances at West End clubs such as the Antilles.

Along with The Sunset, this was a key venue for sessions by West In-

LORD KITCHENER

COURTESY GETTY IMAGES

dian musicians, and as gifted as the singers featured on Melodisc, Lyragon and Parlophone discs are, their recordings would be greatly impoverished without the accompaniment of the musicians who worked at these clubs. The importance of Rupert Nurse as musical director cannot be overstated, but there was also the input of other musicians from Africa and England, underlining the fact that London in the 1950s held a cornucopia of global musical talent. The sessions presented various configurations with names that often maintained African-American titular conventions reaching back to minstrelsy and swing, an indication of the depth of cultural knowledge amongst West Indian musicians. Calypso Serenaders brings to mind Ethiopian Serenaders. Calypso Rhythm Kings nods towards Fats Waller's Rhythm Kings and Benny Peyton's ensemble, The Jazz Kings.[9]

A cursory roll call of the members of these and other bands who backed the calypsonians includes saxophonist George Roberts; guitarists-quatroists Fitzroy Coleman and Brylo Ford; pianist Russ Henderson; double bassists Neville Bocarut and Rupert Nurse; percussionists Reuben Francois, John Maynard and Clinton Maxwell. All of these were part of a second wave of West Indian jazz musicians, following the likes of Ken 'Snakehips' John-son, Leslie Thompson and Leslie 'Jiver' Hutchinson, from the 1930s and '40s. Surviving members of that earlier generation played with the new. Guitarist Cyril Blake and reed players Bertie King and Freddy Grant all contributed to Melodisc, and they had been in Britain since 1920, 1936 and 1937, respectively. Thus the historical lineage was rich.

Inevitably, the seismic changes that occurred in Black music in the Americas between the 1930s and the 1950s permeated the development of calypso in Britain, meaning that the players who worked with singers like Kitchener, Terror and Beginner drew on a very wide vocabulary. Elements of New Orleans, Dixieland, swing and bebop are heard in the arrangements of Rupert Nurse, who'd had the experience of playing with visiting American artists when still in Trinidad. Jazz had been blended with calypso since the 1920s, as Sam Manning's work attests, but the Melodisc sides brought more ingenuity to the scores.

Nowhere is this more apparent than on the label's signature piece, "London Is The Place For Me". Whilst it is Kitchener's song, and as unforgettable is the lead vocal is, it is the performance of Freddy Grant's Caribbean Rhythm Kings that defines the music. Although Denis Preston is credited as the supervisor of the session whether he, Grant, Nurse or another musician, wrote the arrangement is not clear. What is indisputable is that the deployment of the double bass, piano, guitar, quatro and reeds complements and enriches a lyric that is celebratory and global in outlook. Kitch calls England's capital "this lovely city", and, a real red, white and blue patriot, places it top of an international league, above "France, America, India, Asia or Australia." No place like home.

Revealing a postwar, pre-independence West Indian mindset, the lyric is important, but does not wholly dominate the sound of the band. After a two bar introduction in which the piano quotes Big Ben's chimes, singer and rhythm section make their entrance and settle into an ambling slow-mid tempo, built on two chugging guitar chords. Straight after Kitch declares the title, just as he reaches the second bar of the verse, Grant starts to improvise on clarinet, offering a response to the singer's call. The heritage of the blues is clear. Thereafter the pattern repeats. Grant finishes his improvisation after just one measure and Kitch returns to introduce the rhyme of "this lovely city" before Grant solos again, so that horn and vocal alternate like a tag-team. Kitch's quite boyish, high tenor is counterweighted by the lower, woody tones of Grant's clarinet, which envelopes the voice. A guitar chord change signals a shift in the melodic line and Grant solos more liberally, simultaneously with Kitch, so now voice and horn are heard together, like two distinct threads that intertwine. And just as Kitch finishes his phrase, "You must come back to London city", the clarinet launches into another solo, this time joined by a tenor saxophone, the two horns dancing together. The saxophone, with its bigger, more muscular sound, finishes by echoing Kitch's vocal line. Thus the emblematic chorus "London is the Place for Me" retains its shape but changes timbre in the song.

The sax-clarinet duet lasts four bars, which is not insubstantial considering that Kitch's verse was just eight, and imparts, by way of the combined texture of the two reeds, a distinct New Orleans flavour to the arrangement. There is propulsion in the rhythm, but it is not overpowering. The 4/4 beat is simultaneously jaunty and leisurely. Thereafter the eight-bar vocal-horn structure is reprised but instead of being followed by another four-bar horn-horn duet, there is a gorgeously twangy improvisation from a quatro before the return of the vocal. Further solos come from the horns and piano before the piece concludes the way it started: the piano returning to Big Ben's chime. We come back to the lovely city. The journey is complete.

Lasting 2:40 minutes, "London is the Place for Me" fulfils the standard pop song criterion for concision, and its buoyant melody and chorus make it instantly catchy. Yet amid the accessibility is great artistry. The clarinet, saxophone and quatro, all reminders that reed and string instruments were brought to Trinidad by Venezuelan musicians back in the 1850s, are deployed with focus as well as flourish. The piano and percussion are rhythmically precise yet brilliantly measured in their dynamics, providing an undercurrent rather than a surge of power. There were many vocal/ instrumental calypso recordings in Trinidad in the 1930s, but the performance of Kitch and his band make the point that calypso is an *arranged* as well as sung form, a vehicle for improvisation as well as strong melodic content, and this song remains the apex of British calypso's 1950s heyday.

Like many significant pieces of music, "London is the Place for Me" becomes a prism through which an individual and the society in which he lives can be viewed. The conjunction of the vocal performance and the musical arrangement, the framing of the singer by the reed players, the ease of the rhythmic flow against the thrust of the solos, creates a finely brushed sonic canvas. Simple as its chorus may be, the song is insightful in terms of what it reveals about the mindset of the post-war West Indian musician and his relationship to art, for the prominence of extemporization around the lead vocal shows that Kitchener and his accompanists are intent on stretching accepted form, on shifting a paradigm towards something more ambitious than a tune. This comes with a lyric whose irony, probably unintended, encapsulates the condition of a generation of Blacks who were to find themselves marginalized. The creeping shadow of the colour bar and the reality of racist violence make the following line bitterly double-edged: "To live in London you are really comfortable/Because the English people are very much sociable."

As much as Kitch was the designated spokesman for the Black community, or rather additions to a long established if not always visible version thereof, other calypso artists brought their talent to bear on audiences throughout the UK. One of Kitch's fellow Trinidadians, the singer and actress Mona Baptiste[10] was also a passenger on the Windrush, and she sustained a career throughout the 1950s and 60s in a number of different contexts. In 1949, the year after her arrival, she became a cast member of the successful radio programme *Variety Bandbox*, and a few years later she worked regularly with the hugely popular big band led by Ted Heath.

Baptiste's success was by no means limited to Britain. There is sadly precious little documentation on how her face and voice initially caught the eyes and ears of German film producers but she was asked to appear as a singer in the 1954 musical *Tanz in Der Sonne* [*Dancing in The Sun*], and thereafter she made a string of 7" singles and 10" EPs that placed her firmly in the show tunes and exotica market, with her accompanists being German bandleaders such as Kurt Edelhagen and Werner Muller, who led a dance band [Tanzorchester] in Berlin. The fact that she sang in passable, lightly accented German on pieces such as "An Der Ecke [Gib Mir Ein Kuss]" and "Wer Mich Kuss, Ist gefangen" made her part of a lineage of black artists who not only performed in European countries but in European languages other than English.

Several of Baptiste's songs were melodies for which the foxtrot was the dance of choice – as indicated on the sleeves of her releases – and she proved adept at interpreting material in arrangements that were largely in the style of US big bands. However, the song that became and remains her signature is "Calypso Blues", originally a minor hit for Nat King Cole in 1949. The piece was co-written by Cole and Don George and it underlines why American jazz artists and audiences were so attracted to calypso as an idiom in the first place. In a manner not dissimilar to Kitch's "London is the Place for Me", the song has a gorgeously understated floating rhythmic momentum and a swish 3-2 clave beat that is grist to the mill of dancers and horn players. An Ellingtonian flourish in the fanfare of reeds introduces Baptiste's lithe, elegant, well-measured delivery of the lyrics. The opening salvo sees her pining deeply for her island.

> Sittin' by de ocean
> Me heart she feel so sad,
> Don't got the money
> to take me back to Trinidad.

As the piece unfolds, Trinidad is idealized as the land of easy living, a place where a single dollar will go much farther than it will in the high-expense pressure-cooker of New York, where local produce pales in comparison to the bounteous fare of the blessed West Indies, the epitome of which – "plenty fish to fill de boat" – has a biblical overtone.

The piece can be interpreted to a certain extent as a reductively American, if not clichéd, view of Trinidad as an archetypal island paradise, but the narrative gains substance in the second verse when it broaches the themes of social honesty. With Baptiste's voice bringing the words to life, with the slightest hint of irony in her tone, the apparently simple text is thought provoking.

> Calypso girl is good a lot
> Is what you see is what she got.

In other words, Trinidad is a place of less hypocrisy America, where false eyelashes and face-paint are symbols of much more than over-the-counter cosmetic enhancement. They lift the veil on a world that is illusory. Words do not match deeds, and appearances, embodied in the outwardly glamorous but nonetheless superficial 'Yankee gal', are ultimately deceptive. While this image can be seen as reflecting a one-dimensional male obsession with female beauty, with looks rather than intellect as focus, with the belief that a woman's role was passive rather than active, it also makes a wider comment on both race relations and prevailing behaviour in a western society. Let us not forget that the composer is a black man, Nat 'King' Cole, and that the Yankee gal is a white woman, specifically a blonde, more specifically a peroxide blonde – 'is black de root is blonde de hair.' Hence the accusation of duplicity extends across the most destructive fault line in American society, the separation of the races. It resonates with a view of Blacks who had newly arrived in Britain: the dominant white society could and did make false promises.

Taken together "London is the Place for Me" and "Calypso Blues" are compelling articulations of the complex relationship that existed between

West Indian migrants and their perception of home. On the one hand Kitch is projecting utopia on a Britannia of splendour and Royal entitlement, on the other hand, Baptiste is freighting nostalgia for a place seemingly untouched by iniquity. One is for the mother country, the other the motherland. Both visions are flawed to differing degrees, and the tension between the two lyrics, the imagined Britain and the remembered Trinidad, seen as they are through rose-tinted spectacles, provides a powerful encapsulation of the emotional quandary that faced a new wave of "coloured colonials".

Contrasted as their lyrics are, the two songs share similarities of musical arrangement. Each is melodically strong, with a highly effective percussive undertow, but it is the use of horns that underlines the considerable musicianship of calypso artists. Both pieces have saxophone-clarinet improvisations that take up substantial space in the overall narrative, especially in the case of "Calypso Blues" where the horn solo stretches to 16 bars, as well as a number of moments where the reeds either double a vocal phrase or create a well-curled counterpoint to it. Instruments are not entirely subservient to the singer. Even more interesting is the way that "Calypso Blues" brings the strength of the band into sharp focus at an early stage of the song's narrative. Baptiste delivers just one verse before she makes way for the solos, taking a back seat for quite some time before she returns. All of which makes perfect sense given the title of the piece. This is a blues, (or a blend of calypso and blues) and one of the defining characteristics of the genre is a fluid relationship between voice and instrument, such as a guitarist completing a singer's phrase, or a horn section, as is the case in "Calypso Blues" and "London is the Place for Me", momentarily coming into the foreground while the singer withdraws.

For the purposes of record industry marketing, this and other songs by Lord Beginner, Lord Invader and the Lion were specific products. The distinctive pink and yellow Melodisc labels have the suffix calypso placed after many of the titles, making it clear exactly what kind of music this is, underlining the status of calypso as a "Speciality" item, destined first and foremost for the West Indian market.

There were parallel developments in Paris, the hub for recordings from the francophone Antilles – Guadeloupe and Martinique, as well as the smaller island of Marie Galante. The output focused on a form of local music that became very popular, the biguine, which dates from the 19th century and reflects the collision of French ballroom music and African rhythms. Although mostly performed at mid tempo, the biguine often has a bracingly insistent drive in its syncopation, with the high and low tambours prominently placed in lyrical arrangements enhanced by vocals and horns.[11]

Distinct as they are, these various idioms, biguine and calypso, and the Cuban rumba, are all part of an rich musical family. The styles issue from shared source materials in folk dance, the propulsive and polyrhymic energy of percussion and the rich melodic role of guitar or banjo and clarinet – to be found in Port of Spain, Pointe a Pitre and Fort De France. Musicians in all these islands also lent an ear to New Orleans jazz. These common denominators made it possible for players from these various locations to collaborate with ease.

This was the case when two of Kitch's compatriots, pianist Boscoe Holder and Russell Henderson, a multi-instrumentalist who played piano as well as double bass, recorded in Paris with the Guadeloupean vocalist Gilles Sala. A dancer as well as painter and musician, Holder led a troupe that was booked at the Gaumont Palace, and the encounter with Sala came about soon after. The collaboration consolidates the idea of a West Indian creativity that reaches beyond territorial boundaries and their imposed European languages, and shows clearly the complex interactions, the flows of mutual influence across a range of ethnicities, including the indigenous Carib, African, Asian and European cultures. This is particularly true of musical styles. The folkloric imagery that frames biguine, such as the dancer dressed *en dame creole*, reflects the interweaving of the Nigerian headwrap and Indian Madras cloth. Similarly, part of the beauty of calypso lies in the sensual meshing of English and French words such as *we* and *fete*, *chant* and *well*.

What history lies behind a beautiful ballad called "Pal'i Flamboyan"? We might imagine this is yet another variant of calypso or biguine in French patois, given that its subject, the flamboyant tree, is common to both the francophone and anglophone Caribbean. We might imagine that the call and response celebration of flora evokes les mornes. We might imagine that the curiously metallic beat that accompany the vocals was made on a discarded oil drum reclaimed from the docks of Port of Spain. We'd be wrong. This is a legacy of the Dutch colonization of Curacao.[12]

Listen to a range of music from right across the Caribbean archipelago, from the Bahamas down to Guyana on the South American mainland, and recurrent components can be heard: insistent bass and treble rhythms – created in Trinidad by pounding lengths of bamboo on the ground, while in Martinique and Guadeloupe the bamboo is mounted on a stand and played with sticks to create high, crisp timbres. The maracas of the Hispanic Caribbean become the jangling percussion of the shac-shac in English Creole and chacha in French Creole becomes cha cha cha in Cuba.

The fact that calypso is a word derived from other words such as kalenda and kaiso, and biguine from bidgin and bele underlines the cultural pulses that flow through differences of language, that made the meeting between Guadeloupean singer Gilles Sala and Trinidadian pianist Boscoe Holder, in post-war Paris, one of a shared creole dynamic.

The Sala-Holder collaboration recorded songs that were termed calypso, bolero, and one piece, "Ces Zazous-la", which was called a calypso biguine.

Paris and London were thus linked by the role they played in documenting the music across the West Indies and showing their parallels and points of creative overlap. Catalogues of anglophone, hispanophone and francophone Caribbean music grew, with songs carefully identified as anything from calypso to rumba to mazurka creole.

West African Music in Britain

Roughly contemporary to the Melodisc, Riviera and Pathé recordings made in London and Paris was the growing "Repertoire Des Disques d'Afrique Noire" assembled by companies such as Philips. This had precedents in the catalogue of the Zonophone label of the 1920s, discussed in Chapter 8, where recordings of African musicians resident in Britain were framed in didactic terms, identifying languages and the components of the recording such as "chorus, castanets, clapping".[13] Three decades later, Melodisc printed labels that had product descriptions that were only slightly different. On the right hand side of the label for the song "Ominira" by the West African Rhythm Brothers is this subtitle: "Highlife sung in Yoruba." The difference was that the Melodisc labelling recognised that African music was evolving and might be listened to for pleasure. The label identified an entirely new genre of music – highlife – of which Melodisc became a major purveyor in the 1950s.

Although it was a compound noun on the Melodisc label, high life was usually presented as two words, and is one of the most enduring forms of popular music to have emerged from Ghana from the early to the mid twentieth century. It is, in fact, a number of forms housed under an umbrella term, but the two main strands are an orchestral, horn-led sound and a guitar-based one, once known as palm-wine music. Instantly recognizable by its layering of sounds – horn or guitar lines spiral around the melodic base, often with concise, chanted vocals – high life echoes the rhythmic traditions of Liberia and Sierra Leone – Christian church songs, military brass band tunes, and jazz. It reflects Ghana's history as a coastal, colonized country that absorbed African and Western influences and made them into something unique. Named to reflect the love of putting some style on the dance floor, high life also became popular in Nigeria, and it was inevitable, given the numbers of West African musicians who were also in the merchant navy and crossed the Atlantic, that it should make its way to Britain.

Because of the media impact of the *Windrush* in 1948, the Black immigration of the postwar period is largely seen as West Indian, but African settlement in the UK is an equally important part of the musical story. It is a settlement with deep roots; West Africans had been crewing on ships and settling in ports since the 1850s.

Percussion, string instruments and, later, recordings were brought by these sailors to cities such as Liverpool, and played in social gatherings in front rooms, basements and halls, in which music played an important part. But it was the arrival of one man in particular who raised the profile of high life in Britain.

Oladipupo Adekoya 'Ambrose' Campbell,[14] born in Lagos, Nigeria in 1919, to a stern Christian preacher father, who encouraged him at an early age to join a church choir. From these church beginnings, Campbell developed as a musician, singing secular music, much to his father's dismay, before making his way to Liverpool as a member of the crew of a cargo ship, *The Elder Dempster*, at the outbreak of the Second World War. His stay was brief, and he returned to Nigeria. However, a second more eventful voyage followed when he jumped ship in Merseyside and subsequently headed to London.

Over the next two decades, Campbell became one of the most important exponents of African music in Britain. His presence drew in a string of skilled players and led to the formation of important bands. He was a trailblazer who brought new sounds and songs sung in West African languages. As well as playing for fellow Nigerians, Campbell recalls: "We used to play for anthropology students, and all that." The phenomenon of being a "colonial curiosity" was still evidently present. More importantly, Campbell was at the forefront of a West African-West Indian artistic cross-pollination that saw him work with Caribbean artists in many different fields.

His first major step in that direction was a 1946 collaboration with Britain's first Black ballet company, founded by two Jamaicans, Richie Riley and Berto Pasuka, which took the name, Les Ballets Negres, in homage, no doubt, to the prestige of France's embrace of Black culture, such as the Parisian La Revue Negre of the 1920s. Campbell put together a group comprising other Nigerians who had been living in Manchester: the percussionist Ade Bashorun and a guitarist whose Anglo-Saxon name, like Campbell's, reflected how deeply cultural colonialism had penetrated West Africa – Brewster Hughes, who sounds like a P.G. Wodehouse character. With Campbell on vocals and percussion, the newly formed ensemble provided a rich musical framework for dance productions whose choreography was rhythmic and vigorous, drawing on West Indian folklore and ritual. The company toured Britain and also appeared in Paris.

These musicians then became the nucleus of a legendary group, the West African Rhythm Brothers, the epitome of the kind of musical universalism that reflected London's position as a meeting place. Other members included two Barbadian horn players – trumpeter Harry Beckett and multi-reedist Willy Roachford – along with a Nigerian pianist, Adam Fibresima. By this time Campbell was also playing guitar, having been taught by Lauderic Caton, the brilliant Trinidadian musician who had worked with Coleridge Goode and Dick Katz back in the 1940s.

A residency at the Abalabi club in Soho, central London, in the early

1950s gave the band a chance to develop a sound in a setting conducive to experimentation. West African expatriates resident in the capital, from students to government officials, as well as Caribbean and white hipsters came to hear the band playing highly danceable music. Mostly performed at mid tempo, high life has an incredibly hypnotic rhythmic quality, primarily because the emblematic instrument, the dundun or "talking drum" (a small tubular device whose skin is struck with a curved stick) creates a gurgle of low, muffled tones that act as a kind of mobile floor under the skips, curls and crisscross phrases produced by the array of other instruments.

Double bass plays tight, minimal lines, sometimes of no more than three pitches; guitars pick, scrape and scratch usually on just two chords; bongos, congas and shekere stitch together the rich percussive fabric that lends body to the ensemble sound without making it excessively heavy. The real genius of high life is that it evokes movement, yet paradoxically suggests a kind of floating or gently hovering sensation. In terms of its overall hazy, wafting nature and abiding sensuality, high life is often very close to calypso. Setting the pulse is the cowbell or woodblocks which are played in a 3-2 clave style, but are also deployed in seven beat lines of 3-2-2 on the brisker, more energetic numbers. This is the metre of Latin, particularly Cuban music, but is in fact of African origin.

The final, crucial component is the vocal arrangement, built on a call and response structure, often with the second line dropping to a much lower pitch. Again, there is a similarity with the chants in calypso. All this makes high life an irresistible blend of drum orchestration and song in which rhythm is a series of running conversations and melody appears in short, swift asides and fleeting interjections. High life performs a sensory sleight of hand insofar as the voices and horns slide and saunter, evoking airiness, while the percussion cuts and thrusts, evoking earthiness. The net result is a simultaneously light and full sound.

With a tight grip on the idiom, as well as a great song-writing ability, Campbell and the West African Rhythm Brothers made brilliant high life recordings on Melodisc throughout the 1950s. Among their anthems are "Emi Wa Wa Lowa Re", "Mofi Ajobi Seyin", "Oba Ademola II" and "Ayami". As can be heard on the above, and the music of similar groups such as Ayinde Bakare's Meranda Orchestra, high life had a kind of balmy sweetness that steered clear of the saccharine and over-sentimental primarily because of the momentum of the drums, regardless of the tempo of the melodic line.

The prominence of percussion in the high life music of Ambrose Campbell evidently struck a chord with leading British jazz musicians such as Ronnie Scott, Tubby Hayes and John Dankworth in the 1950s. Bands with a guitarist, two standing horn players and two or more seated percussionists provided a feast in polyrhythm, linking to the work of talented Latin percussionists such as Chano Pozo, Ray Barretto and Candido Camero who had played with the great American modernists Dizzy Gillespie and Charlie Parker.

Of all the British musicians who committed to the rhythmic complexity of Africa and its diaspora, none was more prominent than the reed player, Kenny Graham, who formed the Afro-Cubists. Graham heard Campbell at the Abalabi club in Soho and evidently took note of the percussionists more closely than any of his peers, because he used between two and three "congueros" in his own music. Although born in London, Graham actually made his professional debut on alto saxophone in Nottingham with Rube Sunshine and His Band, before moving to London where he played with a variety of dance orchestras, of which the best known was that led by Jack Parnell. As was the case with other musicians, Graham's career was put on hold while he served in the armed forces during the war, but the Afro-Cubists, launched in the late 1940s, were a great addition to British jazz that recognized the musical importance of the colonies.

Usually deploying at least three if not four percussionists – who were generally Africans or Caribbeans such as Frank Holder – Graham made crisp arrangements of enduring bebop or Latin compositions such as "Barbados", "El Manisero" and "Poinciana" on the albums that the Afro-Cubists made in 1950s, *Mango Walk*, *Caribbean Suite* and *Tenorama*.[15]

The influence of Campbell was also heard in some of the short-lived groups formed by Caribbean musicians on the London scene such as the St. Vincent trumpeter, Shake Keane, who briefly led the High Lifers. The general impression that emerges from surveying the Black music scene in London in the 1950s is one of the liberal interaction of different nationalities and an attendant intermingling of styles. The effect of this musical miscegenation on several visiting Ghanaian players, such as the great E.T. Mensah and Guy Warren, was decisive. Both would go on to make music that was breathtakingly adventurous in its synthesis of African music and jazz, with the latter moving to America where he played with several great improvisers and bandleaders before eventually returning to Africa.

An "affable personality"[16] and something of a founding father, Campbell was still the person for club owner Ola Dosunmu to turn to when the Abalabi closed. Dosunmu had run the old place with his wife Irene, and they subsequently launched a new venture called Club Afrique, whose name reflects the kind cultural kudos attached at the time to France (existentialism was much in vogue).

Campbell's former bandmate, Brewster Hughes, had a band called Starlite Tempos that played there, and Caribbean musicians were featured, too, before the club shut when the Dosunmus moved to Lagos.

Up until the late 1960s, Campbell remained a strong presence on the London scene, but there was another musician who had a similar trajectory. He, too, had arrived in Britain on a merchant ship, also with an Anglo-Saxon second name. This was Ginger Johnson who, like Campbell, was a Nigerian and had a priest for a father, though his was Muslim. Orphaned as a boy, Johnson started to play drums when he moved from his birthplace of Ijebu to Lagos. As a seaman who arrived in England in 1943, Johnson initially found work in a munitions factory in Birmingham and then moved to London and began to play percussion for jazz musicians such as Ronnie Scott and Kenny Graham before working for a long time with Edmundo Ros, who led a band playing a light, very polished version of Latin music for the posh crowd living the high life at the Palladium.

Johnson established himself as one of the most skilled conga players in the capital, and when he started recording under his own name for the Melodisc label it was clear that he had become an able bandleader. All of his Melodisc sides are outstanding, none more so than "African Jazz Cha Cha". As the title suggests, it is truly diasporic, seamlessly fusing "Motherland" and "New World" beats, a panorama of the Black Americas.

Between them Ginger Johnson and Ambrose Campbell proved to be two of the founding fathers of African music in Britain, and the guest appearance of the latter with the Rolling Stones at their famous 1969 Hyde Park concert brought enormous exposure. It was an echo of Campbell's memorable performance in central London two decades earlier on VE Day in 1945. Then, Campbell and other Nigerians, armed with guitars and drums, had mingled with the joyous crowd in Piccadilly Circus to mark the end of the Second World War and added their own West African rhythms to the wild outpourings of joy. Tellingly, they were later described by a reporter as a group of "West Indians",[17] which was how most early Black Britons tended to be seen.

Looking back on all of the excellent recorded documentation of the London music scene in the 1950s, much of it thanks to labels such as Honest Jons, it's hard not to be astounded by the quality of the music, both in terms of its idiomatic richness and its execution. The coalescence of African, African-Caribbean and African-American styles on a single piece of music betrays a spirit of adventure among the musicians. What is most impressive is that the majority of the bands sound as if they were well rehearsed, no doubt because they spent a lot of time performing in clubs. According to those who witnessed the unfolding of events at first hand, this was down to the availability of premises at affordable prices, possibly because many were still in a state of disrepair after the war. John Jack is one of the stalwarts of the British jazz record industry, having founded the excellent independent label Cadillac records in the early 1970s, making an invaluable contribution to the marketing and promotion of countless artists over the decades. In the 1950s, he was a young man working at Dobell's record shop on Charing Cross Road, in central London; he was also playing trombone for jazz bands. He has a clear recollection of Soho at that point in time:

> There were general rehearsal places and clubs around. A lot of these places started just after the war, property was very cheap. Various enterprising people picked up basements. You'd find a basement here doing some jazz then further up the street there was another all night cab drivers place upstairs up on the second or third floor – a Greek Cypriot social club-cum-cab drivers café. There was lots going on.[18]

Jack also recalls how strong friendships were formed that ran across racial lines, with music as a unifying force.

> I remember that a lot of the West African musicians were seamen. [Like Ginger Johnson and Ambrose Campbell]. The first one that I befriended was Ambrose. It wasn't unknown for us at the weekend, with the mother and father gone away for a few days, to go home and have a party just playing and playing music. We'd clamber on to a number 9 or 73 bus, and go back to Barnes [in South London] and just play in the night, much to the delight of my aunt living next door.[19]

Whilst rich cultural interaction was one feature of the evolution of British jazz in the postwar period, there was also an area of sharp division. This was between those who embraced the newer, progressive idiom of bebop and the "traddies" who were drawn to the older New Orleans (or Dixieland) style, two schools, which were characterised by different rhythmic and harmonic characteristics as well as different choices of instrumentation.

By and large, bebop set great store by the saxophone and piano while Dixieland lionized the clarinet and banjo. Such clashes of tradition and modernity are a recurrent feature of most art forms that are dynamic rather than static, and the factionalism that occurred on the British jazz scene was inevitable given that jazz was really an umbrella term that included a range of approaches. The real point is less that the clarinet became identified with trad and the sax with bebop as the fact that decades into the future both instruments would still be part of the present and future of jazz. Jazz history is circular rather linear.

However, as the members of the British jazz scene of the 50s remember, there was the fiercest loyalty to the preferred school amongst listeners. This was probably exacerbated by the fact that jazz was a form of music that still required effort to acquire. Enthusiasts had to go specialist record stores or place orders for titles that they read about in magazines, or heard in the "Rhythm" clubs, so it was not surprising that cultish attitudes set in. The result was sniping when territorial lines were crossed.

"I was seen as a trad because of the bands I was in," Jack says, remembering the divisions. "I'd be hanging out with Ambrose [Campbell] going down to a bebop club, people would tut and say "Oh, there's a noted traddie among us." Tony Hall, a committed "modernist" also recalls this polarization: "I don't remember any crossover *at all*. It was them and us."[20]

Polarization did not always hold among the musicians themselves. And while trad, which enjoyed a boom in the 1950s, catapulted the 3 Bs – Kenny Ball, Acker Bilk and Chris Barber – to a star status never quite achieved by bebop artists, there were interesting collaborations between the camps as the years went by. Barber recorded with one of the brightest lights of the bebop scene, the superb alto saxophonist Joe Harriott, and Bilk with the respected modernist pianist, Stan Tracey. The musicians themselves often recognised continuities. Almost all of them recognised the centrality of the blues to jazz expression; what also sometimes brought modernists and trads together was the embrace of calypso. The choice of one of trad's key champions, the trumpeter Humphrey Lyttleton, to close his sets with an uplifting calypso, and also record with London-based "island" players such as the Guyanese clarinettist Freddy Grant in the popular Grant-Lyttleton Paseo band, was one such example.

In addition to collaborating in the studio, though the musicians aligned to each movement mostly performed before their specific constituencies in different venues, occasionally the *freres ennemis* would find themselves playing under one roof. As Jack recalls:

> A place like the Latin Quarter was a good example [of a cheap post-war venue] – the premises were on Greek Street in Soho. The National Federation of Jazz Organizations opened on the ground floor; Chris Barber and Dixieland was on the first floor, Don Rendell and bebop on the next, and the top floor above the café was the homebase for Ginger Johnson and West African bands. On a good night on Saturday all three floors had things going on. It was possibly before its time.

Viewed through the prism of jazz history, the supposed antipathy between the above is a subject worthy of enquiry and analysis, but the promoters, producers or club owners will tell you, whether they were trad or mod, all jazz musicians were coming to be seen as less viable commodities in relation to other forms of music. The inescapable reality of the late 1950s and early 1960s was that jazz was starting to lose commercial ground to pop, and it could be argued that the various Musician Union bans on the presence of American musicians had exacerbated the situation by depriving the jazz scene of the international stars who were necessary to grow the domestic market.

Furthermore, some adepts of classical music still dismissed the validity of jazz artists. Slurs on the wildness of their playing were not uncommon, something exemplified by the throwaway remark of a piano tuner who arrived at the One Hundred club, in Oxford Street, central London, a mecca for both mod and trad musicians. He could not resist saying that he pitied the "poor beast" for the unholy syncopation it endured from cussed souls intent on making it "hot". The quip was a reminder that disdainful attitudes that had greeted the arrival of jazz in the previous decades died hard. In the 1930s, there was a trend for printing postcards that derided the music as cheap entertainment. In one a drunkard is seen traipsing from one public house to another under the caption – "He's suffering from syncopation, wandering from bar to bar."

Suitable Work For Them?

The central question of race relations of the mid 1950s, and to a large extent still today, was employment, and the tragedy for many of the West Indians who arrived on the *Windrush* was that they were not given the chance to enrich British society to their full potential. They were not allowed to apply any of the skills acquired in the Caribbean. Craftsmen were offered positions that made no use of their craft and science graduates were not allowed to practise science.[21]

Over the years the narrative that recruitment drives were undertaken by the London Transport Executive and the British Hotels and Restaurants Associations to bring in West Indians to rebuild a broken postwar Britain has become received wisdom, but whilst such initiatives were taken, post-*Windrush*, in the mid 1950s, what was regarded as problematic by politicians of both parties – with a few honourable exceptions – and by xenophobic sections of the national press, was the prospect of large scale unregulated immigration and the concentration of non-whites in Britain. The *Windrush* passengers appear to have caught the nation unawares, and whilst Britain *needed* Black workers, that did not mean that they were *wanted*.

At first, finding work was not necessarily a problem. As Clinton Edwards, a Jamaican ex-R.A.F serviceman, explains: "The first job I got as a welder, instead of doing welding they gave me a wheelbarrow and a shovel. After a couple of weeks my arms were sore, so I packed it in and re-enlisted in the R.A.F. I knew what to expect in the R.A.F."[22] This was a time of almost full employment and factories and office were almost always recruiting. Others who travelled with Edwards recall being offered as many as five jobs on their first visit to their local labour exchange, but the discrepancy between what the West Indians thought themselves capable of doing and what employers presumed they could actually do was very marked. Another arrival, John Richards, declared: "The average person knows you as a colonial and that's all. You cut cane or carry bananas and that's it."[23]

Such attitudes came from the top. On 8 June, just a few weeks prior to the docking of the *Windrush*, George Isaacs, head of the Ministry of Labour, gave a blunt view of the new arrivals:[24]

> I have no knowledge of their qualifications or capacities and can give no
> assurance that they can be found suitable work. I hope no encouragement
> will be given to others to follow their example.

This degree of suspicion in the field of employment resonated with
discrimination in other areas such as housing and social intercourse.
To not trust a colleague on the shop floor is to not love thy neighbour.

In this respect, black musicians, regardless of how fragile his or her position
in an arts or entertainment industry might be, were at a relative advantage.
They at least had the opportunity to prove their worth. Historically, even
when subjected to the reductiveness of minstrelsy, black musicians exercised
their creativity and had some space to develop their self-expression. The
tambo 'n' bones players paved the way for modern drummers; the banjo
players developed rhythmic finesse; the hoofers created steps that are still
part of contemporary choreography. Thus, even if his performance was on
a pavement in front of bemused, indifferent or hostile passers-by, the black
musician was in a better psychological position than the skilled or professional
black worker denied access to the workplace without so much as an "audition".

Nobody could refute the fact that Lord Kitchener played a guitar and
sang, because these were material, empirical facts. But did employers
imagine that an Aldwyn Roberts could be an engineer? A bank manager?
A lecturer? The failure of imagination of those with power inevitably
fostered an obsession with how to contain this bunch of Blacks who were
both of Britain and from somewhere else. What the state fell back on was
regulation, surveillance and control. For example, one of London's central
West Indian communities, that of Lambeth, came into being because, after
restrictions were put on the number of Windrush arrivals to be placed
in hostels, the migrants were swiftly shunted into an abandoned air-raid
shelter in Clapham, before settling in Brixton.

The other main area of West Indian settlement in the city was Notting
Hill, or as it was formerly known Notting Dale, primarily because the dilapidated housing was cheap, and, more to the point slum landlords such as
the viciously exploitative Peter Rachman[25] were ready to take advantage of
the desperation caused by the refusal of others to accommodate migrants,
as symbolized by the infamous "No Irish, No Blacks, No Dogs" sign
hung in the windows of rooming houses. Hence, dozens crammed into
crumbling, unhygienic tenements, knowing that a box room was better
than a door being slammed in their faces. The phenomenon of multiple
occupancy increased Rachman's profits, but tenants sometimes only had
a single room in which to eat, sleep and have some semblance of a private
life, let alone entertain. Sometimes a washing line with sheets had to be
hung in the room to divide the adults' sleeping area from the children's.
This restriction of space was compounded for the 7,000 West Indians in
Notting Hill by the colour bar operated in many local pubs.

It is not surprising then that social functions organised within the black community assumed great importance, and the record player, usually a large cabinet with an arm the size of a rudder and a needle like a screwdriver, took pride of place in the West Indian front room, comforted by at least one religious icon on the wall, usually placed next to the mandatory "My island" black velvet scroll.

While many played discs in the privacy of their own home, small communal spaces known as shebeens came into existence. These pop-up social clubs were nothing more than a makeshift bar in a basement or a front room, but they had the all-important ingredients of a record player and a willing disc jockey who would spin the latest blues, jazz and calypso singles. Occasionally there might be a singer, guitarist or horn player, but the sounds were mostly spinning off the latest vinyl disc. The music had to be good and the drinks cheap.

Notes

1. For the statistics see Mayerlene Frow, *Roots of the Future*.
2. For Ray Ellington, see the sleeve notes to *Ray Ellington Quartet and the Three Bears* (Avid label, 2000); and a profile in *Checkers* magazine, 1948.
3. See Wikipedia: Rum_and_Coca-Cola.
4. See the sleeve to Lord Burgess & His Sun Islanders, *Calypso Go Go* (Pye, 1967).
5. See the sleeve to Various Artists, *Calypso at Midnight* (Rounder, 1999).
6. See the sleeve notes to *London is the Place for Me: Trinidadian Calypso in London, 1950-1956* (Honest Jon's, 2002).
7. See Ralph McDonald's *You Need More Calypso* (Polydor, 1985).
8. The chantwell originates from the tradition of having a solo singer lead a group of slaves when they sang work songs in the fields.
9. This was the group clarinettist Sidney Bechet joined after leaving the Southern Syncopated Orchestra.
10. For the information on Mona Baptiste see //mischalke04.Wordpress.com/2011/04/14/mona-baptiste-die-madchen-aus-de-mambo-bar-1959.
11. For information on French Caribbean music see John Cowley, *Creole Music of the French West Indies, A Discography, 1900-1959* (Bear Family records, 2002).
12. Hear this on Groupe Folklorique Rincon (Melodie Populaire De Bonaire) on the album *Féérie Des Antilles-Folklore Des Îsles Sous Le Vent* (2004).
13. See Various Artists, *Living Is Hard* (Honest Jons, 2008).
14. For the information on Campbell, see Val Wilmer's excellent essay

on Ambrose Campbell featured in the booklet of *London is the Place For Me, 3* (Honest Jons, 2006).

15. Kenny Graham's other recordings such as *Moondog Suite* (MGM, 1956) are also well worth investigating.
16. Wilmer, op. cit.
17. Wilmer op. cit
18. Interview with the author, Charing Cross, London, 2013.
19. Interview with the author, Soho, London, 2013.
20. Ibid.
21. See the film *To Sir With Love* (Columbia, 1967), which dramatised the struggles of the Guyanese physics graduate E.R Braithwaite who fell back on teaching after being refused work in his chosen field.
22. http://www.bbc.co.uk/history/british/modern Windrush-Arrivals.
23. http://www.bbc.co.uk/history/british/modern Windrush-Arrivals.
24. David Kynaston, *Austerity Britain 1945-51* (Bloomsbury, 2007), p. 274
25. Notorious for the exploitation of West Indians, Peter Rachman was himself an immigrant. He was born in Lvov, Poland. Furthermore he was the son of a Jewish dentist and thus his relationship with people from the Caribbean provided a depressing counterpoint to the uplifting West Indian-Jewish union that existed in jazz in the 50s.

13 CALYPSO, CREOLE, CRICKET, CONFLICT

Big business is bossed mostly by Americans, Englishmen, Syrians and
Chinese with a sprinkling of Indians. The real Jamaicans are only in
the island these days, to use a Jamaican phrase, "fi mek up numbers."
— R. Donaldson, "A Jamaican In London", *Checkers* magazine, 1948.

After the match I took my guitar and called a few West Indians, and I
went round the cricket field singing and dancing. So while we're dancing
up come a policeman and arrested me.
— Lord Kitchener, on the aftermath of West Indies victory over England
in the 1950 Test series.

During the infancy of the BBC, there was an emphasis on real-time
events, from football matches to coronations and above all concerts.
BBC Radio transmitted hours of live music and its cathode ray cousin
followed suit, which meant opportunities for popular African-American
artists of the day during the pre and postwar years. In October 1947,
Adelaide Hall,[1] a major figure from the Harlem Renaissance who settled
in Britain in the 1930s, caused a sensation when she was filmed at the
Radiolympia Theatre, but prior to that she had appeared with Nigerian
bandleader Fela Sowande[2] in *Harlem in Mayfair*, a show from the club
she opened in London, the Old Florida. As film and television historian
Stephen Bourne states in his important *Black in the British Frame*, early
British television also shone a light on, "a small, but important group
of Africans and Caribbeans."[3]

Among them were the dancers and musicians already noted – Leslie
Thompson; Leslie 'Jiver' Hutchinson; West African Rhythm Brothers;
Cyril Blake & His Calypso Band and Ray Ellington. These were some of
the artists who appeared on cultural programmes that reflected the "colonial talent" that was to be seen in London, which, until the early 1950s,
was the only place in the country where TV programmes could be viewed.

Particularly important in the Black presence on early TV was the Trinidadian actor-singer-director and all-round cultural activist, Edric Connor,
who became a key figure in postwar British broadcasting after he arrived
in 1944. Connor recorded West Indian folk music and shared his extensive
knowledge of the subject on radio shows like *Traveller's Tales* and *Music
Makers*. In the subsequent decades he made significant contributions to

film and theatre. He had the voice and physique for audio-visual platforms, and recognizing an obvious talent in its midst, the BBC afforded Connor many opportunities to present Caribbean culture; the body of work that he put together in the immediate postwar years is really quite incredible. Connor was a great adept of Trinidadian calypso and Jamaican mento, and he championed these genres to a wider audience.

Serenade in Sepia was one of the most popular television programmes Connor made, running between 1945 and 1947, and featuring another vocalist, Evelyn Dove. It was a showcase for classic Caribbean folk music, with the two singers performing a varied songbook. Thankfully, footage of some of his appearances on the show have survived, and it is quite thrilling to watch him bring gravitas to a piece such as "Water Boy", because his powerful voice is complemented by a commanding stage presence.

Connor shared a television studio with other trailblazing artists in 1946. Singing calypso songs, he appeared on shows that featured the Jamaican dance troupe Les Ballets Negres and the Nigerian musicians of the West African Rhythm Brothers led by Ambrose Campbell. While these broadcasts reflect the inroads made by black music into the mainstream media in postwar Britain – for nothing was more prestigious than a BBC transmission – the wider sociocultural and political framework around these artists remained ambiguous. To say that the progress of Edric Connor at the BBC pointed to a genuine engagement by editors and programme makers with West Indian culture is moot. The exotic was still well to the fore.[4]

Hugely charismatic in *Serenade in Sepia*,[5] Connor comes across as the archetypal "son of the soil". He sports a bandanna and is surrounded by open-shirted acolytes who gaze at him as if he were a village prophet. Most alarmingly, the studio set, possibly Pathé or Pinewood, is stuffed with fake palm trees intended to denote a "small island". Vocally, Connor is magnificent. Visually, he is cast against the tropical canvas of the western imagination. The same image would also be recognizable in the form of Harry Belafonte, the American whose worldwide success would make him "the king of calypso".

A dynamic performer, regardless of any prevailing reductive expectations, Connor was proactive on many fronts. He went on to form a talent agency with his wife Pearl that was instrumental in providing opportunities for other people of colour in the performing arts and literature. However, the work he did himself, which covered a wide range of activities that would justify the catch-all term "star of stage, screen and recording studio", was no less worthy of note, particularly as it gave him the platform to represent West Indian culture on his own terms. The two albums Connor made in the mid 1950s are hugely important insofar as they reflect the richness of West Indian folk music and the depth of its historical roots. *Songs from Jamaica* and *Songs from Trinidad* are timeless collections that underline how the descendants of slaves lived and fashioned their own morality tales and parables, which often chime with the Black experience in America. There are a number of the "work songs" that accompanied everyday labour, such as "Day Dah Light" – the banana loaders song – as well as picaresque ballads like "Sammy Dead Oh", which tells of a plantation owner who has been "obeah'd" by some of his treacherous neighbours. Also fascinating are chants borne of the imagination of Blacks, who, still clinging to the belief systems of Nigeria, make overt reference to deities such as Shango and Ogun ("Ogoun Belele"). Furthermore, many of the songs highlight the development of Creole, whereby Standard English is reshaped in new ways to acquire a distinct rhythmic identity and inflection. The Empire says, "Tears fall from my eyes", the colonies say, "Wata come a me eye". The Empire says, "Some are crying", the colonies say, "Some a bawl". The Empire says, "He's a hard man to kill", the colonies say, "He's a hard man fi dead". This language, uncompromising in its punchy, straight-down-the-line transparency, is given a sharp focus on these recordings because Connor's sterling baritone voice is accompanied by a group of backing singers, The Caribbeans, and pianist Earl Inkman, rather than a full band. With no drums or string instruments in the arrangements, the beauty of the vocal phrasing, which is often as percussive as it is melodic, comes into its own. Interestingly, the lyrics of these songs, scores and their "translations" were also made available in a book that was published by Oxford University Press.[6]

Connor's ubiquity on BBC music programmes of the early 1950s evidently caught the eye of producers as far away as Hollywood, which led to one of his most high-profile, though brief, film appearances.

His performance in John Huston's 1956 film version of Herman Melville's *Moby Dick*, with a script by Ray Bradbury, starring Gregory Peck as Captain Ahab and featuring a scene-stealing cameo by Orson Welles (and a great white rubber whale made by Dunlop tyres) cemented Connor's journey from the calypso tents of Port of Spain to regular appearances on British radio and early TV.

Connor was cast in the role of the harpooner, Daggoo. He has precious little screen time and only a few lines of dialogue, but he makes a lasting impact with his performance of a Jamaican traditional song "Hill An' Gully Rider", which is heard during the first whale hunt. The tune is overdubbed with remarkable clarity, to give the impression that the sailors are lifting their voices to the sky as they lean back and forth to make their long, wooden oars slice the onrushing surf. The camera focuses on Connor for barely a frame as his solo voice is heard rising majestically above those of his shipmates whom he leads in song.

The emotional power of "Hill An' Gully Rider" stems from its structure. It uses the basic call-and-response model that underpins field hollers, work songs, Negro spirituals, blues ballads and Caribbean folk music.

Call and response transmutes into a melodic context, the most universal of human activities, the dance of conversation, whereby one statement is made as an invitation to another. So when Connor sings "Took my horse an' comin' down", the chorus has to sing "Hill An Gully" because this upholds an implied narrative logic – in the same way that the call of "Oh, happy day" gains emotional plenitude as the response to "When Jesus washed… (my sins away)". Call and response is about statement, but it also celebrates the art of listening.

Secondly, call and response offers rhythmic variety. The attack of Connor's solo lines in "Hill An' Gully Rider" contrasts with the crew's exclamations to create a distinct shift in momentum. Connor sings in relatively medium-fast tempo and they come back with markedly slower, more languid notes that have the effect of anchoring and shoring up his delivery, so as to make the entire phrase more conclusive. The single voice and the chorus are united in their emotional make-up but each curls around the beat in a different way.

Thirdly, call and response offers tonal variety and textural contrast. Connor's timbre is bold and piercing, but the crew-members, singing in unison, create a broader wave of noise, as if the song's energy is expanding as more people join in. It's not so much that the crew-members sing. They chant. They drop into a lower register, fuller, darker, a more bass-heavy presence.

Connor had a specific cultural agenda in bringing "Hill An' Gully Rider" to director John Huston. As his Connor's wife Pearl later explained:

> Hill an' Gully Rider is about the undulating land in Jamaica, but it was the undulating sea of *Moby Dick*, the ocean where they were looking for a whale, where Edric introduced the song. And it is a lyrical, lilting song, a beautiful thing that John Huston loved straight away. And Edric was always trying to do that, introduce Caribbean music into the films he worked on, and letting people know about our songs.[7]

Lasting approximately 90 seconds this performance is a seminal moment in the history of black music in Britain, precisely because it reached beyond Britain. It involved, as his wife commented, a superlative act of cultural intelligence, for packed cinemas around the world heard West Indian music in a classic American story.

The song was also a reminder of the musical role that Blacks had played on transatlantic merchant ships throughout the 18th and 19th centuries, as outlined in Chapter 2, when their fiddling, singing and drumming entertained crews during their long months at sea. In Melville's original text, the character of the "Negro cabin boy", Pip, is a tambourine player, a detail that Huston faithfully brought to his adaptation. Connor's singing brought a spotlight to the black maritime musician whom history often casts into shadow.

Striking as Connor's performance in the "Hill 'n' Gully Rider" sequence is, one has to wonder how much greater an impact he could have made had he been given a speaking part. He did have more substantial roles in films such as *Fire Down Below* (1957) and *Virgin Island* (1958), dramas set in the Caribbean that cast him alongside American stars Rita Hayworth, Robert Mitchum (who also recorded a calypso album, *Calypso Is Like So*), Jack Lemmon and Sidney Poitier. But while Connor made headway as a film actor he knew that British television had a pivotal role to play for the burgeoning black community at the time, as the issue of the "colour bar" became ever more pressing.

Although the BBC was initially responsive to Connor's ideas on how best to present West Indian culture, there was increasing tension between him and the Corporation when his vision became more politically adventurous and sought to reach beyond the realm of "light entertainment", to the extent that the relationship deteriorated in the post-war period. Amanda Bidnall chronicles events in *The West Indian Generation: Remaking British Culture In London 1945-1965*: "He was an immediate success at the Corporation, but when the afterglow of military victory had subsided and concerns about racial strife replaced the celebration of empire in the late 50s, the BBC increasingly rebuffed Connor's efforts to create and broadcast meaningful work."[8]

Presentation for Black music and Black performers in pre and postwar Britain was a thorny issue. While the stereotypes of tropical people surrounded by exotic landscapes and casual clothing was the norm, there was great formality, if not exaggerated eloquence, in the way many spoke. Listen to interviews of the Jamaican double bassist, Coleridge Goode, who appeared in the 1947 television programme *Jazz is Where You Find It* and you hear a man with a professorial tone of voice, his diction in no way suggesting a West Indian background. It's tempting to declare he is out-Britishing the British, but maybe it's fairer to say that he was de-West Indianised by the influence of a colonial education and mindset. Black artists of his era all seem to sound like statesman in waiting.[9]

Goode, in his excellent autobiography, *Bass Lines*, evokes the horror his classical-music-loving father would have experienced had he known that his son had forsaken his engineering studies in Britain to play jazz. The deep attachment of the Caribbean middle class to European concert music and the cultural appurtenances that came with it – gentlemanly manners, sartorial elegance, perfect elocution – reminds us that islands like Jamaica were much more than just ruled by the mother country. They were fully immersed in its baptismal waters.

An even more striking example of the phenomenon can be found in a short film *West Indies Calling,* produced by Paul Rotha in 1943 and based on the radio series, *Calling The West Indies*, a wartime broadcast in which Caribbean serviceman and women sent messages to the islands. Edric

Connor was an early contributor. Lasting just under 14 minutes, the film, which was commissioned by the Ministry of Information, carries a heavy whiff of propaganda and "jolly good show" bonhomie about West Indians who have made "common cause with us."[10] Somewhat inevitably, the strains of calypso ring out, all sliding horns and skipping drums courtesy of Al Jennings' orchestra, and the credits inform us that the "speakers" are two West Indian servicemen, Carlton Fairweather and Ulric Cross, as well as the great Trinidadian cricketing legend, Learie Constantine and the Jamaican broadcaster, Una Marson. As for the larger cast, it is simply "West Indians in Britain." Marson introduces her co-speakers who then praise the colonial war effort. Blacks are shown in munitions factories and in the armed services toiling to help defeat "Hitler and his gang". They are happy on assembly lines with white colleagues. Racial harmony is implied. Then another calypso, this time with a very plummy, English-sounding vocal rings out. It gives way to a quite appalling commercial dance number. It is as if Black music is being "whitewashed" by a diligent BBC censor. What emerges from the film is how absolutely Oxbridge the West Indian speakers sound, though all of them were born on the islands. There is no trace of a Jamaican, Bajan or Trinidadian accent. Presumably, they were not encouraged to stray into the vernacular. The whole thing appears an elaborate construct, like the palm trees and bandannas that formed Edric Connor's backdrop in *Serenade in Sepia*.

Whether they were performing "authentic" West Indian music or recounting the wartime West Indian experience, Connor and Marson evidently had to observe strict conventions, namely that folk themes had to evoke a degree of primitivism, while serious political content required an ultra formal tone. Una Marson's own poetry shows something of this split in consciousness. There are poems whose models are Victorian, but also poems, such as "Kinky Hair Blues" that use Jamaican patois. How far colonial imprinting reached into the psyche of West Indians is graphically illustrated by an anecdote about another highly influential radio programme, in its earliest days produced by Marson, *Caribbean Voices*, which ran from 1943 to 1958. When poems or stories by Caribbean writers were read by Caribbean readers with regional accents, some listeners in the West Indies objected.

Caribbean Voices helped to launch a cornucopia of literary talent, notably Sam Selvon, Kamau Brathwaite and V.S Naipaul. But what made *Caribbean Voices* very different from the other BBC programmes was its exceptional commitment to the West Indian voice. Much of this was to the credit of the programme's second, visionary, producer Henry Swanzy, leftish in politics and utterly committed to the development of Caribbean writing and writers on their own terms. On the surface, Swanzy's much repeated preference for writing that had "West Indian colour" sounds similar to the tropical exotica of programmes like *Serenade in Sepia*, but in reality what he meant was writing that was truthful in language and range of reference to the places and societies of its setting. His commitment was to West Indian writing for West Indians, for the West Indian listener, even if it offended the ears of the Anglicised West Indian middle class. Swanzy, was, for instance, one of the earliest promoters of the patois poetry of Louise Bennett – as well as the gritty stories of Sam Selvon about the seamier side of urban life in Port of Spain.[11] Bennett's work began in the 1940s and had an important influence on coming generations of poets, writers and thinkers who realized that the creole subversion of English was an asset, not a liability. Perhaps more immediately, Bennett was influential because recordings of her verse were issued on the Melodisc label, and these works greatly inspired Edric Connor.

Caribbean Voices thus played a priceless part in revealing what was not an obvious truth for the British establishment, namely that West Indians could and did write, and that their stories, worldview and philosophy had a cultural resonance greater than that of a wartime message from a serviceman or woman to their families listening intently on the island.[12] Swanzy's programme also showed, too, what was constraining in other areas of BBC broadcasting, where an interest in the West Indies as a cultural region establishing roots in the UK gave way to a limiting preoccupation with race and mixed marriages. The visionary nature of the Swanzy period is shown by the fact that it took many years for the higher education institutions in the Caribbean to catch up with what it had done. It was not until the 1970s that the University of the West Indies began teaching Caribbean literature and scholars such as the brilliant Barbadian Edward, later Kamau Brathwaite, fought for the acceptance of "nation language" in which the specifics of "black talk" would gain greater currency. [12]

But Britain's Black population was not solely dependent on official channels like the BBC for its self-image. One of the most important post-war developments was the emergence of Black journalism and magazines where Black people could read about Blacks as written by Blacks.

Launched in 1948 and costing 1 shilling and six pence, *Checkers*, published by Edward Scobie, was a groundbreaking publication; it was billed as Britain's "Premier Negro magazine" and it covered the arts, politics and social issues. Editorial standards were high and the design, graced with earnest portraits, was tasteful. Furthermore, *Checkers* was an international title. It was available on subscription in "Great Britain, Northern Ireland & Colonies." The Arts coverage was particularly strong. In the inaugural edition were features on Nigerian sculptor Benedict C. Enwonwu, African-American actress Hilda Simms and Guyanese jazz saxophonist Wally Stewart. There were also thought-provoking opinion pieces that give the magazine a transatlantic flavour: "The Status of the Negro in the United States" and "A Jamaican in London". The latter article, written by one R.

Donaldson, who sadly does not have a biography on the masthead, is an intensely moving account of the hardships experienced by West Indian immigrants. It ends with an unapologetically sharp denunciation of racial prejudice and a reminder that the subsequent disenchantment of the Negro is heightened by the social injustice prevalent in the West Indies. The article also shows standard English and Black talk bumping heads, as the author finds that there are certain things that cannot be expressed in "proper" language. Cultural authenticity and political polemic elide in the use of creolised English to indict Jamaica's pernicious racial hierarchy. "Big business is bossed mostly by Americans, Englishmen, Syrians and Chinese with a sprinkling of Indians. The real Jamaicans, are only in the island these days, to use a Jamaican phrase, 'fi mek up numbers'."

For a Jamaican journalist in 1948, this use of creole in a piece of formal English prose was daring. It looks forward to the writing of a pioneer such as Sam Selvon who not only accurately transcribed the Trini-talk of his characters – phrases like "Ma, you had me in one set of confusion this morning"[13] – as West Indian novelists had been doing since the early twentieth century, but in *The Lonely Londoners* (1956) narrating the whole novel in a creole-inflected Trinidadian English.

Running to just 24 pages, *Checkers* may have been relatively slender, and it only ran for five issues, but even a cursory trawl through its content reveals a magazine that made an earnest and effective attempt to give a voice to the Black British community and chronicle the social and cultural changes that resulted from mass migration, not least in asserting the legitimacy of other varieties of English.[14]

Calypsos, as in future years reggae was to do, demonstrate that West Indian vernaculars have a breadth of vocabulary that can be used with metaphorical and allegorical depth. Calypsonians used words that the English would not know, as well as using known words in ways they had not thought of. Race relations was a theme that exercised the minds of both Lord Kitchener and Lord Beginner in the 1950s, and the contrasts in the form and content of the language used on the former's "If You're Not White You're Black" and the latter's "Mix Up Matrimony" is fascinating.

Kitchener makes a number of excellent points about the phenomenon of the mixed-race woman who rejects her blackness, from attempts at hair straightening to a denial of African roots, but he also goes to the heart of the culture wars: language. When Kitch sings "You speak with exaggeration/To make the greatest impression", he is denouncing superficiality and recognizing the political need for straight-talking, which is the essence of calypso.

Beginner's treatise on love across the colour line has a different linguistic character. The title itself breaks with Standard English. "Mix Up Matrimony" is a union of a creolised term and a very formal English word. Beginner uses the recognizable, for metropolitan English listeners, formulation of mixed marriage in the first verse of the song, but he switches to mix-up matrimony in the second, and this signals an important duality, as he bounces freely between registers. "Mix up" exists because creole culture moulds vocabulary in a specific way, giving rise to compound nouns or adjectives that often have a sharp rhythmic impetus. "Mix up" swims in the same stream of invention as *cook up, jump up, mash up* and *nice up*, where the two-syllable punch of the word is a crucial part of its communicative power. Creolised English is characterized by such new conjunctions.

The history of the use of patois by calypsonians in the colonial period (when British governors could censor or ban) is a complex one. But what is striking is the linguistic freedom exercised by artists from an early stage in the development of the music. Beginner stands in the lineage of other calypsonians who reflected social realities through the language of the people. For example, Sam Manning, who lived in London two decades prior to Beginner, infused his lyrics with a deep Trinidadian-ness. In his 1925 song, "Brown Boy", he says of a ruffian who has slapped him about, "He black mah eye." The Standard English rendering of "He gave me a black eye" rhythmically would not flow.

"Mix Up Matrimony" is an upbeat song in which Beginner foretells a multi-cultural utopia that is not just confined to Britain – "Racial segregation universally fading gradually"– a cautious optimism that marked the thinking of some with regard to the issue of miscegenation at the dawn of the 1950s. This was broaching a hot topic at a time when the event of a son or daughter announcing the existence of a black partner could be explosive. Details in the song point to Beginner's Trinidadian cultural identity, as well as his worldview. In the first verse he sings "Chiney" instead of Chinese, but so rooted is the word Chiney in the Trinidadian vernacular it would have been unthinkable to replace it by Chinese, just as it would have been for Beginner to sing "two races" instead of "two race" as he does in the second verse. In this case the Standard English plural would have derailed the metric carriage and reduced the overall musicality of the stanza. But the real value of "Mix Up Matrimony" lies in its conjunctions of vocabulary. Matrimony is as proper as mix up is improper.

Some calypsos are more creolised than others, such as the frankly raucous turns of phrase in Mighty Terror's "Women Police", his suggestive love letter to the girls in blue – "I do anything to get arrest", "I hugging up mah police" "I could run straight and bite up one". Beyond the rich colour of the vocabulary, the audacity of the lyric – proposing to make overtures to a British policewoman – reflects his imagination as a writer. This is rooted in the essence of Trinidadian "picong", which places a premium on repartee and the exercise of invention when expressing the commonplace.

Many of the calypsos Melodisc and Lyragon put out in the 1950s have a similar linguistic and intellectual punch, and many broached subjects in their immediate environment – public transport, the authorities, race relations – as well as the iconic social events of the decade – the 1953 coronation of Queen Elizabeth, immortalized in Young Tiger's "I Was There (at the Coronation)" – upholding the *sine que non* of calypso as commentary on the here and now. The rise of the Black British calypso at roughly the same time as the West Indian novelists and poets found outlets for their work in London was not coincidental. It was an intriguing anticipation of the later but similar development of British reggae in the 1970s, by groups such as Steel Pulse, Aswad and Misty in Roots.

The meeting point between Kitchener, Beginner, Tiger et al and some of the writers is revealed in the many acrobatic turns of phrase in Sam Selvon's 1956 novel *The Lonely Londoners*,[14] the definitive account of the postwar immigrant experience: "It's not we that the people don't like… is the colour black." This is the great line that Kitch never wrote, but an utterance that could feasibly feature in one of his verses. This writer-singer kinship is also present in Selvon's choice of character names. Sir Galahad, the constant thorn in the flesh of the narrating protagonist, Moses Aloetta, has a mythical resonance. It is the stuff of legend, and as such chimes closely with the calypsonian who named himself Ivanhoe.

It is because of the parallel developments of the West Indian novel, the West Indian calypso and the West Indian radio broadcast, as exemplified by *Caribbean Voices*, that the late 1940s and early 50s is such a crucial stage in the history of Black culture in Britain. So much of the spirit, the personality of a Kitch or Beginner is in Selvon's writing (and even in V.S. Naipaul's earlier work) and so much of Selvon's intellect is in their singing. One was long form, the other short. One had a typewriter, the other a guitar.

Lyrically, calypso was, from its earliest incarnations, confrontational. Its use of coded language to outwit those in power upped its richness. But it was also about the chronicling of events and the depiction of daily realities in all areas of human existence, particularly those that drew focus to the individual, the way that he or she shaped his or her own destiny and the way that was in turn shaped by those with power. Which is why love and politics are essential themes in the calypso canon.

A subject that also captured the imagination was cricket, because it was an activity that had multiple strands of meaning. It was much more than sport. It was much more than spectacle. The cricket match in the West Indies, in a pre and postwar context, was a deeply political drama in which ruler and ruled, colonist and colonized, were drawn together on a stage with obvious gladiatorial connotations of hurling a leather ball towards the body of adversary who defends himself with a wooden bat, whose sleekly carved shape is weapon-like.

Cricket was also a site of racial struggle. Initially it was the preserve of the elite in the West Indies. The first sides to represent the region in international matches in the 1880s were dominated by white players; it would have been unseemly to allow the underclass to take part in an activity synonymous with refinement, and it was not until the 1920s that Blacks started to make the national team. As C.L.R. James recalls in his seminal study of cricket and its social ramifications, *Beyond A Boundary*,[15] clubs in Trinidad such as Queen's Park and Shamrock were exclusively European. Other clubs were for "brown" Trinidadians, others for Blacks. The first West Indians, in the eyes of the British ruling class, were not black. They were white.

The idea died hard. For example, when the Ministry of Information was explaining to the British public who West Indians were in the 1943 short film *West Indies Calling*, the narrator declared that "they are of a dozen different races," and then stated that they were "descendants of the British and French and Spanish adventurers who opened up the New World" *before* evoking "the African slaves who were brought across to work on the sugar plantations, Chinese shopkeepers, Hindus and Moslems from India." The camera zoomed in on white West Indian servicemen *before* showing any black person.

Race aside, in a context of colonial fragmentation, the West Indies cricket team was a powerful federalizing agent in Caribbean life. It was where the islands came together, each contributing their best players to create a regional superpower.

Prodigiously gifted players such as the legendary 3 Ws – Clyde Walcott, Everton Weekes and Frank Worrell – and the spinners – Sonny Ramadhin and Alf Valentine – signalled the coming of age of West Indian cricket in the 1950s. The success of the West Indies team established the men from the islands as a force to be reckoned with. Cricket became a source of West Indian pride. The pitch was thus a theatre where colonial subjects could defeat the former masters.

The visual drama of the game – the tricksy nature of the spin bowler; the athleticism of the fielder; the physical threat of the fast bowler; the Herculean sweep of a master batsman – were all grist to a calypsonian's mill. Unfolding slowly – between every ball the players and spectators have to wait as the bowler walks back to his mark – cricket offers scope for unbroken observation and attention to detail – which is precisely what defines the best calypsonians.

Recorded in London in 1950, Lord Beginner's "Victory Test Match" (also known as "Cricket Lovely Cricket") is one of the best examples of the genre. It hails the triumph of the West Indies over England in the 2nd match of the Test series, when players such as Clyde Walcott produced match-winning performances in the presence of King George VI at Lords, cricket's HQ. Beginner's use of word-play is impressive and his reference to the West Indian team's sense of ease has a sharp irony, given the fact that the right to belong in Britain, to enjoy the rights and privileges of citizenship, had been challenged by the Labour Ministry's mealy mouthed declaration that no "encouragement" would be given to further waves of migration.

> West Indies was feeling homely
> Their audience had them happy.

Of course, the reason why the tourists felt at home was because there were so many West Indians in the crowd. Whether they felt at home is another story.

By way of witty couplets that bring together key moments in the match, with the ensuing emotion experienced by the crowd, Beginner assumes the role of commentator as well as storyteller, and shows his keen eye and irrepressible linguistic prowess. True to form, he mixes registers, moving seamlessly from the creolised line "They gave the crowd plenty fun" to the formal phrasing of "The king was there well attired."

Later, there comes an even more impressive conjunction of formal and creolised expression, as Beginner starts to praise the W.I. players:

> But Gomez broke him down
> While Walcott lick them around.

To lick is one of the most expressive verbs of action in the West Indian vernacular, and although it firstly denotes "to beat or physically assault", the deeper implication is that a designated foe is being resoundingly defeated or that a task is being completed with efficiency and satisfaction. Which is why lick is often turned into the phrasal verb as in *He lick down the door* or *He lick down the man*. So Beginner's formulation *Walcott lick them around* brings into play the emphatically vivid image of the enemy, the England cricket team, being laid low in a comprehensive way, something which the British might express as *Walcott smashed them all over the park*. But that does not have the same flavour as *Walcott lick them around*. That is what would be heard in a rum shack in Port of Spain or a shebeen in Notting Hill or Moss Side, not a BBC commentary box.

Beginner goes on to evoke the galvanizing, unifying power of cricket among the Caribbean islands, and joyously revels in victory following the dismissal of the English batsman, Cyril Washbrook.

> When Washbrook's century had ended
> West Indies voices all blended

With his closing verse, Beginner paints a masterful tableau that has great sociopolitical depth. Beyond the symbolic victory over Empire, the Test series provided an opportunity for members of the West Indian community located up and down the country to assemble. Although the contest reached its conclusion at Lords in London, one of the other matches took place at Old Trafford in Manchester, which gave Blacks from Liverpool, Manchester, Birmingham, and beyond, the opportunity to experience this sporting and political event as a collective entity. So the line, "West Indies voices all blended", refers both to the union of different islands in the West Indian team and the various Caribbean communities found in Britain. That single line, so incisive in its simplicity, marks out "Victory Test Match" as one of the seminal theme tunes to a national manifestation of Blacks living in postwar Britain. Cricket, rather than London, is the place for me.

West Indian voices also blended in song when euphoric fans scrambled onto the outfield of Lords to demonstrate the joy they could not contain. They began to sing. It turned into a carnival road march. Exultation could have turned to expulsion. Alarmed by the sight of mostly young black men taking part in a pitch invasion, the very sight of which invoked the deepest paranoia of the wild or "savage" behaviour that defined a colonial vision of Africa and the West Indies, the police readied for action. However, a senior official from the MCC – Marylebone Cricket Club – in a wise moment given that police interventions on the cricket field in the Caribbean had provoked riots, advised the police not to intervene. The friends of the tourists were allowed to sing their songs. They could have their moment in the sun.

For the crowd it was about the right to free assembly and movement in public spaces. As Beginner sang: "Hats went in the air/People shout and jump without fear."

Lord Kitchener was also present at the game and he reported:

After the match I took my guitar and called a few West Indians, and I went round the cricket field singing and dancing. That was a song I made up. So while we're dancing up come a policeman and arrested me.

And while he was taking me out of the field, the English people boo him, they said 'Leave him alone, let him enjoy himself! They won the match, let him enjoy himself.' And he had to let me loose because he was embarrassed. So I took the crowd with me singing and dancing, from Lord's, into Piccadilly in the heart of London..."[16]

A black musician with a guitar leading others in an improvised celebration. Sounds familiar? Just five years prior to the Test Match, the Nigerian bandleader Ambrose Campbell had led his ensemble through the streets of Piccadilly on VE Day. Victories in a world war and a sporting event may not be comparable, but jubilation when one is far from home is an essential human need. Those in power, possibly mesmerized by the sound of calypso, were able to recognize as much.

Notes

1. Stephen Bourne *Black In The British Frame* (Cassell, 1998), p. 81.
2. Fela Sowande was an excellent jazz organist-pianist as well as a composer and played duets with the legendary Fats Waller in London in the 1930s.
3. Stephen Bourne *Black in the British Frame*, p. 81.
4. Footage of *Serenade in Sepia* is widely available on the internet.
5. For Connor's view, see *Horizons: The Life and Times of Edric Connor* (Ian Randle Publishers, 2007).
6. *Songs from Trinidad* (Oxford University Press, 1959) came with sheet music and a long informative preface by Connor.
7. *Tropic Magazine*, March 1960, p. 12.
8. Amanda Bidnall, *The West Indian Generation: Remaking British Culture in London, 1945-1965* (Liverpool University Press, 2017).
9. See Anne Spry Rush's perceptive account of the West Indian middle class, *Bonds of Empire: West Indians and Britishness from Victoria to Decolonisation* (Oxford University Press, 2011).
10. *West Indies Calling* can be found in the internet: https://www.youtube.com/watch?v=DcLkGHpw7nY Pathe News.
11. See Glyne A. Griffiths, *The BBC and the Development of Anglophone Caribbean Literature, 1943-1958* (Palgrave MacMillan 2016).
12. See Kamau Brathwaite, *The History of the Voice* (New Beacon Books, 1984).
13. Sam Selvon, *The Lonely Londoners* (Longman, 1956) p. 82.
14. *The Lonely Londoners*, p. 89.
15. C.L.R. James, *Beyond A Boundary* (Hutchinson, 1963). It is worth noting that James's masterwork, *The Black Jacobins* (1938), was an essential text for politically-conscious artists such as Robeson (who in 1936 took the lead part in the stage play that James wrote on Toussaint L'Ouverture and the Haitian revolution.
16. David Kynaston, *Austerity Britain, 1945-51* (Bloomsbury, 2007) p. 516. See also Anthony Joseph's recent *Kitch: A Fictional Biography of a Calypso Icon* (Peepal Tree, 2018).

14 SCALING DIZZY HEIGHTS

"I really don't remember how we met, but when I heard him I knew he was different, and I blagged Decca into letting me record him."
— Producer Tony Hall on Dizzy Reece, born Kingston, Jamaica, 1931, arrived London, England, 1948.

By the 1950s the main product of the music industry had changed. Once sheet music had been the dominant format in which songs were disseminated, but record companies were increasingly marketing the vinyl record, which, in the case of innovative jazz artists such as Dizzy Gillespie and Charlie Parker, was crucial. Few people would have been able to recreate their music on a piano in their front room using dots and dashes on a stave, as they could do with Broadway tunes. Even when based on such a tune such as Cole Porter's "Love For Sale", Parker's teasingly wry saxophone solo, though set to the chord changes of this song, had to be *heard* so far did it deconstruct the familiar melody. Music like Parker's indeed raised the question of why publishers and writers should receive greater royalties than an improvising artist who had eclipsed the original composition, which had served as a point of departure for a new creative flight of fancy.

The individuality of performance was one of many factors that fostered this transition away from sheet music. In the postwar period, listening to vinyl discs or tuning into concerts on the radio had a cultural currency that made the ritual of a family singalong around the piano lose its appeal. The shift to vinyl was also a shift from 78 rpm, fragile, three-minutes-a-side records, to the long player in the early 1950s, with around twenty minutes a side. This obviously allowed for more extended compositions in post-war jazz. Even so, live concerts remained a crucial part of the career of a jazz artist because there was relatively little money to be made from album sales, primarily because markets and avenues of promotion were less developed than they are today. The BBC had "gramophone interludes" rather than whole programmes comprising recorded music – which made little sense given the abundance of brilliant albums being made by Parker and others – and this issue became one of the key battles fought during the development of popular music in the decades to come.

If jazz artists were to make a breakthrough from the local to the national and the international, their work had to be presented in a range of formats. They had to play all over the country *and* have albums to their name in order to gain any kind of foothold in the new media, such as music magazines like *Melody Maker*. The album was a calling card that raised profile, increased demand and hopefully brought in more gigs.

From a cursory glance at the mechanics of the music and record industries of the late 1940s and early '50s, it becomes clear that the musicians who made albums and went on tour had to be supported by at least one if not several people oiling the wheels of their career: booking agent, club owner, promoter, producer, talent scout. All of these formed a crucial interface between the artist and the general public.

Talent alone did not suffice. Of all the game-changers in an artist's career, the one that tends to count above others is the presence of a good manager. This can explain why some musicians are able to "make it" and others do not. It was not until the mid 1980s, for instance, that Andy Hamilton found himself a good manager in the shape of Alan Cross. He had survived as a musician but memorable as Hamilton's gigs were reported to be, they had no resonance outside of the Midlands. His major handicap was lack of representation and as a result he did not record until the 1980s, so vinyl albums bearing the name Andy Hamilton & The Blue Notes were just not available.[1]

It is worth pointing out that in the 1950s, musicians did not have home studios and that the cost of recording was frequently prohibitive. Hence the power of the labels – who had access to studios, engineering equipment and a network of pressing plants – to control the products of those actually making the music. This power was one of the reasons why there are many tragic stories of cynical exploitation, particularly of the young and naïve, or those who made themselves vulnerable through drug addiction so that they would sign away their creative endeavours for a paltry sum to secure their next fix.

Just as the BBC was a powerful gatekeeper (with a monopoly at that time as far as radio was concerned), so the major record labels, of which there were four in Britain – EMI, Parlophone, Pye and Decca – had a distinct hierarchy and stratification that reflected the realities of the British class structure. Bosses and executives had usually attended public school, as did those who worked in the department of Artist & Repertoire, the nerve centre of the record industry.

A&R men sourced new artists and had a huge say in who was given a recording contract and who wasn't, and in some cases what the precise nature of their artistic output would be. However, if stories of heartlessly manipulative A&R men forcing their charges to record monstrosities in the world of pop were legion, they were less so in jazz. Even so, there was not a clear boundary between A&R as talent scout and A&R as producer or supervisor of a recording session, who might advise on the repertoire or the tempo of a piece. A &R men also provided players and engineers with the right sustenance.[2]

A&R men were a vital part of the record label's in-house team, but there were also freelancers who, on hearing a musician they thought worth recording, would put that name forward to a major record label or one of its subsidiaries. Whilst there were many clubs and concert halls in the regions, the boardrooms, offices and bulk of recording studios were located was London. An artist such as Andy Hamilton, without a capable manager or A&R to shout for him in London, was at a substantial disadvantage.

If we turn our attention to Tony Hall, one of Britain's great jazz talent-scouts and producers, we can see how the destiny of one of Andy Hamilton's compatriots unfolded in an entirely different way. Hall was an example of a music industry executive who was very much "on the scene", having been a popular MC at the Flamingo club in Wardour Street in Soho. He was also a respected record reviewer.

It was in London in the early 1950s that Hall first came across a Jamaican trumpeter barely out of his teens. His name was Alphonso Son "Dizzy" Reece (1931-), who like many significant post-war Jamaican jazz and ska musicians received lessons in theory at the Alpha Boys School, an institution for "wayward youth", run by strict nuns who believed in the redemptive power of arts and culture. "Maybe in a club?" came Hall's reply when I asked him in his smart West End office in 2013 exactly where he first heard Reece. "I really don't remember how we met, but when I heard him I knew he was different. And I blagged Decca into letting me record him."[3] Note the terms in which the history is couched. To blag is to lobby, to press the case for something or somebody in whom you believe.

Hall was true to his word and his association with Reece lasted for many years during which time Reece created a body of work that marks him out as one of the key figures in postwar British jazz. Hall worked for Tempo records, a subsidiary of the Vogue-Decca corporation, and first showcased Reece by way of a series of 10" releases, such as 1955's *A New Star*, a title which makes abundantly clear how the English A&R man saw his West Indian protégé.

Bebopper that he was, Reece had nonetheless had a thorough grounding in jazz history while growing up in Kingston. By his own admission, New Orleans, Dixieland and swing trumpet pioneers, from King Oliver to Buck Clayton[4] via Louis Armstrong had been early sources of inspiration, and like many of his peers he had debuted in swing dance bands. At the tender age of just fourteen he was second trumpet in Jack Brown's Swing Stars in Kingston.

Arriving in England on the *Windrush* in the summer of 1948, Reece made a fairly inauspicious start on the London jazz scene and is known to have spent time in the regions, in Liverpool and possibly Birmingham. But he returned to London. And here is one of the great ironies of Black music in Britain: Andy Hamilton went to Birmingham because he had heard that Dizzy Reece was there, while Reece was finding his way into the record business in London, the place where, professionally speaking, Hamilton really needed to be.

What is well documented is Reece's move to continental Europe, where he had the opportunity to hone his craft and in the space of four remarkably active years, from 1949 to 1953, when he sojourned in France, Germany, Holland and Italy, where he was able to sit in with American legends such as Don Byas and the lesser known Jay Cameron.

Reece came back to London in 1954 and worked with Tommy Pollard and Jamaican compatriot Wilton "Bogey" Gaynair among others. With Tony Hall's patronage, he started to put together an impressive portfolio of recordings under his own name and as a sideman with the likes of the brilliant multi-instrumentalist, Victor Feldman, whose father Robert had opened the Feldman Swing club on Oxford Street in the early 1940s. This later became the 100 Club and employed a young Tony Hall as an MC.

It was with Feldman that Reece made some of his most impressive playing, none more so than on 1956's *Progress Report*, a disc that warrants a place in the pantheon of modern British jazz. Assembled from several sessions whose personnel included feted players such as tenor saxophonist Ronnie Scott and drummer Phil Seamen, as well as the lesser known pianists Terry Shannon and the wonderfully named Johnny Weed, this is a superlative album for a number of reasons.

Considering that the line-up changed on all of the three sessions cut in April, July and December, the work is remarkably coherent. This is really a compilation of Reece's music, which is unusual given the fact that whole albums were often recorded relatively quickly in those days, with the best bands knocking off several tunes in a day or an afternoon. *Progress Report*[5] sees Reece confirm his allegiance to bebop, explicitly so on one of the school's great exam papers, Charlie Parker's "Scrapple from the Apple" as well as a few originals cut from a similar idiomatic cloth, such as Reece's "Chorous" and Feldman's "Momentum". All of the trademarks of the bebop jazz model – brisk tempos; 32 bar themes; rapid chord changes; trading of 4 bar statements – are used liberally, but the classic sound of bebop was altered in several ways. For the most part, the quintet with a trumpet-saxophone front line was the bebop norm, but Reece only used this for two pieces. A far less common configuration of trumpet and guitar, the latter played by Dave Goldberg, was used on two pieces but on three songs Reece was backed only by piano, double bass and drums – then not a greatly used set up.

Bebop had weaned listeners on the full, weighty sound of trumpet and saxophone as a powerful joint force, from Dizzy Gillespie and Charlie

Parker to Kenny Dorham and Sonny Stitt via Fats Navarro and Eddie "Lockjaw" Davis. Trumpeters, notably Miles Davis on his overlooked *The Musings of Miles*, did lead saxophone-less quartets, but the format was not as widespread as the quintet where brass combined with reed. The saxophone, especially a tenor, could provide a tonal weightiness and darker timbres to offset the bright, more pinched sounds of the trumpet, an instrument whose natural range is higher. Even without the reed alongside him, Reece does not sound thin or wispy.

His variety of timbres is wide. He moves assuredly between a radiant clarion call and a more dimmed, quite slurred tone. Reece also took good advantage of the trumpet's lower range to create a purring warmth that significantly enhanced the emotional charge and lyricism of his performances.

"Now", a Reece original, is a minor blues with a jaunty, yet wry character, in which drummer Phil Seamen and double bassist Lloyd Thompson mark the 4 to the bar groove with a gossamer lightness of touch. The piece sees Reece play with dramatic verve, highlighting the slightly off-kilter nature of the melody by a supple handling of time, and variations in his attack on a phrase, which can be subtle or stark. Several times he makes marked jumps in volume, or syncopates vigorously, starting a new figure either ahead of, or well after, the downbeat. He is playing with, not just on the pulse.

During Reece's opening and closing statement of the melody, he makes the occasional fleeting pause in his phrases or sustains and gives more body to a note over a few beats, introducing a flash of colour without being overly showy. Or he holds back a touch. When he launches into his improvisation, he alternates lengthy, fluid statements and clenched, clipped lines that are teasing and elliptical, as if he is wont to intrigue the listener rather than tell all at once. There's no rush to a climax.

As the best "comping" pianists do, Victor Feldman both supports and extends ideas. His movement between soft and punchy chords matches Reece's varying stance and with the two men working on a similar wavelength, the leader's 64 bar solo has a supportive framework in which to evolve. At several junctures Reece gives a low, slightly muffled moan to contrast sharply with his gleaming high notes, but the peak of the improvisation is a thrilling moment at the end of bar 41, during which the trumpet acquires a distinctly nasal, grainy sound that strongly implies the yearning cry of Middle Eastern music. This was entirely logical, given the fact that Reece had shown an interest in non-western music and culture from an early stage of his career. His desire to investigate the quartertones common to Arabic voices and strings was an integral part of his development, which became explicit when he recorded the majestic album *Asia Minor*[6] in 1962.

Universal as Reece's musical interests were, America was nonetheless of major importance to his career development in the mid 1950s, and going there raised his profile further. Some critics had been dismissive of Reece's earliest recordings, but others recognized the originality of his approach. Rather than base his playing on Miles Davis alone, he was combining that model with others and creating his own aesthetic, which, with its occasionally provocative if not disruptive impulses, became almost a form of "ugly beauty".

Miles Davis, though, played a bigger part in the Reece story than most have imagined. "Eventually, I sent some recordings over to Miles and Miles spread the word around New York about Dizzy,"[7] recalls Tony Hall. Given the fact that by the mid 1950s Davis had enormous stature in jazz, his endorsement of any musician carried weight, so his words brought attention to Reece. "He has soul, originality, and above all he is not afraid to blow with fire."[8]

Reece's personality had some of the traits familiar in artists who are single-minded in the work they produce. Hall described him as being "very picky. The white musicians found him to be difficult at times, but it was probably because in his own way he was a perfectionist and he had his own standards, his own chord changes and if other people didn't like them that was really too bad. They were his, and those were the changes that he wanted to play."

Hall pulled more strings. "I also got Alfred Lion on Dizzy's case. Ultimately I got Dizzy his contract with Blue Note." Indeed, the *Blues In Trinity* album was Reece's 1958 debut for the label that remains to this day one of the most iconic in jazz, and whose enormous cultural resonance can be heard in the way that its slogan "The finest in jazz since 1939" has been obliquely adapted by progressive imprints in hip-hop such as Okayplayer whose strap line is "Giving You True Notes Since 1987". The history is there in the contemporary slogan.

London may have been the centre of the record and the music industry in Britain, but New York was the jazz capital of the world, and to have the opportunity to make albums for a label as prestigious as Blue Note was a substantial accolade for a London-based player. At the time relatively few Britons were able to do this, even though two of Reece's collaborators took similar steps. Tubby Hayes recorded albums in New York with the cream of the city's bebop scene, while Victor Feldman emigrated to America and saw his career flourish by way of highly prestigious sideman gigs with Miles Davis, Shelley Manne and Julian 'Cannonball' Adderley. The latter can be heard gently ribbing the pianist's English accent on his classic live performance of "The Chant".[9] Reece recorded 1958's *Blues In Trinity* at the Decca studios in London. It was a memorable session with notable transatlantic personnel – American trumpeter Donald Byrd and English saxophonist Tubby Hayes are the other star horn players – and it further cemented the international status of the still young Jamaican. Thereafter, Reece left London for New York in 1959, and his and Feldman's cases illustrate how some players will always gravitate to what they see as the location that will best serve them artistically and professionally, assuming that they are given the chance to do so.

Though Reece was ultimately lost to the UK, prior to that his leadership of multi-racial bands was significant at a time when the magnitude of cultural and political change wrought by immigration was becoming apparent. The musical relationship between Reece and Feldman, a black West Indian and a white Englishman, was a symbol of an understanding that reached beyond colour, a ray of beautiful art made away from the shadow of bigotry.

A Woman, Black and Successful

If Reece's career showed the importance of far-sighted managerial support, he had a musical peer whose career showed that a black woman could be no less focused and successful. Indeed, in monetary terms, the pianist Winifred Atwell (1914-1983) was undoubtedly one of the most successful black artists of this period. Hers was an example of just how far an artist of colour could go when talent was combined with the patronage of a producer and a proactive label. That Atwell achieved this as an instrumentalist and a woman is quite remarkable.

From its first stirrings in the late 19th century, jazz had been mostly a male preserve, certainly in terms of the major instrumentalists. Women soloists and bandleaders were far less common and there was a great deal of scepticism around the ability of those who did come to the fore, such as the excellent trumpeter, Valaida Snow, an artist who performed in America, Great Britain and Europe in the 1930s. She showed that the misogynist admonition that "Woman ain't supposed to play no horn!" was good only for ears made of cloth. There was also Lil Hardin, at one time married to Louis Armstrong, a brilliant pianist who taught her husband a great deal of music theory. What was at issue was the lack of opportunities that women had to express themselves in whichever way they saw fit.[10]

Hence the emergence in 1950s Britain of a female artist who was not a singer, but a player with a good command of her instrument, who became a star, is a noteworthy one. Winifred Atwell based this achievement not only on her skills, but her ability to captivate an audience through her personality as well as her music. It helped that her backwards-looking musical style, was one that a popular audience felt comfortable with. Bebop, in Britain at least, was a minority pleasure.

Atwell was born in Tunapuna, Trinidad, then a large town near Port of Spain best known as the birth place of the Marxist writer C.L.R. James. A child prodigy, Atwell initially trained as a pharmacist but moved to America to study classical music at the age of twenty-six, before coming to Britain to take up a place at the Royal Academy of Music, where she became the first woman pianist to gain the highest grade for performance. In order to put herself through college, Atwell played theatres and small clubs in London, and her speciality was a style that was a throwback to the kind of early 20th century jazz that had been performed as part of the musical, *In Dahomey*, which toured Britain back in 1903: ragtime. She had apparently learnt jazz on the American military bases in Trinidad.[11]

Atwell was a skilled exponent of the genre with a penchant for attacking her right-hand lines with great vigour, so that they sounded like bell chimes set to the chord progressions of the blues. She quickly came to the attention of Decca producer, Hugh Mendl, a Radley old boy who had worked as a song plugger before making the move into A&R. His discovery of Atwell launched his own career as a music industry executive with vision. (He also played a role in the signing of the future icons of British pop, who based their style on African American blues – The Rolling Stones.) Mendl produced Atwell's 1952 hit, "Black and White Rag", a jaunty, irrepressibly cheery piece that she performed on a honky-tonk piano, a battered upright that had tacks or nails punched onto all of the regular, felt-padded hammers, which gave the instrument a clanging, metallic sound that enhanced its percussive nature. "Black and White Rag" is credited with starting something of a fad for honky-tonk piano playing throughout Britain, and it consolidated Atwell's rising commercial status.

Tension between the legitimacy of the classical world and the perceived illegitimacy of forms of popular Black music had been prevalent in the West for many decades, so Atwell's decision to deploy "the other pianna", this beaten-up device, was in a way subversive. She serves as a reminder of the fact that there was a strong classical music tradition throughout the West Indies, and that those who subscribed to British cultural norms would have wanted their children to choose Handel and Elgar over Armstrong and Basie. Some would have been positively alarmed to know that their children had been corrupted by jazz.[12] Some West Indians would only have given Atwell their seal of approval had she performed Grieg rather than "boogie" music.

So here was a classically-trained pianist using her skills on an instrument that some would have deemed beneath her, and any assumption of a wilful gimmick on Atwell's part could not disguise the fact that her honky tonk tunes actually placed her in a rich and influential cultural continuum. She gave a bastard sound beauty, she told us bad meant good, a tenet of the blues, the foundation of the future idioms of funk and rock.

Between 1952 and 1956, Atwell had no fewer than eight singles in the British top ten, of which "The Poor People of Paris" raced to the top of the charts. She became the first Black artist to score a number one. As her career unfolded, Atwell became a phenomenon, selling in excess of 20 million records, and selling out tours of Australia where she broke box office records to rank as

WINIFRED ATTWELL

one of the country's top earners. Atwell's immense popularity indicated that there was a market for nostalgia. "Black And White Rag" had been written by the American composer George Botsford in 1908. Her command of ragtime and its outgrowth, boogie woogie, was solid, but her approach would have drawn indifference if not contempt from the leading jazz soloists of the day, because she had none of the advanced harmonic or rhythmic ideas of bebop innovators such as Bud Powell[13], who expanded the language of jazz piano between the early and mid 1950s. This would not have mattered to Atwell, because she was winning over the British public with one more monster seller, "Let's Have Another Party" (1954). She made people smile. Her songs had an undeniable feel-good factor, and that was partly due to the sound as well as the sheer brio with which she performed. What jumps out is their tonal brightness, as if the right-hand phrases are glittering into life, while the bass chords lend a strong sense of backbone to the sharp rhythmic flurries. Her accompaniment of drums and guitar was deployed lightly, with the former mostly using brushes rather than sticks, so that Atwell's bustling work on the keyboard is the prominent element for the listener.

Today, some of her music retains charm. But she sways easily between infectious ditty and tiresome kitsch. On the one hand, a song such as "The Poor People of Paris" is a cloying number whose slush quotient is upped by the ill-advised use of a whistle-like countermelody, for which a producer should have had his *oignons* well and truly *rotied*. On the other hand "Five Finger Boogie" is sweetly zestful rhythm playing. But regardless of the creative value of her work, Atwell was an artist of integrity whose sharpness of execution never wavered. There is an absolute precision in her recorded performances that can be ascribed to her advanced training. She was, after all, a classical musician who happened upon a pop career rather than a pop musician aspiring to reach the level of a classical musician.

And there were other brilliant women like Atwell across the West Indies, who played a classical repertoire to a high standard, but who did not devote themselves to music because of other talents. There was Barbara Wilkins, who hailed from Brown's Town Jamaica, a brilliant student who obtained a B.A in social science at McGill University, the 'Oxford' of Canada, and went on to study law. In 1948, she became a member of the Inns of Court in London and subsequently gained entry to the Bar. But one of her great loves was music, and she also found time to study that formally. In 1938 she was awarded a Gold Medal from the Royal School of Music in London for having scored the highest marks in the final grades of piano among students in the West Indies. She then came to Britain to further her musical education in 1939, but the outbreak of war saw her return to Jamaica. However, she continued to excel musically, passing the Intermediate Arts Examination of London University by correspondence. She also played cello in the Jamaican Symphony Orchestra.

Wilkins's story indicates the dynamism of a woman of colour who was a mere historical footnote. Her story also reminds us of the degree of control Britain exerted over education in its colonies. The exams taken were found only in the "mother country". The official term that was used to describe Barbara Wilkins was "external student".

Notes

1. Interview with author, 2015.
2. Musicians and producers have confirmed over the years that the sustenance could be anything from food to alcohol to narcotics.
3. Interview with the author, Soho, London, 2013.
4. Buck Clayton was a key member of the Count Basie big band between the mid 1930s to the mid 1950s.
5. Dizzy Reece, *Progress* Report (Jasmine, 1956).
6. Dizzy Reece, *Asia Minor* (Original Jazz Classics, 1962).
7. Interview with the author, Soho, London, 2013.
8. Sleeve notes of Dizzy Reece, *Asia Minor*.
9. Cannonball Adderley, *The Chant*, (Riverside, 1960).
10. This was a commonly held view among leading American jazz artists, particularly the pianist Geri Allen (1957-2017), who the author interviewed several times between 1998 and 2004.
11. For the biographical material on Winifred Atwell, see *Checkers* magazine, November 1948.
12. In his autobiography *Bass Lines* Coleridge Goode tells of how horrified his classical music-loving father would have been to know his son was playing jazz.
13. Bud Powell was one of the greatest pianists in the history of jazz, and his influence on a host of significant players, notably Bill Evans, Chick Corea and Herbie Hancock was immeasurable.

15 NORTH BY NORTH WEST

The band at The Nile was a rehearsal high-life band. And that was the strangest high life you've ever heard because it was a mixture of African-Caribbeans, Africans, white guys... all sorts who used to play there, so it really was quite groovy, quite jazzy.
— Saxophonist Tosh Ryan on The Nile club, Moss Side, Manchester.

I was in The Capital playing [opposite The Nile]. It was packed out and this high commissioner from Ghana came over and said "Boy, they'd love you in Ghana... [with your] high life." But it's calypso we were playing.
— Vocalist/guitarist Ossie Roberts.

"Shebeen" is a nice example of linguistic cross-fertilization. Some may associate the word with the rickety, tin-roofed, after-hours drinking dens of township South Africa, but it actually derives from the Gaelic "sibin", which means moonshine whiskey. Thus the word straddles communities that were both subjected to social stigma. Although the shebeens of Notting Hill in 1950s Britain noted in the previous chapter, with their blues in the basement, are an integral part of Black London's musical history, they were by no means exclusive to the capital. They were also found in Bristol, Birmingham, Leeds, Liverpool and Nottingham, wherever there was a quarter where West Indians were ghettoised by discrimination in housing.

The exploitative methods of property owners were the same everywhere. In Manchester, Moss Side, an electoral ward located roughly two miles to the south of the city centre, had become a blighted slum in the 1950s. By the end of the decade, a series of articles in the *Manchester Evening News* by Barry Cockroft examined the challenges of life in the city for immigrants. His insights resonated with the views of those who lived there. "Vice was raising quite a stench in this jaded relic of a once respectable Victorian suburb long before a calypso rang out among the flaking walls."[1]

West Africans and West Indians, who collectively numbered 10,000 Manchester inhabitants (along with 6,000 Poles), found themselves concentrated in Moss Side, which white people were leaving in favour of newly-built council housing in Withenshaw. With this exodus came the opportunity for landlords to let the crumbling rows of terraced houses, which were often in urgent need of refurbishment. Multiple occupancy of single rooms, inadequate leisure facilities and fluctuating employment prospects made life bleak for Manchester's Black population. Yet first hand accounts from the period suggest that the Black community made compensations for itself. As well as the shebeens in which Black music was heard on records, there also developed a network of clubs and a plethora of live bands. Tosh Ryan, a baritone saxophonist born in Withenshaw, who became part of the burgeoning music scene in Moss Side, recalls:

> The only kind of upside of all of this, was what was taking place in the social life, which was absolutely vibrant. You could hear music coming out of buildings all the time. That's what I liked. It was like looking at some kind of history of Harlem where people were sat on steps because the houses were pretty similar. They had big steps and people would sit outside and music would be playing constantly. Calypso, jazz, African... all sorts.
> Going into Moss side, it was like entering a whole new world because at the same time there was the 'beat culture' going on; all that American influence of Kerouac and Ginsberg was part of this whole fusion It wasn't just a music scene, it was a whole cultural bubble it was amazing."[2]

Jack Kerouac and Allen Ginsberg were the celebrated "beat" writers who came to prominence in the 1950s, drawing on the revolutionary energy of bebop and modern jazz to fashion what became known as the counterculture, in opposition to mainstream America. Whether Blacks, immigrants, political radicals or homosexuals, the marginalised were a vital part of the canvas these writers sought to depict, and the phenomenon of arty intellectuals "slumming it", as they had once done in Harlem, was also part of the scene in both Notting Hill and Moss Side.

There could be no greater evidence of the status of Moss Side as a brown town than the story of Whit Stennett, a key figure in Black Manchester, who travelled from Jamaica in 1959 and later became a mayor in the metropolitan borough of Trafford. In his very engaging autobiography *A Bittersweet Journey* he recalls how, without discussion, a taxi driver took him straight to Moss Side on arrival in the city. There was no need to ask where to go. The fare was black. [3]

Stennett depicts Moss Side as a place where the Black community was closely knit, where grocers selling yam, sweet potatoes and breadfruit became unofficial "liming spots"[4] after men tried their luck at the Labour Exchange on Aytoun Street. Beyond the wedding parties and dances, organised by a man named Gilbert Barrett, it was really the shebeens that were the crux of social life in the black community.

There had been a black population in Manchester from the mid 19th century, but the community really became more conspicuous when it became a focal point for Black political activity in the late 1930s. A dynamic Guyanese lecturer and entrepreneur, George Thomas Griffith, who adopted the name Ras Tafari Makonnen after committing to Ethiopian resistance following Mussolini's invasion in 1935, had emerged as a lightning rod for black solidarity in the city. He opened a chain of restaurants that became a hub for West Indians, Africans and African-American troops in nearby bases, and the accrued revenue from venues such as the Cosmopolitan was funnelled into political activity, particularly the Fifth Pan African Congress that took place in Manchester in 1945, with fellow organisers Trinidadian George Padmore and future Ghanaian president, Kwame Nkrumah, dedicated to the total liberation of Africa and the West Indies from colonial rule.[5]

The first four meetings of the Congress had taken place in London, but Manchester became a suitable location for the fifth because of a growing synergy of cultural initiatives and events. While Black GIs flocked to Manchester to socialize, Makonnen was producing pamphlets and a monthly periodical *Pan-Africa*, focusing on "African life, thought and history", and he opened a bookshop to sell this and related titles. Certainly, the Fifth Pan African Congress was a landmark event; it was scheduled around the same time as the meeting of the World Federation of Trade Unions in Paris, and had an impressively wide span of participation. Twenty delegates were sent by fifteen organizations in West Africa, six represented organisations in East and South Africa, thirty-three came from the West Indies and thirty-five from a variety of organisations in Britain. The pioneering African-American writer and civil-rights campaigner W.E.B Dubois, Mrs Marcus Garvey, Jomo Kenyatta, and Dr Hastings K. Banda were all present in Chorlton Town Hall.

The 1950s were, of course, a pivotal moment in world history precisely because the key issue of the human rights of ethnic minorities, of colonised people, of women became more pressing. It was a time when Blacks were struggling for equal rights in the USA – and the British were committing the most despicable atrocities in Kenya.[6] It was a time when voices of dissent articulated the grounds of the struggle, none more influential than that of the revolutionary Martiniquan psychiatrist-author, Frantz Fanon, whose seminal 1952 text *Black Skin, White Masks*,[7] was acutely relevant to understanding the trauma of the post-slavery condition of Blacks and colonials.

It was Algeria's bloody and protracted struggle for independence from France, a conflict in which Fanon was directly involved,[8] that became the signal for the flames of decolonisation to spread throughout Africa and the West Indies, and for the emergence of inspirational national leaders such as Kenya's Jomo Kenyatta, Ghana's Kwame Nkrumah and Nigeria's Nnamdi Azikiwe. This was a fulfilment of ambitions laid decades before, not least in the relationship of the singer-actor-activist, Paul Robeson who, as noted above had known and bonded with these leaders when they were students in the 1930s. This was the context in which the Fifth Congress took place.

Illustrious as some of the people present at the Manchester Congress were, it was not just about the intelligentsia and the Black politico-literary class talking shop. The Congress had a proletarian character, or a leaning towards Black working class struggle that was reflected the involvement of many trade unions and workers organisations, from the Negro Welfare Centre in Liverpool and the Trinidad Oilfield Workers Trade Union, to the Grenada Labour Party and the Gold Coast Railwaymen's Union. The Fifth Congress can be seen as a high point in the history of Black Manchester, but that history was also marked by a more continuous activism that was transforming the cultural life of the city.

As Tosh Ryan recalls, high life was the staple musical diet at Moss Side clubs such as The Nile, a very popular haunt run by a man known as Teacher Sunday – Teacher because he was a conscientious educator, Sunday because that was the day of his birth – an anglicisation of West African naming practices. What his birth name was is unknown.[7]

Dozens of musicians regularly pitched up at jam sessions at clubs such as The Nile. Sadly the names of many have been lost, but one was a Nigerian percussionists known as Beezy Bello, who became known for his excellent work on the talking drum, an instrument that requires a great deal of dexterity to draw out its full range of timbres.

The human geography of Moss Side played a part in the cultural explosion of the mid 1950s that carried over into the following decade. The area was small and the central thoroughfares such as Princes Road and Denmark Street were easy to negotiate, which meant that West Africans and West Indians were bound to mingle, and that any musicians, black or white, would have had no trouble hearing about the sessions that were taking place in the clubs.

Tosh Ryan makes several important points about the fluidity of the musical vocabulary heard at The Nile:

> It was basically people playing a mishmash of American blues, really. A lot of that happened because it was easier [music] for people to play together. The band at The Nile was a rehearsal high life band. And that was the strangest high life you've ever heard because it was a mixture of African-Caribbeans, Africans, white guys… all sorts used to play there so it really was quite groovy, quite jazzy. There was a crossover in clubs that just kind of happened naturally, by the way of things.
>
> I mean to start off, you would get a bassist playing a particular type of Caribbean rhythm, then you'd get an African drummer, and then you'd get these would-be, wannabe jazz players on horns, all trying to mimic what they heard on record, so it wasn't really definable. I'd have difficulty saying what it was. It did have quite often a high life flavour. There was good food too. I mean you'd get goat and stuff."[8]

Culinary delights were also available at another popular haunt that attracted revellers and musicians in equal measure. The Lagos Lagoon, "run by a really nice guy called Mr Salau", was an all-night venue that got going in the small hours. The idea was for the clientele to eat in the restaurant that served traditional African food before enjoying several sets of music until the break of day.

From accounts given by Ryan and other musicians of the era, the Moss Side music scene had an all-night, Greenwich Village-type intensity, because people could walk easily from one venue to the next. A typical evening would start at the Lagos club, then move on to the Edinburgh near Alexandra Park, before concluding in one of a number of basement shebeens that sold bottles of Guinness for a few shillings and featured a disc jockey spinning calypso or blues until five o' clock in the morning,

Inevitably, there were a few underworld figures operating in the area, the most memorable of whom was a character called Don Tonay who took over a huge old Edwardian house on one of the streets near Denmark Road. The result was a local scene within a local scene that nonetheless attracted punters from outside Manchester. As Ryan recalled:

> In that building there was a room where people used to play, just anyone could get up and play. There was a barbershop and a café that only sold jelly! That was the centre for a completely racially-mixed scene. It was really good. That kind of thing existed all around that area, in the shebeens, that was where the parties used to take place. It was where visiting people came from Birmingham and London. You'd get people travelling up for various parties and they'd all be in that particular area, around Moss Lane, Fairnell Street or Monton Street. It's a very concentrated area really. It was a real hub."[9]

Apart from the Nile, other notable clubs in Moss Side were The Reno, from which the hardiest patrons did not quit until eight in the morning, and The Capital, located above a car showroom called Capital Cars. This was where local jazz musicians, such as the drummer Bruce Mitchell, used to play after finishing gigs in the city centre. This venue presented music every weekend, occasionally during the week. Here African and Caribbean musicians, high life and calypso, rubbed shoulders, so that Trinidadians and Jamaicans often found themselves performing to audiences who hailed from Ghana and Nigeria as well as the West Indies. Sometimes the musicians would be playing one thing and the punters hearing another. Jamaican guitarist-vocalist Ossie Roberts, a regular performer in Moss Side clubs who had arrived in Manchester in 1961, recalls: "I was in The Capital playing [opposite The Nile]. It was packed out and this High Commissioner from Ghana came over and said "Boy, you know that they'd love you in Ghana... [with your] high life." But it's calypso we were playing."[10]

Whether this experience of cultural overlap was paralleled in other cities where African and Caribbean musicians worked in close proximity has not yet been properly researched, but on the evidence of Manchester it probably did. Supporting Roberts' account of calypso-high life fusion is a recording made in London by the St. Vincent trumpeter Shake Keane for the Lyragon label. An outstanding improviser with a gorgeous tone, Keane was a poet, an inquisitive, cultured man who was interested in a wide range of things beyond music. His recording was called "Trumpet High Life",[11] which shows how he was drawn to African sounds, whilst the description on the label reads "Calypso Instrumental".

Whilst the jam sessions in its clubs were remembered fondly by those who witnessed them, the Moss Side scene of the 1950s and early 1960s is another example, much like Andy Hamilton in Birmingham, of how talent can be concentrated in a small area, but remain mostly unknown to the outside world. Chances are that an album of local talent recorded *Live at the Nile* would have entered the canon of Black music in Britain, bequeathing an invaluable record of how a specific scene developed. But no Manchester session was ever committed to tape. Without the oral testimonies provided by the musicians who were there, much important history would have been lost. The identification of the venues and players of the day will hopefully act as a springboard for future research into the heritage of Black Manchester.

It is also worth pointing out the existence of "shebeen stars", often self-taught rather than formally-trained players, who held down a day job and attended jam sessions as much as a form of relief from the working week as from a genuine love of making music. Just as there were musicians who didn't play outside of the basements of Notting Hill, so there were musicians who did not venture far beyond Moss Side. This is not surprising. The standard of playing in the jazz clubs in London's west end or Manchester's city centre was so high that sitting in with the most accomplished exponents of bebop was not something to be ventured lightly, especially if there was a big-name visiting American horn player against whom a local rhythm section was testing its mettle.

What the history of Moss Side shows is how much the quality of life and morale of an immigrant community can be improved by the existence of spaces for the creation of artistic excellence as well as social cohesion. Respect is rightfully granted to artists, activists and scholars in the realm of Black history in Britain, but the role of those who ran the clubs deserves greater notice. Such individuals had to be highly motivated, wily, resilient and resourceful.

According to residents of the black quarter of Toxteth, Liverpool, there was an abundance of music in many homes because of the wide availability of 78 rpm recordings brought in by seamen. Their precious cargo was exempt from sales duties because of an astute piece of maritime administration: shellac discs were classified as ballast. The existence of discs fresh off the boat enhanced Merseyside's black music resources.

This meant that Liverpudlians often heard much sought-after new works by leading American jazz and blues artists before they made their way inland to other cities such as Manchester and Birmingham.

As has been previously noted, Liverpool was, along with Cardiff, one of the oldest Black communities in Britain because it was an international port, through which passed, and in which settled, seamen as well as civilians from the colonies. The *Windrush* was not the only ship that brought West Indians to Britain in 1948. Later in the year, in September, another vessel, the *Orbita* docked in Liverpool with 108 Jamaicans aboard and they quickly fell into the city's lively multi-cultural life.

As well as what could be heard at home, Black Liverpudlians were keen patrons of clubs. In Toxteth, in the Liverpool 8 district, they were spoilt for choice One estimate was that there were around 23 clubs operating in the mid 1950s, frequented by seamen from the colonies, whites, new immigrants and African-American GIs who were stationed on the nearby base at Burtonwood (who also went to Manchester in their leisure time). These GIs were another source of jazz and blues records.

Among the 'L8' clubs, the Pink Flamingo, Dutch Eddie's and the Palm Cove were all very popular, but if ever there was a sign of how Black Liverpool was seen by the local media, it was the language of the *Evening Express* on 11 January 1955, after Lord Derby made a visit to the Stanley House Social club: "Lord Derby went into Liverpool's jungle last night to listen to Negro spirituals and calypsos."

What would the journalist have written had Derby visited the New Colony Club? This was run by a Trinidadian calypso singer, Lord Woodbine.[11] One suspects that the opportunity for puns based on the meeting of two Lords of very different circumstances would have been too tempting.

Lord Woodbine's beguiling stage name reflected a characteristic calypso irony. Woodbines were a low cost, unfiltered high tar smoke[12] from the Wills Tobacco company, and the conjunction of the name with Lord is a brilliant oxymoron in its espousal of society grandeur and commoner economy. Whether Lord Woodbine was an invention of the singer himself, or a nickname bestowed on him by friends is immaterial. The point is that it stuck because it had the essential quality of charm.

The naming had other resonances. During both World Wars, the prime market for the cigarette was soldiers, and the calypso singer (born Harold Adolphus Philips in Laventille, Trinidad, in 1929) fitted into one of the key lineages of Black British cultural history: he was a member of the armed services. Woodbine joined the RAF in 1943 and stayed in Europe for the duration of the war. He returned to Trinidad after his tour of duty in 1947 before coming to Britain on the *Windrush*. After brief sojourns in Clapham, south London and Wellington in Shropshire, Woodbine settled in Liverpool and soon started to make an impact on the music scene in

Toxteth. As well as singing at the New Colony, he played guitar and steel drums in the All Caribbean Steel Band, which appeared regularly at two more highly popular venues in the area, Jokers and the Jacaranda.

The portrait that emerges from the available accounts of Woodbine's life is that he was an all-rounder who recognised the need to find performance spaces and create scenes rather than go cap-in-hand to known venues and promoters with the hope of scoring a gig. There is a consensus that he ran several shebeens in Liverpool, and that he could easily switch roles from barman to security. In that role, any punter with an understanding of calypso naming might have well dubbed him Lord Cutlass[13] in tribute to his weapon of choice, for the sword is mightier than the high tar cigarette. More seriously, it was a symbol of Woodbine's roots as a working-class Trinidadian, born to disadvantage and the poverty and violence that went with it.

Like many musicians who did not have the support of a credible manager and record label, Woodbine had to take a variety of jobs to make ends meet, and if he was a noted "shebeen star" in L8, that didn't stop him from painting and decorating, driving lorries, working on the railways or repairing televisions.

Given the informality of the club scene of which Woodbine was such an integral part, it was inevitable that younger musicians gravitated to him, and the aspect of his life that has become more widely known – when it was recognised as such – is the role he played as a mentor to four teenage white musicians who called themselves the Silver Beetles, before becoming the Beatles. Paul McCartney, George Harrison, John Lennon and Stuart Sutcliffe were so intent on being taken under Woodbine's wing that they, he reportedly said, "made themselves orphans"[14] so that his attention to the aspiring stars would be secured. The strategy worked.

Club-goers who frequented the Jacaranda paint a picture of the young Beatles as eager to the point of being pushy, taking any opportunity to climb on stage. But Woodbine had sufficient patience, if not affection, to give them some basic advice on how they could improve the band, the most significant being the recommendation that they acquire a competent drummer to supplement the three guitarists and bassist. This is a wholly credible theory given the place of percussion in calypso.

Lending further credence to the narrative that Woodbine treated his "boys" with generosity, perhaps realising that they were musically limited and needed a guiding hand to bring them up to scratch, is the fact that he cut them in on some action that he found on the continent. The steel band in which Woodbine once played, the Royal Caribbean Steel Band, was noticed by a German sailor when it played at the Jacaranda, and the band was then invited to appear in Hamburg, after which Woodbine, realising that there were more gigs to be had there, took up residence on the Reeperbahn, and was soon locked in negotiation with local agents to bring over more Liverpudlian talent, the first of which was an energetic black blues singer by the name of Derry Wilkie, about whom more in a later chapter.

In an act of generosity, Woodbine drove the Beatles, the original four with new drummer Pete Best, to Hamburg in a minibus so they could have a crack at the club scene. This was an invaluable stage in their development, before their fortunes were boosted by a new manager-fixer-business mind, Brian Epstein.

Undoubtedly, Woodbine and Allan Williams, one of his early business partners, played a central role in the formative years of the Beatles, providing them with advice on musical matters and the bookings needed to improve and refine their ability as players. The input of other black Liverpudlian musicians, such as the guitarists Odie Taylor, Vinnie Tow and Zancs Logie, was also instrumental in widening their basic musical vocabulary, particularly a knowledge of chords, which later served their song-writing.

As was the case with Birmingham-based Jamaican tenor saxophonist Andy Hamilton, Woodbine went unrecorded, so one can only speculate on the kind of material that he performed, but as a calypsonian who also played steel drums, a combination that was rare, it is possible he would have been backed by a "pan man" as well as a rhythm and horn section. Had he settled in London and fallen in with other West Indian musicians, the Melodisc label might well have documented some of his output.

Sadly, Woodbine faded into obscurity later in his life and died in poverty, and although his name should always be associated with the Beatles, he remains unknown for the majority of their fans. His place in the history of British popular music is not what it should be. There are two conclusions to draw. Firstly, that there was no place in the British music industry for a black A&R-supervisor-producer in the postwar years, for it is clear, given the part he played in providing a solid musical grounding for the Beatles, that he could have had a shot at that kind of position within a management company or record label. But the idea of Black executives in the British entertainment industry had no currency in the early 1950s, especially if they did not have the credentials and polished manners of privately educated young men. A class-conscious pop music industry was not going to empower mere Black colonials at a time when the management roles were mostly taken by members of the elite[15] whilst the bulk of artists were commoners.

Nevertheless, it is clear that the music played in Britain's West Indian communities had an impact on budding practitioners of pop. In the accepted historical narrative, a group such as the Beatles drew inspiration from African-American blues, and while this is certainly true, it should not deflect attention from the fact that calypso was another influence, both being folk forms in which rhythm and storytelling predominate. It may be objected that there are few explicit traces of calypso in the Beatles' body of work, – other than "Ob-la-di, Ob-la-da" – compared to the strong resonances of the blues, but I'd argue that the time spent in the company of Liverpool's West Indian musicians was invaluable because they knew how to attack the beat of a tune with sufficient vigour to affect an audience. Calypso was able to teach pop all these things.

Listen to the strong Latin-Caribbean flavour of a Beatles piece such as "Day-tripper" and the results of this education is clear enough. One might also surmise that awareness of Woodbine's music encouraged McCartney and Lennon to open the door to other forms of world music, such as Consuelo Velazquez's "Besame Mucho", a haunting bolero that they openly acknowledged as an inspiration for their writing.[16]

The Beatles, of course, went on to change the face of popular music in the following decade, while Woodbine faded into obscurity, tragically burning to death in a house fire.

Notes

1. The series of reports was entitled "Strangers In Our Midst", *Manchester Evening News*, June 1958.
2. Telephone interview with the author, October, 2013.
3. Whit Stennett, *A Bittersweet Journey* (Batsford, 2007).
4. Liming spots are places to congregate and hang out, from the Trinidadian vernacular "to lime".
5. On the Pan-African Congresses, see *The Oxford Companion to Black British History* (Oxford University Press, 2007), pp. 359-361.
6. See David Anderson's *History of the Hanged, Britain's Dirty War in Kenya* (London: Orion, 2005).
7. Frantz Fanon *Black Skin, White Masks*, 1968 (London: Pluto, 2008).
8. Fanon was a member of the Algerian National Liberation Front.
9. Telephone interview with author, October, 2013.
10. Ibid.
11. Ibid.
12. Featured on Various artists, *London Is The Place For Me 5&6* (Honest Jons, 2012).
13. See Alan Clayson, "Lord Woodbine", *The Guardian*, 10 July, 2000; James McGrath, "Phillips, Harold Adolphus (1929-2000), *Oxford Dictionary of National Biography* (Oxford UP, 2012).
14. The nickname for Woodbine cigarettes was "gaspers", which tells you everything you need to know about their quality.
15. See Simon Napier-Bell's *Black Vinyl, White Powder* (Ebury, 2002).
16. This has been publicly acknowledged by the Beatles.

16 ORIENTAL BALLS FOR ABSOLUTE BEGINNERS

We used to play all over the country – Birmingham, Manchester, Reading,
you name it. People were so glad to know that there was a sound system
here because of what they were used to in Jamaica.
— Duke Vin

He has for all the older people the same kind of hatred psychos have
for Jews or foreigners or coloureds, that is he hates anybody who is not
a teenager.
— Description of Wiz, *Absolute Beginners* by Colin MacInnes

Chapter 15 noted the growth of a Black music scene in Manchester.
One contribution to that growth came from the presence of the US
military. There were "Yanks" deployed all over the country. Among the
units were official bands as well as musicians who had played before
they were drafted, and continued to do so when on leave. A notable
talent was Robbie Robinson, a black GI billeted at the American army
base in Burtonwood in Cheshire. This housed some 18,000 personnel
during the war and the immediate postwar period. It was during that
time that Robinson made a name for himself on the Manchester jazz
scene as a drummer.

What gave him an advantage over his peers was the tuition he received
from one of the great exponents of bebop drumming, the American Art
Taylor, whom Robinson saw once a month when he returned to Newark,
New Jersey on what the military authorities termed a transport flight.
This was time well spent. As the drummer for leading soloists such as Bud
Powell, Miles Davis and John Coltrane, Taylor had the kind of fluid dynamism required to match their formidable improvisatory skills as well as the
intricate ensemble arrangements they were writing. Bebop drummers had
to reinforce the darting, rhythmically inventive lines and improvisations
of the "front line" by playing jumpy, uneven patterns on the snare and
bass drum while keeping regular time on the ride cymbal. They had to be
simultaneously on and off the beat. They drove the ensemble forward but
also cunningly disrupted its carriage. Those who saw Robinson play, paint
a picture of a musician at the top of his game, who also had the aesthetic
allure of a Miles Davis, meaning that he was "a very handsome guy, always
extremely well dressed."[1]

Along with the well-respected local pianist Joe Palin and an expatriate Swedish double bassist, Trond Svennevig, Robinson became part of a trio that is widely recognized as one of the great bebop ensembles to have emerged from Manchester in the early 1950s. They were an integral part of a modern jazz movement developing in the city. If London had the Flamingo, Club 11 and Ronnie Scott's, Manchester had the Left Wing, Club 43 and the Carlton Club a.k.a The Reno.

Notable musicians who rose to prominence in the early 1950s Manchester jazz scene included drummer Bruce Mitchell, trombonist Eddie Warburton and trumpeter John Rowland. Robbie Robinson had a certain kudos as an African-American who had learnt with a master player on the other side of the Atlantic, and no less respect was shown to his compatriot and fellow serviceman, who was also stationed at the Burtonwood base, bassist Major Holley.[2] Although these players appeared in Manchester's dedicated bebop clubs such as Club 43, some of them also went to the African-Caribbean venues like the Nile on Moss Side, so the stylistic range in the black quarter widened with the presence of beboppers in among the high-lifers and calypsonians. Culturally mixed as the scene was, the long shadow of segregation was nonetheless cast over the way a key part of the clientele, American GIs, went about organizing a weekly night out on arrival in Manchester from the Burtonwood military base.

Saxophonist Tosh Ryan, who played many of the clubs in question, has an important story to tell of this divide: "There'd be a coach of black servicemen and a coach of white servicemen and they separated from where the bus came in. The black guys would move south towards Moss Side and Rusholme and the white guys would end up in the city centre around the bars, clubs and hotels. But the black guys would go towards especially Club 43, which was going south on the Oxford Road, and they had a real influence on local music."[3]

As was the case in London and other cities, bands would often appear at several venues in one evening, and some musicians became proper nighthawks who could move from the 43 to the Left Wing and possibly end up at the Nile. One such, a Ghanaian drummer by the name of Sammy Nelson, was remembered for his percussive and polyrhythmic ability, while another musician who stood tall on the Manchester modern jazz scene was a Trinidadian tenor saxophonist whose name is still said with a reverential hush to this day, Julius Hasford.[4]

Hasford, Robinson and others made Manchester an essential jazz city, but the arrival of Lord Kitchener in the late 1950s gave them a veritable calypso star. Exactly why he left London is the subject of speculation – to all intents and purposes his life in the capital was a fulfilling one. He had a substantial fan base, performed in clubs and recorded on a regular basis. One story was that Kitch went north for the sake of a local woman by the name of Marjorie, whom he would fête in song, and recent research indicates that he indeed married Marjorie and later went back to Trinidad with her – though it seems the marriage foundered over Kitch's continuing activities as a ladies man. One thing that stands out in all of the archive photographs of Kitch is how impeccably dressed he was: box suits, silk ties and buffed leather shoes were *de rigueur*. Maybe more than vanity was at stake.[5]

Many musicians have made the point that there was a psychological pressure on black men to ensure that they were never seen looking anything less than their absolute best. "We wouldn't dream of not wearing a suit to play in a club in those days, but I think we all felt we had to look extra sharp because there was this whole thing about West Indian workers being lazy, casual and unreliable, so we really had to be the opposite."[6]

Kitchener appeared at clubs such as The Nile and on at least one occasion led an 11-piece band with a hefty horn section that enabled him to develop the kind of jazz sophistication in the arrangements of his music that had marked his sessions with Rupert Nurse in London.

Another of the musicians with whom Kitchener worked, who had also come to Manchester from the Caribbean, was the saxophonist Eric Deans. In the 1940s he had been a prime mover on the big band scene in Kingston and had led a hugely popular swing orchestra with several excellent soloists, the most promising of whom was a young guitarist by the name of Ernest Ranglin, who would go on to make his mark on Jamaican and British music in the next decade.

Guitar was the instrument that Kitchener used when he was singing his own songs, but the double bass was what he played in other musical settings, and it was the big "bull fiddle" that he used when he was a part of Deans' jazz groups. If the band launched into a calypso number, Kitchener sang, but they mostly played instrumental tunes. Deans was known as a brilliant arranger and sight reader who believed firmly in the discipline of writing out parts for the various members of his group and watching magic emerge when the sound of the different instruments came together as one, and in that respect he can be seen as an Ellingtonite with a belief in "band as instrument".

Regardless of the regular shows that they did in Manchester, musicians like Deans and Kitchener could not rely on work in the city to sustain them. Kitchener, for instance, joined a touring circuit that took him to Britain's best known chain of holiday camps. Calypso went all the way to Butlins.

It is reported that Kitchener opened a club in Manchester but this is not actually true. Towards the end of his sojourn in the city – he returned to Trinidad in 1962 – he became increasingly less active, and according to some, he rarely left his home in Whalley Range, an area adjacent to Moss Side with better housing.

If Kitchener's time in Manchester has only recently been documented, then the names of players like Robbie Robinson and Julius Hasford have been all but forgotten, not to mention Floyd Grainger, Chris O'Brien, Mike Falanga, none of them well known beyond Manchester jazz circles. Yet in the 1950s some of the above *were* recognized nationally. Robinson was named best drummer in a 1957 poll of *Melody Maker*. Hasford also had coverage nationally, as well as locally, and the Left Wing, the club where they both played, made the pages of the *Daily Mirror*. Hence the question of why these musicians, and the excellent white players in Manchester, did not make a bigger splash on the British jazz scene has to be broached.

A major handicap was a lack of support from the recording industry. Their work was not documented and distributed on a national scale. The music industry was still exclusively centred in London. There wasn't a producer/A&R man in Manchester to do for Robinson what Tony Hall did for Dizzy Reece in London. The Mancunian jazz musicians lacked a champion who could open the commercial doors. London was the magnet to which substantial talents where drawn, and one can only imagine how British jazz would have been impoverished if Tony Kinsey, one of the leading drummers on the bebop scene, had elected to stay in his native Sutton Coldfield in the West Midlands rather than move south. It was a situation that affected both black and white players with ambition. The highly talented Deniz brothers, Frank and Joe, left Cardiff for London; Coleridge Goode left Glasgow for London; Tommy Wilson left Birmingham for London. We have noted the cautionary story of Andy Hamilton who stayed in Birmingham.

London may have remained the commercial epicentre of the recording world, the place where album deals were signed and sessions booked, but Black communities in the capital and the regions were bound together by the distressing common thread of ghettoization. They were consigned to specific areas of a particular city where the quality of housing was poor and the sense of insularity pronounced. Cardiff had Bute Town; London had Notting Hill; Manchester had Moss Side; Liverpool had Toxteth; Birmingham had Handsworth; Leeds had Chapeltown; Nottingham had The Meadows; Bristol had St. Pauls. And whilst West Indian and African immigration had a major impact on the music scenes of these cities, the problematic place of the black migrant in British society was not a concern that could easily be put to bed.

At the levels of both the cabinet and the shop floor, attitudes to black immigration hardened. In 1948, the Colonial Secretary, Arthur Creech-Jones, referring to the *Windrush*, coldly stated that further movements from Jamaica or elsewhere in the Empire should be "detected and checked before they can reach an embarrassing stage."[6] This antipathy towards "coloured colonials" met the tragic illusions many West Indians had about their place in the Metropole. Their lives in the islands had been so pervaded by British products and services that they thought they would feel at home in England, a feeling encapsulated by the sight of a newly arrived *Windrush* passenger clutching a box of Special K breakfast cereal.

But by January 1951, a ministerial committee was established to consider the possibility of "limiting coloured immigration". A few months later Sterling Metals, an engineering firm in Coventry, "came under such union pressure that it unequivocally declared at a works conference that "it was their main desire to recruit white labour." The Suez crisis of 1956 had put economies around the world in deep recession, and as jobs became scarce the scapegoating of black workers increased.

But despite such hostility, the attraction to a life outside the West Indies did not diminish, strengthened by the depressed state of postwar economies on the islands (Jamaica was also recovering from the ravages of a 1944 hurricane), and the high levels of unemployment that many returning servicemen encountered. This was no doubt why some *Windrush* passengers saw Britain as a permanent home rather than a location for a short-term sojourn during which they'd earn big money. There were those who had declared: "My children would not grow up in a colony."[7] There was also the fact that many of the departing West Indians were cosmopolitan in outlook – they had been in the services after all – and saw the limitations of their current lives. Jamaican ex-airman Arthur Curling: "After you reach a certain time in life, you think you want to get away from the control of your parents. I had a reasonably good job in Jamaica and things were looking up. It just a matter of the island is too small. You don't realize how small until after you've travelled." But in Britain there was the struggle for a career, of trying to lay down roots, and raise a family. Another immigrant, Wilfred Greaves, movingly explained: "The English do not understand how we feel. How can you just go back and leave what you have built in England? Our children were born here, live here and will remain here. Barbados is in my head, in my memory." [8]

Unsurprisingly, many migrants have stated that the hardest thing about life in the mother country in the 1950s was how "two-face" some white people were, being outwardly polite but inwardly contemptuous, publicly preaching tolerance but privately wishing no son or daughter would bring home a "darkie". This was not just talk over port at the gentleman's club or brown ale in the pub. It was debated on national TV.[9]

Xenophobia was very much part of the mood of the nation, as the *Sunday Pictorial* revealed in January 1947. Quizzed on the forthcoming marriage of Princess Elizabeth and Prince Philip of Greece, 40% of respondents declared themselves against on the grounds that he was "a foreign prince", which is why he had to become Philip Mountbatten RN. What makes a study of the national psyche more intriguing is the fact that another poll taken in the Spring of 1948, just a few weeks before the arrival of the *Windrush*, found that 42% of all Britons wanted to emigrate. History tells us that there is nothing like unhappiness at home to make you hate those who come from abroad.

Even so, the music of Africans and West Indians was embraced by Britain. As the Guyanese singer, Frank Holder, claimed, West Indian music helped to make people "relax and let themselves go… you know I think that calypso helped to loosened them up a bit."[10]

Calypso did, in fact, catch the ear of the well-to-do and the stories of the interest taken in the music by members of the royal family[11] underscored its prestige and reminds that there was a tradition of high society professing a weakness for Black culture that reached back to the Prince of Wales taking banjo lessons from James Bohee and the Fisk Jubilee Singers finding favour with Queen Victoria.

Switch On, Sound Travels

There was progress of a kind in the access of West Indians to the national media – but one that still presented barriers as much as opportunities. As BBC radio had broadcast concerts by Leslie 'Jiver' Hutchinson's jazz big band in the 1940s, BBC television in the mid 1950s also produced programmes that featured black musicians, the two most noteworthy being *The Winifred Atwell Show* and *Tonight*, a current affairs magazine that had a calypso performance by vocalist Cy Grant.

Atwell's programme was significant insofar as it was something that she herself fronted and reflected the enormous popularity that she had attained in Britain, reflected in the colossal sales of her records, not to mention the substantial kudos she had drawn from an electrifying performance for Queen Elizabeth at the Royal Variety Show in 1952. The fact that Atwell had her own show consolidated her status at a time when the phenomenon of the pop star-turned TV personality-host was slowly gaining traction.

As for *Tonight* it was a major boost for Grant, a Guyanese singer, actor and broadcaster, who, like many other West Indian artists, had been a serviceman. He was in fact one of the few to make officer grade in the R.A.F.[12] On the programme Grant sang a calypso based on a text written by producer Bernard Levin on a news story of the day, which nicely added to the history of calypso as a vehicle for political comment. Grant showed how far and well the genre travelled.

Later, he presented his own television show, *For Members Only*, in which he sang, played a guitar and interviewed various guests. Here a parallel can be drawn between Grant and Edric Connor, archetypal black Renaissance men, mentioned in an earlier chapter, insofar as both were all-round talents who worked extensively in radio and television and indefatigably championed the folk culture, both song and story, of the West Indies.

Grant's output was eclectic, to say the least, and reflected the wide range of music in which he had been interested since childhood. Because his native Guyana, although part of the West Indies, was in close proximity to South

America he had been exposed to Latin music, particularly Brazilian bossa nova, as well as the songs of the African and Indian populations of his homeland. Grant was also drawn to blues, jazz and British folk music, and the albums he recorded between the late 1950s and mid 1960s such as *Cy Grant Sings*, *Cool Folk* and *Cy and I* (with English pianist Bill Lesage) are very much the work of a singer whose commanding, eloquent voice, with subtle Caribbean inflections, could be effectively deployed on any kind of traditional material, be it "Yellow Bird" or "Green Sleeves", as well as on material that was of a more modernist hue. For example, Grant's rendition of "Moanin'", an anthem of the 'hard bop' movement spearheaded by the likes of Art Blakey & The Jazz Messengers, was well measured, as was his take on the enduring show tune "Feelin' Good", set to an elegiac arrangement by Le Sage.

All of which symbolized Grant's desire to spread his wings, stylistically, rather than be confined to one particular genre of music, and unfortunately his career struck a parallel with that of Connor insofar as he also found himself limited by the perceptions of producers in the world of television and film.

Grant's ambitions to present his own show in which he would do something other than sing West Indian music, and thus escape the typecasting of which he was all too aware, were not fulfilled, as the BBC did not countenance that kind of role. Calypso had enabled Grant to make his breakthrough on national television but it also subsequently put a glass ceiling above his head.

Some years later he would voice his frustration on how his career unfolded.

"I had made two films from either side of '56…'58. I'd been in two very big television plays, so my career as an actor had been quite established, but I found that people saw me purely and simply as a calypso singer. At the time I resented it very much because it… devalued what I… wanted to do."[13]

Regardless of the barriers they faced, Grant and Connor, whether acting, singing, holding a microphone or addressing a camera, found their work was much needed because they filled something of the void left by the absence of that essential role model, Paul Robeson, because of his inability to continue to visit Britain as he had done during the preceding three decades. In the USA anti-Communism took its McCarthyite form and Paul Robeson, as an unrepentant socialist, was one of its victims. He had visited Russia several times where he was greeted as a hero by both the common people and the Politburo. But by drawing attention to America's iniquities while in the bosom of its sworn enemy in the Cold War, Robeson committed the sin of being both black and red. He was an arch black traitor to Uncle Sam. Washington struck a decisive blow. Robeson's passport was revoked in 1950 on the grounds that it was "contrary to the best interests of the US", presumably for fear that he might be an agent of subversion. He was now marooned. Although he was not formally placed under house arrest, the dynamic of his life as an internationally recognized artist – the ability to reach audiences around the world – came to an abrupt halt. But whilst the singer was prevented from leaving the States, his voice was nonetheless able to travel. Robeson performed for his British fans by way of the technology of the day – a transatlantic cable phone line. Supplied by technicians from the Post Office, the connection lasting all of 23 minutes was billed as a special service and cost $255. This was heard by around 900 people who filled St Pancras Town Hall in London on the 26 May 1957 to hear Robeson, installed in a New York studio with pianist Alan Booth, perform a set consisting largely of gospel and folk songs such as "Water Boy", "Didn't My Lord", "This Little Light of Mine" and "Deliver Daniel" as well as Schubert's "Lullaby". Fed through the latest high fidelity cable the sound was excellent and Robeson, then 60, was in good voice. There was another telecommunications-enabled concert at the Porthcawl Pavilion in Bridgend, Wales for the 10th annual miners Eisteddfod on October 5, 1957.[15] More than 5,000 people came to hear Robeson sing. The numbers were a testament to the enormous impact that the black artist had made on the people far from his home. If there is a corner of some foreign field that is forever England, then here was a place in the valleys of Wales that was resolutely African-American.

Taking it to the Streets

The outstanding interpreter of the post-Windrush West Indian British experience is, as noted in Chapter 13, Samuel Selvon in his novel *The Lonely Londoners* (1956). One British novelist who captured some of the nuances of this complex sociocultural canvas was Colin MacInnes. A diehard jazz fan who knew the world of the West Indian community in Notting Hill well, MacInnes wrote a highly influential novel, *Absolute Beginners* (1959), that evoked the cultural flux in 1950s Britain.

In particular, MacInnes conveys the incandescence of the new phenomenon of youth culture, a term that marked the place of the teenager in a world in which adults no longer enjoyed an unchallenged hegemony; adolescents had purchasing power and were being recognised as more than children who owed obedience to their parents.

They became part of a world of factions segmented by tastes for different varieties of music and fashion. MacInnes vividly chronicled the volatile energy of the postwar youth in need of outlets to satisfy its desires and opposition to their elders. As the author says of one of his key characters in *Absolute Beginners*, Wiz: "He has for all the older people the same kind of hatred psychos have for Jews or foreigners or coloureds, that is he hates anybody who is not a teenager."[16]

But the new youth culture was not immune to hatred towards Jews, foreigners or coloureds. This was evident in the sight of teens running amok in Notting Hill, West London, during the race riot of 30 August 1958, which came barely a week after similar events in Nottingham. It is worth noting that there was also wanton destruction of several Cypriot cafés in West London around the same time, a dark prelude to the main event and a reminder that swarthy Europeans could as easily become a target.

The riots said many things about Britain. First and foremost there was race hatred of the most naked kind, marked by the desire to physically assault any person of colour who happened to be walking down the street.

But the sheer wildness, if not euphoria, of the many pitched battles also seems to have been a challenge to social norms and received wisdoms about what the nation should be and how it should behave. Decency and decorum were disrupted by juvenile delinquency. It was not a protest against poverty – teens had never had such purchasing power. Well-waged boys and girls had disposable income that topped £850 million per annum. Bright and shiny materialism was taking hold, and there were no doubt tensions between ration-generation parents and advertisement-targeted youth, weaned on a diet of 45 rpm singles, coca cola and sharp clothes. *Vogue* magazine wrote: "When people of the older generation see a boy in sharp clothes with his hand in his pocket, they are apt to suppose he is reaching for his flick knife", though this is followed by the explanation that "in fact he is more likely to be digging out the price of a bottle of a Coke."[17]

For the most part, the records favoured by the violent youth intent on nigger bashing in Notting Hill was rock & roll. This was a grotesquely contradictory and tragically ironic phase in the postwar cultural evolution of Great Britain. This new genre was another outgrowth from the deep roots of Black music, the blues, which also found favour with West Indians. The sad paradox lay in the resemblances between the "Teddy Boys" and the Black youth on whom they pulled their flick knives. White teens liked "record parties" and black youth "Sound system dances." Each each had their allegiance to 45 rpm vinyl recordings that drew on similar sources.

This was a time of rapid transition and, in hindsight, the heaviest burden of the Windrush was that they arrived in Britain at the time when the country needed to face up to the loss of empire and the uncertainties of identity this involved. For some, the arrival of West Indian migrants was no doubt a reminder of that loss of status. It was a country undergoing a shift from being a society of collective class loyalties to one that was emphatically consumerist, a society where growing disposable income would bring a greater sense of self, but where the other might equally well be identified by the cut of their cloth as by the colour of their skin.

Add to the confluence of these various kinds of social change the activities of far-right groups like Sir Oswald Mosley's Union Movement and the White Defence League and you have a country that was ripe for disorder.

In the case of both the Nottingham and Notting Hill disturbances the spark for the violence was lit by the sight of a black man in public with a white woman. "Mix Up Matrimony" was a calypso, a taboo, and a source of conflict.

While the Nottingham riot lasted a few hours and involved a white mob of up to 1,000, there were several thousand more on the rampage in Notting Hill, where disturbances lasted for a fortnight, during which time 140 arrests were made. The members of high society who had taken to slumming it in the area's calypso shebeens were nowhere to be seen when running battles were fought in the area, so the local Black residents had to defend themselves as best they could. Among the now legendary stories of West Indian solidarity, the tale of "reinforcements" arriving from the other London black enclave of Brixton is the most uplifting. Crossing town to lend a hand to the *bredren* under siege was not the kind of cricket that the new Blacks in town had signed up for, but they grabbed bats and took to the streets.

Equally impressive was the contribution of West Indian women in the resistance. This has been largely overlooked, as has their essential role in the black community, as a creative, financial and maternal force. "Island" women, many of whom followed their husbands to Britain after a year or so of delay, had great organisational skills as well as considerable physical strength. Toil in the fields, toil in the market place, toil in the yard and toil in the kitchen were deeply rooted elements in the historical experience of many Caribbean women, as is a refusal to bow to the desires of abusive men, be they black or white.

One striking photograph taken during the fighting shows a short black woman in a plain blouse, knitted hat and palm-tree print skirt standing on her doorstep with a black man frozen behind her. Had Sam Selvon, the Trinidadian author of *The Lonely Londoners* been observing the scene he might have written of her: "She talking to two policemen. She have them under heavy manners. She armed and she dangerous." Had Colin MacInnes, author of *Absolute Beginners*, observed the scene he might have written of her: "She's tooled up." She is indeed carrying a quite fearsome hatchet. Her grip is firm. The sharpness of the blade in her hand contrasts with flatness of the sensible shoes she is wearing, suggesting she might well be an NHS nurse. If there are *big-tree* racists in her yard then she holding *a small axe.* And anybody who has seen the inch-perfect accuracy with which a West Indian auntie or mother can split a coconut with a cutlass in one stroke will know that the woman in this historic photograph is not carrying her weapon just for show. She is ready, willing and able. As the apprehension etched on the faces of all the men, black and white, around her, attests, *is not joke she making.*[18]

The riots had a soundtrack. The first wave of mob violence occurred during a party held by the popular sound system men King Dick and Count Suckle. As the chants of "Kill the Niggers! Keep Britain White" rang out, the 45 rpm single that was spinning on a Ferguson record player was a calypso called "Oriental Ball". I haven't been able to find the lyrics of this calypso, but the implications of its title are apposite if one considers the connotations of "oriental" in the British psyche, as signifying the archetypal foreigner, whereas "balls" in West Indian and African-American slave history were the lavish dances hosted by the plantocracy in the Great House.

Notes

1. Robbie Robinson's strikingly photogenic appearance is confirmed by several pictures in Bill Birch's *Keeper of the Flame, Modern Jazz in Manchester 1946-72.*
2. Major Holley is a highly respected double bassist who worked with jazz legends Coleman Hawkins, Dexter Gordon and Charlie Parker.
3. Telephone interview with the author, October, 2013.
4. Julius Hasford is a revered figure on the Manchester jazz scene, but sadly there is no recorded documentation of his work.
5. See Anthony Joseph, *Kitch* (Peepal Tree, 2018), for an in-depth portrait, including his years in Manchester and his marriage to Marjorie.
6. An opinion expressed numerous times over the years by both West Indians and African-American musicians.
7. David Kynaston, *Austerity Britain, 1945-51* (Bloomsbury), p. 275.
8. Stephen Pollard, *Ten Days That Changed The Nation* (Simon & Schuster), p. 4.
9. http://www.bbc.co.uk/history/british/modern Windrush-Arrivals
10. See Panorama's groundbreaking 1956 documentary *Does Britain have a Colour Bar?*
11. Interview with the author, Wallington, 2013.
12. This resonates with royals taking an interest in jazz in the 1920s.
13. Grant was one of the very first West Indians to sign up in 1944. See his fascinating mixture of autobiography and philosophy, *Blackness and the Dreaming Soul: Race Indentity and the Materialistic Paradigm* (Shoving Leopard, 2007).
14. Quoted in Amanda Bidnall, *The West Indian Generation*, p. 104.
15. Peoplescollection.wales/casgliedyweincymru.co.uk
16. Colin Macinnes, *Absolute Beginners* (Allison & Busby) p. 13.
17. Chris Pearce, *The Fifties: A pictorial Review* (H.C Blossom) p. 95.
18. www.blackpast,org/gah/nottingham-riots-1958.

17 BRITISH STEEL FROM ABROAD

I was listening to the news back home in Barbados about more and more gangs [in Moss Side]. Being a physical sort of person I came up to see what was going on. I had a brother, sister, uncle, I sort of ...I came here to help.
— Curtis Bellamy, Tropical Heatwave Steel Band, Manchester.

To walk and play is a difficult thing to do.
— Russ Henderson, steel pan soloist, London.

Distressing as the riots were, they did not match the tragedy that occurred less than a year later. In May 1959, a 32 year-old Antiguan carpenter, Kelso Cochrane, was stabbed to death by a group of six men on his way home in the Notting Hill area. The murder, which remains unsolved to this day, was a landmark for a number of reasons. The consternation that came in its wake led to an extensive questioning of race relations in Britain. A committee led by Amy Ashwood Garvey, former wife of Marcus Garvey, was set up to compile a detailed report on the subject.[1]

There was a show of inter-racial harmony as 1,200 mourners, black and white, attended Cochrane's funeral in London, though, somewhat ironically, the last shot of the Pathé newsreel of the solemn and moving procession was a billboard on a wall in Ladbroke Grove bearing the legend 'He Is Coming. Mosley Speaks.'

Despite the initial claims of the Metropolitan police that Cochrane's murder was not caused by the victim's skin colour, it was eventually seen as a racist murder and received more media coverage than any of the other crimes of this type – the earliest of which reached back to 1785 (John Dean mutilated aboard a ship bound for Bristol) – that tarnish British history. The murder coincided with the coming of the age of television, so a crime that concerned mass migration was given mass media coverage.

Notting Hill had actually seen anti-racist demonstrations in 1958 in the wake of the riots, and the sight of protestors walking up and down the streets carrying sandwich boards with the legend "No Little Rock here!" – a nod to the infamy of segregated schools in Arkansas – underlined the parallels that were being drawn between the expanding Civil rights movement in America and worsening race relations in Britain. Sensitive media coverage was crucial to the cause of equality.

Cochrane's death became a national tragedy. Those households with televisions could discover a world beyond their doorstep, regardless of where they lived. As Judith Richardson, from Durham in the north east of England, recalled:

> Watching on those early televisions they saw a very dignified West Indian crowd dressed completely in black, walking slowly behind the cortège up to the cemetery in Kensal Rise and were very moved by what was happening. People were really so shocked. Yes, it was the first race murder to be reported in the mass media; it did make an impact. I was lucky enough that my parents had a television. [Cochrane's death] spread around the country because it happened at Whitsun time. He was 32, a carpenter. He was murdered on this holy day and people saw the similarity between him and Jesus Christ, and they were horrified to find out what had happened, because at that time you very seldom heard of a knife crime.[2]

Brought up in a rural area, Judith reported that she had not seen a black man in her childhood, except the occasional Arab seaman on Newcastle docks. With no prompting, she also noted that several local ministers felt a prick of conscience that churches could and should have done more to help the integration of West Indians in Britain. They had not been greatly welcomed. We had this conversation in the Tabernacle community centre in Notting Hill, a location that has been an outlet for Caribbean culture, and a major part of Judith's life since she moved to Notting Hill in the wake of the Cochrane tragedy. At the instigation of Donald Soper [later Lord Soper] of the West Mission, the Methodist church, and other Christians in Notting Hill, a house in Blenheim Crescent was offered for volunteers from around the country who were willing to move to London and improve the lot of West Indians.

Teachers, social workers and Quakers accepted the invitation and set about drawing up campaigns to foster community harmony and avert any further breakdowns in race relations. Judith was among the party, and after settling in the area, she met a 24 year-old Trinidadian by the name of Selwyn Baptiste who had only been in London for a few months, but was beginning to make a cultural impact in Notting Hill. The two became a couple, which then required no small amount of fortitude.

"I think if I'd known how difficult it was gonna be I might not have had the strength to go through with it!" Judith said with the most wry of smiles. "You find ways round it. I mean in the early days it was better for me to phone for a taxi so they could hear my English voice."[3]

Baptiste had enrolled at the Dartington College of the Arts, near Totnes in Devon, to study music but found the course was too narrow in its subject matter, with an overriding emphasis on European classical music. Within a few months he decided to drop out and commit himself to a very personal musical agenda in London.

Baptiste was a virtuoso on the steel pan. Three months prior to his arrival in Britain he had won a major artistic accolade as Best Pan Soloist at the Trinidad carnival, a title that acknowledged outstanding skill in a field that included eighty-six contestants. Baptiste came from La Romaine, near San Fernando in the south of the island, and had to overcome considerable local snobbery when he first arrived in Port of Spain as a boy to pit his skill against the notoriously competitive older players who were based in the pan heartland of Laventille. His triumph said much about his resolve and strength of character, as well as his musical ability.

In Notting Hill, Baptiste began to combine his skill as a pan player with a desire to improve local community education work. He taught children to play the instrument and, with Judith's support, though she was primarily focused on housing and "getting people out of the terrible one-room accommodation", he set about increasing the presence and appreciation of pan in the area.

"He could not only play the pan, he could also make the drums," Judith pointed out. "We wrote round to oil companies and got them to provide us with drums, which he fashioned over the fire at the adventure playground, and his first band was the Adventurers, after the playground [Acklam Road]."[4] Baptiste's tireless development of pan as a means of social cohesion is a key part of British cultural history. Even today, attend a performance by a pan group and you'll see audience members walk over to the instruments and cast an eye over their curved surfaces, once the music has stopped, because they are intent on seeing how the device works. The steel drum does not *look* like an instrument.[5] Therein lies its subversive power.

Around 1967, the band moved its base to the nearby Metronomes club, and became Metronomes, which, to this day, remains one of the most esteemed ensembles in the steel band movement in Britain. Baptiste's initiative was paralleled by the work of other expatriate Trinidadians, even though there was not always the same degree of community activism involved. For example, the All Caribbean Steel Band, which featured both an excellent pan soloist by the name of Gerry Gobin and calypsonian Lord Woodbine (see pp. 16-217), was active in Liverpool in the late 1950s, appearing regularly at Jokers and the Jacaranda, two popular venues in Toxteth.

As F.I.R. Blake records, a few years before the All Caribbean Steel Band surfaced in Liverpool, The Trinidadian All Steel Percussion Orchestra appeared at the South Bank Centre in London as part of the 1951 Festival of Britain, a series of cultural events intended to provide a "tonic for the nation" after the years of post-war austerity. It's worth noting that the still colonial government in Trinidad were reluctant to support the sending of the band, evidently feeling that steelband was not a fitting representation of Trinidadian culture. Nonetheless this 11-piece steel band came to Britain and played. What its audiences heard was music that was distinguished by its eclecticism. There were calypsos such as "After Johnny Drink Mih Rum", Latin-inflected numbers such as "Jamaica Rhumba", and, in keeping with the Imperial times in which the event took place, a rendition of "God Save The Queen". Possibly the most impressive moment of the concert was the interpretation of a demanding piece of classical music, Toselli's "Serenade", which, coming from such "crude instrument", may well have surprised audience members.

The presence of Toselli in the T.A.S.P.O. repertoire was to be expected because, from its genesis in the 1930s, the steel pan had been used to perform both folk and "art" music, and historians of the instrument cite the landmark moment in the 1940s when Winston "Spree" Simon played several passages of Tchaikovsky's *First Piano Concerto*. Spree is largely regarded as the inventor of the modern day pan, because he was one of the first to take a discarded oil drum and create a basic tuning system for it by heating and shaping the metal surface. He, in turn, was building on the fact that since the 1900s, Trinidadians, especially at carnival, had used household and industrial objects, from bottles and spoons to biscuit tins, salt boxes, lengths of tram line and car hubcaps, to create percussion groups, with players often using the term "irons" to designate the miscellaneous devices deployed to make music. As noted above, there were also "tamboo bamboo" bands in which various lengths of bamboo were pounded on to the ground to create pitches that ranged from booming bass up to singing soprano.

Steel bands evolved from this desire to bring tonality into a percussion ensemble, and it is significant that the term steel pan is interchangeable with steel drum; the most skilled exponents of the instrument are as much purveyors of rhythm as melody. At the heart and soul of their aesthetic, *dey beat pan*.

By the 1950s, when T.A.S.P.O. appeared in London, steel pan culture had grown in Trinidad to the extent that there were numerous highly skilled bands in Port of Spain, where fierce rivalry often led to violence. The eleven players who travelled to Britain were among the best pan men in the city, drawn from different bands, who had to set aside differences to bring dignity to the instrument, and by extension, the "coloured colonials" they represented.

Nathaniel Joseph Griffith, a former member of the Trinidad Police Band, a reputed centre for musical excellence on the island, was assigned the task of instilling discipline among his potentially volatile charges and conducting and arranging the repertoire. Most significantly, Griffith ensured that the pans were all set up chromatically. This was liberating for the musicians. The possibility of playing semi-tones as well as whole tones, of shifting pitch up from a C to a C sharp or down from an E flat to a D, widened the expressive palette and provided a greater range of harmonic colour. Introducing these nuances was vital to the development of pan as an instrument on which increasingly complex chords could be played.

This meant that there are two indispensable elements in the culture of pan: the tuner and the player. There is a fine art to both disciplines. Accordingly, as much kudos is bestowed on those who work or hammer the pan before it is touched in performance as is bestowed on the virtuosi who make it sing. The status of the former is high, especially when the leading exponents have been able to extend the sonic range of the instrument and in some cases add new members to the pan family. Western pop music has accustomed us to the idea that tuning an instrument is of relative insignificance, a task performed mid-concert in a split second by a guitarist or bassist who just fumbles with a peg to bring an errant string to order. This is absolutely not the case with pan. The tuners have to work assiduously to fully prepare the instrument.

Pan is a generic term, but each steel drum is built to enable an orchestra to cover upper, middle and low register, hence the existence of tenor, double tenor, double second, cello and bass pans. A player has to find the right tuner for his particular pan because he knows that it is only then that he will have any hope of obtaining exactly the tones he has been hearing in his head. Sound tuners look at the steel as a flexible material. Hence the idea of using a curved surface, that crucial step of "sinking" the pan, thus turning it from a convex to a concave shape, lead to a dramatic improvement in terms of pitch quality.

Standing tall here was the revered figure of Ellie Mannette, a founding member of the Invaders steelband and a visionary who has been one of the great innovators of steel pan design since the 1940s. Mannette was a key member of T.A.S.P.O. precisely because of his status as a master tuner, a skilled "sound architect". Steelband historian Dr F.I.R. Blake provides an excellent insight into just a few of Mannette's many achievements. "To the envy of many other steel bands at the time, his tenors were better than anyone else's in volume, range and timbre, and his cellos sounded like organs."[6]

Sharing tuning responsibilities with Mannette in T.A.S.P.O. were Andrew De La Bastide, Philmore 'Boots' Davidson and Sterling Betancourt. The latter opted to stay in London, after the ensemble had played an engagement in Paris after the F.O.B. concert, and he went on make a historic contribution to the development of pan culture in Britain. Although pan is very much ensemble music, playing solo has been part of its culture, particularly for a tuner who inevitably develops a close relationship with the device whose sound he has shaped. Betancourt began to play solo at venues with West Indian patrons such as the Colherne pub in Earls Court, West London, as well as the Paramount in Central London, usually in the breaks taken by bands that were booked for the evening.

Eventually his path crossed that of a fellow Trinidadian who arrived in

London in 1951, Russ Henderson, and the bond between the two men may have been fostered by the fact that they were both interested in the art of tuning. Betancourt applied it to the pan while Henderson was studying piano tuning. He was also an aspiring jazz pianist with an immersion in steel pan culture when he grew up in Port of Spain. He was taken to "pan yards", the all important storage area and rehearsal space, by a player called Chick Springer. Nobody earned money from pan. Springer was a professional barber. The fact that players learned pieces without sheet music also improved their listening skills and powers of memory, which are essential tools for any musician.

Betancourt and Henderson started to play together because the pianist had the idea of integrating pan into the jazz gigs that he had started to do in London. "With my band that I had already, I just put the steel band inside it, that was 1952," Henderson told me in 2012. We spoke in the music room-cum-study of his home in West London, where an old school "Invaders" style pan took pride of place next to numerous piles of manuscripts, books and concert programmes.

"I had a resident job in a club as a pianist, but while we were playing I'd get up and do a steel band thing, then everybody would go back, with tunes that Sterling could play on the tenor. In 1952, we recorded "Ping Pong Samba". Sterling was on tenor, me on piano, Fitzroy Coleman on guitar; that was the first recording of pan music and conventional instruments."[7]

The title of the piece had little to do with table-tennis, for ping pong was the name for the earliest, small, high pans, and it had a particular resonance for Henderson because, as a young boy, he attended competitions in Trinidad to find the best exponent in the field, and saw his friend Chick Springer triumph.

Henderson and Betancourt worked extensively throughout the 1950s in variable configurations. Betancourt taught Henderson how to play pan and the addition of another pan player, Irwin Clement, and later Ralph Cherie, marked the birth of The Russell Henderson Steel Band, and after initial gigs in London's clubs they were requested for smart functions like Oxbridge balls.[8] Kitted out in tuxedos and bow-ties or morning suits and cravats, the band looked the height of high-society sophistication. Sartorial elegance besides, they also did something that with the pans that had not been seen at the Festival of Britain in 1951.

"Up til when T.A.S.P.O. came here, they had to sit down and play with one stick," Henderson explains. "They had no stand. I introduced stands in London, but I started off with 'pan round the neck' too. When I used to go round those pan yards, there were no stands. They were sitting down on a box or something, that's how they played."[9]

The change to the pan round the neck style, where a long strap kept

the instrument upright in front of the player, like a cinema usher with a
cigarette tray, brought no end of musical challenges.

> With the strap, visually, it's nice to look at, but it's not better because what
> happens is that the pan, when it's against your stomach, it deadens some
> of the notes. It's not so bright. It's like you putting your hand against the
> pan, [and so] you killing some of the notes. When the pan first came
> in, they all tuned in a certain key, mostly F, but when it was around the
> neck, certain notes, like a low C, it was dead. I raised the pitch, tuning
> in G, because the pans were round the neck. Lots of people can't play
> with the pan round the neck. There's a special competition in Trinidad
> for pan round the neck because only a few people could do it. To walk
> *and* play is a difficult thing to do.[10]

Henderson might also have added that the control of the mallets used to
strike the surface of the pan is not at all easy in motion. Developing a wrist
action so that the sticks hit the metal with the right weight and emphasis
takes years when a player is stationary, let alone walking, and in some cases,
executing a series of choreographed steps.

During that musically fertile period in the mid 1950s, when Henderson,
Betancourt and Irwin were taking pan upmarket, Henderson also wove more
elements of jazz into compositions in which he brought steel drums together
with a piano trio, guitar or a horn. These were musicians who understood
the aesthetics of pan as well as the principles of jazz; they were not forcing
a marriage. This nascent "pan jazz" was a development that paralleled the
work of Wilfred Woodley, who formed a group with similar instrumentation
in Trinidad, but, sadly, there is no recorded documentation of its work.

Henderson was a vital link between the two forms, insofar as he had
the same passion for the piano as he did for the steel pan, and was happy to
move from one to the other, realising that both were capable of providing
the richness of timbre needed to broaden the expressive range of Caribbean music. Although pictures of Henderson with "the pan around the
neck" are iconic, the many action shots that exist of him sitting in front of
a keyboard, smiling broadly as he plays, are of no less importance as they
provide a more complete portrait of him as a musician, as concerned with
the intricacies of harmony and melody as he was with the complexities of
polyrhythm.

A limited amount of improvisation took place among Trinidadian steel
bands, as players took it upon themselves to spontaneously embellish a
given melody with a flurry of concise, additional notes. Because of the
restricted tonal range of the pans, the lines were short, but the players
espoused the idea that a theme could invite variations. Older Trinidadians
refer to this technique as *ramajay*. If this was an important foundation for
the innovations of Woodley and Henderson, then one should also bear
in mind that, throughout the pre-war and post-war period, jazz made its

presence felt in Jamaica and Trinidad by way of broadcasts, recordings and tours by leading artists.

Talent shows for up-and-coming local players were also regular. In 1948, just three years before leaving Trinidad for England, Henderson entered and won a competition for jazz small groups judged by a brilliant visiting American pianist, Wynton Kelly, another manifestation of the West Indi-an-African-American cultural nexus. Kelly, though a New Yorker, was of Jamaican parentage.

Henderson subsequently got to know the man who underpinned modernist solos with a deep blues feeling and made his mark as a bandleader in his own right, as well as a sideman to legends such as Dinah Washington, Charles Mingus, Freddie Hubbard, Dizzy Gillespie and Miles Davis.[11]

"I showed Wynton a few calypso tunes, [any song] that was like the song of the time," Henderson recalls. "I became very good friends with him, he came to my house and showed me a few things. I was amazed to see his hands flying all about! My theme song is "Robin's Nest", composed by Charles Thompson. Wynton showed me that."[12]

Decades after, this piece is still the ringtone on Henderson's telephone. If Henderson's jazz sensibility was strengthened by that engagement with a stellar American improviser, there was also a sense that pan was being pushed in new creative directions in the West Indies, Europe and America. The integration of steel pan into dance productions in these territories between the late 1940s and mid 1950s was particularly important.

Three key performer-choreographers put steel drums on stage. Beryl McBurnie with *Carnival Bele* in Port of Spain; Boscoe Holder with his *Bal Creole* in London; and his brother Geoffrey Holder in Truman Capote's *House of Flowers* in New York. Geoffrey Holder[13] subsequently reprised his character of the mischievous voodoo loa, Baron Samedi, almost 20 years later in the New Orleans-based James Bond film, *Live and Let Die*.

McBurnie's initiative was especially admirable as she had to overcome barbs from some in the arts establishment in Trinidad who felt that the use of pan in theatre would lower the tone, because of the stigma that still clung to steel pan in the late 1940s. By placing steel drums in the setting of the Little Carib Theatre, she was bringing cultural legitimacy to an instrument that was demonised by the middle class, because of the violence that was associated with the early steel bands. In the poorest parts of Port of Spain, known collectively as "Behind The Bridge", each downtrodden district required a band to cement its own identity, security and self-worth, and regular clashes took place over borders, with the cutlass and bottles as weapons of choice. To the outside world, the bloodletting may have appeared wanton, but the pan men were mostly uneducated youths whose lives had been blighted by harsh authoritarianism. Bands took names such as Invaders, Desperados and Cross Fire precisely because they saw themselves as bandito-outsiders who were engaged in a form of trench warfare with a police force that held them in contempt, and an establishment happy to let them rot in the slums.

Members of the Hell's Yard band found themselves jailed for the heinous crime of "being in a procession of more than 20 persons". As well as this denial of the basic right to assembly, arrests were common if sticks were seen in a youth's back pocket and judges swiftly increased sentences once it became known that the defendant was a pan man, commonly seen as "badjohns". To romanticize or sanitize these figures would be wrong because these men were by no means paragons of virtue, but that should not mask an essential truth: they were the product of a dehumanizing environment, who also produced music of beauty.

Earl Lovelace's novel, *The Dragon Can't Dance* (1979) provides a brilliant insight into the mind of the badjohn by way of the character of Fisheye, and the novel explains how the vehicle of the steel band provides an outlet for the energies and frustrations endured by Fisheye in his grim daily life. Too often the badjohn was dismissed as a thug, with little thought given to the circumstances of the deep and divisive socio-economic hierarchies of a colonial society. What is also a reality is that a degree of violence framed the transition of West Indian culture from the islands to the Mother country.

When assault and battery were visited upon the black community by white racists in Notting Hill in 1958, just as the likes of Sterling Betancourt and Russ Henderson were developing pan in London, those African Caribbeans who had come from the rough-around-the-edges world of the steel band or the ghetto byways of Port of Spain would have been seen as a comforting rather than a threatening presence, even to the black bourgeoisie who would have snubbed them at home.

There is incontrovertible evidence that pan men resident in other parts of the country did indeed answer a call to arms and flex muscle in situations where *their* people had come under attack. So to the stories of West Indians in Brixton travelling to Notting Hill to offer strong-arm assistance to besieged fellow Blacks in 1958, one should add the case of Curtis Bellamy, a steel drummer who arrived in Manchester in 1961.

> I was listening to the news back home in St. John's Barbados, about more and more gangs [in Moss Side]. Being a physical sort of person I came up to see what was going on," he said when I met him in Moss Side, Manchester in the autumn of 2013. "I had a brother, sister, uncle, I sort of [fearing for their safety]… I came here to help. They came here in 55, 57, at different times in the 50s. I saw a few incidents; how they were terrorizing the place, picking on Blacks, more and more gangs. The leader was Mosley. They used to have meetings at Alexandra Park Gates, the followers used to be there. It was a dangerous time.[14]

Alexandra Park Gates was right in the centre of Moss Side with its well-established African-Caribbean community, and if Oswald Mosley's Union Movement, as it had done in Notting Hill in 1958, wanted to poison race relations in Manchester, then this was the place to do it. A 1960 photograph of Mosley, who openly espoused the doctrines of Hitler and Mussolini, standing on the platform of a flat-bed pick-up truck with two loud-speakers and a union jack, chin jutting forward, whip hand emphatically raised, shows a demagogue intent on preying upon the most base fear that all humans have of the other. It should also be noted that the tabloid press ran numerous scare stories to entrench the association of a black ghetto with crime and depravity. The irony of a musician from a British colony travelling to the Metropole to shepherd his loved ones out of harm's way, in what was supposed to be a more advanced, if not *civilized* society, would have been lost on the tabloid press.

But protecting family members in a hostile climate was not the only priority in Curtis Bellamy's life. He had to find work and accommodation. After securing a room in Moss Side, he was hired at the Morris & Ingrams foundry where he made the kind of baths that wouldn't have looked out of place in the sci-fi film sets of the day. Later, Bellamy found employment in Smiths and then the Walls factories, while he made his way on the Manchester music scene. Later, he moved to Whalley Range, where Lord Kitchener lived for several years, and before long he found a number of other steel pan players working in Manchester, such as fellow Bajan Jason Waldron. Bellamy became a member of Starlanders Steel Band and played at clubs like the Capital, the Lagos and the Nile in the early 1960s.

> "Yes, I started out going to clubs, playing and also singing calypsos like "Kingston Market" for Starlanders, which was Joe Leader's band. I'd been playing pan since I was thirteen in Barbados but I did more singing for Joe. He and his brother Secki were two of the main pan players at the time, they were from St. Kitts There was another player from St. Kitts, Tex Matthews, we all played together, then Secki formed his band."[15]

Joe Leader had been in Manchester since the late 1950s and was a dynamic force in developing groups, and his 7-piece Starlanders (pan with vocals) proved popular. With calypso well established at Manchester clubs like the Nile for years, it made sense for a steel band to feature singers, and Bellamy and his bandmates were able to gig regularly.

Leader's was not the only pan ensemble active in Manchester. There was also the much respected Trinidadian Arthur Culpepper who had arrived in 1957 and led a band called Silver Century, which would evolve into another combo in the 1960s that Bellamy also joined, The Caribbean Syncopators. Here was a historical reference that perhaps only older music lovers and historians would have understood, harking back to the ragtime heyday of the early 20th century, such as Will Marion Cook's Southern Syncopated Orchestra. The application of an archaic term like Syncopator to a Caribbean ensemble in the north of England was a highly intriguing piece of cross-cultural time travelling.

Throughout the 1960s and beyond, the steel band movement continued to grow into a national rather than just local phenomenon confined to the capital, and pioneers such as Sterling Betancourt, Russ Henderson and Selwyn Baptiste. Many other skilled steel drummers from Trinidad settled in the North and the Midlands and began to lead bands, and if Culpepper and others were active in Manchester, then mention must also be made of Victor Philip in Birmingham, St. Clair Morris in Leeds and Terence Noel in Leicester. Steel band was too important for West Indians for it to be confined to one city.

Notes

1. Mark Olden, *Murder in Notting Hill* (Zero, 2011).
2. Interview with the author, Ladbroke Grove, London, January, 2014.
3. Ibid.
4. Ibid.
5. This is an observation based on attendance of many steel pan performances. One audience once asked a pan player if he had any "secret" pedals to make the instrument sound so "electric".
6. Dr F.I.R Blake, *The Trinidad & Tobago Steel Pan: History & Evolution* (Self-published, 1995) p.166
7. Interview with the author, Kensal Rise, London, 2013.
8. Val Wilmer has taken excellent photographs of the band in this attire.
9. Interview with the author, Kensal Rise, London, 2013.
10. Interview with the author, Kensal Rise, London, 2013.
11. See Wynton Kelly, *Kelly Great* (VeeJay, 1960).
12. Interview with the author, Kensal Rise, London, 2013.
13. Holder's turn in *Live And Let Die* is pantomime-ish to say the least, but his screen presence is nonetheless commanding.
14. Interview with the author, Moss Side, Manchester, 2013.
15. Ibid.

18 DO START THE CARNIVAL

"I can remember the first carnival, when you walked down to Potternewton Park and I heard the sound of the steel band. I was walking behind this old lady, a West Indian lady. She was so excited. She put she hands in the air and she shout, 'Lord I haven't heard anything like this for 15 years!'"
— Arthur France, founder, Leeds West Indian Carnival

"We used to meet at the Speedy Bird café on Sundays, drinking fish tea and Red Stripe beer and listening to calypso music with a paraffin heater to keep warm.
— Roy Hackett on the Commonwealth Coordinated Committee, which played a major role in the birth of St. Pauls' Carnival, Bristol.

Despite the financial and cultural hegemony of the south, the disparities of class and wealth were and are no less manifest in the provinces. Manchester, once the industrial powerhouse of the North, had its own moneyed elite, "the Cheshire set". It wasn't only Londoners like Russ Henderson who were asked to play for "society events" – as Curtis Bellamy told me in 2013:

"Yeah, 'the Cheshire set', that was mostly posh people who gave us gigs back in the day. We did weddings, functions, golf clubs, cricket clubs around places like Knutsford, mostly. It was people who were bankers, actors, or they'd inherited family businesses. They used to come down to the Great Western [in Manchester], listen to the band and then book us. The money was good.

"We used to have a great time. Sometimes they'd have big parties and they wanted a steel band, so they'd set up a marquee on the lawn the size of a football pitch. You always knew you were in a different world because when you went to the house they had the kind of carpets that were so new and deep that you'd just spring right up in the air when you put your foot down. I have to say they looked after us well."[1]

But appearing at a select private functions was not really what steelbands were about. Like calypso singers, steel bands come into their own in the intense and intoxicating context of carnival, a socio-cultural highpoint of the year for which elaborate preparations were made. The arrival of carnival in England was as inevitable as the arrival of steel pans. One reinforces the other. Carnival is not just something that West Indians do. Carnival is what West Indians *are*.

By the time that Mancunian steel bands such as Starlanders and Caribbean

Syncopators were gigging throughout Lancashire and Cheshire, the first foundations of Carnival, as it is known today in Britain, with its significant global reach, had already been laid in West London. From the mid 1960s the event that is now branded as the Notting Hill Carnival grew from very humble origins, with its initial attenders far lower than the million plus that now stream through the streets on August bank holiday weekend.

However, what is considered to be the inaugural appearance actually took place indoors, with bright lights illuminating a series of performances and a dance floor that was enthusiastically filled by several loose-limbed couples. BBC Television was on hand to film proceedings, complete with an impossibly plummy-voiced presenter who can be heard saying these immortal lines. "In a famous London ballroom a West Indian get-together... a Caribbean carnival they call it, I believe."[2]

Such was the introduction to a film of what is considered to be the very first version of Carnival in Britain. It took place on 30th January 1959 at St. Pancras Town Hall. The emotional distance that the script conveys by its euphemism for outsiders, foreigners, or blacks – in this case *they* – suggests that this "get-together" – surely the dullest epithet for Carnival imaginable – stood well outside British social norms. Some explaining had to be done.

The film is an important reminder of the Black community's still marginal status. It echoes the wartime Pathé newsreels that sought to give an insight into *who* West Indians were, and why they were relevant to the mainstream – with a strong anthropological resonance.

After the titles, there is footage of masqueraders in full costume, impeccably dressed dancers and musicians playing congas. Next comes a close-up of the souvenir programme, "A Caribbean Carnival, directed by Edric Connor", and below that line is the key credit: "Organized by *West Indian Gazette*." Edric Connor we have already met; the *West Indian Gazette* was a black newspaper established in 1958, a follow-up to the magazine *Checkers* of 1948.

The *W.I. Gazette* was the brainchild of Trinidadian journalist-social campaigner, Claudia Jones.[3] Born Claudia Vera Cumberbatch in Belmont, Port of Spain, Trinidad in 1915, Jones moved to Harlem, New York with her parents at the age of eight and became a journalist and civil rights activist. For the best part of her adult life she was a mighty thorn in the flesh of the American establishment. Deported for her communist beliefs,[4] Jones arrived in England in 1955 and realized that establishing a newspaper could provide cohesion for a Black community that was struggling to find its feet.

Jones' experience of fighting racism in America, as well as her strong ties with political artists such as Paul Robeson, made her a galvanizing figure in the struggle of Blacks in the UK. The shockwaves caused by the race riots in Nottingham and Notting Hill of August 1958 gave Jones and other leading members of the community food for thought on what was the place of people of colour in British society. As an internationalist, Jones sought to locate the British struggle in the context of the struggle for independence in the colonies. While the oft-reprinted photograph of Jones, leaning over a typewriter, telephone and ballpoint pen in hand in the *Gazette's* Brixton office, paints a compelling picture of a dedicated and dynamic woman, it is the *Gazette's* headlines, *What Now for the West Indies?* that properly locates her life.

She saw that the complex political relationship between the islands and "the mother country" was not separate from the explosion of violence against Blacks in Nottingham, Manchester and the capital. West Indian expatriates found themselves straddling two precarious and changing worlds. Just as the islands themselves were on the cusp of change, expatriate West Indian communities were in the process of changing Britain.

On the one hand, "A Caribbean Carnival" at St. Pancras Town Hall might be seen as a morale booster for a beleaguered community, but carnival was also the assertion of a deeply-rooted strain of resistance within the West Indian psyche. West Indians from slavery onwards had fought for the right to hold Carnival against banning orders, state violence and repeated pro-hibitions, which had previously targeted drum dances, and the practice of obeah. Wiser slave-masters recognised the utility of carnival as an occasion for releasing social pressure, so slaves were granted the right to take part in song and dance, and mimic their masters by daubing themselves with flour, but such acceptance was also matched by dehumanizing exclusion.

One of the earliest documented records of Carnival reveals the most specific and divisive of racial hierarchies. In 1881 L.M Fraser wrote:

> The population of the Colony was divided into the following categories, Whites, free persons of colour, Indians and Slaves. The free persons of colour were subjected to very stringent regulations... and were compelled to keep to themselves and never presume to join in the amusements of the privileged class. The Indians kept entirely aloof, and the Slaves, except as onlookers... or by special favour when required to take part, had no share in the Carnival, which was confined exclusively to the upper class of the community.[5]

If blacks were prepared to fight the police for their place in Carnival, leading to riots in Trinidad in 1881[6] then it was not surprising that they would parade their art of resistance in the wake of a race riot in Britain in 1958. Carnival has always been more than an expression of the desire to "jump up". It is the assertion of the right to *show* oneself and to *be* oneself, two rights that were problematic for West Indians in 1950s Britain. This was why an apparently insignificant part of the St. Pancras event was actually one of the most significant: the beauty contest. This gave black women the opportunity to celebrate who they were at a time when there was little recognition of this in the mainstream women's press. A supporter of hairdressing salons run by West Indian women, Claudia Jones also put beauty tips in the *Gazette*, which was a way of telling her sisters that they were attractive.

While the Notting Hill riots had proved that black women were prepared to show their physical strength in the face of violence,[7] the election of the "Carnival Queen" conveyed the message that they were not aesthetically inferior to Europeans, and gave black women an opportunity to be visible. There was a stark absence, for instance, of black women on the covers of jazz albums in the mid 1950s, even when the musicians were black. White models were deemed more suitable. It took the lobbying of artists of the stature of Miles Davis to persuade white-run labels to change this disgrace.[8]

Whatever the gender politics of beauty contexts, Jones was very much a pragmatist. Hence the political capital from the St. Pancras beauty contest was supplemented by putting hard currency from the Carnival to good use. As Ansel Wong, a former chair of the Notting Hill Carnival, explains: "Claudia Jones saw carnival as a process by which she can celebrate people's achievements. She agreed that the proceeds from the sale of tickets for the carnival shall be used to pay for the legal fees of those people arrested during the Notting Hill riots the year before."[9]

But the rise of carnival was not just a matter for the West Indian community. It's clear that it was part of the attraction that Black culture exerted on the mainstream. In Nottingham and Notting Hill, controversy around a racially mixed couple had sparked the violence, but months later the dance floor at St. Pancras was filled by Blacks and Whites of both sexes. A picture of miscegenation was there in stylish monochrome.

The varied bill of the cabaret at that historic inaugural edition of the Carnival featured music and dance, with the jazz guitarist, Fitzroy Coleman, calypsonian Mighty Terror and choreographer Stanley Jack all making contributions. Choreographer-musician Boscoe Holder and Connor himself also took part, though it is not entirely clear in what capacity. What was important was the audio-visual richness of the spectacle; the stimulus for the eye and ear were of equal magnitude.

Following St. Pancras, other indoor Carnivals took place in subsequent years in central London locations such as Porchester Hall and Seymour Hall, a venue that held up to 2,000. What boosted these events was the presence of the emerging calypso stars from Trinidad, the most sensational of whom was The Mighty Sparrow. His 1956 composition, "Jean And Dinah", which dealt with the subject of prostitution fostered by American military bases on the island, proved him to be an incisive socio-political commentator. For the privilege of seeing this star at Carnival in 1962, punters had to pay two shillings and six pence.

Significant as these events were, they were not true carnival. For that to happen, the music had to be heard in the open air, as musicians, dancers, masqueraders in costume and the following crowds took to the streets. But given the negative press and paranoia that framed the Black community in the late 1950s, the authorities would have probably resisted giving permission for a procession of West Indians in the open air. Indoor events "contained" the Black presence.

But Carnival could not be held back and the landmark year in the history of carnival in Britain came in 1964. Immigration had become an even bigger political issue. The 1962 Commonwealth Immigrants Acts effectively limited entry to labour from Africa, Asia and the Caribbean by way of an employment voucher system, which was in turn dubbed "the Colour Bar Bill" by Claudia Jones.

It was at this point that Carnival broke out of halls and went onto the streets, and it was significant that this should have been initiated by a social worker, Rhaune Laslett, an *enfant du monde* of Russian and Native American heritage, since it displayed a depth of unity amongst the diverse community of Notting Hill. Although six years had passed since the riots, the neighbourhood was still a largely impoverished ghetto with a fearsome reputation. The plight of many of the local Portuguese, Irish, Russian and Polish families was not significantly better than that of West Indians.

The 1964 event was a celebration first and foremost for local children of various nationalities. There was a mixed bill of entertainment that included an African drummer, clowns, and a steel band led by Russell Henderson. A small part of Portobello Road, one of the central arteries of today's Notting Hill Carnival route, was given over to Laslett and the performers and the proceedings were reported as joyous.

Another inspirational community worker, Judith Baptiste (met in Chapter 17), makes the point that the event was part of a drive to raise cultural awareness among children. This underlined the fact that immigrants were laying down roots, so the focus had to be not so much on the Windrush generation as on their offspring. She recalls:

> There was Russ Henderson playing enthusiastically. And these little children who didn't know what had hit them, but they were loving it, jumping up and moving and learning about their roots, which was so important to know where they've come from.
>
> Not only black children. I went round to a lot of primary schools, and had a little exhibition that I put on to show them where they came from. I arranged trips to the Commonwealth Institute in the High Street [Kensington], which had wonderful tableaux of different countries, but in particular Trinidad and Tobago. It was really good because there were balconies around. That was a lovely setting.[10]

Baptiste's husband Selwyn also held many events at the Institute and it was the combination of these initiatives and Laslett's first Carnival that really fostered the growth of the present day Carnival. Baptiste's steel band, Metronomes, later emerged as one of the key ensembles at the event. But it was the appearance of Henderson's trio of pan players (Sterling Betancourt, Ralph Cherrie and himself) at the 1964 edition of Carnival that made the landmark moment when they embarked on a spontaneous procession around the area, moving to Holland Park, Bayswater and Westbourne Park before returning to Portobello. They had a joyful crowd in their wake. This captured the essence of Carnival as it is defined in the West Indies. It involved *movement*. People were in a parade, improvised as it may have been. They *followed* the music of the pan men, or as they express it in Trinidad, they were on a road march. This is an assertion of power. It is an exercise of the right of assembly that had, at that time, a political resonance for Carnival-goers aware of the history of the event in Trinidad and the police harassment of pan players all year round.

Although the tradition of the tent, where calypso singers come to perform their best songs, is crucial, the event reaches its apotheosis in an exterior space, where movement frees up the body and increases the likelihood of dance. To walk, after all, is to take a first step on the road to a "jump up".

Henderson's procession through West London was seminal and it struck a chord with the event that took place more than a decade before – the parade that Lord Kitchener led following the victory of the West Indies cricket team over England at Lords in 1950. Here was another musician reacting spontaneously to what he saw and leading the people on a grand excursion, as he set his commentary on it to a piece of original, extemporized music. The police kept a watchful eye on events and in both cases, wisely elected *not* to stop the carnival. Had they done so they would surely have been the subject of a *piquant* calypso.

The people who contributed to the planning or the performance of the early editions of Carnival, both in the halls and on the road – Claudia Jones, Edric Connor, Rhaune Laslett, Russell Henderson, Selwyn and Judith Baptiste to name but some – have an essential place in the pantheon of contemporary British culture, because the event has since become a worldwide phenomenon.

Carnival has created its own vocabulary. The formal designation of the costumed and processional event as "a masquerade" has been replaced by the diminutive "Mas", but, more importantly, it is conjoined to a verb of energy. To do Mas will not suffice. You have to *play* Mas. This is a brilliant encapsulation of Carnival, because it conveys theatricality, release and physical engagement. You play games. You play tricks. You play the fool. All of this is manifested in "Mas".

Of the many things left behind in Trinidad, the loss of Carnival was arguably the cause of the greatest emotional pain. It was why one of the most meaningful calypsos of the Windrush era was Mighty Terror's "No Carnival In Britain", recorded in 1954, exactly ten years before Laslett, Henderson et al went into action. Terror's song had a haunting lament:

> Yes, I does cry when the time comes
> No Mas here in Great Britain.[11]

The real significance of Carnival in Notting Hill in 1964 was the fact that it was soon reinforced by other similar initiatives outside London. "Mas" soon spread to places where there were motivated individuals with organizational skills.

Leeds, in West Yorkshire, had made headlines for a significant breakthrough around the time of the first Notting Hill Carnival. Its football team, Leeds United, fielded the first ever person of colour to play in the final of the FA Cup in 1965. This was the brilliant South African left winger, Albert Johanneson, but if the Black community in Leeds had taken heart from his achievement, the lot of the majority was dire. With a population of around 500,000 in the post-war period, Leeds, formerly a major cloth-making city, now in decline, had a relatively small Black presence, but significant Irish and Jewish minorities. Numbers from the Caribbean increased to around 4,000 by the late 1950s. Most of the new arrivals were young, male and single, with trades – carpenters, clerks, mechanics, ex-servicemen and teachers.

As in other cities, immigrants were concentrated in one area, Chapeltown, just north of the centre of Leeds, often living six and more to a room in large, often dilapidated Victorian houses, where landlords saw the opportunity to turn a quick profit.

Like many other West Indians, Arthur France, who came to Britain in 1957, held strong to the belief that he was travelling to the centre of the universe. Like many other West Indians, the young man from Nevis ended up in a particular city because of a family connection – his sister's journey preceding his own by a few years. His voice cracked a little when he told me in 2013:

> When I first arrived I had mixed feelings, I mean the place was so damn cold. It was amazing, because growing up in the Caribbean we always look at England as the mother country, this special place that everybody wanted to come to, but the place was just damned cold, and pretty unfriendly. We were living in these dingy rooms in houses… the whole thing, well, it was just so disappointing.[12]

Finding work as a porter for British Rail, France settled into a Black Leeds community, which was dominated by citizens from St. Kitts and Nevis, two of the Leeward islands, and he soon experienced discrimination as Black people tried to make a social life for themselves.

> You couldn't go to the clubs if you were black because a lot of people wouldn't let you in. We had many battles with them. There was no law, so they could tell you to piss off. There was a club at the bottom of Chapeltown called Prince Edward where most of the black people used to go and have a drink, so there were one or two. There were *lots* of

problems with different clubs. But even the churches were racist. Some of them just simply didn't want you to "darken" their door.[13]

But exclusion did not dampen the spirit of the Black community in Chapeltown, and around the late 1950s and early 1960s two steelbands by the name of Caribbeans and Esso were formed. Being a diehard lover of pan, France also co-founded the Gay Carnival Steel Band (later to become Wilberforce) with his cousin, while another local ensemble that rose to prominence at around the same time, Invaders – formed by a friend of France's known as Prentiss – took its name from the famous Trinidadian steel band led by Ellie Mannette. France saw steel bands as an essential rallying point for West Indians living in Leeds. "I never actually played pan, but I was fascinated by it. I managed the band. I take the steel band in our culture very serious. The pan is not a joke. We know it is a positive thing."[14]

With pan culture established in Leeds, it was only a matter of time before France took steps to launch carnival in the city. Like Claudia Jones, he recognised that the black community in Chapeltown was in need of uplift and he looked to anything that could foster solidarity and collective well-being. "The carnival starting… well, I thought we needed something that would bring us together. The best thing was the carnival," France said, as if it were a statement of the obvious.

However, he made a point that is highly revealing of the complexity of the West Indian mindset as shaped by colonial rule. What carnival represented to the people was one thing, but they were not unaware of the way they would be perceived by the ethnic majority. He explained, his voice sometimes weary:

> Some people were interested and some were not. My sister and a few friends had an organization called African Caribbean and Asian, and they had dances, but I felt we needed something more than that for community spirit. The last Sunday in November 1964, I had 27 people in my bedsit and we set up The United Caribbean Association. I said we should have a carnival and they thought I was crazy! They just went and threw me out of the meeting!
>
> A lot of them had a complex about us being out in the street. Some felt carnival would degrade our people because it's dancing in the street. It was like 'Oh, you bring us here for the white man to *laugh* at us.' Carnival had a deeper meaning for me because I thought it was a celebration of emancipation from slavery. So it took me about three years to make it happen."[15]

Shocking as the objections to Carnival from *within* the black community may seem, they remind us of the struggle that West Indians had to make to define their own cultural norms outside of the colonial constrictions that had existed for so long. As noted in Chapter13, some West Indian listeners complained about the use of West Indian readers on the *Caribbean Voices* radio programme.

Perseverance paid off for France. On bank holiday Monday, 7 August 1967, the first Leeds West Indian carnival took place under a cloudy sky. France, assisted by a number of friends and family, wanted to model the event as closely as possible on carnival as he knew it in Nevis, and marked a route that would take several steel bands through Potternewton Park. He recalled:

> Steel band was built for carnival, it's part and parcel of the whole thing. The sound and the whole rhythm is just amazing. So, all the more reason to stage a steel band competition.

For the inaugural competition, three ensembles entered: Gay Carnival and Invaders from Leeds, and St Christopher's from Birmingham. The latter was the eventual victor. France remembers them having to make two trips to Leeds in a transit van with their bulky instruments strapped to a luggage rack on the roof of the vehicle.

All of the bands were the relatively small, six-piece units consisting of two tenors, two double seconds, and cello and bass. Their repertoires were a reminder of the eclecticism of pan culture. Invaders played "Drink to Me Only with Thine Eyes", Gay Carnival played "Pan in G Minor" and St. Christopher, "Elizabethan Serenade". Deep in the heart of Yorkshire, once the county of coal and textiles, immigrant musicians played classical music on discarded objects from the oil industry – a collision of art, race and recycling.

Intent on recreating a real West Indian carnival, Arthur France also organized a calypso competition. Singers, hailing mostly from St. Kitts, took part and the calypso king was Lord Silky, a charming entry in the pantheon of calypsonian names, which referred to his sartorial elegance, namely the fine cloth used to make the shirts in which he performed. Silky saw off Lord Smiley, Lord Prince and the Mighty Chuka. As the conquering hero recalled when we spoke in 2014, it was Arthur France himself who personally put the word out around Leeds' Black community that the first Carnival needed vocalists and bands: "Yeah, I was at the youth club in Chapeltown, just hanging out and he asked if anybody wanted to sing, and I jumped at it because I had done a bit of singing back home in St. Kitts. We used to sing Kitch songs that we heard on the radio, we'd just practise in our spare time really."[16]

Earning his living as a joiner, Silky did not see music as a profession, but was happy to perform when the opportunity arose. Interestingly, Silky's choice of material expressed feelings of nostalgia for his homeland *and* pride in the "mother country" just as Kitch had done on "London Is The Place For Me". Silky recalled:

> For the calypso competition I sang a song from home called "St. Kitts is My Borning Land", but I changed the lyrics in places. I put in "England is my home in every way/No matter what people say/In England I bound to stay." I suppose that's what I was feeling at the time, really. Carnival,

in any case, was something that was special, to have it in Leeds. The whole event was so exciting, I think everybody was ecstatic because it so reminded us of being back at home in St.Kitts.[17]

Silky's recollections make it clear that the 1967 Leeds carnival was a crucial moment in the history of its Black community. But as far as France was concerned, it was really the impact that the carnival had on the first wave of older West Indian immigrants in Leeds, those who had arrived in the early 1950s, that made the whole endeavour, including the scepticism that he had to overcome from within the Black community, more than worthwhile. He recalled:

I can remember that very first carnival when you walked down to Potter Newton Park and I heard the sound of the steel band. I was walking behind this old lady, a West Indian lady. She was so excited. She put she hands in the air and she shout, "Lord I haven't heard anything like this for 15 years!" It was quite a moment.[18]

15,000 people attended the first Leeds West Indian carnival in 1967. The police presence was limited because it was a community event under the aegis of the local council, to whom France had to apply for permission. Quite apart from fostering greater solidarity in the Leeds Black community, the event also drew West Indians and Africans from Birmingham, (some no doubt in support of their pan homeboys, St. Christopher's) and Manchester. "They heard of a carnival, they got excited," France recalls. "I suppose they all knew what was going on."

This record of the establishing of West Indian culture in Leeds cannot omit mention of the contribution of St. Clair Morris (or Mr Morris as he was known to all) who founded the Paradise Steel Band a few years later and took steelband music to virtually every school in Leeds. Much loved, Mr Morris sadly died in 2017 as this book was being prepared for publication.

Only forty or so miles separate Leeds from Manchester, and transport links by bus and rail were good. Movement of Blacks between the two cities was frequent and in some cases the trips were cultural reconnaissance missions. France recalled:

Yeah, there were groups in Manchester that we became aware of in Leeds. If we wanted to organize a dance, we were told to look at these guys in the Denmark, which was the pub where most West Indians went, and we went there, found them and they came down and played for us. They were quite good. We basically went to where black people hang out in Manchester to find any kind of good music.

Caribbean camaraderie across the north was enhanced by such trips. With poor intra-island transport communication, few West Indians had the chance to travel *within* the region, so Britain was not only the place where Blacks met Whites, it was the place where Blacks met other Blacks. Petty inter-island rivalry existed, but it was mostly outweighed by the solidarity that arose from the blanket discrimination that most West Indians faced.

Though the media tended to equate West Indians with Jamaicans, (as encapsulated by a 1955 Pathé newsreel entitled *Our Jamaican Problem*), the West Indian population in Britain was in reality diverse. "It was here that I met Jamaicans, Bajans and Trinidadians for the first time, and felt OK with them," says France. "We were all in the same boat with regard to the racism. Basically, you see a person on the road and if you looked alike, and shared some similarities, then you get along well."

One thing that challenged many West Indians was the local accent. France recalls how he had to adjust to what he heard in the streets of Leeds, how much it differed from the English he'd heard in St. Kitts:

> The Leeds accent? I find it was funny. I mean it wasn't the BBC. But there were also black people from Yorkshire with a *completely* different accent. I remember people from Castleford with a deep Yorkshire accent, but you got used to it. They'd say "dost tha nae?" instead of "do you know?" Me, I find it funny listening to people in Barnsley. Joe Williams the comedian, he made it because he was a black man with such a deep northern accent. It was a real novelty.

It worked the other way, too.

> Yeah, I mean it's the same as white people born in the Caribbean with a deep accent. We saw a white man at Headingley cricket ground once in 1963. [France started to chuckle] And he came up to us and we thought, "Oh, here we go, what does he want with us?" But then he started talking to us and you couldn't have heard a deeper Caribbean accent.[19]

Divided by race, black and white West Indians can still be bound by culture.

In 1968, just a year after the first Leeds event, Carnival also began in Bristol. Much like Liverpool, the Southwestern port was a vital thoroughfare in the slave trade and had a population of Africans that reached back to the 18th century. That history is written into venues such as the Colston Hall (named after Edward Colston, a wealthy slave trader) and street names, such as Black Boy Hill and White Ladies Road in Clifton, which reflected the trend of well-to-do women strolling into town with exotic young slaves trailing in their wake.

By the mid 1960s, the black population in Bristol numbered around 3,000, of which a large swathe had served in the armed forces. West Indians became mostly concentrated in the area of St. Paul's, north-east of the city centre, which had been the home of affluent slave traders in the 18th century, but had since fallen into decline, following extensive damage during the Blitz. As elsewhere, the "coloured quarter" of Bristol had poor housing and social facilities and a reputation as a dangerous place. As elsewhere, West Indian immigrants were refused entry to pubs in the centre of Bristol, which led to a very localized social life centring around shebeens, private parties, dances and weddings. But whilst there was social segregation, it did not prevent some immigrants, who had arrived in the most precarious circumstances, from reversing in their fortunes. This is best illustrated by the case of the St. Claire family from Barbados.

Joseph St. Claire arrived as a stowaway some time before the 1939-45 war. He earned a living as a herbalist and dentist. He was also a lay preacher and wrote original spirituals that were sung by his son Reuben, a member of the Bristol Home Guard during World War II. Joseph's daughter Naomi was also a singer, who adopted the stage name Eve. Sadly there is little information regarding where she may have performed, but her existence, as does that of her father, points to musical activities in Bristol that have passed under the radar of any promoters or impresarios

Precious little documentation exists of other Bristol-based Black artists who were active between the 1940s and 1960s, but it is known that a steel band appeared at the first St. Paul's Carnival in the summer of 1968. The event lasted a week (June 15-22) and was billed as the St. Paul's, Montpelier and Easton Festival. The programme reveals an admirably wide range of activities with a strong emphasis on sport, arts & craft. There were school & scout displays as well as music and dancing, judo and karate demonstrations, a dominoes tournament at Baptist Mill Youth Club. Revellers, once they had followed the carnival procession from Lower Ashley Road to City Road and on to St. Nicholas, could enjoy a pan group at the Mayfair Suite, at the grand dance on the final evening. The organizing committee's mission statement was forward-thinking in recognising the desirability of cultural diversity:

> The purpose of the festival is to provide a scene on which the interest and variety of the culture and life of the peoples in the area can be displayed and enjoyed. We hope it will also lead to better understanding, greater respect and increasing harmony in this community of communities.

So there was an Indian *mela* as well as Irish and West Indian concerts at St. Barnabas Hall, and the 1969 carnival reinforced this spirit of inclusion. There were "Concerts of speech, music and dancing by Burmese, English, Indian, Irish, Pakistani and West Indian groups" as well as steel, jazz, pipe and brass bands and "even we hope a barrel organ". On the executive of these early organisations of Carnival were people who have now passed into local legend – Bernard Hall, Colin Tennent and Carmen Beckford, a Jamaican community worker who went on to become the director of the Bristol Race Equality Council. Another was Roy Hackett, a Jamaican who initially worked in Liverpool in the early 1950s before moving to Wolverhampton, London and then Somerset, where he worked at Britain's first atomic power station, Hinkley Point. Hackett settled in Bristol by the end of the decade.

The St. Paul's carnival had strong roots in socio-political issues. Hackett, with a close friend, Owen Henry, had established a pioneering action group in the city in 1962, the Commonwealth Coordinating Committee, which subsequently evolved into the Bristol West Indian Parents & Friends Association. Their mission was to improve the living and working conditions of the Caribbean community in whatever way possible.

In an interview conducted for the Bristol Archives in 2012, Hackett pointed out the soundtrack to the birth pangs of the CCC, which took place in the kind of Spartan surroundings that West Indian migrants knew only too well. "We used to meet at the Speedy Bird café on Sundays, drinking fish tea and Red Stripe beer and listening to calypso music with a paraffin heater to keep warm."[20]

Aware of the substantial financial gains generated by the Notting Hill carnival today, and the thorny issue of the kind of business model that would benefit all relevant contributors, Hackett expounded a few essential home truths based on his own experience. In the beginning, making money was not on the agenda:

> The festival was never a business. It was a community event. We had people who were from the outside come in and help us, but 90% of the people that ran the festival were from the community. They were shopkeepers, carpenters, shoemakers – everybody did their little bit. We went with caps in hand, begging pennies and half a crown. If one gave five shillings, that was a whole lot of money! We begged and got favours from people who had lorries and they gave us their time and vehicles to get the festival people on the floats. All of this was given us. All we had to do was pay the driver for the day."[21]

This local commitment was in keeping with the original manifesto of the St. Paul's Carnival: "increasing harmony in this community of communities."

The second carnival had a "United Nations display and parade of the fashions and dress of the world", and this resonates with the work done by Judith Baptiste.

Looking at the histories of the carnivals in Bristol, Leeds and London, it is clear that a desire for community cohesion was the driving motivation. Carnivals chimed with community desires, but their existence owed much more to the determination of individuals such as Claudia Jones, Rhaune Laslett, Selwyn and Judith Baptiste, Arthur France, Carmen Beckford and Roy Hackett. All understood that culture and politics were inextricably linked, and that percussion and procession could do more than entertain Blacks in Britain.

Notes

1. Telephone interview with the author, May 2014.
2. British Pathé newsreel.
3. See footprintsoflondon.com/2014/02/claudia-jones-and-the-notting-hill-carnival/
4. Claudia Jones was deported from America in 1951 after being convicted of 'un-American' activities under the Smith act. She was refused entry to her native Trinidad and offered entry to Britain on the grounds of compassion. For more on Claudia Jones see Carole Boyce Davies, *Left of Karl Marx: The Political Life of Black Communist Claudia Jones* (Duke University Press, 2008).
5. Quoted in John Cowley *Carnival, Canboulay and Calypso* (Cambridge: Cambridge University Press, 1996) 20-21.
6. For further reading, see John Cowley *Carnival, Canboulay and Calypso*.
7. I'm thinking of the unknown warrior woman described in Chapter 15.
8. See Miles Davis, *The Autobiography* (London: Picador, 1990).
9. https://archiveshub.jisc.ac.uk/data/gb1443-wong
10. Interview with the author, Ladbroke Grove, London, January, 2014.
11. Mighty Terror, "No Carnival In Britain" is reissued on *London Is The Place For Me* (Honest Jons, 2002).
12. Telephone interview with the author, March, 2014.
13. Ibid.
14. Ibid.
15. Ibid.
16. Telephone interview with the author, August, 2014.
17. Ibid.
18. Telephone interview with the author, March, 2014.
19. Ibid.
20. Bristol Archive Records, 10th September, 2012.
21. Ibid.

19 FASCINATING PEOPLE, GREAT MUSIC

West Indian? You must be joking, I come out of the East End. The first music I heard was Bow bells.
— Kenny Lynch as Sammy Coin, *Dr. Terror's House of Horrors*.

1963 was the year of the Bus Boycott. What ignited the protest was the refusal of the Bristol Omnibus Company to hire African-Caribbeans and Asians in their crews. There was no law against it at the time.

Roy Hackett, Owen Henry, Audley Evans and Prince Brown formed the West Indian Development Council to challenge the stance taken by Omnibus and subsequently appointed Paul Stephenson, a youth officer for Bristol City Council, as their spokesman. Widespread action, including a number of marches, meetings and a four-month boycott of Omnibus followed, during which time high-profile figures declared their support for the movement. One was the cricketing legend and Trinidad & Tobago High Commissioner, Learie Constantine. Another supporter was the Bristol East MP, Tony Benn, who pleaded the cause to the new Labour party leader, Harold Wilson, who, when he became prime minister in 1964, introduced the first Race Relations Act. Harold Wilson apparently told Paul Stephenson that it was the Bus Boycott that strengthened his resolve to legislate against race prejudice in the field of employment.[1]

Beyond the debates, newspaper articles and television documentaries on the topic of "the colour bar", there was, between the late 1950s and early 1960s a wave of feature films that dealt with the subject of West Indian immigrants and their place in British society. Some of these movies paint their politics in very broad stripes and lack the cultural and sociological nuance to present Blacks as they saw themselves, rather than as they were viewed by an English writer – none of the scripts were by Blacks – yet they are interesting documents of the time. Their recognition of the violence that could stem from prejudiced responses to sexual relations between the races, as well as the resistance to integration in the workplace is invaluable. They also signal the strong presence of Black music in British film.

Basil Dearden's film, *Sapphire*,[2] released in 1959 – and principally distinguished now for its fine modern jazz soundtrack, written by Philip Green and performed by the John Dankworth band – is a thriller centred on a mixed-race girl found brutally murdered on Hampstead Heath in London. That Dankworth, one of the young champions of the British bebop scene, should have his name on the credits was pertinent. He was married to the singer, Cleo Laine, who was of mixed race, and he also employed West Indians such as Guyanese percussionist-vocalist Frank Holder in his band.

Harmonically rich and rhythmically supple, the Dankworth band's playing, particularly that of his horn section, perfectly captures the shadow, angst and pathos of a story of hate corroding a seemingly normal English family. However, while *Sapphire* makes an earnest attempt to examine attitudes towards race, and particularly interracial relationships in post-Windrush Britain, it also reflects enduring cultural stereotypes of Black people, above all their apparently "special" relationship with music.

During their investigation into the death of the young girl, Superintendent Hazard and Inspector Learoyd pay a visit to Tulips, a hip basement club in west London. The house band plays a brisk Latin blues in the style of Dizzy Gillespie, with bustling brass and crisp bongos to the fore. On the dance floor are various West Indians who may have been connected to Sapphire. Their soubriquets are revealed by an African bartender: Johnny Fingers, Johnny Hotfeet, Johnny Rags, Johnny Tiger, each matching either a precise gesture or sartorial trait. The latter sports a bright red sweater with a big cat on the chest. The West Indians dancers actually included the distinguished artist, dancer and choreographer, Boscoe Holder (1921-2007) and the actor and future film maker, Lloyd Reckord.

As an evocation of the Caribbean proclivity for nicknames this is resoundingly clunky and lacking in imagination. In Trinidad a person would be dubbed Batman, Bosey-back[3] or Bambam Head if there was anything conspicuous about their physiognomy, demeanour or behaviour. A man might be dubbed Motion if his pace was so leisurely it suggested a form of slow motion. These are all credible West Indian nicknames. Johnny with the functional suffix is blandness incarnate. If the only thing that a Johnny does is smile, dance or strike a pose, he's a rent-a-black. Had the Johnnys been Sonnys, Errols or Winstons, common West Indian names of the day, the scene would have had more weight.

Black club owner Tulip – "That's what they call me" – makes his appearance soon after and when asked about Sapphire he points out an olive-complexioned girl, and refers to her as a "lily skin", a prevailing colloquialism for mixed race. What follows trumpets the stereotypes of black culture.

"Once they hear the beat of the bongo…" says Tulip, but before he can finish his sentence, the band breaks down to just percussion and the camera pans to a "chick" on a bar stool who shimmies in her seat in submission to the music. There follows a sweeping shot of the dance floor where the party crowd is all wide smiles, flailing limbs, and blindingly bright clothes. Finally we see a close-up of hands flitting across the skins of the bongo drums. Tulip rounds off what he meant to say: "No matter how fair is the skin, they can't hide that swing."

Any doubts on what this rhyme really means are dispelled by the abandon on the dance floor, whose barely veiled sexual frisson is heightened by a flash of underwear beneath the rising whirl of a skirt. Erotic charge; giddy, entrancing sounds; a brush with the boys in blue: the elements of the tableau paint all things black in the colours of danger and abandon, where rhythm – what mainstream culture had identified as *the* Negro phenomenon from the days of ragtime in the 1890s – is a force that is irresistible. The dance floor is thus the place where "authentic" blackness will out. It is the bongo that will arouse even a "diluted" descendant of the Congo and the explicitly African nature of the music in this scene, where the focus is on Black people, marks a notable contrast to the more introspective orchestral jazz played elsewhere in the movie.

Because *Sapphire* hinges on the hatred that a mother has for the mixed race girlfriend of her son, and, by implication, the social scandal that will ensue from this controversial union, it nonetheless has its place in the canon of British cinema that broaches the subject of inter-racial relationships. This is evidently deeply rooted in the national psyche – the precedent being Shakespeare's *Othello*.

A more important work in British cinema that recasts the Bard's tragic tale of doomed romance between the Moor and Desdemona is the 1962 feature, *All Night Long*. Again directed by Basil Dearden, the film transposes the action to the world of jazz musicians in London and weaves the key themes of ambition, infidelity and jealousy into a script that presents Othello as an expatriate African-American trumpeter, Aurelius Rex, Desdemona as Delia, his wife, who is also a singer, and Iago as a drummer, Johnnie Cousin. Intent on forming his own band, Cousin (Patrick McGoohan) asks Delia (Marti Stevens) to become his vocalist, and when she refuses his overtures he tries to convince Rex (Paul Harris) that his wife has been unfaithful to him with the manager Cass (Keith Mitchell). The drama unfolds at the lavish home of promoter Rod Hamilton (Richard Attenborough). The original trailer of the movie puts the emphasis on glamour, as Hamilton, immaculately turned out in a tuxedo and chauffeur-driven to an upscale West End club, declares enticingly to camera. "Tonight I'm giving a party and I'd like you to come along, you'll meet some fascinating people and hear some great music."

Using the single location of Hamilton's large, opulent flat is an excellent plot device as it acts as cipher for both domestic drama and music industry intrigue. The fact that there is a piano and space for a band as well as a mezzanine in which mind games can be played out certainly heightens the tension throughout the movie, which provides a comment on the ruthlessness of artists attempting to further their careers as well as the trope of a beautiful woman who is the object of male desire, and as such liable to arouse mistrust and be subjected to casual retribution.

Interracial love is an added dimension, but, as much as certain audiences may have been disturbed by the sight of a tall, muscular black man laying his hands on a white woman, the story, crucially, affords the Black lead character (Rex) a status that is absent in *Sapphire*. He is a famous bandleader, married to the "fabulous" Delia. He is part of a power couple. Man and wife are photogenic. A very credible performance by Paul Harris lends substance to Rex as a character who is as much undone by the malice lurking under the glossy surface of the jazz world as he is his own insecurities and lack of judgment. From a historical point of view, Harris is interesting insofar he was part of a long line of African-American performers who had plied their trade in mainland Europe as well as Britain. Born in Los Angeles, Harris followed in the footsteps of Paul Robeson by appearing in *Showboat* at the Los Angeles Greek theatre in 1949 before moving to Paris in the 50s where he performed in the musical *Free and Easy*. *All Night Long* was his first major film role.

Compelling as the Shakespearean story of *All Night Long* is, it is also the brilliance of the featured bands that really marks the film out. The great music promised by Hamilton was no exaggeration, and it is the appearance of several of the leading exponents of late 1950s modern jazz, drawn from both America and Britain – double bassist Charles Mingus, pianist Dave Brubeck, drummer Allan Ganley, saxophonists Tubby Hayes and Johnny Dankworth – that would have struck a chord with the considerable fanbase of each. It's also worth noting that American jazz musicians were in increasing demand to perform soundtracks for international films, including British films such as *Alfie*, scored by tenor saxophonist Sonny Rollins.

Indeed the excellent soundtrack of *All Night Long* featured tunes such as Brubeck's "It's A Raggy Waltz", which retained some of the flavour of his hugely successful *Time Out* album of 1959, as well as original compositions such as "Fall Guy" by Dankworth. The bulk of the score is by Philip Green, as was the case in *Sapphire*, and he is again adept at using the vocabulary of post-bop, in all its harmonic-rhythmic finesse, and infusing fraught, sometimes sinister orchestral detail that enhances the tension on screen.

Hence brass and reeds, with their large palette of tones, featured prominently in the compositions. So, too, does the bongo drum, cipher of blackness in *Sapphire*, which Green shows to be tremendously effective in conveying a sense of danger as well as excitement. In the film's trailer, the very first sound heard is the pinging, incisive, hi-tempo attack of the percussion instrument, which, when played solo, catches the ear for the distinctly crisp, curt nature of the notes. The bongo, along with the conga and timbales, is essential to the polyrhythms of the Latin jazz themes, and creating a surging momentum; it vividly evokes a relentless escalation of angst, a breathless frenzy, elements that frame the story.

That the drama should unfold against the backdrop of the jazz industry, a place in which the issue of equality had been a vexed one for many
decades, was to be applauded. Racially mixed jazz groups in both Britain
and America (which, incidentally, had been led by three of the featured
bandleaders – Dankworth, Mingus and Brubeck) could not disguise the
fact that black musicians still fell foul of racist policemen or club owners,
and record companies still regarded white musicians as easier to market.

How remarkable this film was in taking black characters seriously is all
the more apparent in comparison to the international blockbuster, *Dr No*,
released in 1962.

This presented a character who was quintessentially British, but gained
dramatic substance from his adventures in exotic lands. Here the country
was Jamaica. The character James Bond. This movie marked the beginning
of one of the most successful film franchises of all time, made a star out
of Sean Connery and gave island music pride of place on the soundtrack.
As the credits roll, the menacing twang of guitar in the iconic 007 theme
segues into a barrage of dense percussion in which bongos, congas, cowbells and shac shac weave a spellbinding polyrhythm. Silhouetted figures
of hip-gyrating women are projected on to a screen of shifting colours as
drums continue to ricochet into life.

Cut to the streets of Kingston where three blind beggars, effortlessly
hip in pork pie-hats and raybans, tap their white sticks on the pavement to
find their way. Folk music takes over. Guitar and percussion are prominent
whilst a soaring flute is used to punctuate the verses and improvise on the
choruses. The lyrics leave no doubt as to what kind of music is playing, as
if the audience didn't already know.

> Three blind mice in a row,
> three blind mice, there they go.
> Marching down the street single file
> To a calypso beat all the while.

The mice are anything but blind or unable to shoot straight. After the
sunny calypso has faded out, the beggars turn assassins and dispatch
British agent Strangways, the death that will bring Bond to Jamaica. In
Dr. No the black man is a lethal force in the broad daylight of Kingston.

If this was a contrast between the beauty of calypso and the brutality
of the action, then later in the film, music performs a more conventional
function. "Under The Mango Tree" is a gentle lovers calypso that is the
backdrop to the moment that Bond catches sight of Honey Rider resplendent
on a beach with a rather impressive conch. On an altogether more upbeat
note is "Jump Up", a composition heard in one of the most memorable
scenes of the film. Trying to solve the mystery of Strangways' death, Bond
has a meeting with his newly acquired sidekick, Quarrel, and an ally, the
American spy, Felix Leiter, at the bar and grill owned by the physically im-

posing but quaintly named Puss-Feller. As the men talk, a band is playing "Jump Up" to a packed dancefloor: it is Byron Lee & the Dragonaires. In 1962 they were one of the top bands in Jamaica.

The scene is memorable for the vibrant tableau it presents. With their vocalist, four percussionists, horns and rhythm section, the band has charisma and the tune bounces along with enormous energy. Built on a standard mento beat, the piece nonetheless has a sound that is substantially different to the works of Kitchener, Invader, Terror et al recorded in the 1950s. This is primarily because of the instrumentation deployed. This is mento music gone electric, on its way to becoming ska. Instead of an acoustic guitar and an upright bass, there is an electric guitar and a Fender Precision bass guitar, the instrument that Lee introduced to Jamaica after he purchased one during a tour of America in the 1950s. These sharper amplified sounds brought a rougher edge to the arrangements. They hardened the marrow of the sound.

What audiences around the world could see in *Dr. No* were current events in Jamaican culture. "Jump Up" was a song written by the British composer Monty Norman, a hot property on the London theatre scene who had scored for numerous productions. He stayed in Jamaica for a number of weeks to work on the soundtrack. "Jump-Up" was a response to what he found when he took in Kingston nightlife.

"When we went to one or two of the big clubs there these wonderful open air clubs where everybody was going wild dancing," he recalled, "they were doing this thing called the *Jump Up*. [Director] Terence Young wanted some melody to give to the Byron Lee Orchestra so that they could play it live and wild while the dance was going on."[4]

Hence *Dr. No* is an example of a British movie that acknowledged the dynamism of West Indian culture and it is obvious that the film's soundtrack would not have made the impact that it did without the input of Jamaican musicians. The colonies had something that could not be recreated by anybody else. No English band could have played *Jump Up* like Lee's, which is why they had a considerable 36 seconds on screen.

The song reflected the evolutionary nature of Jamaican culture as a snapshot of Kingston circa 1962. Published in 1958, Ian Fleming's novel *Dr. No* has no "Jump Up". The original scene in Puss-Feller's bar features "a calypso trio in sequinned scarlet shirts softly improvising on "Take Her to Jamaica Where the Rum Comes From."[5] If James Bond 007 was licensed to kill, then Byron Lee was a necessary shot in his cool cinematic arm.

There is no definitive record of the input of several other great Jamaican musicians to the soundtrack, but it is most likely that guitarists Ernest Ranglin and Lynn Taitt, actually an expatriate Trinidadian, and percussionist-trombonist Carlos Malcolm were among those who were involved in the sessions on the island.

Impressive as the film is, in terms of its soundtrack, location and casting, *Dr. No* nonetheless flags up a very definite racial hierarchy with regard to its characters. The dust jacket of the original Ian Fleming novel presents Jamaica as a place where "the sun shines, the palm trees wave, the calypsos throb" in line with the prevailing image the island had in the western imagination, and from the outset it is clear that Bond, the superior European, will exercise authority over the locals and vanquish the titular villain, who is "a Chinaman, or rather half Chinese and half German." Two sworn enemies for the price of one.

Interestingly, Fleming references miscegenation and racial tension in the West Indies in the original story, all the while stirring several diehard stereotypes into the pot. The Colonial Secretary who hosts Bond at the upmarket Queen's Club in Kingston says "the Jamaican is a kindly, lazy man with the virtues and vices of a child"[6] before contending that the mixed-race Chinese Negroes – Chigroes – are a cause for concern because "they've got some of the intelligence of the Chinese and most of the vices of the black man." Although this statement did not make the final screenplay of the film, it is telling that it was published in a book by a best-selling author who had captured the post-war public imagination. Naturally, there is talk, on screen, of "native superstition", and Bond has to bark orders at Negro fishermen.

Bond is one of cinema's ultimate imperialist figures. He echoes the Victorian "great white hunter" and the jet-set playboy of the western world who meets no resistance from foreigners, be they super villains or nubile women, on whatever part of the globe where he elects to pitch up. In fact, Fleming's adventure is careful to distance the sources of the culture that provides the novel's and film's setting. For as much as *Dr. No* shines a light on Jamaica and Jamaican music, there is no focus on the living reality of Jamaicans, who are denied any status as drivers of the narrative. They have their designated locations for socializing, such as Puss-feller's bar, while the British expats have theirs, the Queen's club. The gap between black and white is visible. The line between the races is drawn in much more than golden sand.

A British movie of the mid 1960s that taps into the same stereotypes of the uncivilized "other", and does it in a childishly ludicrous way, is *Dr. Terror's House of Horrors* (1964). At best one might suspect an element of parody of the clichés of *Dr No*. The film is constructed from a series of vignettes in which strangers on a train are invited to glimpse their tragic destinies by the eponymous fortune-teller, who may be a cheap charlatan or Lucifer kitted out by Dr. Who's wardrobe assistant. As a period piece, the film is cracking fun and the amateurish, frankly fright-free nature of the frights – none more so than a vengeful triffid that looks like a black plastic prop from *Blue Peter* – makes more for camp comedy than scary movie.

The third story, *The Devil's Music*, is that of a London jazz trumpeter, Biff Bailey, played by Roy Castle, who takes a trip to the fictional Caribbean island of Paiti, and, being a curious sort, attends a local religious ritual held deep in the jungle. Gripped by the throbbing polyrhythms of the percussion that accompanies the ceremony, he transcribes what he hears and upon his return to London, he plays a new arrangement of "an ancient voodoo tune" during a performance with devastating consequences. A storm is unleashed, the club wrecked. Black music equals black magic equals big trouble. When you mess with things you don't understand…

The stereotypes that mark the beginning of the story are treacle-thick. On his arrival in Paiti, Bailey and his musicians see a band with a rhythm and horn section and two steel drummers, kitted out in the mandatory, colourful floral shirts.[8] Appearing with them is a suave black singer who croons a bouncy, upbeat calypso, every bit as bright as the garb sported by his fellow band members. The number, "Everybody's Got Love" is performed by a singer called Sammy Coin, who is played by Kenny Lynch. At the time Lynch was quite popular, having enjoyed some success with several hit singles in the four years prior to the release of *Dr. Terror*. Lynch did very passable covers of hits by American artists such as The Drifters ("Up On The Roof") as well as his own original compositions such as "You Can Never Stop Me Loving You". He had a pleasant voice modelled on Nat 'King' Cole and Frank Sinatra and could hold a tune with precision and good dynamics.

Familiar as Lynch was, his character, Sammy Coin, plays interestingly around the cultural stereotypes. When he's singing "Everybody's Got Love", he adopts a Caribbean accent, which is recognized as such by Bailey, who equates it with racial authenticity. "I dig that calypso music, man. It's good sung by a real West Indian." Coin instantly refutes any such notion: "West Indian? You must be joking. I come out of the East End. The first music I heard was Bow bells." His voice is as cockney as pie and mash.

Over in a flash, it is tempting to dismiss the exchange as light-hearted banter written by a script writer who knows that success is contingent on making something, especially a song, appear real. Yet the dialogue scores a bulls-eye on the central problem of identity politics for Blacks born in post-war Britain. That is to say: how can you be considered British when you don't *look* British and can sing a calypso like a "real" West Indian? Coin has to *state* that he is a cockney rather than be recognized as one by a white fellow compatriot. Kenny Lynch was actually born in Stepney, East London, to Jamaican parents. In other words he was a *real* Eastender. That's not the point, though. He is still seen as black before he is seen as British.

Bailey's ignorance is compounded by Castle's woeful attempt at imitating a West Indian accent, his mimicry falling between Scots, Geordie and Indian. The crudity of Castle's turn as the jazz musician in search of a new beat that will lead him down the road to the devil's music does not make for comfortable viewing these days. Everybody is playing for laughs, yet there are several home truths that emerge from *Dr. Terror*'s direction and casting.

Above all, it points to the fact that the residue of minstrelsy still stalked British entertainment. Although the voodoo worshippers comprised a troupe of black dancers and extras, the high priest was played by a white actor, Lionel Jeffries, who was blacked up for the part. This was a time when the most popular television series in Britain was *The Black and White Minstrel Show*. Launched in 1958, it had a peak audience of a massive 18 million.

The fusion of black exotica and erotica, the sexual charge snaking through "the beat of the bongo" evoked in *Sapphire*, is delineated more explicitly in *Dr. Terror*. The cultural clichés are elephantine. As soon as he arrives in Paiti, Sammy Coin reduces Bailey to drooling when he describes a voodoo ceremony: "Out in the woods, drums beating, girls dancing, wild, frenzied… very few clothes on." But if in the film, the black woman is sexually enticing and inspires lust, the black man is physically threatening and inspires fear, so much so that when Bailey is back in London, he is "spooked" by a tall, stocky black man who does nothing more suspect than emerge from a telephone booth.

What exacerbates the Grand Guignol caricatures in *Dr. Terror* is the fraudulence of its premise. In the early 1960s very few, if any, British jazz or pop groups played residencies in the West Indies. The traffic was all in the other direction. This is why British culture changed so much.

Badly flawed as it is, *Dr. Terror* is nonetheless a showcase for British culture in a state of transition. The film is something of a summit meeting for early 1960s London-based jazz and calypso artists. Bailey's backing band is actually a quintet led by Tubby Hayes, a brilliant multi-instrumentalist who emerged as one of the leading exponents of British bebop. There was also a bearded, bespectacled trumpeter in the band. This was Shake Keane, an excellent soloist from St. Vincent, who made a name for himself on the London jazz scene through his work with West Indian, African and British musicians. The steel band featured in the Paiti club scene was that of the Trinidadian pioneer, Russell Henderson. His compatriot, Boscoe Holder, choreographed all of the dance scenes. The musicians can't be held responsible for the crassness of the script – and the music in the film is generally outstanding.

Hayes, Henderson and Keane were all at the height of their powers and epitomize everything that was progressive in modernist British jazz in the mid 1960s. Somewhat mischievously, the screenplay slips in a joke at the expense of the trad jazzers towards the end of the story, just as the club is being trashed by the mysterious hurricane. Sammy Coin sharply admonishes Bailey for meddling with dark forces beyond his control and quips: "Who do you think sent that wind? Kenny Ball?" This is a cheeky dig at the trumpeter who was a trad jazz icon. The other sharp wisecrack in the dialogue makes a meaningful point about the relationship between art, commerce, and race. Bailey is accused of stealing from the voodoo god Dambala and is angrily told that the rhythms are centuries old, to which the trumpeter cheerily says: "Ah well, if it's that old, then it's out of copyright!"

The scene would have had resonance for West Indian artists of the time. There was the infamous case of "Rum & Coca Cola", the calypso written by Lord Invader and Lionel Belasco that *was* stolen by Morey Amsterdam, then recorded by the Andrews Sisters to become an international hit in 1945. The tone is frivolous, but Bailey's punchline raises the issue of the appropriation and exploitation of the original creative capital of ethnic minorities, whether West Indians or African-Americans, a matter vividly evoked in the title of Frank Kofsky's important book *Black Music, White Business.*[9]

But given the levity of *The Devil's Music*, and the stereotypes it panders to, the issue of the brazen theft of rhythms from "small islands" is not one that contemporary audiences would have recognised.[10]

There were other films that indicated that calypso and jazz could be effective parts of the vocabulary of British cinema – as they had already been used in British television. In 1956, *A Man From The Sun*, a drama-documentary exploring the lives of West Indian migrants in London featured superb music by Trinidadian calypsonian, Young Tiger, aka George Browne, and his compatriot, the virtuoso guitarist Fitzroy Coleman, as well as the acting talent of Guyana's Cy Grant – already mentioned for his witty calypso songs on the *Tonight* show a year later.

Following in the footsteps of the *Devil's Music* segment of *Dr. Terror's House of Horrors* (1964) was another film of racist hokum, *She* (1965), adapted from the colonialist fantasy of the Victorian novelist Henry Rider-Haggard, about a white woman who rules with an iron hand over black people in what is an unspecified part of north Africa.

In one scene where a captured member of the British expedition is about to be put to death, amid a frenzy of ceremonial dancing, there are tight close-ups on masks and writhing bodies amid the insistent polyrhythms of several drummers, whose repeating lines, spread out across bass and treble pitches, unleash a wave of energy at high tempo. The man playing the talking drum was a well-known figure on the UK jazz scene: Ginger Folorunsho Johnson, whose work is discussed at greater length in Chapter 23.

She had an orchestral score by James Bernard, but no film composer could have produced the music Johnson provided for the scene, just as no English band could have played a calypso like Russ Henderson's in *The Devil's Music*. In other words, the superficiality of the stories, their stereotypical depiction of people of colour, was counterpointed by the authenticity of the Black music featured in these films. The movies are disposable. The sounds are not. Ironically, Johnson does not feature in the film's credits, unlike Bernard, and this omission epitomises the marginal status of African music in cinema and popular culture, despite the recognition of its necessity by the film's director and producer. The prevailing wisdom would have been that the music of Johnson was for specialist rather than mainstream markets.

Nothing much had changed in a film made at the end of the decade– 1968's *Salt And Pepper*, a ham-fisted caper starring two Americans, jazz singer and civil rights activist Sammy Davis jnr and actor Peter Lawford. It was another attempt to bring some of the glamour and sexiness of "swingin" London' to the big screen. As was the case with *Sapphire*, the soundtrack was by John Dankworth, composed largely in the modern jazz idiom, yet the tone of the story was altogether more light and whimsical, mindful perhaps of the success of the burgeoning Bond franchise and the general public's taste for racy tales of espionage. Chris Pepper (Lawford) and Char-lie Salt (Davis) play the owners of hip nightclub where the last words of a murdered Asian girl reveal a plot to overthrow the British government. The black and white heroes fly to the defence of the realm under threat of a shadowy enemy.

Inverted as the racial references are – one expects the white character to be Salt and the black Pepper – the film nonetheless makes a certain amount of capital from collision of foreignness and Britishness, as the two protagonists are very much Americans in Albion. The presence of "dusky maidens" imparts to the location a certain tired frisson that is only somewhat rescued by John Dankworth's artfully orchestrated score.

All the films discussed in the chapter represent an interesting point of engagement between British culture, Caribbean islands nearing independ-ence, and West Indians in London. At the least they provided employment for Black musicians.

Notes

1. "West Indians claim 100% support for bus boycott", *Bristol Evening Post*, 30 April 1963.
2. *Sapphire* won the Bafta for Best British film in 1959.
3. Bosey-back is a creole term for hunch back, derived from the French *bossu*.
4. Stephen Bourne, *Black In The British Frame* (London: Cassell, 1998) 103
5. This substantiates my earlier point about nicknames in *Sapphire*. Puss-Feller is much more vibrant than Johnny Rags etc.
6. *Inside Dr. No* documentary (Special edition DVD of *Dr. No*, MGM 2003).
7. Ian Fleming, *Dr. No* (London: Pan, 1958) pp. 34-35.
8. Many hotel bands in the Caribbean are still dressed like this.
9. Frank Kofsky, *Black Music, White Business* (New York: Pathfinder, 1998).

20 THE BEAT TURNS BLUE

By South African standards I'm a criminal in marrying Cleo [Laine].
When mixed marriages do occur, people inevitably start talking about
the children.
> — John Dankworth, alto saxophonist and composer.

In 1962,Britain passed the Commonwealth Immigrants Act. Entry
to Britain was restricted to those with employment vouchers, which
were only granted to citizens from former colonies who had particular
skills and professional qualifications. Fanned by the right-wing press
and neo-fascist groups, the issue of controlling borders, containing
the number of arrivals from abroad and preserving a British national
identity became major political issues.

In 1962, after fourteen years in London and Manchester, Lord Kitchener, one of the most celebrated of the Windrush passengers, returned to
Trinidad. Given his sizeable contribution to the catalogue of calypso in
Britain in the 1950s, his departure marked the end of an era, a signal for
new sounds to be heard.

In 1962, the year of *Dr. No*, Britain said yes to the demands for independence from Jamaica and Trinidad, and four years later for Barbados and
Guyana. Ghana had been the first African country to gain independence in
1957. Even now, the West Indies and other parts of the ex-colonial world
are *still* coming to terms with the effects of decolonization. This was less
about any change of relationship between the former colonial power and
the new independent nation, more about confronting the social structures,
institutions and culture they inherited – all this within the context of a
free-market, global capitalist economy dominated by American capital.
For Britain it was about having to recognise a vastly diminished place in
the world, something that the decision to exit from the European Union
suggests has not yet happened.

Some older West Indians maintain that the end of Whitehall rule would
only have been constructive for the peoples of the islands if their standards of
living had been maintained, if not improved, because political independence
is nothing without economic stability. One of my neighbours, Mr Bill, who
arrived in Britain from Jamaica in 1962, told me: "Jamaica… you know with
independence it go down because of the economy, is like American business

tek over." With endemic levels of poverty, underemployment and widening social inequality, crime has flourished on the island.

Regardless of the tragedies that unfolded in the post-independence era, it is important to note the joy with which independence was heralded in song, as in Lord Brynner's "Our Nation's Calypso", Lord Creator's "Independent Jamaica" or Kitch's "Birth of Ghana" – the latter particularly important because it consolidated the Afro-centricity and pride in blackness that he had expressed elsewhere in his output.

Parallel with the gaining of independence and the sometimes halting steps towards decolonisation in the ex-colonial world, the USA witnessed an upsurge in Black political assertion that manifested in struggles for desegregation, civil rights, equal employment rights and an assertion of pride in blackness and in African origins. It was an upsurge that reflected the impact of the Second World War and later the Vietnam War, continuing internal migration and urbanisation on Black lives.

In the newly independent ex-colonies and in the USA, this political ferment was expressed through new musical forms, whether soul music from the USA, reggae from Jamaica or Afrobeat from Africa, and these new militant musics shaped both musical tastes and music production elsewhere in the western world, not least in Britain.

In the USA, the huge movement of people from the South into the Northern cities coincided with the electrification of the guitar, and fresh, game-changing forms of urban music grew from this. It was a period when, for the first time, popular black music began to reach a wider audience. By the mid 1950s, the music industry had coined a new term to designate most black popular music; it was called rhythm & blues, a replacement for the limiting term "Race Music". The change was important because it recognised that Black music should not be confined to Black audiences, but it also built on musical forms that were directed towards Black listeners. In the days of minstrelsy, the demand from white consumers had been strong but limiting; by the 1950s the Black audience was big enough to determine the evolution of Black music that was both "more Black" but also had a wider appeal.

R&B was a generic name that designated a range of styles, but recognised that the blues was the bedrocks of African-American music. There were doo-wop close-harmony vocal groups, solo blues shouters, hard-riffing electric guitarists and honking saxophonists whose riffs had been partially shaped by the swing grooves of the 1940s big bands. As a catch-all genre, R&B reflected the exciting cross-fertilization of jazz, gospel and blues. Indeed, a key feature of many R&B songs was the horn solo, sometimes stretching to as many as sixteen bars, after one or two sung choruses, as well as totally instrumental pieces, all of which underlined the place that brass, reeds and rhythm sections had in black music.

R&B was hugely popular in the West Indies, particularly the saxophon-
ist-vocalist Louis Jordan, and New Orleans musicians such as pianist-vocalist
Fats Domino and pianist-vocalist Professor Longhair and less remembered
stars such as Joe Liggins. Audiences all over the region were charmed by
their combination of shuffling rhythms and spirited vocals, which, in the
case of all of the above, often had a humour that chimed with the calypso
or in Jamaica the mento aesthetic.

Jamaica, which was also undergoing a massive process of urbanisation
as the population of Kingston virtually doubled during the 1940s, emerged
as a creative pacesetter and local artists used the U.S. template to mould
their own R&B, often called JA boogie. The prime exponents included such
engaging vocalists as Owen Gray and Alton Ellis. Because of the growth of
the DJ-led sound-system culture in the dance halls, there was a demand
for recordings made in Kingston as well as America, where selectors had
originally sourced their discs, and the hottest new Jamaican songs on vinyl
soon began to make an impact.[1]

Ever aware of changing trends, Emil Shalitt of Melodisc, the London-based label that had been in the vanguard of calypso in Britain, founded
a new label, Bluebeat, in 1960, to purvey JA boogie to a market of West
Indian immigrants and white hipsters interested in black music. With Laurel
Aitken (whose "Boogie Rock" was the inaugural Bluebeat release) moving
to England in that same year, the new Jamaican sound had a figurehead
who could expand a growing fanbase by way of high energy live gigs as
well as a steady stream of recordings.

Even though entry to the UK was by no means as easy as it had been in
the days when Kitchener and Beginner boarded the Windrush, Jamaican
artists were still making the journey, and since by the late 1950s plane travel
had become the norm, artists moved backwards and forwards with greater
frequency. Apart from Aitken, other key expatriates from the period were
the singer Dandy Livingstone and a number of instrumentalists, the most
notable being trumpeter Eddie 'Tan Tan' Thornton, and trombonist Rico
Rodriguez, both of whom would go on to become prolific session musicians
in a wide variety of genres.

Sigmund 'Siggy' Jackson was appointed as label manager/A&R man for
Bluebeat and he built a substantial catalogue in a relatively short space of
time. By 1967 the number of 7" singles Bluebeat issued topped over 400,
which is a phenomenal output for a record label by any standards. The vitality of Bluebeat came from the way it tapped into a talent pool in Britain,
recording in London, but also actively sourced music in Jamaica. It was, in
real terms, an international operation.

Licensing agreements were also made with many leading labels based
in Kingston, Shalitt's imprint charted a pivotal change in the character of
Jamaican music, capturing its shift from imitation to original creation.

What started as a form of R&B became something else called "ska". Jamaican artists were never satisfied by their ability to implement American musical templates. They understood the resonant chord changes of the blues, the irresistible contagion of shuffling, boogieing piano figures, the scales on which bass lines were written, the emotional charge of the vocal "shout", the drama of trickily scored, jazz-inflected horn lines. This was not surprising given the high standard of playing expected of musicians who had worked in the hotel big bands in the swing era of the 1940s. They had absorbed this vocabulary and let it flow into the folk music of mento, with its concise, bitter-sweet riffs.

Gradually musicians in Kingston began to develop a distinctive approach to the pulse of R&B, in which the use of the offbeat was the defining feature of their playing. But it was more than just accenting the 2 and 4 in a bar that enabled them to personalize their music. There was a particular sharpness that could be heard in the way the offbeat note burst into life before it almost instantly popped into silence. Older Jamaican musicians have used the term "chop" to shed more light on their methodology. They attacked the offbeat in such a way to create a cutting sensation. It was clipped and curt, like a sharp kiss of the teeth.

The freshness of ska's aesthetics came from its roots in Jamaican popular culture in both music and language. The very word ska was not Standard English; ska was Jamaican music that was freighted by language to be found nowhere other than Jamaica. This fact has political weight. Wherever it actually comes from, the word ska brings to mind words such as *cha*, *rass* or *rah*, meaning that it serves an exclamatory role, in much the same way as *hey* or *whoa* do in Standard English. "Me nah know exactly what it mean," Mr Bill said, "But dem man, all the musician, they did just find new words. That's what they did. And if the feeling was right, then the word, it just catch on." Ska had something fresh to say as well as to sound, and brought a new term that British fans had to learn to pronounce. To this day they have mostly failed to do so, softening rather than toughening the sound. It must be hilarious for Jamaicans to hear clueless little Englanders say *scar* instead of *skiagh*. The proper rendition of the word has the same hardness and boldness that defines the performance of the music.

Ska marked an empowering into urban and electrified song of Jamaican popular culture, as adventurous musicians in Kingston went about adapting the titles of classic American tunes to assert their own new "ting". Hence the romantic ballad "I'm in the Mood for Love" became "I'm in the Mood for Ska". An everyday idiomatic saying "the sky is the limit" became "The Ska is the Limit". A satellite had to became a Skatalite. Beyond the Jamaicanising of African American R & B, ska also became a public expression of Black pride, racial protest and a desired relationship with Africa that came with the Rastafarian faith of some of its leading musicians.

The Skatalites[2] were one of the defining exponents of the new music. A group of extraordinary players, which included trombonist Don Drummond, saxophonists Tommy McCook and Roland Alphonso and organist Jackie Mittoo,[3] excelled at combining haunting melodies with pulsing rhythms and their classic tunes such as "Guns of Navarone" shored up the popularity of ska in Britain. Music on Studio One, the Jamaican label for which they recorded, became as sought-after as Bluebeat.

Like R&B, ska was an instrumental as well as vocal music, and the Skatalites were the boss players at the summit of their art. They showed how richly expressive a three minute horn-led song could be when performed by soloists whose role models were jazz icons like Charlie Parker and whose skills matched those of any American jazz musicians. The result was a tightly channelled virtuosity.

Alongside the rise of such musicians came the ascension of Jamaican producers such as Duke Reid, Clement (Sir Coxsone) Dodd and Prince Buster, who all made their names as the lords of the sound system, but then started to use musicians to make recordings of their own. Of the three it was Prince Buster who had the most direct connection with Britain. As the name suggests, Cecil Campbell stood in the lineage of West Indian artists who re-imagined themselves as royalty, though the second part of his stage name was a spin on the name of Jamaica's first post-independence prime minister, William Alexander Clarke Bustamante.

Buster produced instrumentals, often featuring brilliant players such as the trombonist Rico Rodriguez, and he became one of the key artists on Bluebeat, spending a lot of time in studios in London, where he got to know both the African and English musicians who contributed to sessions for the label. His friendship with the Nigerian high life guitarist Ambrose Campbell and the English R&B/jazz organist Georgie Fame is an enduring symbol of fruitful cultural exchange.

While Buster's 1963 album *I Feel The Spirit* was a landmark in ska, especially for the haunting "Soul Of Africa", featuring Rodriguez and consolidating the strain of Negritude and Rastafarianism that had flowed through much of the work of the Skatalites, Buster excelled on singles where his irrepressible, larger-than-life personality came into play.

1964's "Al Capone" was a brilliant song that strikes a perfect balance between its constituent parts. It was an instrumental coloured by flashes of the spare but incisive use of words. Buster announces the subject so grandiloquently that he raises expectations of a detailed account of one of America's great anti-heroes: "Al Capone's guns don't argue." Then he throws a delicious theatrical grenade into the air as the piece explodes into life as an instrumental with all of the *talking* done by saxophone and trombone solos. The real weapons are the horns. The brass and reeds provide a devastating sonic attack. Buster's imagination catches further fire as he increases rhythmic tension by imitating the razor-sharp cut of the guitar against the thrust of the brass instruments, his voice mostly on the down-beat whilst the other players jockey on the up.

Buster's vocal effects belong to the historical lineage of jazz artists – Louis Armstrong being the obvious example – who use their voices to recreate the sound of instruments, and although he employs a relatively simple rhythmic pattern, the result is striking because he is emphasising the role of the guitar in bluebeat music, demonstrating the way it slices, scrapes and grinds.

In the final few bars of the tune, Buster chants "Lick it… lick it", a call to arms. To lick the beat is to nail it, to play it well. That's what a producer would tell a musician in the studio. But it also implies the idea of licking down a rival, disposing of a foe as a seasoned gangster would do – a brilliant convergence of musical commentary and dramatic irony. When Buster speaks in the first person role of Capone, he adopts a cool hauteur akin to the most British of British secret agents abroad: "Don't call me scarface!" The name's Buster, Prince Buster. License to *skiagh*.

Quite apart from the beauty of the musical arrangement of "Al Capone", the bravado with which the piece is executed is remarkable. Buster's sheer boldfacedness encapsulates why Jamaica was able to produce such musical riches at this time. There was a confidence among emerging artists that was not dissimilar to that of the Trinidadian calypsonians of the 1950s, whereby a black man could step right into an historical white persona and uphold this icon on his own terms. Busta is doing more than caricature Capone. He is drawing a clever parallel between the undeniable glamour of the underworld and the swagger of the musician searching for a new sound. "Al Capone" could not fail to capture the imagination of teenagers in Britain as well as in the West Indies. It is escapist, inventive, confronta-tional, thrilling and daring. It channels the blues heritage of the badman Negro, the hot tempered and trigger-happy roughneck immortalized by the mythical Stagolee, but it also forecasts a strain of Black popular music some decades ahead, for *Al Capone* is nothing if not a wry foreshadowing of gangsta rap. The persona of the 1980s Cuban mob boss, Scarface, was hugely influential on American rappers in the 1990s, and here was Buster presciently bringing his antecedents to life in the 1960s.

Popular as the Bluebeat label was among Black communities in Britain, the mainstream commercial breakthrough of ska came from another source. The young location scout on the film, *Dr. No*. Chris Blackwell,[4] was now working as a record producer in Jamaica. He had set up his own label, R&B, which subsequently became Island Records. He enjoyed success with artists such as Laurel Aitken, but was spending more time in England, licensing Jamaican music to willing partners. Blackwell found a fifteen-year-old singer from Clarendon called Millie Small, who had chalked up a few hits

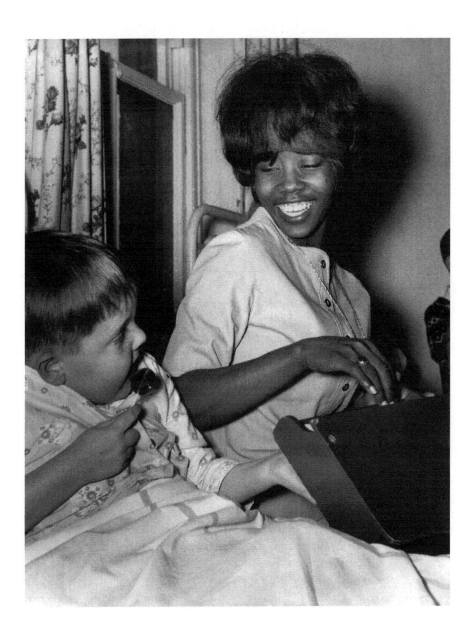

MILLIE SMALL

COURTESY TRINITY MIRROR / MIRRORPIX / ALAMY STOCK PHOTO

on Studio One in a vocal duo with Roy Panton. Blackwell accompanied Small to London in 1963 so that she could take lessons in elocution and dance. Then in 1964 he asked her to sing "My Boy Lollipop", a charming song that had been a minor hit for New York R&B singer Barbie Gaye. The arrangement and guitar work on the piece came courtesy of the Jamaican virtuoso, Ernest Ranglin. He had played with the seminal orchestras of Val Bennett and Eric Deans as well as The Skatalites and Prince Buster, and his ability to improvise as well as write harmonies was absolutely flawless. He is one of Jamaica's greatest ever instrumental soloists.

Blackwell took Ranglin to London to record "My Boy Lollipop" with Small and they transformed a slice of appealing R&B into irresistible ska and the record quickly became a worldwide phenomenon, selling in excess of 6 million copies. It was the first piece of Jamaican music that went global under the aegis of a producer who had taken his first steps on the set of a quintessentially British film, made on location in Jamaica, whilst the song itself was originally American, revealing yet again the complex cultural chain that still bound the peoples of the Old and New World, the fragmenting Empire and the emerging independent states of the West Indies.

Easy as it may be to dismiss "My Boy Lollipop" as a fluffy, lightweight love song, with its teenie rhymes of "sweet as candy/sugar dandy", it is anything but a trite piece of music. Its power derives from the clever juxtaposition of soft and hard sounds and the contrast of Small's adolescent, sweet vocal, fluttering in the high register, and the mature stance of the rhythm and horn sections, which work solidly in the mid and low. It is a light-hearted song but not entirely lacking in muscle. Rhythmically, it is an astutely constructed piece. The bass swings in quarter notes against a relatively straight drumbeat to create a sensation of gentle motion, but the guitar is dispensed in sharp, taut eighth notes, slashing into the cushion created by the other instruments. The masterstroke is the terse central horn motif, which plays a dual rhythmic and melodic role. Comprising just four notes, it is one of the great pop "hooks", insofar as its chipper brightness evokes both seduction and innocence. However, its real value lies in implying a vocal complement to Small's singing, almost as if she is funnelling a girlie shriek of "I love you so" right into the brass. The hook also underscores the momentum created by the choppy guitar figure, and one can hear how the horn arrangements have assumed a similarly curt, staccato character. They are deployed with concision. They are ska'd, not R&B'd.

Although not required to be virtuosic on "My Boy Lollipop", Ranglin unveiled his full improvisatory skills during his stay in London, as he became part of the house band at Ronnie Scott's jazz club. This launched his international career in earnest. He was heard by dozens of visiting musicians as well as music lovers, went on to work extensively in Europe, often with the gifted Jamaican pianist Monty Alexander[5], and he recorded

ERNEST RANGLIN

two fine albums in the mid 1960s for Blackwell's Island label, *Wranglin'* and *Reflections*. They underlined his exceptional gifts. His improvising was measured and expressive, and indebted though he was to American jazz greats such as Charlie Christian and Wes Montgomery, Ranglin had a certain spikiness in his comping and a tonal flourish that are absolutely his own.

Ska would not scale the commercial heights of "My Boy Lollipop" again but its enormous sales showed the potential of West Indian music beyond the West Indian market, and highlighted how musicians from the former colonies could create something fresh and vibrant .

The way Small's song was promoted showed the importance of doing more than concert performances. Blackwell scored a major coup in getting the young Jamaican singer on television, particularly on the vanguard show, *Ready, Steady, Go*. This not only presented the biggest names in pop but also showed a studio full of teenagers dancing to the sound of their heroes. In the words of those who were on hand to witness the birth of the show, it appeared to present something akin to "chaos."[6] "My Boy Lollipop" was thus heard on a programme that helped to break epochal acts such as the Beatles and the Rolling Stones.

Looking back at this pivotal period in the history of Black music in Britain, it is clear that Jamaican music came into its own. It was bolstered by the arrival of Small, Aitken, Ranglin, Rico Rodriguez (who gigged with the popular R&B artist, Georgie Fame) and others. Ska was a new sound; it broadened the repertoire of steel bands up and down the country, as well as giving the soundmen another type of beat to mix into their sets of calypso, jazz and R&B.

Along with the production and distribution of ska and reggae on the Bluebeat label came one of the major and lasting developments of West Indian, in particular Jamaican, popular culture: the sound system. This was the event at which records are played to an appreciative audience in a way we now take for granted, but in its time was revolutionary. Now, several decades down the line, in the era of the superstar DJ, the principle of choosing songs with a degree of discernment had been enshrined as an art. From the 1950s onwards, Jamaicans had done vastly more than play records. They would *present* them.

The likes of Tom The Great Sebastian, Sir Coxsone and Duke Reid saw that the difference between live and recorded music could melt away in an adequate setting with a charismatic DJ. In Jamaica, the assembly of powerful, custom-built speakers, record deck and microphone (to announce the tunes in style) became known as "the sound system". Such was the popularity of such sessions and their relatively low costs compared to live bands that they rapidly became economically viable. It was visionary thinking on the part of the first pioneers of what would become a lasting part of Jamaican culture that has survived many changes in the forms of Jamaican music from ska, bluebeat, rocksteady, reggae, dancehall, ragga and so on. Inevitably these cultural forms travelled to Britain.

With the expansion of the West Indian community, so came the growth of venues and performance by the "sound man" or "selector" whose job it was to spin the right tunes. But it involved more than that. There was the MC, master of ceremonies, who had to announce them, bill them, talk them up, big them up, nice them up, creating a palpable sense of expectation and excitement before the needle hit the record. This was more than a jukebox. The soundman's reputation depended on being able to imbue a social event with a sense of action theatre.

Chief among the UK pioneers was Duke Vin, whose name reflects the trend among sound men for adopting aristo monikers, just as the calypsonians named themselves as Lords. Arriving in London in 1954, Vin launched his sound system the year after. It soon became a national outfit, playing shuffle blues records to baying crowds across the country. "We used to have very good times. And all these people who used to follow the sound – if we went to Birmingham, they used to come from London. We used to play all over the country – Birmingham, Manchester, Reading, you name it. People were so glad to know that there was a sound system here because of what they were used to in Jamaica."[7]

Vin's recollection of the loyal allegiance to "a sound", resulting in the movement of West Indians from one city to another, reiterates how whilst Black communities had dispersed throughout Britain, they were still unified through music.

By the time "My Boy Lollipop" was a hit, the pop revolution was well underway, and the BBC was forced to adapt. It had been slow to recognize that the Jaggers & Richards and Lennons & McCartneys were the voices of a new engagement with culture that was aeons away from the fossilized form of "light entertainment". Teenagers wanted to see their peers with guitars and do the latest jivey, twisty dances being shipped in from Black America. Rock & roll, which exploded in the early 1950s, had shown that rhythm & blues could be repackaged under a new name (and with white musicians playing Black music) and find favour with a mass audience that took its cue from American radio disc jockeys such as Alan Freed, who understood that Black culture was a limitless source of creativity.

Rock & roll became associated with youth rebellion, a threat to the adult world, and a danger to a racially intolerant America because of the Blackness of its source, the blues, but it was a short-lived commercial phenomenon that by the late 1950s was on the wane. Nonetheless, it had represented a form of cultural change with its edginess, wildness, dissent, individuality and demands for gratification. Both rock & roll and R&B records became the educational tools for aspiring pop stars to learn their trade. By placing the needle on the vinyl again and again, a musician could study, master and adapt a Chuck Berry guitar lick. By listening to white American singers imitating black American singers, white British singers could imitate black American singers – and if they were smart enough they'd just listen to black American originals. Singers and bands were becoming the epicentre of a young person's world and the material artefact underpinning it, the vinyl recording, which as a lightweight 45 rpm 7" single could be easily carried and stored, was an essential object of desire.

Hence the deep sense of allegiance fostered by the sight of a Bluebeat logo, with its noble silver laurels stylishly stamped on a dark background above a song title, or the feel-good glow that was experienced when Georgie Fame, who had played on sessions for the label, told the world he would spend an evening with his pretty baby "playing records, the sounds of groovy Hi-Fi" on "Yeh Yeh". The song, a glorious slice of Latin-flavoured R&B with astute interplay between the lead vocal and tenor saxophone, topped the charts in 1965. Like "My Boy Lollipop", it was a cover of an American tune (by jazz great Jon Hendricks). On the record sleeve there was a picture of Fame with a bottle of Coca Cola. With the song came a lifestyle and a product to which the kids could relate. It was undeniably *their* culture.

Yet amid the rise of R&B, and its American and West Indian offshoots, rock & roll and ska, an inalienable truth of the entertainment industry endured: that there remained an unreconstructed taste for the familiar, for novelty, easy-listening, romantic ballads or Broadway show tunes; a catchy melody still seduced, especially if it came from a popular film. This is why, in 1964, in the middle of Beatlemania, Julie Andrews' "A Spoonful Of Sugar" and Doris Day's "Move Over Darling" were major hits. The former was unbearable kitsch, the latter breezy sophistication. There was also a taste for jazz-inflected torch songs. Two seminal figures in the history of black music in Britain fitted in different ways into these older show-business oriented popular musical forms. Both were charismatic mixed-race women who debuted in the 1950s and flourished throughout the 1960s: Cleo Laine (1927-) and Shirley Bassey (1937-), the former at the jazz-oriented, the latter at the show-tune end of the spectrum.

Laine,[8] the daughter of a Jamaican father and an English mother who grew up in Southall, Middlesex, emerged as one of Britain's most accomplished singers who showcased her talent in a wide variety of settings. London audiences enjoyed her appearance in new plays at the Royal Court Theatre and a national television audiences warmed to her regular slots on the satirical programme *That Was The Week That Was*, and those who still kept faith with the wireless heard her in *The Island*, a "radio opera" written by Bill Russo and Adrian Mitchell.

Laine also worked extensively with the great bebop saxophonist and composer, John Dankworth, whom she married in 1958 after appearing with one of his earliest groups, the Dankworth Seven. Their creative partnership hit something of a peak on 1965's *Shakespeare and All That Jazz*, in which Shakespeare's words were sung by Laine to Dankworth's music. It showed Laine's ability to handle the most sophisticated material. She had a great combination of power and restraint. Dark, imperious and occasionally aloof, Laine's voice had enormous personality, impressive range and quite masterful tonal control.

Her solo work bore this out. In 1961 her single, "You'll Answer to Me" climbed to number 5 in the British national charts, showing that it was possible for her to achieve crossover success without compromising artistic integrity. It was an intriguing song built on a bluesy guitar hook, played softly rather than stridently, that was further cushioned by high trills of strings, which contrasted effectively with the low, sombre tone of the lead vocal. There is poise in Laine's delivery, and instead of punctuating every other line with showy octave leaps, as do some vocalists with little sense of light and shade, she weaves in the most subtle brush-strokes on the canvas of her voice, drawing out a line-ending or lowering pitch just a touch to acquire a faintly masculine quality. The lyric is an admonition to a love rival and Laine is skilled in the way that she imparts a calm, controlled menace into the grace of her performance. By the time she reaches the climactic line ("You'll regret the day you were born"), she is utterly believable.

The cultural identity of her vocal is interesting. Her delivery is predominantly accented *à l'Americaine*, as was the norm at the time, but when she sings the word *answer*, her enunciation of the last syllable clearly leans towards an almost R.P like '*sir*' rather than the '*sah*' that would be expected of a Stateside diva. There is a distinct Britishness that surfaces in Laine's tone that makes it clear that she was not attempting to be a native New Yorker. Not that her identity was without problems. Her own white mother had been disowned for marrying a black man, and Laine's marriage to Dankworth had to be kept secret from both of their families until after the ceremony at Hampstead Registry Office. With admirable candour, Dankworth had made the point in an article published in *Tropic* magazine that this was at least preferable to the institutional racism found in other parts of the world. "By South African standards I'm a criminal in marrying Cleo. As a man I loathe any form of racial or social discrimination."[9] This statement was pertinent given the equivocal stance that the British government had taken with regard to the apartheid regime, and indeed many UK companies still traded with the former colony. Dankworth backed his words with concrete action and was one of the first artists to donate record royalties to victims of apartheid and to reject extremely lucrative offers of work in South Africa. This was not a fashionable stance in the early 1960s.

He was also fully aware of the social stigma attached to mixed-race children, or as they were known at the time in Britain, 'half-caste'. "When mixed marriages do occur, people inevitably start talking about the children. Not fair to the kids they say," he continued in the *Tropic* article. "The poor little things are going to be born under a handicap."

The two children that Dankworth and Laine had, double bassist, Alec, and vocalist Jacqui, grew up to become successful jazz artists in their own right, but there was certainly an element of truth in the statement, given the prevailing prejudices of post-war Britain.

Early 1960s British social realist films such as *The Wind of Change* and *Flame in the Streets* confronted the subject head on and revealed how virulent could be the reaction of a brother or mother to a daughter bringing home a black man, even if he flouted stereotypes and was gainfully employed in a respectable profession. The key point made by these dramas was that such bigotry was part of wider upheavals, such as intergenerational conflict and the struggle between management and unions in the workplace. The focus of resentment was not just connected to a fear of all things black, but a deep unhappiness with a society in a state of flux.

There was outright offensiveness suffered by mixed-race children when they were described as "mongrels". Judith Baptiste remembered some of the comments that were made about their son, Wyn. "People would say to me, totally unaware of the implicit snub, 'Oh well, he's not *very* brown, he could pass as Italian,' as if that was something to be thankful for." Tragically, such attitudes still exist.

Beyond musical circles, cosmopolitan London was still some way off in the future. But there were communities where mixed-race couples and children went further back in time. One such location was Tiger Bay in Cardiff, where the marginalization of being mixed race was probably less significant than poverty and class. Here, it was the matter of poverty that was most pressing for Shirley Veronica Bassey,[10] the daughter of a white housewife and an African seaman.

Faced with the prospect of a dead-end job in a local factory, she put her preternaturally strong singing voice and self-confidence to good use, and made her way into the world of entertainment as a chorus girl in revues such as the successful 1953 show *Memories of Jolson*.[11] Bassey moved to London when she was 18, and went on to appear in shows such as *Hot from Harlem,* where she emerged as a performer with the kind of charisma and arresting stage presence that could win over the most exacting audiences. Bassey also successfully managed the gruelling induction of the variety circuit, where a singer would be thrust under the spotlights in front of rows of pensioners who had been given complimentary tickets to ensure the theatre was at least half full, especially on the notoriously tough mid-week slots. A record contract followed.

From the late 1950s onwards, Bassey became a sensation. The combination of the blinding sequins, rafter-raising voice and signature poses, none more iconic than the mock drama of the arms held to both sides of the face as if steadying herself against the torrid emotional shocks detailed in her love songs, made her burst out of TV screens and into the nation's hearts.

Yet if this undoubted X-Factor afforded Bassey star status at a time when journalists, gushing as they were, had no qualms in describing her as "a girl from a back street in Cardiff", who didn't have a Welsh accent, Bassey's studio recordings had undeniable artistic substance. Her body of work, like that of other singers from the era, was relatively eclectic. Perceived and marketed as a popular entertainer, Bassey gave both accomplished renditions of jazz standards such as "I Cover The Waterfront" and "Night and Day" as well as easy-listening fare like her first number one, 1958's "As I Love You".[12]

Calypso-styled music was also something that Bassey did well. Of the material that she recorded in the first stage of her career, two songs stand out – "Fire Down Below" and "Kiss Me, Honey, Honey, Kiss Me". Both are sharply arranged pieces of dance music in which clanging percussion is prominent in the mix. The latter in particular has an irresistibly catchy chorus in which Bassey taps into the ribaldry that is one of the staple ingredients of West Indian folk music. She even found herself banned by the BBC for the cheekily suggestive slant of her debut single, "Burn My Candle at Both Ends".

All of these songs seem like warm-ups to the performance that remains Bassey's signature to this day: "Goldfinger", the Leslie Bricusse and Anthony Newley title song of the third James Bond movie, released in 1964, a landmark piece of pop. Bassey's tone is an appropriate blend of camp theatricality and stern authority, hardening for the key word "gold" to underline the fact that in the jet-set world of suave spies, swish motors and expensive jewellery, people, especially nubile women, get a gold paint job, and then perish. To make us believe in the story of death and glamour, Bassey has to do more than just belt out verse and chorus. The over-the-top delivery is necessary to evoke the excess of the story, but emotional depth is reached only because the singer also manages to convey a blend of cynicism and weirdness.

The drama is all there in her handling of the word "Goldfinger". The first syllable is taken as a full-on Bassey blast, as she draws deep from her low register, but then shifts towards a higher, slightly more nasal timbre on the last two syllables, the effect of which is bring duality to the whole palette of the song. The story is about glitter and danger. What turns you on will also bring you down. Yes, she is vamping it up, but there is also a degree of nuance, a range of emotion brilliantly paralleled by the masterful melody and arrangement by the very gifted John Barry.[13] His score is unsettling and alluring. The strings and horns are majestic, grandiose and eerie.

Culturally, the song "Goldfinger" bridges a number of different worlds. It fits the easy-listening market, but also shows how African-American and European classical music both stream into the genre. While the billow and swirl of the strings flag up the influence of Vivaldi, the focused holler of the brass is all Ellington and the jazz tradition of horns inflected towards the human voice. The iconic *Wah wah wah* triplet on the second bar of the verse is a tip of the hat to the quivering vibrato effects of the Duke's star trumpeter, Bubber Miley. Jazz was indeed a key constituent of Barry's aesthetic and "Goldfinger" reminds us that the vocabulary of the big band can be effectively deployed within a cinematic context where concision in connecting image and sound is essential. "Goldfinger"[14] is a dense, multi-layered piece, but it is not an epic composition. It lasts a mere 2:49 minutes.

The historical-geographical framework of the music could not have been more British: a girl from humble origins in Tiger Bay going global on the back of a dazzlingly glamorous film franchise whose first exotic location was a former crown colony, Jamaica.

Notes

1. The sources for this account of the development of Jamaican music include Steve Barrow and Peter Dalton, *The Rough Guide to Reggae* and to Colin Larkin, *The Virgin Encyclopaedia of Reggae* (Virgin Books, 1998). See also Michael de Koningh and Laurence Cane-Honeysett, *Young Gifted and Black: The Story of Trojan Records* (Sanctuary, 2003).
2. Hear The Skatalites, *Guns of Navarone: Best Of* (Trojan, 2003).
3. Hear Jackie Mittoo, *The Keyboard King at Studio One* (Universal Sounds, 2000), Don Drummond's Don Cosmic (Studio One, 2017), Tommy McCook's *The Authentic Ska Sound of Tommy McCook* (Moonska, 2009).
4. A young Chris Blackwell can be seen dancing in the Puss-feller's bar scene in *Dr. No*.
5. Hear Monty Alexander's *Rass!* (MPS, 1974).
6. Simon Napier-Bell, *Black Vinyl, White Powder* (London: Ebury, 2002).
7. See "Duke Vin, Obituary", *The Telegraph*, 23 November, 2012.
8. On Cleo Laine see Michael Church, "Caribbean Cleo? The Amazing Cleo Laine", *Caribbean Beat*, Issue 13, Spring 1995, and "Passed/Failed: Cleo Laine", an interview with Jonathan Sale, *The Independent*, 10 June 1998.
9. *Tropic* magazine, March, 1960, p. 12.
10. On Bassey see, John L. Williams, *Miss Shirley Bassey* (Quercus, 2011).
11. *Memories of Jolson* was based on the life of Al Jolson, "The World's Greatest Entertainer", who performed in blackface.
12. Hear Shirley Bassey, *The Best of Bassey* (Contour, 1970).
13. Hear the John Barry soundtrack to *Beat Girl* (Columbia, 1960), featuring Adam Faith. I find the entire *Goldfinger* soundtrack (United Artists, 1964) masterful, especially the instrumental version of the title track.

21 GOSPEL TRAIN: RUNNING ALL THE WAY HOME

She was very flirtatious and talked a lot about Jesus. And she was pretty
good at knocking back the brandy too.
— George Melly on Sister Rosetta Tharpe.

Going down to the river and drown… my sorrows.
— Derry Wilkie

In 1960, 777,411 automobiles were manufactured and sold in Britain.
– Anglias, Cortinas, Minis, neat and tidy, wholesome vehicles fit for
those who were unable to afford 007's much more grandiose Aston
Martin. Yet public transport still played a major role in keeping the
nation on the move, and if buses, with their West Indian conductors,
were integral to popular consciousness, then trains, which took families
to all-in holiday camps on the coast, with their uniformed, ever smiling
and sunny hosts and entertainers, were still very much part of the
modern world.

Trains could also be the last resort for the disenfranchised and destitute.
A carriage could provide shelter for a homeless man. This was the fate that
befell Wilbert Augustus Campbell in the early 1950s, before he managed to
turn his fortunes around and became Count Suckle (1931-2014), founder
of one of the most revered sound systems in Britain. The lord of the dance
once had to bed down among the milk and papers.[1]

More broadly, the train had deep associations with the blues in America;
it was the mode of transport for the pioneering exponents of the music
back in the 1920s and 1930s, who, for the most part, were from the wrong
side of the tracks, working the land for precious little in return. Jumping a
freight train with a guitar in hand or a mouth organ in the pocket to head
for the cities was a reality reflected in many songs.

The Granada TV producer Johnny Hamp played on these associations
when he staged a concert in May 1964 at a disused railway station in
Chorlton, south Manchester.[2] On the bill was a string of African-American
musicians, including Sister Rosetta Tharpe, Muddy Waters and Sonny Boy
Williamson. They were gospel and blues legends. It was a landmark event
in British musical history. Due to appear at the Manchester Free Trade Hall
in the evening, the artists were coaxed into playing at the station, specially
kitted out with sacks, crates and even some livestock (chickens and goats

rather than hogs and steers) to create "authenticity" as Hamp imagined it. Exponents of black popular culture were expected to wear overalls not suits.

Several hundred people turned up for the performance, as news of the event started to circulate, and the resulting TV broadcast, *The Gospel and Blues Train*, was a resounding success. James Chapman-Kelly, just sixteen at the time, was there on the day, and recalls: "It was incredible because we loved these blues players in those days. People only heard about the concert through word of mouth, but there was a huge crowd and it inspired people to go off and make their own music."[3]

The Granada recording and the crowds that turned out signalled the decade when British popular music turned Black, whether its inspiration was folk blues, electric blues from Chicago, deep south soul or Motown. There was scarcely a rock or pop group that emerged in this period, from the Beatles to the Stones, whose inspiration wasn't Black music coming from the USA.

If listening to records was an essential part of the learning process of an aspiring rock musician, then seeing these artists in person was the equivalent of an audience with the pope. Access to recordings is one thing, but having the opportunity to see an artist on stage, to see their body language, gestural idiosyncrasies, their sense of self, is really quite another. The significance of the superb blues guitarist T-Bone Walker lay as much in the unique way that he held his guitar – practically at a right angle to his body, treating it almost like a keyboard he could slash into from above – as it did in the startling sounds that he was able to produce.

The Musicians Union's decision to ban American jazz artists from appearing in Britain in the 1930s was borne of a protectionist impulse that displayed a huge blindness to what stimulates a lively music scene, where new directions come from both within and without. The loopholes used to circumnavigate the ban, from jazz artists being invited for charity events or being "upgraded" to classical musician status, may be notable for their convolution, but they are also a sad indictment of institutional myopia.

"Chorltonville" was thus significant because it met an obvious desire on the part of Mancunians to experience the blues live and direct. Moreover, the concert has to be seen in the wider context of visits by other exponents of the genre in the 1950s, when the likes of Josh White, Sonny Terry & Brownie McGhee and Big Bill Broonzy arrived on these shores, some like White undertaking well-received national tours and appearing on BBC broadcasts. These artists were often billed as "variety performers" in order to outfox the MU hounds whose prohibition of American music specifically covered artists who were categorised as blues as well as jazz.

Among the most fervent evangelists of the blues in Britain was Chris Barber (1930–), a trombonist who was one of the spearheads of the trad jazz movement discussed in Chapter 12, and while he may have turned away from the new avenues opened up by bebop, his recordings highlight a desire to reflect some of the heterogeneity of Black music, hence the reprise of spirituals as well as blues and rags in his repertoire.

As modern jazz became increasingly demanding, the appeal of blues as a simpler form is understandable. Blues artists were in general vocalists. They sang songs. Lyrics that sketch out the human condition, either with frivolity or gravity, can touch the emotions of a wide audience when performed with conviction, and that held true for Broonzy or Waters, whose work dealt with everything from racial persecution to sexual gratification – all with a wide range of nuance: defiance, sarcasm, jubilation and irony. Beyond that immediate appeal, there was also an element of the virtuous pleasures of championship, of the rediscovery of artists whose excellence had been hidden by racial discrimination in the public media and the segregation of "race records". There was something romantic in discovering a guitar maestro like Robert Johnson whose 1936-37 recordings were highly influential on a whole generation of rock and blues guitarists when his recordings were reissued on the *King of the Delta Blues Singers* album in 1961.

Roughly contemporary to UK appearances by such blues artists was the advent of skiffle, the movement of acoustic folk blues that came about when Lonnie Donegan, the banjo player in Barber's band, enjoyed a major hit in 1955 with "Rock Island Line", a song by the prolific Louisiana-born singer, Leadbelly (1888-1949). This was another example of Black music in America, even with a rural, acoustic lexicon, reverberating beyond the temporal and spatial boundaries in which it was created. Tempting as it is to dismiss skiffle as light-hearted, posing little threat to middle-class values, it foregrounded the idea of relatively inexperienced musicians taking steps towards creating a personal identity. The onus on using cheap, it not makeshift instruments, such as a washboard or a box for percussion, or more ingeniously, a one-string bass, evoked the resourcefulness of early Negro music, where anything that came to hand – whether part of an animal carcass or discarded pieces of wood, could be fashioned into a music-making device. The success of the Carolina Chocolate Drops in our own time is an indication of the continuing appeal of such early Black music. Moreover if skiffle brought a new form of happy-go-lucky pop to the charts, then it also showed how the lines of sonic demarcation between genres could be easily blurred as instruments seen as representative of one style could surface in another. For instance, the clarinet, so symbolic of trad jazz, was also heard in folk and calypso, and the banjo linked these to bluegrass and country music. Common to all was the double bass, with a deep, cavernous, sensual sound and a purity of tone that suited an unamplified aesthetic in which the hard raking of fingers across a fretboard and the whirring vibrations of the bow were all part of the rootedness of music with a strong historical foundation.

But while the blues is planted in the dark psycho-emotional soil of desolation and fleeing from the slave master's hellhounds, it is also a mobile form, mischievously invested with both trickery and alchemy. It has a "mojo", a theatrical super-naturalism. It works on sonic as well as sexual expectation, which makes a mutation from one sound to another, an acoustic to an electric chord, a powerful cry to an even more powerful scream, seem both surprising and inevitable. It's there in Muddy Waters' (1913-1983) yearning, his individuality ripping open a straitjacket of modesty and asserting Black pride on "Mannish Boy", his superb song of resistance to a static existence and its attendant tedium. He is *made* to move. He is a rollin' stone. The acoustic world could not contain such bravado and magnitude of ambition.

So, the blues' voltage-assisted explosiveness became a key part of a new lingua franca in popular music, the brash abrasiveness of a Fender Strato-caster – a kind of nails-on-the-blackboard screech at convention. These instruments provided an altogether more dynamic and dangerous sensation than that of the acoustic instruments favoured by folk and skiffle, whose champion, Donegan, was really part of the music hall tradition, as can be heard in his 1965 hit "My Old Man's a Dustman", whose clatter of corny cockneyisms would have brought a comfortable sense of the rightness and inevitability of the British class system.

But skiffle did provide a way into popular music for a number of young bands in the 1960s, chief among them Liverpool's The Quarrymen. Don-egan's aesthetic was really a staging post rather than a finishing school, and as the young Merseysiders matured into the Beatles they turned away from artisanal acoustics to state-of-the-art electric technology. It was the sound of their trinity of electric strings – two guitars and bass guitar – that came to define them, just as it did countless British groups who took their cue from the many intertwined strands of Black American music.

A sense of possibility came with the arrival of r &b and gospel in 1960s Britain. Whether at concerts in BBC studios in London or at railway stations in Manchester, the themes of African American songs, whether sacred or profane, struck a chord among teenagers. As Mick Jagger said: "There was something about the sound"[4] when he tried to put his finger on what drew him to the blues. The extent to which he and his peers understood the complex relationship between the literal and the figurative in the blues, where an apparently transparent statement such as "I'm a man" could have meanings beyond the obvious, is a moot point. However, Jagger and co were sufficiently perceptive to recognise that a voice fired in the furnace of Jim Crow America, that flamed in the fire of minor-third guitar chords, offered a magical template for the future of popular music. Easier to learn to play at a basic functional level than the trumpet or saxophone (the iconic instruments of jazz), the guitar, which formed the backbone of the blues band, readily become the heart and soul of a new British pop, driven by the ambition of (in the main) young men who saw that these American models could create a sensibility that would define their generation. There was much strumming of the six-string and striking of preening poses in the bedroom mirror.

As the idea of youth as a demographic and a market gained traction, artists were needed who differentiated themselves from the entertainers whom their parents liked. The Rolling Stones were important for their studied non-conformism and unabashed sexuality. Jagger clearly understood the carnal power of dance that was part of the act of some black performers. It enabled a performer of limited vocal ability to ascend to iconic status. Using print and broadcast media effectively, the Stones manager, Andrew Loog Oldham, was able to exploit the growing synergy of music and fashion, enshrining the image as well as the sound in popular consciousness – a key factor in expanding the market.

Whilst ignited by the embrace of Black music, the evolution of the Stones and others took place against a backdrop of complex race relations. The question of exoticisation and stereotyping stalked some concerts by blues artists, to the extent that performers who arrived in suits rather than the denim overalls associated with the "country Negro" were met with disappointment. Such shackling expectations were contemporary with detonations of racially motivated violence on Britain's streets, the worst of which took place, as noted earlier, in Nottingham and Notting Hill Gate.

Pop music cracked open the generation gap, but issues of social identity that encompassed purchasing power and skin colour were also bubbling up in the lyrics of some groups who made their breakthrough in the 1960s. "Substitute" by The Who was one such thought-provoking snapshot of life in Britain that raised discomfiting questions for which there were no quick and easy solutions.

> "Simple things you see are all complicated/I look pretty young but I'm just backdated/I look all white but my dad was black/My fine-looking suit is really made out of sack."

Quintessentially British as this song was, its tenor is entirely traceable to the blues. The piece is predicated on the same pithy imagery, linguistic pirouettes and sardonic reality-checks as Big Bill Broonzy's "Black Brown And White", a song where the use of the word "brother" is brilliantly layered with sarcasm and solidarity, empathy and alienation. The blues opened creative doors through which young musicians kept walking.

From the early 1960s onwards, musicians in both the north and south of Britain – Alexis Korner (1928-1984) and Cyril Davies (1932-1964) in London, John Mayall (1930–) and Victor Brox (1940–) in Manchester – became indefatigable champions of the blues and their bands provided opportunities to younger players. These musicians were instrumental in keeping this older form of Black American music in the consciousness of younger audiences. They did this on the basis of high standards of musicianship, and Korner's Blues Incorporated Band acted as a finishing school for a raft of future guitar heroes such as Keith Richards, Jimmy Page and Eric Clapton.

Because the epiphany of Jagger and Richards bonding over blues records at a train station has become so anchored in our consciousness, we tend to forget that the blues had already worked its way into the minds of other significant thinkers decades before the 1960s. The Stones may have taken their name from a Muddy Waters song and directly modelled their work on his musical strategies, but the substance on which they drew was much more than just musical. The blues is worldview, attitude, character and above all story, and as distant as Louis Armstrong's jazz may seem from Muddy Waters' urban R&B, he had encapsulated the blues in the 1920s and the world took note.

Sadly, the blues as a form can sometimes be reduced to cliché, though even in the 21st century there have been artists who have found fresh things to do with the idiom. For the most part based on a formula, a set of established patterns of chord changes and stanza construction that at worst can be applied with as much repetitive regularity as a car assembled on a production line, at best the blues has reflected on the most vexed of moral dilemmas, existentialist speculations or projection of feelings upon inanimate objects, whether a packing trunk or a lonesome room. Perceptive commentators have long seen that the blues can act as code and context for moments of intense psycho-drama.

Aldous Huxley writes in *Brave New World* (1932): "The Synthetic Music Apparatus was producing the very latest in slow Malthusian Blues, they might have been twin embryos gently rocking together on the waves of a bottled ocean of blood surrogate."[5] He doesn't evoke a Malthusian sonata or a Malthusian aria, but a Malthusian Blues – to which the unborn are doing nothing as mundane as embracing, hugging, cuddling or snuggling. No, like some genuine Black Americans in a juke joint on a Saturday or a house of praise on a Sunday, they are "rocking".

Here, the blues has become the anthem for the wretched souls of the Hatcheries destined for planned obsolescence in Huxley's bleak dystopia of a future of extreme biological and social control, where thinly veiled jazz allusions, from "sexophones" to "a super-cornet solo",[6] also feature. It is also a racially differentiated world in which a black man is an "Epsilon-Plus Negro porter."[7] It is impossible to think that Huxley had not heard Louis Armstrong's music, and reflected on the significance of the word "blues" as it appeared in such landmark recordings as 1928's "West End Blues".

Huxley imagined human beings as expendable, graded assembly line products. It was a terrifying vision. Muddy Waters would have called it real life on a Mississippi cotton plantation. That's why the blues changed Britain. It wasn't just that pop could not resist its sounds in the post-war years, literature had already acknowledged its dramatic charge in pre-war times. The blues had permeated progressive minds because of the depth of its humanity, the sanctity of its emotion and the honesty of its exponents, whose very names could convey the dynamics of our daily behaviour.

Muddy waters are what every individual stands in and occasionally moves out of at points in their life. It is an intensely levelling metaphor, providing empowering solace for the empty-pocketed and the broken-hearted. You'd rather drink muddy water than crawl on home to that woman. And she'd rather drink mo' muddy water than take your sad ass back.

The power of lament in the blues is matched by its capacity to uplift, by way of confidential admission and by congregation. When a man or woman lays down their sack of woe before another, they entertain the possibility of a burden being shared. And if the voice and lyric are the essential tools of this exercise, then so is the guitar because of its relative democracy. Strike the right two chords and you have the makings of a blues new world. A man or a woman can write songs with a guitar. A man or a woman can go places with a guitar.

For a generation of post-war teenagers who did not want to be like their parents, the guitar, with its variety of expressive possibilities was an weapon of great power. The instrument was even banned in some British public schools because draconian housemasters saw it as a symbol of revolution that would undermine the existing social order. Imagine their horror at the sight of a musician playing the instrument with his teeth or behind his head, or a pianist hitting the keyboard hard enough to break it apart while cocking his leg on the wooden frame of the instrument as if to commit a sex act on it. Imagine how easily an existing racial prejudice could be reinforced if these exponents were black and the viewer only felt comfortable with musicians of colour in the environment of a minstrel show. It was one thing if such images came from across the Atlantic, another if it was a black man who sang in a ruggedly bluesy voice on stage, but talked just like John Lennon off it. The black Scouse rhythm & blues hero in question was called Derry Wilkie (1941-2001) who announced himself as "the first spade singer in town".[8]

Born in Toxteth, Liverpool, Wilkie was one of the great personalities of what was known as the early Merseybeat scene, who fronted a band called Derry and the Seniors, which convincingly captured some of the wildness of black popular music in its transition from rhythm & blues to rock & roll. Little information exists on Wilkie's background, but the consensus is that he was the son of Nigerian migrants who discovered at an early age that he had a strong voice and a stage presence to match. The Seniors played in Hamburg, Germany in 1960 prior to the arrival of the Beatles, but although recognized as a combo with an eye-catching front man, they never consolidated their talent by way of a steady run of hit singles, though they were actually one of the first Liverpool beat groups to go into a studio and make a record.

Following the departure of two of its founder members, the group reformed with saxophonist Howie Casey as the leader of Howie Casey & The Seniors, with Wilkie sharing vocals with another youngster, Freddie Folwell, who would later find fame as the zany television comic, Freddie Starr. Among the 45s they issued in 1962 is "I Ain't Mad at You",[9] a vibrant cut of rock & roll in which crackling guitars and a throaty saxophone set up a lively backing for Wilkie to deliver a vocal performance that has the vigour to bring an archetypal tale of a lovers' tiff to life. The song also has several well-realized ideas in its arrangement. The curtain-raiser is high camp but cute. A bar of rakish guitar and the clear slap of the snare drum are the R&B equivalent of a town crier's "hear ye" for all the latest headlines on who's been running around with whom. A longer drum roll starts the introduction in earnest, the whole band snaps into life and four bars later Wilkie can be clearly heard issuing a very knowing "huh", which is brilliantly executed by the way that it suggests the raised eyebrow of a man who thinks a woman is maddening and stimulating in equal measure. The chorus is instantly catchy and easy to internalize as a kind of folk wisdom on the numbers game in the world of relationships.

> I ain't mad at you
> Don't be mad at me
> One and one is two
> Two and one is three.

Spare as the language is, it's a clever computation of infidelity – the intractable love triangle, an equation of wants and needs that don't add up. "I Ain't Mad at You" sets that eternal conundrum to the rhythms of the nursery rhyme, which makes the point that people in the grip of lust often behave like excitable children in a playground.

Yet if Wilkie's handling of the refrain strikes a balance of playfulness and assertion, then he also makes a statement with cultural and historical weight in the line: "Going down to the river and drown… my sorrows" – a reminder that the blues flows from the same wellspring as gospel, above all the biblical Jordan, the symbolic place where a lost soul can be saved and redemption found.

Sadly, Derry & the Seniors did not enjoy great commercial success with singles such as "I Ain't Mad At You" and the band went through many personnel changes, eventually leading to its break-up, though its work as a pioneering force on the Liverpool scene is indisputable. The character of Wilkie's voice was in line with a fundamental shift in Black music. The flash of intensity he conveyed was part of the bigger emotional storm created by electrifying preachers and singers who brought ecstatic feelings to worshippers in Black churches.

When vocalists carried this sacred energy deep into the profane world of the blues, the result was exhilarating. Sam Cooke and Ray Charles were the instigators. Scandal greeted them both. When Charles wrote a song that explicitly blended godly and ungodly language – "Hallelujah, I Love Her So" – seduction in the name of the Almighty was just too much for some folk to bear. Others related strongly to the combination. It was the dynamic that leads a man to look at a woman whose erotic attraction has pushed him past the point of distraction to joyfully holler: "Lawd have mercy!"

The turbulence of the sacred and the profane coursed through Sister Rosetta Tharpe's performance at Chorltonville in 1964. She was a gospel singer who *was* the blues, as the trad jazz singer, George Melly, who worked with her at several other concerts in Britain, remembers well. "Offstage she was very flirtatious and talked a lot about Jesus. And she was pretty good at knocking back the brandy too."[10] She was evidently a complex being impelled by both spiritual and secular desires.

Rosetta Tharpe, born in Arkansas, daughter of the legendary singer-preacher Katie Bell Nubin, was one of the first gospel artists to achieve success in the pop world in the late 1930s with "This Train", and she exerted an enormous influence on rock & roll stars such as Little Richard and Jerry Lee Lewis. With Charles, Cooke and the young James Brown, she laid the foundations of what would become the defining leitmotiv of Black popular culture in the 1960s: *Soul*. This signified self-empowerment, the call for social justice and cultural pride central to the Civil Rights movement. It led to the epithet "soul" being prefixed to everything from food to handshakes to brothers and sisters. Musically, soul designated a shift in R&B as it absorbed more of the ecstatic surge of the church, just as the increasing use of electric instruments such as the guitar, bass guitar, Fender Rhodes piano and Hammond B-3 organ introduced harder, tougher timbres. Soul was still the blues, but it was the blues for today. Black music in America in the 1960s was producing one new dramatic aural sensation after another, and one can only imagine how thrilling it must have been for a teenager to hear for the very first time the slinky organ purr its way into life on Booker T & the MGs' "Green Onions"[11] or James Jamerson's[12] bass guitar wrangle sensually over countless Motown anthems. These were sounds that marked the era, sounds that would shape music in Britain, Black and White, for decades to come.

Histories of the UK music industry tend to evoke the obsession of the major labels in the mid 1950s with the creation of a domestic Elvis, the black-sounding white boy whose whiteness was manna from heaven for a less than progressive music industry that sought to market Black culture without Negro packaging. A more fascinating question is: Who would have been Britain's Ray Charles? – one of Elvis's many black role models. The obvious candidates *ought* to have been the son of a black immigrant family in London, Liverpool or Manchester. After all, West Indians had been weaned on the good rocking of Saturday night sound systems and the holy rolling of Sunday morning church services.

Be that as it may, the whole point about Black music in Britain is that it has *not* been restricted to that constituency, so the idea of a white boy who could sing black was not so much an eventuality as a probability, given that the record-buying culture provided all with the same raw materials to learn from, and there were now many more chances to see "the real thing" on stage. The destructive essentialist myth that *all* Blacks sing soul as a kind of divine right because of the accident of race was offset by the reality that some Whites sing soul because of a god-given talent as well as extensive cultural immersion. We should be no more surprised to listen to a 7" single, hear a gospel-stamped tenor roar into life and then look at the record sleeve to see a bunch of skinny Caucasian teens, than to see a formally-attired black man conducting a symphony orchestra in a gilded concert hall.

What matters is that Steve Winwood's lead vocal on "Keep On Running" by the Spencer Davis group was a thing of vibrant beauty. Here was superlative Black music made in Britain by a young white group from Birmingham, a city that had been touched by Jamaican musicians like Andy Hamilton and whose sound system DJs had been targeted by the distributors of Melodisc and Bluebeat because of the sizeable West Indian population that had significantly enriched the city's social and cultural life.

Set to a stompingly powerful backbeat, "Keep On Running" was one of the great pieces of progressive music of 1965 in the way that it blended the soulfulness of Winwood's voice with the roar of Spencer Davis's guitar, a sound that gave a rougher, more rugged edge to keyboard-based R&B, but more importantly extended the explosive nature of Ray Charles' performance on 1962's "I Got a Woman".

Incredibly, Winwood, who, like Ray Charles, was an excellent pianist and organist, was just thirteen years-old when he was drafted by his older brother, bassist Muff, into a trad jazz trio, Muff's Mojo Men, a name redolent of Black folklore. Thereafter they met Spencer Davis, a guitarist and teacher of German, and the quartet became a group under his name, playing at Birmingham venues such as The Golden Eagle. Initially, their repertoire comprised covers of American blues and soul legends from Muddy Waters to Ray Charles, but they subsequently branched out and investigated the music of other artists.[13]

They made a connection with Chris Blackwell, the Jamaican entrepreneur-producer who had enjoyed enormous success with Millie Small's "My Boy Lollipop". Blackwell could see that Winwood was star material after hearing him sing with the group in a club in Birmingham, so he signed them to Island Records, and set about launching the band in earnest. As-

JACKIE EDWARDS

COURTESY PICTORIAL PRESS LTD / ALAMY STOCK PHOTO

SPENCER DAVIS GROUP

COURTESY GRANAMOUR WEEMS COLLECTION / ALAMY STOCK PHOTO

tutely, Blackwell matched Winwood's great voice to a great song, "Keep On Running". The composer was Jamaican – Wilfred 'Jackie' Edwards (1938-1992),[14] a charming singer from Kingston who learned his trade listening to American radio broadcasts and who, after winning local talent contests, chalked up hits in1959 with the singles "Your Eyes Are Dreaming" and "Tell Me Darling". Edwards had a gift for writing original melodies, and he travelled to London with Blackwell to help him establish Island records by writing songs and, as legend has it, riding red double-decker buses so that he could deliver boxes of singles to the small record shops in town.

"Keep On Running" bucked convention. The majority of 1960s British groups assembled their repertoire by covering tunes by a successful American artists, but here the original was by a far less well known West Indian, and Edwards' melody was as good as anything that had been written by such an iconic figure as Ray Charles. What is also fascinating is the light that the two versions of "Keep On Running" cast on the complexity of black music straddling Britain and its former colonies. Edwards was an artist whose sweet, quite boyish voice was equally suited to ska as it was R&B and he had recorded in both styles. His version of "Keep On Running" has as propulsive a groove as the Spencer Davis hit; the key difference is the supporting role of the horn section in the Edward's cut, memorable for the three-note motif on the bridge, a punchy lick that vaguely recalls the brass hook on Millie Small's "My Boy Lollipop", and grabs the listener from the start.

Davis & co replaced the horns with vocals. It was an inspired decision. The sound of the band members intoning "Hey, hey, hey" creates a simple but artful burst of harmonies. These form a dramatic gateway to the second stage of the song's narrative, announced by a change of key in the middle eight. This marks the shift of emotional weight from the assured determination of the teenage suitor to his now desperate humiliation. "Hey, Hey, Hey" is all bright, upward energy while the new lyric turns sharply downwards: "Everyone is laughing at me/it makes me feel so sad". The "hey, hey, hey" thus plays a trick, suggesting hope, but instead revealing despair. This is pop at its most masterful. Conquest and defeat in the love game are matched by the contrasts in musical and emotional tone. Somebody must have imagined the horn line of Jackie Edward's version could work as a vocal line, and this underlines the crucial role of arranging in popular music, where the choice of instruments and sounds can be so decisive.

The two versions of "Keep On Running" sketch out a framework of possibilities for British pop in the mid 1960s. On the one hand Jackie Edwards hails the orchestral paradigm, where production values are high, and the artful scoring of horns or strings is essential to defining the character of a song. Spencer Davis posits the leaner, tougher model of the guitar-led band, where the attack of the vocals or the tones of the electric instruments are paramount. This version has more grit, more attitude.

"Keep On Running" also makes an important point about the history of black music that is sometimes overlooked. It often has beautiful *melodies* as well as strong rhythms. What Edwards did was craft gorgeous verses that have a perfect balance of long, floating notes, especially the elongation on "runn…ing", and shorter, busier phrases ("One fine day") that raise the energy levels in line with the song's surges of emotional intensity. Such is the richness of the theme that it could be sung *a capella*.

Although the distorted "fuzz" of the guitar is prominent in Davis's case, what really defines the rhythmic carriage of the song is Muff Winwood's bass guitar, an instrument that was still young in 1965 – the first models being manufactured in 1951 by Leo Fender. It is very prominent in the mix and has a weight to match that of the baritone saxophones that once featured on many R&B tracks. The hard pounding of the low end in the intro, with the thick, bulbous A, E and G notes like bouncing bombs on the pulse of the song, is thrilling for the sense of imposition and threat created. It is this combination of the electric bass and guitar, providing boom, shudder and screech that really defines what became known as "beat" music – think Beatles, Animals, Stones, Manfred Mann, Yardbirds. Loud, hefty guitars, bulky backbeats and hormonal vocals generated waves of excitement, often through the simplest of lines. The magic was in the Beatles wailing "Yeah… yeah…yeah" and Spencer Davis hollering "Hey, Hey, Hey…", which was why pop was so accessible and universal. A "Yeah" and a "Hey" were variations of breath coming from the same universally understood body of expression, and their alterations and combinations, from 'Hey yeah' to 'Ha yeah' to 'Hey Ya!' provided almost limitless raw materials.

The "Arghs" and "Aws" and "Woahs" and "Woohs", which were such a vital part of the blues, carried over into mainstream pop, epitomized by the Beatles out-shrilling the Isley Brothers when they covered "Twist And Shout" (1964). These exclamations, sounds that had no definitive phonetics, words that were not for the dictionary, consolidated the energy of informality, the potency of the ordinary, the thrill of non-musicality. You didn't have to be classically trained to be able to nail a "Wooh!"

While the journey of the song "Keep On Running", from Kingston, Jamaica to Birmingham, England, says much about the cultural shifts underway in post-Empire Britain, the stylistic transformation also reflects the irrepressible dynamism of Black music, its pace of change. The Edwards original was orchestral, but it is not hard to hear the residual influence of close-harmony vocal music in it, even though the style of doo wop, which had been hugely popular between the mid and late 1950s, had lost much ground as R&B turned into soul at the dawn of the 1960s.

However, one piece of doo wop-influenced music that conquered British pop in that period came from a St. Lucian singer and musician who settled in London in the mid 50s, Michael Emile Telford Miller, who performed under the stage name of Emile Ford.[15] Following in the footsteps of other West Indian musical expatriates with engineering skills, the Trinidadian guitarist Lauderic Caton and Jamaican bassist Coleridge Goode (who had built prototype television sets and amplifiers), Ford, a graduate of Paddington Technical College, devised a machine that could play backing tracks for live performances – an ingenious forerunner of the modern day karaoke set-up.

He also formed Emile Ford and the Checkmates and started to make inroads into the prime-time television circuit in the 1950s, appearing for six consecutive weeks on *Sunday Serenade* and enjoying a number one single in 1959 with a cover "What Do You Want to Make those Eyes at Me For", a piece that had been a hit for Ada Jones and Bill Murray in 1917, but was reborn with the vocal ornamentation that characterised the doo wop sub-genre. Ford's delivery, pleasant rather than idiosyncratic, and his group's understated performance, struck a chord with British listeners, and he and the Checkmates recorded several successful albums before they disbanded in the 1960s, after which he moved to Sweden.

Apart from its seductive quality, its evocation of sighs and whispers in a lover's ear, doo wop was an appealing development in Black popular music because it could be effective when performed *a capella* as well as with a rhythm and horn section. There wasn't a need for any equipment if four or five decent voices could harmonize well and this proved the case among black military personnel. Though few of them were actually recorded, there were doo wop groups to be found on American army bases in Britain in the 1950s. When they had time to socialise, four or five guys could perform a kind of spontaneous gig known as a "street corner symphony".

There were exponents outside the bases, too, and one of the most accomplished British doo wop groups of the 1960s was to be found in Liverpool: The Chants.[16] Formed in 1962, this was a five-piece vocal ensemble comprising brothers Joe and Eddie Ankah, Nat Smeda, Alan Harding and Eddie Amoo,[17] all school friends from the Toxteth area who appeared regularly at venues such as the Cavern, sometimes with members of the Beatles providing backing. As was the case with Wilkie, they never really got going as recording artists, and their discography is frustratingly meagre even though they were together for over a decade. Like U.S. groups such as The Coasters, The Penguins and The Drifters, The Chants had fantastically lush, creamy harmonies, very pretty melodies and a discreet, if not understated, rhythmic backing.

Watching vintage footage of the group performing "I Could Write A Book" in Liverpool is thrilling. Slickness of sound matches slickness of presentation. The group members sport matching beige collarless jackets, crisply starched white shirts and ties and black, straight-leg trousers. They stand in a row, stretching arms and bending back and forth in simple choreographed moves. They are packed snugly together as if huddling for warmth, so when their voices blend, the close harmony is mirrored by the close positioning of all the band members. They lean right towards centre-stage, shoulders pointing inwards as their rich unison lines become tighter and tighter, curling around the song's tonal centre. The visual becomes a reinforcement of the aural. Even more intriguing is the fact that the audience comprises mainly beehived teenage girls, many of whom stare dreamily at the group as their scat vocals of "degga degga degga degga doo wah ah" ring out in between the verses of the song. It's all sophistication, reminding us that Black vocals do not always have to be screamed into life, that there is room for nuance. The Chants are all gilded charm laced with understatement.

Urbane, slick, polished, they were part of a tradition of African-American vocal ensembles that excelled both *a capella* and in orchestral settings and for whom matching outfits – evening wear rather than easy casuals – were a vital part of their image. Looking and sounding as good as the Chants did, it's a wonder they were not more successful, but the issues of management, marketing and changing trends in Black music probably conspired against them. They did not manage the kind of change that transformed one of their role models, the Detroit group The Temptations, when they signed to Berry Gordy's Tamla Motown, from a doo-wop ensemble to the adventurous soul group who sang "Papa was a Rolling Stone".

For British teenagers at the cutting edge of style, Motown became the indispensable cachet of hipness, and fashion-conscious teenagers took to the label's logo to an even greater extent than they had done with Bluebeat and Studio One. Motown records had the blues, but there was also an artful integration of the tradition of Broadway balladry, pop and jazz, with its great orchestral flourish in the arrangements, so that the end product was a savvy blend of sophistry and grit, elaboration and earthiness.

In the early 1960s, Motown groups such as Martha Reeves & The Vandellas and The Supremes had commercial success in America and Britain, and their cultural importance was down to more than great songs. They were extremely well turned out, thanks to the grooming and deportment classes the artists received, and they had stop-in-the-name-of-style dance moves, in which each member of the ensemble had clearly designated steps, which made a huge impact on youth-oriented TV shows.

These attributes resonated potently with a British "modernist" or mod culture in which the cut of a mohair suit, the sheen of Chelsea boots or beef-roll loafers, the marble-column stiffness of sta-prest trousers, the hue of a button-down shirt, the precise tilt of a porkpie, the tightness of a check mini skirt, the curve of high heels and the rise and swirl of a lacquered beehive had become matters of importance. Preening youth for whom the possibility of achieving distinction through dress, of being *the* face picked out in the crowd went with having money to spend. Social success could come by way of a material object – a car or scooter, or the kind of stylish clothing sported by jazz musicians that could be seen on the sleeve of a Blue Note record.

Knowing the latest moves had such kudos that many clubs employed dancers to stand on stage, often next to the DJ, and show their peers exactly how to do what the black kids in Detroit, Chicago or, indeed, Kingston, Jamaica were doing. The tradition of songs named after the steps of the day, from The Cool Jerk and The Hucklebuck to The Locomotive and The Mashed Potatoes ran deep, because Black America was the land of a thousand dances. The ingenuity in how to move mirrored the creativity in how to sing.

Inevitably, Motown came to Britain with an action-packed multi-artist revue in March 1965. Featuring Smokey Robinson & The Miracles, The Supremes, Little Stevie Wonder, The Temptations and Martha Reeves & The Vandellas, the tour had no fewer than 20 dates including London, Glasgow, Wigan and Newcastle, but the low attendance for some gigs was a sign that at this point, the popularity of Motown was still a sub-group phenomena, and that the label had not yet worked out how to promote their shows abroad. So poor were ticket sales outside of London that Georgie Fame was added to the bill. This is significant because it shows how competitive the British beat movement was in relation to groups from the USA. The likes of the Beatles, the Kinks and Gerry & The Pacemakers had amassed huge fanbases.

Even so the real British devotees of Motown were in their element, convinced of the historic nature of the moment. Apparently the tour came about in the first place largely because a committed R&B enthusiast, Dave Godin,[18] who founded the Tamla Motown Appreciation Society, wrote to label boss Berry Gordy, and raised the idea of appearances in Britain. Now a membership card of the T.M.A.S. is as treasured a piece of memorabilia as a ticket stub for one of the historic 1965 gigs on the British tour.

Notes

1. Chris Salewicz, "Count Suckle – Obituary", *The Independent*, 10 June 2014
2. "When the Blues train rolled into Chorlton", *Manchester Evening News*, 18 January 2013.
3. Ibid.
4. Interviewed on BBC Radio 4's Front Row, 2016.
5. Aldous Huxley, *Brave New World* (Longman, 1932), p. 64.
6. Aldous Huxley, *Brave New World*, p. 28.
7. Aldous Huxley, *Brave New World*, p. 83.
8. See www.triumphpc.com/mersey-beat/archives/derriewilkie.shtml., and see *Mersey Beat*, 23 July 1964.

9. Featured on Various artists, *Calypsos, Boogies, Rockers, Ballads & Bluebeat* (Rockhistory.co.uk, 2013).

10. https://alternativestovalium.blogspot.co.uk/2006/02/interview-with-george-melly-jazz.html. And see on Tharpe, *The Godmother of Rock and Roll: Sister Rosetta Tharpe*, BBC 4, 24 May 2011.

11. Booker T & The MGs were hugely influential on many British 'beat' groups, particularly the Small Faces.

12. Jamerson was part of the brilliant Funk Brothers house band that made an invaluable contribution to the Motown sound.

13. spencer-davis-group.com

14. See Jackie Edwards, *I Feel So Bad: The Soul Recordings* (Castle, 2006). And see Obituary: "Jackie Edwards", by Lloyd Bradley, *The Independent*, 1 Sept. 1992.

15. "Emil Ford, legendary St Lucian artiste, dies in London", *Los Angeles Sentinel*, 21 April 2016.

16. See Youtube, 23 October 2008.

17. Amoo later found fame as a member of the 1970s soul group, The Real Thing.

18. Dave Godin is a highly respected DJ-curator of soul music and considered one of the UK's foremost authorities in the field. See his compilations, *Dave Godin's Deep Soul Treasures Vol 1-3* (Kent, 1997-2000).

22 BLACK ROCK, BLACKS ROCK

"We never had much time to rehearse proper because the boys were working. Sometimes they left work and went straight to the gig."
— Ossie Roberts, Soul Brothers, Ossie & The Sweet Boys, The Alphabets

Martha Reeves & The Vandellas' "Dancing in the Street", one of the signature Motown hits in the 1960s, was a great ode to happiness, to the kind of untrammelled joy that arrived when Black cultural expression and high record sales coincided for the good of all – "There'll be swingin', swayin' and records playin'". But the song also came to resonate with the riots that set alight Los Angeles and Detroit, ignited by the police brutality prevalent in African-American neighbourhoods.

The year before the release of "Dancing in the Street" the inspirational Civil Rights campaigner Medgar Evers had been assassinated in 1963, part of the tragic bloodletting that occurred as White America wrestled with the refusal of Black Americans to be second-class citizens, culminating in the deaths of Martin Luther King, Malcolm X and lesser-known white activists such as Revered James Reeb. All this took place against the divisive backdrop of the Vietnam War, for which African-Americans were disproportionately drafted. Shut out at home, then shot at abroad.

That conflict was much more than a national trauma for the USA. It reminded the world that the legacy of imperialism involved large-scale loss of life as decades of slicing up overseas territories sparked power struggles and attendant cycles of violence. The Vietnam War of the 1960s grew, of course, from the anti-colonial Indo-China War of the 1950s when the co-lonial power was France. International protests against the Vietnam War, notably at the U.S. Embassy in London in 1968, were defining social and political events of the decade.

But nothing was clear cut in the struggle to decolonise. The granting of independence to countries formerly under British rule brought to a head massive problems as well as opportunities. The civil war that ravaged Nigeria was a calamity waiting to happen. Nigeria, as a British dominion, had been more or less created by the ambitious industrialist George Taub-man Goldie in the late 19th century, and the complex issues of ethnicity, religion and politics created by this yoking of dissimilar peoples and cultures had never been adequately resolved during the colonial period. What made things worse were the behind-the-scenes roles played by Britain and other world powers such as the Soviet Union and France, lending support to opposing sides according to their own national interests.

Whilst the Vietnam War eclipsed the Nigerian Civil War or Biafran War, as it was known, in the attention it received, the latter was also one the great geo-political calamities and human catastrophes of the 1960s. It is believed that from 1967 to 1970 between 1.2 and 3 million died in Nigeria, not to mention the legacy of orphaned children consigned to a life of malnutrition and displacement.

Far away as these conflicts seemed from the music scene in the UK, their effects were nonetheless marked. In the USA, the influential composer Lawrence D. 'Butch' Morris, saxophonist Frank Lowe and violinist Billy Bang[1] were just a few of the African-American jazz artists packed off to Vietnam. In Britain, some Nigerian musicians resident here were not content to follow the news of the Biafran hostilities from the safety of the BBC World Service. So they swapped horn and guitar for rifle and pistol.

The Mancunian saxophonist, Tosh Ryan, a regular collaborator with West African musicians at Moss Side clubs such as The Nile, recalls that there were many departures from the musical scene because of the Biafran conflict. "Yes, a lot of my friends went back to fight in the Biafran war. They were just gone very quickly, really. It was a sad thing to see, because people that you'd seen in good circumstances, you had known on stage with smiles on their faces playing music, had to leave in fear for their families and loved ones back at home. The whole thing was tragic."[2]

Yet whilst music and war seem contradictions, for some of the poor and the disenfranchised, particularly in the USA, the military offered stability, and sometimes an improvement in circumstances for those who were still searching for a direction in life. And some of the musicians who signed up did not let their muses go. They still played guitar. They sang. Occasionally, their destinies followed a course that few had predicted.

Courtesy of the US Army

The middle of the 1960s saw the arrival in Britain of two artists linked by their experience of the military. One was still wearing fatigues, but the other displayed a sartorial flair ill-suited to the homogeneity of khaki. Geno Washington's[3] (1943–) and Jimi Hendrix's (1942-1970) names are seldom mentioned together, but they are bound by the common denominator of their brief military experience. Hailing from Evansville, Indiana and Seattle, Washington, respectively, Washington and Hendrix both enlisted in the air force. In 1962, roughly a year into his service, during which time his musical proclivities were neither appreciated nor encouraged,[4] Hendrix was discharged from the 101st

Airborne after sustaining injury from a parachute jump. Washington maintained grade A physical condition and worked as a U.S.A.F. gym instructor – no doubt one of the reasons he was able to deliver such incredibly energetic stage performances.

Washington, the singer, was rooted in gospel whereas Hendrix, the guitarist-vocalist, was deeply anchored in the blues, but had a maverick, outlandish, if not surreal spirit that nudged his self-expression towards shock and awe. In his formative years, this earned dismissals from several R&B bands whose leaders felt that he was stealing their thunder, or committing the heinous crime of refusing to cut his hair.

Washington was brilliantly of his time. Hendrix was of a time to come, though, ingeniously, he never severed his umbilical cord to time past. He said that he was always looking for "today's blues", but what he really found was "tomorrow's blues for today." Musically he stretched time.

Washington, initially stationed from 1965 at an air force base in East Anglia, did one-off gigs as a guest vocalist with R&B bands in London before he came to the attention of the guitarist Pete Gage. Gage thought that the singer would be the perfect front man for a new combo – Geno Washington & The Ram Jam band, a well-drilled soul ensemble fuelled by Washington's relentlessly gutsy, uplifting vocals.

Issued in December 1966, their debut album *Hand Clappin' Foot Stompin' Funky Butt... Live!* was a substantial seller that spent 38 weeks in the album charts, the result of the strong support the band garnered from their endless round of gigs. The album was recorded in concert, and showed that Washington and the Ram Jammers were a very engaging covers band who could play the Motown and Stax hits of the day with great proficiency and feeling. None of the repertoire was original.

In contrast, Jimi Hendrix, who came to London in 1966, although he made his breakthrough with a reprise of the brooding folk-rock standard "Hey Joe", was essentially defined by his own writing. The originals recorded on his two landmark albums – *Are You Experienced?* (1967) and *Axis Bold As Love* (1967) – showed how excitingly the blues and R&B vocabulary that Hendrix had learned in his youth could mutate and expand in the mind and hands of an imaginative artist. His guitar/vocal-bass-drums three-piece unit, the Jimi Hendrix Experience, remains one of the greatest examples of a small group capable of producing a molten orchestral power that succeeded in vividly capturing the tenor of the times.

The term guitar hero is inadequate for Hendrix. His virtuosity with the six-string guitar is inseparable from the imaginatively wrought lyrics, focused drama of the voice and a wide range of sculptural, tonal distortions from his embrace of technology. Hence the cracking and cleaving of the wah wah pedal on "Voodoo Child [Slight Return]" is not an addition to the heart-stopping image of a mountain "chopped down with the edge of my hand" but a foretelling of it. Mass, so powerfully expressed in the image of the steep, high rock, is one of the defining characteristics of Hendrix's aesthetic, and the chords that follow the snarled intro convey the quality of air-sagging weight, the kind of oppressive high summer humidity where sweat can feel solid rather than liquid. This sensation of thickness and heaviness marks a logical progression from the crashing bulk that is summoned by the bass guitar on some of the defining pop records of the mid 1960s, a key example being Spencer Davis' "Keep On Running". Listen to that bass next to the guitar on a Hendrix cut and you hear how the pop of the era is hardening up tonally, from low to high register. Physicality of this kind had been part of the electric blues of Chicago since the 1940s. One has only to listen to Muddy Waters for confirmation. But Hendrix, along with other British groups like The Yardbirds, The Who, Stones and Cream pushed further down the evolutionary road of a new sensibility in rock, in which an even greater density of tone and volume would materialize.

Further, beyond the guitar hero image, Hendrix never forgot his role as a team player, and whilst attention has tended to focus on his lead guitar work, his quality as a rhythm guitarist should not be overlooked. The way that Hendrix accompanied other musicians, such as when he comps behind the saxophones and trumpets on the jazzy "South Saturn Delta", and enhanced the percussive attack of a song, particularly by foot-stomping his pedals, remained part of the core vocabulary of Black music. His roots in R&B were never denied. But Jimi used them in a different way to his peer Geno. The former largely found chordal and textural richness in the guitar; the latter in a horn section. Yet the strength of the blues was encapsulated in both their personal aesthetics. They were related but they were very different.

Both Hendrix and Washington returned to the States by the late 1960s, but programmers were astute enough to put them on the same bill prior to their departure. Audiences who attended a spectacular event called Barbeque '67 at Spalding in Lincolnshire would have seen them along with Cream, Zoot Money's Big Roll band, Pink Floyd and The Move – a line-up that showed that the rich heterogeneity of popular music. Its spectrum of soul and rock, and new offshoots such as psychedelic rock had led to neither a partitioning of styles, nor of Blacks and Whites. Rock as a genre was rapidly evolving to reflect major issues in politics and society, just as blues had done, while state of the art technology was bringing forth radical new sounds, certainly in the hands of Hendrix. The strain of experimental thinking that galvanized him and some other groups of the time showed that there was no clear division between what might be seen as pop and what could be called art.

So many of the iconic images of Hendrix show him on stage with a stack of towering speakers behind him. Inevitably, he, and the likes of

Cream, made rock synonymous with the stadium, yet Hendrix's aesthetic also contained the finesse and understatement of his ballads. There is the eruption of "Voodoo Child (Slight Return)", but also the deep pathos of "Little Wing" – an indication of both the complexity of Hendrix's character and the emotional resources of blues culture. As Huxley intimated in *Brave New World*, the blues is at its most gripping as a "slow" tune, the format that can manifest vivid confessional states and lay bare the deepest feelings. In the electric church that Hendrix creates in his playing, he presents rock as a form of music that can successfully accommodate both introspection and aggression.

Rocksteady with a Slower Beat

Nothing may seem farther removed from Hendrix than the West Indian music that he probably heard while he was living in West London. Slow songs have always had a place in West Indian culture; ballads and crooners were hugely important in the rituals of courtship and romance. The great popularity in West Indian homes of country & western and pop-jazz balladeers, from Jim Reeves to Nat 'King' Cole and Billy Eckstine was a reflection of this. Tales of heartbreak, love, loss and longing were the foundations for seduction at a basement club or a dance. Music played at slow tempos gave the chance to get close to somebody who was worth getting next to at a house party or "blues".

For West Indian ears, there was a clear divide between the heaviness of a Hendrix-style electric guitar and the lightness of strings and brass and at this point in time there was a preference for the latter. The texture and tempo of music in Jamaica was changing. Ska had evolved into Rocksteady, which was slower in rhythm, with, as the name suggests, a mellowness and leisure in the beat that made it greatly appealing to dancers. Although it featured a heavy bass guitar, often played with forthright syncopation, rocksteady was also an unabashedly romantic music, as typified by stellar vocal groups such as The Paragons whose 1967 hit "The Tide Is High" was an example of the continuing quality of writing and arranging in Kingston. Like ska before it, rocksteady also found favour with British listeners, both West Indian and beyond. When people were right in the heat of the "blues", a rocksteady tune signalled the moment to "just lean up somewhere or… on somebody… and rock…nice and easy." [5] Many rocksteady hits were silky songs, laced with violins, a key feature of "The Tide Is High", tugging gently at young lovers' heartstrings.

It is easy to forget that British rock and Jamaican rocksteady were more or less contemporary. Between them they highlighted the complex, multi-faceted nature of African-Diasporic culture in its American and Caribbean manifestations. To rock could mean to make a loud, manly (Muddy Waters) sound, to convey aggression, but it could also mean to tantalize and tease, to move in a sensual and relaxed (Ken Boothe) way, in line with the lyric "take your time/there's no need to hurry."[6] Rock, like swing had done before it, was now beginning to fulfil the dual function of noun as well as verb. It was a genre and a behaviour.

Hearing musicians play hard and heavy rock music was not wholly to the taste of West Indians for whom rock signified a steady form of dance music, though that didn't mean that they could not appreciate the work of a rock artist who had sufficient emotional intelligence and tonal delicacy to realize that music played with a restrained energy could also have tremendous communicative power.

Manchester Again

Variety was something understood by Oswald Roberts, a Jamaican vocalist-pianist who had arrived in Manchester in 1961. Roberts was a joiner by trade who played music in his spare time, having learned the rudiments in the Salvation Army in his native Kingston. He became a member of an R&B group, The Fiestas, subsequently the Soul Brothers, who gigged regularly around town. They also played rocksteady because: "At gigs that we did we had to play any and everything, like a whole range of songs people liked."[7] Invited to London to make some demos for Polydor, the ensemble morphed into Ossie & The Sweet Boys and landed a support slot to none other than the Jimi Hendrix Experience at the Speakeasy in 1967. Ossie had a close-up view of the man and his music. "He was very, very quiet, just sat there on his own in the club, with his little bottle of spirit, very mellow, you know".[7] Roberts also has a strong memory of how he feels Blacks in Britain actually perceived the rock star's repertoire.

"'Hey Joe' was the main Hendrix song that West Indians liked, that was one of our favourites… because it was very *slow*, with a nice melody. He wasn't playing that much, and at the time the West Indians didn't listen to *bang, bang, bang*… they listen to the *arrangement*. There wasn't a lot of chords, but the arrangement was there. It's like the rocksteady, sometimes it's only two chords but you can follow it."[8]

Ossie also puts Hendrix's Speakeasy performance in a wider context of Black music. "What I heard on the night, it was excellent, for the limited amount of musicians," he noted. "Just the three of them! I was amazed at the sound. I never heard the guitar played like that, apart from the soul guys like Steve Cropper, when he was with Booker T. Sure, Hendrix had a connection to R&B and soul, and he could play jazz as well," Ossie continued. "I heard him play a few things I never expected, it was not *only* rock. I call him a versatile musician; it's like when I first heard Chuck Berry.

It's mad, mad, mad, loud, loud, loud, but I saw the other side with him playing his Nat 'King' Cole. I saw Hendrix the same way, I heard the soul in his music. It meant something."[9]

Mancunian, African-Caribbean soul singers sharing the bill with African-American rock guitarists in London is a good symbol of the geographical movement and stylistic alignments of the mid 1960s, and the brief intersection of the destinies of Ossie and Jimi also points to the transience of the period because their paths would soon diverge. Roberts returned to Manchester while Hendrix headed back to the States.

Although the 1960s is generally regarded as the moment when any one with a guitar, two chords and a decent tune could make it, the truth was that many with more than a modicum of talent did not. Effective management and the iron will to seize on any opportunity was essential, as was holding one's nerve under pressure. Recording sessions couldn't be fluffed and good producers and engineers were also vital.

Ossie recalls that the original members of his first group, the Soul Brothers, "couldn't cope with the studio" or the idea of cutting tracks in London, which is why they stayed in Manchester, leaving the singer to go ahead with the aid of the keyboardist and guitarist from the Vagabonds, the band of the popular Jamaican soul vocalist, Jimmy James, who had also shared bills with rock acts such as The Who and Hendrix. Hence the revamped Soul Brothers had little rehearsal time and, inevitably the chemistry wasn't there. "My boys in Manchester would have done a better job because we knew each other," Ossie reflects. "But they got cold feet. I got teed off myself and came back up north."[10]

Of all the obstacles that a young band had to clear, the question of their mindset is perhaps the most intriguing. For many groups with good stage presence, the onus was on playing the hits of the day. They were flesh and blood jukeboxes who had to bring to life what people were listening to on the radio. There was no immediate incentive to write original material as the already popular song, rather than the new artist – certainly in the eyes of the major labels and publishers who held such power in the music industry – was the saleable product. In part, they were absolutely right because the phenomenon of the covers band, be it the 'Bootleg Beatles', or an Elvis tribute act, still appeals to large numbers of people in the 21st century, because everybody has their song, and a real desire to hear it or, impelled by a karaoke fantasy, sing it themselves.

Yet the first or third person narrative from a new perspective, in a new setting, in a musical framework with new instruments such as electric guitars, with their unapologetic hardness and loudness, constituted an irresistible paradigm in post-war pop. The three minute rock & roll song was a template for a must-hear story in the hands of a skilled raconteur. Chuck Berry's "Johnny B. Goode" is a masterpiece because it depicts a three-dimensional character. It is an engrossing vignette that paves the way for other burgeoning writers because it conveys the circumstantial drama of the "country boy" who "never ever learned to read and write so well" but who "could play the guitar just like ringin' a bell." Denoting triumph in the face of adversity, the lines show that an apparently blighted life can be transformed by talent which can be shared with the world.

Those who followed suit had to believe that they were capable of producing something worthwhile, and that there would be a demand for it when they did. A tale of teenage sexual angst that also cleverly evoked the modernist totems of the car, radio, TV, cigarettes and "girl reaction" was waiting to be told. The Rolling Stones did so with "Satisfaction" and its significance is not just that it is a great song, but that they had the chutzpah to perform it when Mick Jagger didn't have a great voice, and they were sufficiently audacious to put the melody into a world populated by great singers from the blues in which the song was rooted. They wrote an original song rather than cover someone else's. Otis Redding would show them just how to sing it in due course, but the Stones had dared to make "Satisfaction" theirs *before* it was claimed by another. They had a resolute desire to succeed, which was facilitated by their presence in London. Ossie Roberts made a vital connection with an up-and-coming music industry mover and shaker from Jamaica whose impact on British music we have already charted, but a combination of diffidence, the North-South divide and the more pressing matter of keeping up with the rent meant it came to nothing.

"Sometime in the early '60s I went to London with a friend and we met Chris Blackwell," recalls Ossie, who after the demise of the Soul Brothers, led both The Sweet Boys and The Alphabets. "We played him a song we'd written and he loved it and he invited us back down. But we never went! We just didn't. In them times, it was very little money a week that you worked for, but work really did come first. It made it difficult for the music. We never had much time to rehearse proper because the boys were working. Sometimes they left work and went straight to the gig."[11]

In a situation where work was hard to find for a West Indian, holding on to any job had to come first. Although a skilled cabinetmaker, Ossie did not have a builder's union card. To obtain one he had to have... So, ironically, in the end Ossie actually earned his living from music because he was unable to secure steady work in the trade for which he was formally trained in Jamaica. By the late 1960s, the unemployment rate among Blacks in big cities such as Birmingham, Manchester, London and Leeds was steadily rising.

Back at home in the West Indies, particularly Jamaica, things were not much better, as the dreams of post-independence sovereignty and shared prosperity crumbled rapidly. Large numbers of young men traded rural poverty for urban destitution, fuelling the phenomenon of the violent "rude boy". This was a subject compassionately treated by Desmond Dekker in his song "007", with its illuminating sub-title: "Shanty Town". Whether one was trying to make ends meet in Kingston, Brixton or Moss Side, to be black was to be poor, to be born a sufferer. There was a middle class in Jamaica, but it was much more likely to be brown rather than black.

This was also the case in other parts of the ex-British Empire. Decolonization had wrought enormous demographic changes all over Africa and the Asian sub-continent, and rapid urbanization often compounded already low standards of living. Yet while poverty could foster rebellion, generations of colonial rule produced people who retained deep attachments to aspects of Empire by way of colonial education and Christianity. Former colonials were likely to have several things in common, chief among them a love of Shakespeare, cricket, tea and, in the West Indies, Christianity.

East Meets West

Two significant musicians from different ex-colonies who came to Britain had some of those very ties: the Jamaican Joe Harriott (1928–1973) and the Indian John Mayer (1929-2004). Both had been born into greatly disadvantaged circumstances in their native lands. Both came to Britain and made a significant impact on "art" music.

Indians had been in Britain since the 17th century when servants were recruited to serve noblemen, and there was also a large number of seamen or lascars in the merchant navy. Indian recruits or sepoys made an invaluable contribution to the British army in both world wars, and many chose to settle in England at the end of their tours of duty. Although 1948 is considered a landmark year because of the mass migration from the West Indies, 1947 had seen the arrival in Britain of Punjabi Sikhs following partition, when Britain's decision to create the sovereign states of India and Pakistan had led to immense population shifts, upheaval and tragic bloodshed. Between the early 1950s and early 1960s the number of people of Indian and Pakistani origin in Britain increased from 43,000 to 112,000. [12]

Fleeing a desperate situation, the majority came with nothing. In some cases the amount of money they arrived with was as little as three pounds, with perhaps a few extra notes sewn into a woman's sari. Poor housing and factory work was the lot of the majority – when employment could be had – because of the prejudice of many employers against traditional dress.

But there were also a few students who gained graduate traineeships in the commercial sector and a number of scholarships for those who had shown aptitude in the arts. This was the case of Mayer, born in the Calcutta slum of Chandni Chawk and forced to take handouts in many places of worship as a boy. He incurred the wrath of his strict, Anglo-Indian Catholic family when it transpired that his precocious ability on string instruments had led him to play violin outside several local Protestant churches.

He came to London in 1952 when he was 22 years old, after being awarded a grant to study at the Royal Academy of Music. Prior to his arrival in England, Mayer had gained a grounding in Western and Indian classical music and his talent later saw him flourish as a violinist with two major British orchestras, the London Philharmonic and then the Royal Philharmonic.

Mayer then began to write original pieces that were culturally adventurous. "Raga Music for Solo Clarinet" was a witty, daring combination of Hindustani and western classical music that was well received in classical circles. Greater prestige and recognition came in 1958 when Mayer composed *Dances of India* for Indian instruments (sitar, tablas and tanpura) as well as flute. The piece was performed by the Royal Liverpool Philharmonic.[13]

Alto saxophonist Joe Harriott[14] came to London in 1951. He was 23 years-old and had already gained a formidable reputation for himself in Kingston, Jamaica as a player of tremendous virtuosity, who drew inspiration from American bebop stars such as Charlie Parker and Sonny Stitt. His playing had the kind of energy and creativity that soon caught the ear of experienced danceband leaders in the city. Like several of Jamaica's ska and jazz legends, Harriott had attended the Alpha Boys School. Harriott found a kindred spirit in the equally adventurous and forward-thinking trumpeter Dizzy Reece.

Britain was supposed to be nothing more than a stopover on a European tour for Harriott as a member of singer-pianist Ozzie Da Costa's band, but he decided to stay, and quickly made his mark on the London scene when he joined modern jazz ensembles led by Tony Kinsey and Ronnie Scott. Able to improvise fluently while negotiating the demanding chord changes of bebop, Harriott worked regularly and by the mid 1950s was leading his own groups and recording mostly in his own distinctive version of the bebop genre. However at the end of the decade, he made a dramatic stylistic left turn. Instead of composing according to the strictly regulated "head-solo-head" structures of bebop, he started to write in a much more mercurial, structurally fluid way, as can be heard on *Free Form* (1960) and *Abstract* (1962).

The composing on these albums was predicated on his conviction that music can convey great imagery – "I want to paint pictures in sound". His work reflected a similar kind of intellectual dynamism to musicians such as the African American alto saxophonist Ornette Coleman, insofar as they were questioning the existing paradigms in jazz. Moving away from set chord sequences appealed to Harriott. Working in a more harmonically ambiguous way fired his imagination, as did introducing melody in the final phase of a performance, so that it appears as the culmination rather than the starting point of a solo. Some of his finest pieces are explorations of an idea that centres much more on subversion than affirmation. For example, "Tempo" is about stillness as well as motion. "Calypso" is *not* a calypso as one would expect, but a playful scrambling of its patented rhythm, a deconstruction-reconstruction of a form that makes much of pause and swerve rather than a steady pulse. "Compound" is essentially a series of intricate conversations between drum kit, congas and bongo which brings forth a number of highly melodic phrases before the arrival of the piano, bass and horns in the coda. It's a bravura arrangement insofar as it plays with the prevailing expectations of jazz listeners. One imagines that the horns will arrive much earlier and that when they do they will signal the *beginning* of the piece in earnest, not its end. In this song, percussion is primary, brass and reeds are secondary. This was not the norm in jazz. Harriott's thinking aligned him loosely to a movement in American jazz that was known as the avant-garde or free jazz, precisely because of its greater organizational unpredictability. This "New Music"[15] moved away from improvisation that was strictly based on chord changes towards a degree of spontaneity that would eventually lead to performances that had no pre-composed parts at all.

Whether avant-garde or not, Harriott was a highly intellectual and cultured individual who envisioned a world in which boundaries between aural and visual expression dissolved, and a song could be a single thought, explored from various angles, rather than a linear narrative. *Free Form* is essentially about the compositional process as a series of implications and enigmas rather than clear statements and resolutions.

Harriott came to work with Mayer by way of the producer Dennis Preston. His Lansdowne recording studio had been a success and his work across a range of genres – jazz, calypso and classical – had given him extensive business contacts and, more importantly, an acute knowledge of the particular strengths of musicians. Preston had recorded both Harriott and Mayer individually, (The former's *Freeform*, the latter's *Nine For Bacon*) and hit upon the idea of putting the two men together.

The result was a 'double quintet' comprising Mayer's personnel – Diwan Motihar (sitar), Chandrahas Paigankar (tanpura), Keshav Sathe (tabla) and Mayer himself (violin, harpsichord) and Harriott's – trumpeter Eddie Blair, pianist Pat Smythe, double bassist Rick Laird, and drummer Alan Ganley. The group made its debut in May, 1966 in Chichester, and in the same year *Indo-Jazz Suite* was recorded. Between 1967 and 1968 two more sets, *Indo-Jazz Fusion I* and *Indo-Jazz Fusion II*, followed. These three albums form a fascinating chronicle of cultural ferment in post-war Britain. Here was a blend of African-American, Indian and European classical forms performed by black, brown and white musicians, hailing from Jamaica, India, Scotland, Ireland, England, and later, Canada (Kenny Wheeler). Here were the East Indies, the West Indies and parts of the Commonwealth creating what marketing now calls "World music" in London.

Mayer's command of the raga, with its fixed scale of notes generating melodic statements and tala, a cycle of beats that differed from the 4/4 structure of jazz, imbued the music with a palpable sense of warp and weft, whereby flurries of motifs hold the attention because of their constant interweaving. Counterpoint is paramount. The brass and reeds are frequently deployed in overlapping lines, like a simultaneous text and subtext, while the percussion moves as a series of odd and even numbers, so that a ten beat tal can be counted as 2.3.2.3, a sequence in which the addition of the extra beat in the second and fourth unit generates a simple but nonetheless effective spike of internal tension.

The result is music that has a wry, subtle stop-start motion, the delicious paradox of the fluid stutter, precisely because the differing sub-divisions in the beat are much like changing inflections in speech. Time, the way it is conceived and observed, is a central foundation of music, because the length of a performance, and the manner in which the players create a pulse, a sensation of regularity or irregularity, consistency or interruption, pushing forth or holding back, depends entirely on choice. The decision to place an accent on an offbeat as opposed to an onbeat, to count a certain number of beats in a bar, or to play at low rather than medium or high tempo, is almost inevitably absorbing. Indian music thus presented more options in the realm of meter. The intricacies of the tala created a stimulating sense of unfolding in time so that movement and momentum were experienced in a very different way to the four beats per bar prevalent in western music.

To hear John Mayer and Joe Harriott perform compositions based on the mathematics of the tala was, and still is, engrossing because it unveiled an assortment of organizing numbers rather a single one. There was no reason why 10, 12, or 9 could not be as important as the blessed 4. Tala reminds us that time is a subjective entity, that its points of departure and closure vary according to the imagination, and that if a cycle has a first beat there are many options as to where the last will fall. All of which conjures a wealth of emotions and ambience. The enormous sense of release, or rather rebirth that is created by the beginning of a new sequence attests to this richness. It is like a life cycle.

Having said that, Mayer occasionally had Harriott's drummer lay down a pulsing 3/4 rhythm that was much more synonymous with jazz, around which the tabla player twirled tricky variations on the beat.

Interesting as the structural and rhythmic finesse of the *Indo-Jazz* series is, the gorgeous timbres of the music also captivate. Harriott, responding to the rhythmic and metric intricacies of the music, reveals a slightly more tempered aspect of his playing, often with a light, dancing tone, as if he wanted to draw flickers rather than fire from his saxophone. As for Mayer, in his role of arranger, he showed an inspired touch in bringing together the flute and sitar, as these offer a thrilling dynamic range. The low velvety purr of the former and the high keening twang of the latter impart a combination of softness and steeliness that is enticing, particularly on *Indo-Jazz Fusions II*, where the woodwind is often like a whistle that drifts around the sitar, whose distinctly metallic, bell-like clangs exude a sense of great authority. Hissing under both of them is the tanpura, the unerring drone that underscores the circularity, the suggestion of the possible eternity, of the raga cycle. This constant bed of sound highlights the darting phrases above it.

These were sensational new sounds in the mid 1960s. Familiar though it is today, the sitar was a great discovery, an instrument that is sometimes lazily described as a 'weird guitar', but which had a very distinct sonic identity, as was proven by its most masterful exponents.[16] The west was opening up to timbres that had not been heard before and the use of the sitar on the Beatles' very beautiful song "Norwegian Wood" was a foretaste of Harriott's and Mayer's collaboration.

Jazz artists from Yusef Lateef to John Coltrane had also turned towards the organizing principles of Middle Eastern and Indian music as a logical extension of their path towards a means of expression that was universal rather than local. A raga scale was as stimulating to progressive improvisers as an Arabic mode or a Russian folk melody. These all presented new points of departure.

The contemporary music industry often draws lines between genres, but the affinity that existed between certain exponents of raga, rock and jazz – their shared hunger for new sounds – was such that the hypnotic sound of an Indian sitar could inspire an electric guitarist as much as a soprano saxophonist. Ravi Shankar, John McLaughlin and Coltrane seemed kindred spirits in unforced musical communion.[17]

If there was a grand fantasy British musical meeting, it would surely have been Jimi Hendrix sitting in with John Mayer and Joe Harriott. They all happened to be living and working in Britain at the same time, all pushing the boundaries between popular and art music. It never happened, but the three can be seen as crucial additions to British music in the 1960s because their "massalas" of blues, jazz, rock and raga still act as templates for musicians several decades down the line. *Axis Bold As Love* and *Indo-Jazz Fusions* are not often mentioned in the same breath, but they are part of the same heritage of ground-breaking recordings of this time.

Obviously, what raised the visibility of Hendrix above that of Mayer and Harriott was the fact that he worked in a genre with bigger audiences, and that his flamboyance drew massive media attention. In an age when there were parts of Britain where the cliché that locals had never seen a person of colour was actually true, his individuality, his blackness on his own terms, would have appeared all the more striking. There is an apocryphal tale of an early gig in Newcastle, hometown of Hendrix's manager Chas Chandler and a place with a minimal black presence, during which Hendrix put his guitar through the ceiling of the venue, much to the delight of the punters, some of whom then proceeded to draw around the hole to mark it for posterity, possibly as a shortcut to heaven.

Two Women Step Out of the Background

While in the 1960s, Blacks in both America and Britain were striving for real social equality, women took up the same fight. Campaigns to end discrimination in employment, particularly on the issue of equal pay, came at the same time as the introduction of the pill gave women more control over their own bodies. In the music industry the position of women was no less difficult and many talented women were not permitted to develop on their own terms – a matter both of male sexism and the absence of women at executive and management level. But women were not silent on the matter. As the singer and mother of three children, Aretha Franklin sang: *All I'm asking for is a little respect... just a little bit... just a little bit.*

But there was a tradition of female blues artists with the brio and raucousness that make them a match for any man. Following Sister Rosetta Tharpe in the mid 1960s, a new face appeared on television pop music shows and on many large stages up and down the country. This was P.P. Arnold (Patricia Ann Cole, 1946–),[18] a member of the Ikettes, the trio of backing singers-dancers who appeared with the ultra-dynamic duo, Ike & Tina Turner. They had one of the great show-stopping revues in R&B and, after several years of touring in the States, landed a support slot with the Rolling Stones in Britain. Hailing from a Los Angeles family of gospel singers, Arnold had an immensely soulful voice and quickly came to the attention of the Stones manager, Andrew Loog Oldham, who offered her a contract as a solo artist with his own Immediate record label. Arnold accepted, quit the tour in 1966 and stayed in London. The decision paid dividends in the short term as the singer enjoyed a string of hit singles, several of which were penned by Paul Korda ("The Time Has Come") and Cat Stevens ("The First Cut is the Deepest"), which were fine combinations of crafted musical arrangements and vocal prowess. Peaking at number 18 in the UK singles chart in May 1967, the latter, with its delicate verse and swooning chorus, is a song that is well rooted in pop consciousness because it has been covered a lot over the years, but Arnold's version remains definitive. She makes us believe that the story in the song is her experience, her heartache, her pain, rather than just an evocation of something experienced by another. She is a convincing storyteller.

Sonically, the arrangement of "The First Cut" is fascinating. Its constituent parts are similar to many Motown songs of the era: strings, electric rhythm section and brass are all used, and the way the pounding backbeat of the chorus shatters the introspective calm of the verse is a classic example

PP ARNOLD

COURTESY PICTORIAL PRESS LTD / ALAMY STOCK PHOTO

of sound used as an echo of emotional content. Yet despite the obvious gospel richness of Arnold's voice, the song retains an Englishness because of the deep folk inflections of the melody. The theme has a kind of down-through-the-ages afterglow and the prominent use of the harp in the first part of the arrangement serves to heighten that implication.

Apart from her solo singles, Arnold also worked with one of the most important British bands of the 1960s, the Small Faces, a group, like the Kinks, with a distinctively English sensibility. While their formative musical culture of rhythm & blues was always audible, co-founders and writers-in-chief, Steve Marriott's and Ronnie Lane's melodic sensibilities often seemed more than a million miles from Memphis, Tennessee or Detroit, Michigan.

"Tin Soldier" was a moody, bluesy Faces song that featured potent backing vocals from Arnold and remains one of the most interesting products of the transatlantic cultural cross-pollination of the day. The Jimi Hendrix Experience, with its black lead singer and white sidemen, had made a multi-racial British rock group a reality, but the sight of the Faces with their hippyish threads, long hair and guitars, and Arnold, with her more conservative coiffure and garb on the set of a French TV show, *Bouton Rouge*, in 1968, crossed the lines of gender as well as race and nationality. The rarity of this scenario underlines how strict was the division between the male beat combo, where each member would be a fan's favourite, and the solo girl singer, instrument-less and backed by a band tucked into the shadows.

As far as transatlantic black female soul singer/white male rocker collaborations are concerned, the other very notable example is that of Madeline Bell[19] and John Paul Jones, bass guitarist of Led Zeppelin. Theirs was an excellent writing partnership that produced "What am I Supposed to Do?", the B-side of Bell's 1968 single, "Picture Me Gone". Like Arnold, Bell had sung in the church as a child and the first group that she joined at the age of sixteen was a gospel ensemble called The Glovertones. However, it was musical theatre that brought her to Europe. She appeared in *Black Nativity*, a show written by African American poet laureate Langston Hughes, which premièred in New York in 1961, before moving to Europe. The 1962 London performance was well reviewed and, as the tour came to an end, Bell, who was born in Newark, New Jersey, chose to settle in the city. The parallel with Arnold's journey was clear.

Blessed with a rich, strong voice and compelling stage presence, Bell was initially promoted as a cabaret artist, and taken under the wing of Norman Newell who had managed and made Shirley Bassey a major star. Patrons at the La Dolce Vita nightclub in Newcastle were able to see Bell on the same bill as Lionel Blair and Les Dawson. But that was not the extent of her artistic ambition and, since that time, Bell has been one of the great eclectics of the British music industry, working across jazz, soul and pop as well as doing theatre and studio session work. Her output has been stagger-

MADELINE BELL

COURTESY PICTORIAL PRESS LTD / ALAMY STOCK PHOTO

ing. From singing on jingles and commercials, as well as being a first-call backing vocalist at the chart-topping end of pop, where she worked with Cliff Richard, Elton John and Dusty Springfield, Bell became the American expatriate artist whose work the British public is probably more familiar with than it realises. But, regardless of how far she has ventured into the mainstream, Bell, who made her solo debut in 1967 with the album *Bell's A Poppin'*, has excelled when working with artists whose core vocabulary is the blues. If the Small Faces did well to enlist the services of P.P. Arnold, then Rod Stewart and Joe Cocker made an equally wise choice in asking Bell to provide backing vocals for them.

What the cases of Bell and Arnold – and Jimi Hendrix and Geno Washington – show is that African-Americans who had talent and the right management team could succeed in the rapidly developing British pop market. More importantly, Bell and Arnold question our understanding of what is termed a "backing vocalist", often faceless and uncredited, a bit-player kept out of the spotlight by the lead singer.

The history of American pop reveals that some of the best black vocalists and harmony ensembles were recorded, but only for their work to be attributed to white singers who would mime to their tracks, and the prevalence of misogyny in the music industry, in which producers, white and black, were largely men, made for a high incidence of exploitation. Bell and Arnold were proof that given the opportunities, the best backing singers could thrive as artists in their own right. They often had the ability to improvise beyond the lines they were given to perform. Bell and Arnold were creators as well as singers.

Notes

1. A poignant expression of the experience of African-American Vietnam vets is the pair of albums recorded by Billy Bang, *Vietnam The Aftermath* (Justintime, 2001) and *Vietnam: Reflections* (Justintime, 2005).
2. Telephone interview with the author, October, 2013.
3. On Geno Washington hear, *Sifters, Shifters, Finger Clicking Mamas* (Marble Arch, 1967).
4. Charles Shaar Murray, *Crosstown Traffic* (London: Faber & Faber), 36.
5. A commonly expressed summary of a typical blues dance.
6. Hopeton Lewis *Rock Steady* (Merritone, 1966).
7. Telephone interview with the author, May, 2014.
8. Ibid.
9. Ibid.
10. Ibid,
11. Ibid.
12. Asian immigration continued to rise with the expulsion of Indians

from Kenya, Uganda and Malawi in the 1960s and '70s. See Mayerlene Frow, *Roots of the Future*.

13. Interview with the author, London, 1998.

14. See Alan Robertson, *Fire in His Soul* (Northway, 2011).

15. New Music was also a term used for avant-garde jazz in the mid 1960s.

16. A complaint I have heard many times from Indian musicians over the years.

17. See John McLaughlin and Devadip Carlos Santana, *Love, Devotion, Surrender* (Columbia, 1973), where both guitarists vividly channel the spirits of Coltrane and Shankar.

18. See www.pparnold.com

19. See www.bell.com

23 DRUMS UNLIMITED

With the ever increasing population of West Indians in Great Britain and the demand for music they like most, RUSS HENDERSON, [sic] who comes from Port of Spain Trinidad, was called upon to make this LP.
— Sleeve notes of Russ Henderson's *Caribbean Carnival*.

We try to get nearer the source, right down to the grass roots of the jungle. All my songs on this record are inspired by the jungle – the sun, the heat, the insects, the abundance of life.
— Ginger Johnson on *African Party*.

As pop music grew in commercial and cultural importance throughout the 1960s, audiences became increasingly drawn to and obsessed by bands as reflections and fantasy versions of themselves. One of the great media masterstrokes of The Beatles was that they were four clearly defined characters who formed what was a musically functional "family" unit, which meant that fans could naturally have their own favourite within the fold.

Everybody knew that Ringo played the drums, Paul the bass, George and John the guitar. Identifying who did what in a group was the most basic sacrament taken by any serious member of the faithful who would part with hard-earned cash for a Beatles doll as well as a 45. The contribution of session musicians who provided rock and pop groups with sounds that were beyond the possibilities of their members was much less recognised. But string or brass players with good sight-reading skills and the ability to execute a scored part or improvise in a given key or time signature could find themselves in great demand. They really could enhance a tune.

One example is the Beatles' 1966 hit "Got to Get You into My Life". This beautiful song showed the importance that the orchestral element of soul music on labels such as Stax and Motown had for the group. A five-piece horn section was used in the arrangement, and on trumpet was Eddie 'Tan Tan' Thornton. Like Joe Harriott, Thornton had attended the Alpha Boys School in Kingston – he was actually in the year below Harriott, and has clear memories of his senior's considerable prowess in the rehearsal room[1] – where he received a solid musical education and learned the art of 'section playing' in an orchestra. He came to England in 1964 and soon started to pick up gigs on the R&B scene in London, most significantly as a member of The Blue Flames, Georgie Fame's band – the singer-organist who knocked The Beatles off the top of the charts that same year with his swinging version of "Yeh Yeh".

Other session gigs in rock and pop followed for Thornton, with The Rolling Stones and Small Faces, who, as noted in the previous chapter, had used the services of the expatriate African-American vocalist P.P. Arnold – a further reminder of the eclecticism, openness and broad cultural sweep of the British music scene in this period.

Another graduate of the Alpha Boys School became a common denominator in the worlds of jazz, progressive folk and the new wave of socially conscious film-making. This was Harold McNair (1931-1971),[2] a flautist who emerged as an impressively versatile musician after his arrival in London in 1960, and whose virtuosity matched that of his close friend Joe Harriott. In London, McNair led his own ensembles, recorded several well-received albums, notably, *The Fence* and *Harold McNair*, and played extensively with the composer-arranger John Cameron. Two of his finest performances came towards the end of the decade in very different situations. In 1968 he made an invaluable contribution to *The Tumbler*, a stunning album by the maverick guitarist-vocalist John Martyn, an artist who brought together folk and rock, often with a marked jazz sensibility. The album finds McNair in brilliant form, complementing the rich melodies with a series of haunting solos that enhance the pastoral but decidedly edgy quality of Martyn's music.

A year later, McNair appeared on the soundtrack of Ken Loach's *Kes*, an outstanding work of social realist cinema. It is McNair's flute that is heard soaring in the aerial sequences tracking the kestrel, the metaphor of the hope and freedom missing in the life of a boy growing up in a poor mining community in Barnsley, Yorkshire. The soundtrack was written by McNair's frequent collaborator, John Cameron, and the combination of the excellent written parts and the superb playing produced inspired accompaniment to the images.

However, not all of the musicians who arrived in Britain from the former colonies came from the kind of modest backgrounds of the Alpha Boys School graduates. Since the 18th century, Royal families and well-off traders in Africa had sent their sons to England in order to complete their education, and the trend continued throughout the later colonial and independence eras.

In several cases a privileged young African was sent to England to qualify as a doctor or lawyer, but drifted into the world of music and entertainment, often to the dismay of the parents. This was the route of the trumpeter-bandleader, Fela Anikulapo Kuti (1938-1997),[3] who arrived in London in 1958 to enrol on a medicine course, but soon swapped University College Hospital for Trinity College of Music. Thereafter he formed his own band, Koola Lobitos, which played a blend of jazz and high life. This later evolved into a trailblazing new genre called Afrobeat, after Kuti toured America, returned to Nigeria and brought an uncompromising anti-establishment stance and criticism of neo-colonial politics into his music. His band harked back to the orchestral richness of 1940s big bands whilst embracing the electric charge of 1960s soul, and Kuti fashioned a dynamic new vocabulary from his creative vision and experience of interactions with and learning from musicians from outside Nigeria. He became one of the great cultural icons of the African continent, but he was just one of several musicians whose talent flourished during a relatively short sojourn in Britain.

Trinity College was also the alma mater of another pioneering musician, the Ethiopian composer and multi-instrumentalist, Mulatu Astatke (1943–), an artist who is credited as the architect of a genre that is still highly influential today: Ethio-jazz. North Wales was Mulatu's first port of call in Britain. He was sent to a private school there in 1959 when he was sixteen, but, like Fela, he abandoned his family's plans for him. They had hoped he would become a pilot, but his gift for music was quickly identified when he was at school, and enrolment at Trinity and then the Eric Gilder School of Music followed. The latter became a focal point for several other African musicians. Alumni included the fine Ghanaian guitarist Ebo Taylor.

While in London, Mulatu, who had already developed a liking for jazz, soul and calypso, became a regular at clubs such as Ronnie Scott's and The Flamingo, and these venues gave the young Ethiopian the opportunity to meet many expatriate West Indian musicians, one of whom was the Guyanese percussionist-vocalist, Frank Holder, known for his work with John Dankworth and Kenny Graham in the 1950s. The two found that they shared a creative vision.

"When Mulatu came over here, I was doing a lot in jazz and Latin American music," Holder recalled when I spoke to him in 2014. "We struck up a friendship and ended up recording together."[4] The Ethiopian musician's ultimate goal was to go to America to learn jazz at the source, but the opportunity to work with Holder who played jazz as well as calypso and rumba rhythms was too good to pass up.

Sometime in 1969, a band consisting of Astatke, Holder and other Ethiopian and British musicians was put together for a session that yielded several songs, the most notable of which is "Asiyo Bellema", which is a superlative piece of British African-Caribbean music. The composition simply bursts with energy, moving along on an Afro-Latin rhythm that is propulsive but not frenetic. The pulse is strong and steady, but the sensibility of the performance is laid-back. This is the great *trompe-l'oreille* of Cuban music.

As is the case in much Latin music and American blues, the bass line comprises a spare motif, built on just three pitches, which repeats over and over to create a solid undercarriage to the dense percussion around it. So high in the mix that it mildly distorts, the bass is a slow, heavy fuzz. Through a thicket of rousing chants from several male singers, a high keening solo vocal improvisation cuts free, accompanied by a series of repeated melodic phrases on a steel pan, played by Holder. The tone has a wavering, slightly whistling quality, which connects to one of the earlier less harmonically advanced incarnations of the instrument that was commonly referred to as a "Corbeau Jack". Holder had this to say about his performance on "Asiyo Bellema".

> "I never used to play pan *really*, I was more congas and bongos. I just watched and listened and applied myself to it. I played other people's pans when I did a show and there was someone on the bill who played pan. I learned enough about pans to play what was required by Mulatu. I mean that was it, to just do what felt right for the song."[5]

This makes the point that the steel pan is as much a drum as it is a melodic instrument, a form of percussion to which any drummer with a vague interest in pitch as well as rhythm can relate.

"Asiyo Bellema" showcases the beauty of the *sound* of the steel drum rather than its possibilities as a device for improvisation. As a piece that blends sounds from different cultures, it raises questions about geo-cultural identity in music. "Asiyo" is a traditional Ethiopian melody that is heard once a year when youngsters pay tribute to their elders, but the arrangement is dominated by the Latin groove set by the percussion and bass, though instead of a vocal chant in Cuban-inflected Spanish, the language is Amharic.[6] Countless steel orchestras in Britain had reprised "Guantanamera" or "El Manisero" ("Peanut Vendor") but none had appeared on an arrangement of a traditional Ethiopian praise song. Mulatu and Holder made music that was not easy to define. It was also an alliance between different generations. By the time he recorded with Mulatu, Frank Holder had been working in Britain for two decades. A seasoned live performer who always saw dance as an essential ally to music, Holder had lived through changing times and heard Black music in its great many guises, from swing to calypso, bebop to steel band.

Russ Henderson Gets Real

The arrival of R&B, soul and ska tempts us to assume that the market for the older forms of Black music dried up, especially as many of the exponents of the new forms benefited from the advent of youth-oriented pop programmes on radio and television. But this was not entirely the case. Calypso, steel band music and jazz did not die. Older people, black and white, who had grown up with these genres, remained record buyers. There were also musicians who built bridges between old and new schools in black music. Steel bands had always sought to play the popular music of the day, so if they observed the rise of R&B, soul and ska, their instinct was to adapt their repertoires and play pan

R&B, pan soul and pan ska as well as a pan calypso and pan jazz. This is exactly what one of Holder's peers, Russ Henderson did.

In 1966, two years after he led a small steel band at the first Notting Hill Carnival, and the United Caribbean Association held a meeting in a Chapeltown bedsit to plan the first Carnival in Leeds, Henderson cut an album whose title contained the key 'c' words: *Caribbean Carnival*. This presented something British that is forever West Indian.

The Allegro record label, a division of the Pickwick corporation, seems to have thought that apart from West Indians, the release would appeal to music lovers whose tastes landed somewhere between jazz, classical music and exotica. Listed on the back sleeve of Henderson's album are dozens of other titles that provide "additional hours of musical enjoyment!", including Bizet's *Carmen*, Charlie Parker's *Yardbird Suite* and *Hawaiian Holiday* by Johnny Pineapple & His Orchestra, a name that conjures up quite nightmarish images. Cinema-goers might have felt a sense of familiarity with the front cover of Henderson's album – a "dusky" maiden standing in a jungle of plastic palms with a tribal mask perched on a log in the background. It is a very similar setting to "The Devil's Music", the laughable voodoo jazz segment in 1964's *Dr. Terror's House of Horrors*, to which Henderson contributed music.

The liner notes on *Caribbean Carnival* observe: "With the ever increasing population of West Indians in Great Britain and the demand for music they like most, RUSS HENDERSON, who comes from Port of Spain Trinidad, was called upon to make this LP. Russ, who has for many years been an active performer in London, had no difficulty in finding top artists from his country with the right feeling and rhythm necessary to produce an authentic recording."

What Henderson thought about the sleeve notes is not known, but the issue of authenticity had been vexed since the days when Rupert Nurse was criticised for daring to bring jazz influences into the realm of calypso. What's more significant is the way the sleeve is couched in terms that connect with the way 19th century minstrel troupes were often presented as "Genuine" Negroes. The more real the blackness, the more spontaneous and "natural" would be the rhythm, the more eye-popping the novelty. Henderson would have been all too aware of such clichés, but his priority was to maintain his artistic integrity and serve his musical imagination. He thus enlisted musicians with whom he had long-standing relationships.

Chief among the personnel for *Caribbean Carnival* were the steel drummer-percussionists Sterling Betancourt and Irwin Clement, who had both worked with Henderson in the 1950s. Sadly, no other rhythm or horn players are identified on the sleeve, but there were two vocalists, Ray Blair and Vernon Neptune, each singing lead on different tracks. The track listing itself was what one might have heard at a dance for West Indians of a certain

RUSSELL HENDERSON

age, and the genre to which each title belongs is clearly stated: "Sammy Dead Oh!", "Marianne" and "Stone Cold Dead in the Market" are calypso. "Peanut Vendor" and "No Ho L'Eta Per Amarti" are steel band. "Walking The Dog" was bluebeat – which was another word for ska – except that the song wasn't. It was soul. The original, a hit for Rufus Thomas that helped establish the Memphis-based Stax label, was in that style, and Henderson's version was faithful to it. This confusion in the labelling of the songs suggests that someone at Allegro records just didn't know their soul from their ska.

Most interestingly, the final track on *Caribbean Carnival* is called "West Indian Drums", and unlike the other songs listed on the sleeve, it is not assigned a genre. On the face of it, the composition is a piece of Latin jazz with a marked African feel in its heavy percussive drive, yet "West Indian Drums" is a composition that falls between many stylistic stools. Like Mulatu Astatke's *Asiyo Bellema* it is a piece of music that is extremely hard to pigeonhole.

Set in a brisk 6/8, the song sways with a graceful momentum, as Henderson plays chunky left-hand piano chords that lock in tightly with the double bass to craft a brawny, supple low end. Cymbals and cowbells ring out tightly on the pulse, while the timbales and congas improvise a series of chattering, tumbling phrases. The wall of percussion builds and builds, then it starts to break down tantalizingly. Roughly a third of the way in the tempo drops. Bass and piano lines lengthen and shift chords as the whole carriage of the piece eases up into a hazy slow motion. The energy of these instruments plateaus out, but then the percussion once more takes centre stage. The conga onslaught is relentless. Suddenly the band whips into double time, and the high BPM brings a new sense of ignition. The locomotive takes off again, turning into an express train as the cowbell becomes the dynamo, its sharp, crisp tone swept up in the faster flowing trail of notes from the timbales whose lines mark momentary pauses for dramatic effect. As the piece starts to fade out to silence, a shaker is introduced to underline the abundance of higher sounds. Piano and bass play very much second fiddle to the full-blooded rampage of the percussion.

Harmony provides the frame; rhythm is the picture. The central image evoked is that of carnival in the relentless barrage of beats, which conveys the endless wave of energy that is created by players and masqueraders hammering away on cowbells, tins and, of course, steel drums and bottles, making music by whatever comes to hand. "Street" instruments prevail over the "salon" instruments. This, given carnival's history as an event that had once pitted slaves against their masters, has a potent cultural resonance.

This is sophisticated percussion music, an important piece because it shows just how "orchestral" instruments such as cowbells, congas, timbales, cymbals, snare and kick can be when they are deployed in complex polyrhythmic patterns driven by a piano riff without being subservient to it. It was the pivotal piece on *Caribbean Carnival* because it underlined the fact that for all the ways of classifying Black music, there was always a sound that was hard to pin down, a sound that was resistant to labels, a sound that was *something else*, even if the presentation of the album with its alluring native girls, masks, jungle palms and, most tellingly, the sub-title "magic rhythms of calypso, bluebeat and steel band" still carried a sizeable freight of exotica. But this was at a time when record companies still marketed steel band albums with the promise of "savage music to awaken the ballroom beast". They saw mileage in the association of Black music with nature, where certain mysteries totally impenetrable to modern western civilization were lurking, to scare and seduce, frighten and fascinate, intrigue and engage.

Ginger Johnson, West African rhythms and British music

Another Black British artist who demonstrates a role parallel to Henderson's, but West African rather than Caribbean, was Ginger Folorunsho Johnson. As noted in Chapter 12, he had been a pioneer of African music in Britain since the 1950s, working with an array of leading jazz musicians, and recording under his own name for the seminal Melodisc label. His contribution to the film, *She*, was noted in Chapter 19. Johnson's "African Jazz Cha Cha" was a nod to the burgeoning relationship between African music and other related forms in the African diaspora, from jazz in America to cha cha in Cuba. Johnson saw that the wealth of rhythms he had learned as a boy in Nigeria could enrich a whole range of other genres, and that an organic and coherent musical language could be born of the marriage of sounds made by traditional instruments such as bongos, congas and cowbell, and western reeds, brass and strings.

"All the music we have today is firmly based on African traditions,"[7] Johnson argued. "So is rhythm & blues – but we try to get nearer the source, right down to the grass roots of the jungle. All my songs on this record are inspired by the jungle – the sun, the heat, the insects, the abundance of life." Released in 1967 the album in question is *African Party*, a recording that has a huge importance in the annals of Black music in Britain. It shows the creative gain that can be made when the usual relationship between rhythm, melody and harmony is questioned if not subverted, so that the first element takes pride of place over the second and third, defying the western axiom that the tune is all important. Johnson argued that R&B, the key development in popular music in the 1960s owed a debt to African music, and for those who cared to lend a discerning ear to Black American music this was a self-evident truth, both in the retentions of rhythm and pitch, and also in the decisive use of Afro-Latin hand drums like congas and bongos, which were deployed to great effect on anything from countless Motown records to a piece of British pop such as The Yardbirds' "For Your Love".

African Party places percussion centre stage. Just as had been the case on Russ Henderson's "West Indian Drums", it is the family of instruments that would be stationed at the back rather than front of the stage in a rock or jazz ensemble that now had a starring role, so that the ear is drawn as much to the dry, hard sound of a palm or stick on the goatskin stretched tight over a conga as it is on the trill or flutter created by the careful manipulation of breath and tongue on a flute or saxophone.

For the most part the horns play relatively short motifs that are often doubled by vocal chants, delivered rousingly over skipping high-life rhythms and concise woodwind solos, none of which detracts from the interplay of the various drums, their accents frequently syncopating so as to imbue the music with a kind of sliding, see-saw activity. All of the fleeting offbeats and end-of-phrase punctuations are almost like micro-solos. On *African Party*, the drums provide light and shade with a series of hypnotic grooves that appear to be constantly moving, spinning, rotating. Eric Sugumugu, one of the percussion section, whose numbers varied from three to five, was a young Ghanaian who had arrived in London in 1965 and joined Johnson after freelancing around town, made this telling observation. "Everything was carefully put together, each drum part was precise. It's because the rhythm was so strong and so precise, so set it's like the rhythm had that feeling of something going round. Like the beat is a kind of circle."[8]

Certainly, the compositions in 6/8 time, such as "Witchdoctor", present the beat as an entity that is swirling rather than proceeding in a straight line, but the other aspect of the percussion that enhances the music was the range of timbres. Because Johnson had worked in so many different contexts over the years, he had acquired many instruments that covered a wide sonic and dynamic range. Bass drums and log drums had low, bulky sounds, but timbales, bongos, cabassa and cowbells were much higher and brighter in pitch, while the mbira, or thumb piano, produced a beautifully hypnotic hum and the "talking" drum a slightly muffled, vibrato moan that was almost like an alto flute. All of these sounds served Johnson's aim of reflecting the organic, living, breathing orchestra of the jungle – "the sun, the heat, the insects, the abundance of life".

Quite apart from being a landmark in Black British music, *African Party* resonated with a number of other recordings made between the mid 1950s and late 60s that either saw Africans collaborate with Americans, black and white, or African-Americans bring African rhythms more prominently into their work. Albums by Guy Warren, the Ghanaian percussionist who, like Johnson, had worked with Kenny Graham during his short sojourn in Britain (*Africa Speaks, America Answers*, 1955), Babatunde Olatunji (*Drums of Passion*

1959), Max Roach (*We Insist! Freedom Now Suite*, 1959), Randy Weston (*Uhuru Afrika* 1960), Herbie Mann (*The Common Ground,* 1960) and Solomon Ilori (*African Highlife*, 1963) were statements of both the primacy of African music, and the desire of members of the African diaspora to identify culturally, spiritually and politically with an Africa that was entering the post-colonial era.

The other very significant figure in this regard was the drummer Art Blakey, leader of the Jazz Messengers, one of the indefatigable spearheads of the hard bop movement whose interest in African and Afro-Latin rhythms led him to hire several brilliant Cuban hand drummers, chief among them Sabu Martinez, and place percussion at the centre of his most experimental album, *Orgy in Rhythm* (1957). Blakey played an important role in establishing the jazz drummer as a bandleader with ideas, cultural and musical, and it made perfect sense that he headlined a high profile summit meeting of the leading practitioners of his instrument in London in October 1968. "Drum Workshop" at Hammersmith Odeon Jazz Expo also included Max Roach, Elvin Jones, Sunny Murray and Ginger Johnson. The presence of the London-based Nigerian at this event was important for its cultural as well as musical symbolism, for here were members of the African diaspora, American exponents of jazz, that country's great invention, meeting an African musician in Britain, the land that had significantly linked the two continents through the slave trade. The intersecting lines of both a past of inhumane oppression and a present of creative dynamism were clear.

Of all the African-American musicians mentioned above the one who was most directly comparable to Johnson was Blakey. The two were figureheads, respected for both their musicianship as well as their ability to identify and recruit significant new talents. Whether Johnson named his group African Messengers as a nod to Blakey's Jazz Messengers isn't known, but the word messenger conveyed a distinct sense of purpose, a dedication to a cause, a mission statement. According to Eric Sugumugu, Johnson was as much a father figure and mentor as he was a musician. There was a considerable age gap between Sugumugu and the other Messengers, but he was made to feel comfortable. "When I came into the band they were older," he recalls. " I was the youngest. But it was cool. But when Ginger played he attracted a lot of musicians, very good musicians. If I had to describe him I'd say he was like a pillar. He was generous too."[9] Sugumugu also recalls that he was a hard taskmaster with high musical standards.

In the mid 1960s, Ginger Johnson's Iroko Country Club in Haverstock Hill, north London, was a restaurant, performance space and informal "hang" that became something of a hub for Black London culture and the celebrities of the day, national or international. The reputation of the establishment spread very quickly. Dennis 'Dee Mac' Johnson, Ginger's son who, as a child, spent many happy hours at the club, recalls:

All the African musicians they'd go straight there. Any big black actors, they went there too. That was the meeting place; that was what the Iroko was. Yet it was open to everybody, not just Africans and Caribbeans. They felt welcome. It had the craziest psychedelic lights on the walls, big paintings, with all kinds of stuff in them. It wasn't something you'd expect to find in an African club. Dad saw everybody in there, Shirley Bassey used to go down there, Elton John used to rehearse down there. Eric Clapton was there because in those days they didn't know much about African music. Ginger Baker? They couldn't get him out of the door, he loved it so much.[10]

Ginger Baker, the drummer in the pioneering rock band Cream, went on to take his interest in African music further in the 1970s when he collaborated with Fela Anikulapo Kuti. Then again Fela, when he was still known as Ransome, was another young musician who often came to kneel at Johnson's shrine. In fact, 'Father', as Johnson was known to many, was something of a magnet for promoters as well as players from a number of different scenes, which was hardly surprising given the enormous clout that he had among African and British musicians who had come into his orbit.

Beyond his musical ability, generosity and charisma, Johnson was an extraordinarily open-minded man who took an interest in youth movements and the counterculture of the mid 1960s, an engagement that was primarily facilitated by his friendship with the legendary photographer and political activist John 'Hoppy' Hopkins, the man who was behind some of the significant 'happenings' of the hippie era.

There were notable points of convergence between the two men, above all the role that Hopkins played in creating, along with the social worker Rhaune Laslett, the London Free School, a pioneering community adult education project in Notting Hill, which provided something of a springboard for the Notting Hill carnival, at which Johnson also appeared. Creative energies were colliding in the city.

Hopkins went on to take a greater interest in alternative and psychedelic culture, setting up with the record producer Joe Boyd the UFO club, an important venue for new experimental rock bands such as Pink Floyd. In 1967 he helped to stage one of the most ambitious countercultural events of the decade: The 14 Hour Technicolour Dream at Alexandra Palace in north London. This multi-genre marathon performance was resoundingly eclectic and featured exponents of blues, rock, pop and poetry. On the bill were Alexis Korner, Soft Machine, Michael Horovitz, Pink Floyd and Ginger Johnson & His African drummers amongst others. Those with open minds would have realised that the battery of drums that Johnson so skilfully deployed created waves of energy that were not dissimilar to the volleys of power chords and heavily distorted electronic effects that were favoured by the likes of Pink Floyd and Soft Machine, and that rock musicians who had an ear for distinctive sounds might have done well to integrate the mighty rumble of the congas booming out at Alexandra Palace.

Another event that featured Johnson was the free concert in Hyde Park, in London on the 5th July, 1969, headlined by the Rolling Stones, with sets by experimental rock ensembles King Crimson and Third Ear Band, but also Alexis Korner, the enduring blues-rock bandleader. Ginger Johnson & His African drummers joined the Stones for the finale of their performance, an eighteen minute version of "Sympathy for the Devil". The picture of a beaming Mick Jagger clapping his hands as the stage is engulfed by the troupe of percussionists is emblematic of western popular culture interfacing with African folk, in front of an estimated quarter of a million people.

This was an extension of the 1968 studio recording of "Sympathy for the Devil", which featured the conga drumming of Rocky Dijon, a respected Ghanaian session musician, who had also worked with Jimi Hendrix and Ginger Baker of Cream. It only takes the most cursory of listens to realise that "Sympathy" is defined by a rhythmic base that is decidedly non-western. While the kit drum is skipping lightly on the pulse, producing a swing that creates kinetic energy through each measure of the arrangement, the conga punches out two and three note phrases, their timbre slightly slurred, as befits the use of the palm rather than a stick, while a shaker frames the beat with a constant trail of sound. This kind of construction would have been instantly familiar to any listener who had taken an interest in modern jazz from the 1940s onwards, particularly the moments when the polyrhythmic richness indicated by terms such as Afro-jazz and Latin-jazz started to come into play. In Britain, the proponents of this had been the likes of Kenny Graham, who hired percussionists such as Ginger Johnson, whereas in America the great bebop drummers such as Art Blakey, Max Roach and Kenny Clarke also either worked with conga players such as Candido Camero or adapted their patterns to their own approach to the conventional drum kit.

Like many of the rock drummers of the 1960s, the Rolling Stones' Charlie Watts drew inspiration from such jazz drummers, musicians who were revered for their skill and imagination in freeing the instrument from the straitjacket of simple time keeping. Watts' statement on the genesis of "Sympathy For The Devil" makes perfect sense. "We had a go at loads of different ways of playing it; in the end I just played a Latin jazz feel in the style that Kenny Clarke would have played on 'A Night In Tunisia'."

Clear as the boundary was between rock and jazz, certainly in terms of audience size and media exposure, there were still exchanges between the two, quite simply because musicians with any degree of ambition or curiosity realised that the contact could produce something that could satisfy a desire for newness. As Ginger Johnson contended: "All the music we have today is firmly based on African traditions. So is rhythm & blues." [11]

For the purposes of marketing, "Sympathy For The Devil" is rock, but its real artistic identity lies elsewhere. It is a piece of music that belongs

DON'T STOP THE CARNIVAL: BLACK MUSIC IN BRITAIN

firmly to the African diaspora. Whether one calls it Afro-Samba, Afro-rock or Afro-Latin rock, there is no escaping the fact that this is a piece of Black music made in Britain that acknowledges a dialogue between various artistic voices developing throughout the Americas. Remove the percussion from the Stones' masterwork and its whole conceptual foundation would crumble. Hence, the appearance of Ginger Johnson & His African drummers at the Hyde Park concert is much more than a rock group embellishing the finale of a high profile gig with exotica. It is rock music that reminds any fans minded to listen closely that the sound of a less popular or specialist market could invigorate music made for mass consumption.

If the Beatles were perceived as antithetical to the Stones – a proposition too facile for its own good – then a common denominator between the two bands was an interest in non-western music. The Beatles loose equivalent of "Sympathy For The Devil" is "And I Love Her". Where the former is a samba, this is Cuban *son* or calypso. You could put the melody of "Yellow Bird" or "Jamaica Farewell" over the beat and nobody would bat an eyelid. There was no Ginger Johnson moment for "And I Love Her", but there could have been the presence of Lord Woodbine's steel drummers. As one time mentor to the Liverpool band, Lord Woodbine would, no doubt, have loved to have joined them on stage. The wistful theme of "And I Love Her" is a pan player's meat and potatoes. Or maybe, to reflect the realities of multi-racial Britain, his or her rice and peas.

Notes

1. When I interviewed Eddie 'Tan Tan' Thornton in 2001, he spoke at length of the esteem in which Joe Harriott was held at Alpha both by his peers and younger boys. What follows comes from an interview with the author, Wallington, South London, 2013.
2. On Harold McNair see Herbie Miller, *Jamaica Observer*, 11 June, 2006.
3. See the sleeve notes to *Koola Lobitos, 1969 Los Angeles Sessions* (Sterns 2001).
4. Author interview with Holder.
5. Ibid.
6. Exactly how many languages are spoken in Ethiopia is hard to pinpoint; there may be as many as 90. Apart from Amharic, other key languages are Tigrinya, Somali and Oromo.
7. Sleeve notes of Ginger Johnson's *African Party*, (Masquerade,1967). Reissued by Freestyle, 2015.
8. Interview with the author, Seven Sisters, North London, 2015.
9. Interview with the author, Seven Sisters, North London, 2015.
10. Interview with the author, Seven Sisters, North London, 2015.
11. Sleeve notes of Ginger Johnson's *African Party*.

24 EXILE ON GERRARD STREET/
DON'T STOP THE CARNIVAL.

This musical has come as a revelation to many South Africans that art does not recognise racial barriers... the first export of indigenous South African theatre will reveal to the rest of the world the peculiar flavour of township life as well as the unrecognised artistic talents of its people.
— *King Kong*, opened at the Prince's Theatre, London, 1961.

That's singing about the police inspectors who tried to stop carnival. It was only after independence that we had our own police, before the inspector was always English. It's against him. It's a political song. Definitely, it was a political song.
— Russ Henderson on "Don't Stop The Carnival".

As outlined in previous chapters, British music has long been enriched by the arrival of musicians pursuing social and economic opportunities not available in the colonies for which this country was then responsible. This chapter charts the arrival and lasting impact on British music of musicians in flight from apartheid South Africa. As recently as 2014, Andrew Scott brought together a mix of British and South African long term emigres to record the album *Duduvudu: The Gospel According to Dudu Pukwana*, in honour of Pukwana, one of those who fled to Britain in the 1960s, and in 2016, the British jazz saxophonist Julian Arguelles released an album, *Let it Be Told*, in honour of what South African jazz brought to British music. Now, it is far from uncommon to hear the strains of township harmonies in contemporary British jazz. What this chapter tells is a story of how racist discrimination, which attempted to separate the "races" in South Africa, actually brought about some remarkable cross-cultural musical fusions in Britain.

In the UK, the story begins with the jazz saxophonist and bandleader, John Dankworth. As noted in Chapter 19, Dankworth had become all too aware of the complexities of racial politics in Britain when he married the Jamaican-English singer Cleo Laine,[1] and throughout his career, he had invariably formed racially mixed bands. Hardened as he may have been to confronting bigotry, Dankworth reeled from the shock of seeing unfettered racial discrimination when he toured South Africa in 1953. "A coloured band who wanted to attend a concert I gave at Johannesburg City Hall put on dungarees and carried brushes and pails in an endeavour to get in as cleaners, but they were prevented from doing so."[2] Appalled by the extent of the prejudice he witnessed, Dankworth turned down an offer of £10,000, a truly astronomical figure in post-war times, to play again in South Africa.

Whilst the independence movements in the 1950s and '60s gathered momentum, South Africa remained the most egregious example of colonialism insofar as the indigenous population was held in a state of dehumanizing second-class citizenship by a government and laws representing the interests of the white minority. These included the "Boers" who were descended from 17th century Dutch settlers no longer beholden to a metropolitan government in Holland, and British-born settlers. This white elite had achieved absolute power in the land to which they had migrated by taking ownership of vast fertile areas of "native" territory. The institution of apartheid in 1948 by the National Party enshrined in law white supremacy and the segregation of the races. The creation of the categories of white, bantu, "coloured" and Asian compounded the horrific nature of this ethnic grading that disenfranchised all non-white citizens, a process that had parallels with the 19th century segregation laws of America where until the 1960s Negroes could not share amenities with Whites in key areas of civic life, whether the restaurant, the bathroom, the schoolroom or the bus.

Inevitably, there was resistance from black South Africans and the freedom movement crystallised in organisations such as the South African Native National Congress, founded in 1912, which eventually became the African National Congress (ANC). Over time the government enacted a raft of legislation such as the Separate Amenities Act, Native Laws Amendment Act, and Group Areas Amendment Act[3] that impinged on opportunities for Blacks to lead normal lives, as they were "racially disqualified", according to the grotesquely twisted language of the day. Yet black domestic workers were miraculously "racially qualified" to ensure standards of hygiene and maintenance in "places of public entertainment"in which all refreshments and seated accommodation were the preserve of white patrons.

As the ANC organised mass protests, the government sought to muzzle its leadership through legal channels, the most infamous of which was the Treason Trial in Pretoria, an indictment for seditious activities of 156 people including Albert Luthuli, the president of the ANC as well as several of his colleagues such as Oliver Tambo, Walter Sisulu and Nelson Mandela. The case dragged on for four years, but in the process raised international awareness of the evils of apartheid. It also affected the thinking of a good many artists in the UK, the USA and Europe.[4]

In Britain there was the creation of the Defence and Aid Fund For Southern Africa, which received donations of £75,000 to help cover the legal fees of the accused. True to his deeply held anti-apartheid convictions, John Dankworth, who by that time had lent his assistance to a UK training scheme for young African musicians, donated a portion of the royalties generated by his recordings to the cause.

Alarming as the Treason Trial was, it was overshadowed by the spectacle of state-sponsored murder when, in March 1960, a peaceful protest against restrictions on freedom of movement was met by wanton butchery. At the Sharpeville police station in Transvaal, armed officers shot dead 69 unarmed Blacks and wounded 180.

In the mass media age, shockwaves reverberated around the world. A BBC report on the event quoted the chillingly unrepentant police commander D.H Pienaar: "It started when hordes of natives surrounded the police station. If they do these things they must learn their lessons the hard way."[5]

British arts organisations, notably the actors union Equity and the Musicians Union, had already forbidden its members from appearing in South Africa, but Sharpeville resulted in a major nationwide fundraising initiative to provide greater assistance to the ANC. *Music Against Apartheid* was launched in the spring of 1960 from hastily set-up headquarters at a popular "mod" coffee bar, the Farm Cellar in Covent Garden, central London. Founded by Pamela Jones, an indefatigable activist who regularly picketed South Africa House, and folk singer Neal Rock, MAA raised money through both live performances and recordings by major figures in folk and Black music either resident in or visiting Britain. The movement was launched by a gala concert in June 1960 at St. Pancras Town Hall in London and there was a subsequent compilation album that was significant for the way it tied together a number of significant historical and multi-cultural strands. There were songs by the Scottish singer Jimmy McGregor, by noted West Indians, the Guyanese Cy Grant and the Trinidadian Lord Kitchener, who was accompanied by the steel pan player Russ Henderson. "Anti-apartheid Calypso", Kitchener's piece, underlined how well this form could comment on international as well as local affairs.[6]

Possibly the biggest name involved was Josh White, the great African-American folk singer and Civil rights activist who sang the composition, "Marching To Freedom", whose lyrics had been written by the Black American poet, Langston Hughes. White, like Paul Robeson was an exponent of "songs of the people" and Hughes was a spearhead of the 1920s Harlem Renaissance.

Further events organised by the MAA involved British folk singers such as Bob Davenport, Ewan MacColl and Enoch Kent, all of whom appeared in another gala concert presented by the Anti-Apartheid Movement at St. Pancras Town Hall in 1963. Also performing was American folk great Peggy Seeger. As renowned as the above were – MacColl recorded for British and American labels and also toured North America with Seeger – the one person on the bill who was most relevant to the evening was a South African, Todd Matshikiza.[7] Alarmed by the drastic turn of events in his homeland, he had moved to London in 1960 and had become a music critic, writing a weekly column for a South Africa magazine, and he broadcast for the African Service of the BBC. There is no information on the exact nature of his performance at the "We Sing of Freedom" concert, but he was a pianist whose mother, Grace, was a soprano singer and his father, Meekly, a jazz pianist, whose bands Todd joined as a youngster. He had gained a diploma in music at Adams college in Natal, and although he earned a living as an English teacher, Matshikiza also began to compose his own original pieces, some of which were choral works and some jazz, to which he had become further drawn, both as a pianist and journalist. He wrote for *Drum*, a society magazine for Black South Africans that gave that community a sense of its own identity and aesthetics, with features on fashion and lifestyle trends in the African townships, the products of rapid and large-scale urbanisation. Matshikiza chronicled the emergence of a vibrant jazz scene in places such as the Sophiatown district of Johannesburg. Large format glossy photos in *Drum* of black men and women in white suits and floral dresses, dancing and looking effortlessly cool, embodied the glamour of Black South Africa. Gangsters and hustlers were also be seen, completing the edginess of this urban tapestry.

Jazz had captured the imagination of local South African musicians since the arrival of recordings of the genre's innovators such as Jellyroll Morton, Louis Armstrong, and Duke Ellington in the 1930s, and the names of early black South African jazz bands, the Manhattan Brothers and the Harlem Swingsters flag up the affinity Black South Africans had with Black American modernism.

But South African jazz also evolved alongside the emergence of new popular styles such as kwela, which was defined by bright, singing melodies played on small tin whistles and marabi, a genre with rugged, repetitive riffing based on no more than two or three chords. Fresh sounds from home and abroad were swirling around the townships.

The rich tradition of choral singing – which as noted in Chapter 4, Britain had experienced through the visit of The African Choir in 1891 – also permeated the lives of many musicians, and this cross-fertilization made jazz in South Africa restless and eclectic, often played in major key signatures with bustling rhythms and soaring crescendos from the brass and reeds.

What also gave South African jazz its edge was the desire of some of its earliest practitioners, such as Kippie Moeketsi, Thandi Klaasen and Jonas Gwanga, to play music that was *not* viewed favourably by the ruling white minority.[8] Traditional music was permitted because it could be accommodated with the patronising, reductive view of "native" expression as something inferior to European norms, but jazz was viewed with suspicion by the authorities for its innovative multicultural modernism, evidence of advanced Black thinking that challenged the fixed categories of apartheid.

Although there were music schools, such as the one Todd Matshikiza founded, many aspiring players honed their abilities playing in shebeens rather than concert halls, so that jazz was an underground and urban phenomenon whose progress was further hampered by the tightening vice of apartheid, such as prohibiting multi-racial group meetings and demolishing Sophiatown to make way for a whites-only residential area. Against these overwhelming odds, Black South Africans continued to exercise their creativity. One breakthrough came in theatre, when in 1959 Todd Matshikiza wrote a musical *King Kong* that charted the fall from grace of the boxing sensation Ezekiel Dhlamini, a talented athlete who had succumbed to the violent gang culture that had taken root in the townships. The show, bolstered by a strong company that included gifted jazz musicians such as Hugh Masekela and the singer, Miriam Makeba, enjoyed runaway success at venues all over South Africa. It eventually attracted strong interest from abroad and a London run was arranged.

Following Matshikiza's move with his family to the English capital in 1960, *King Kong* opened the following year on February 23rd at the Prince's Theatre in London. The production was a showcase for the talent of South African artists, but it also highlighted the conflation of race and the exotic in mainstream arts. The album sleeve of the London cast-recording bore the sub-title "All African Musical", a term that echoed the 1930s when the popular swing orchestras of the day were billed as "All Colored" or "All West Indian".[9]

King Kong was also sub-titled an "All African Jazz Opera", and the affinity that Matshikiza had for African American music was heard in the overture to the opera. The orchestra gives a clear indication of the impact that Duke Ellington had on South African jazz musicians. Bathed in a doleful yet sensual atmosphere, the piece is defined by the hazy sound of a clarinet whose ethereal, legato tones drift into being, and are intermittently thickened by several slow choruses of louder brass that recall the music that the great American bandleader made during what is commonly referred to as his "jungle" period.

Around the half-way mark, a short piano motif signals a distinct shift in mood and both the rhythm and horn sections become louder and then the choir makes a dramatic entrance, singing a number of rousing, soul -stirring choruses that inject a colourful exuberance into the air before dropping out for the return of the clarinet, which draws the song to a wry, pithy conclusion with a piercing high note that evaporates into the closing roar of the horn section.

"Sad Times, Bad Times" is an interesting piece of music in many respects, above all because of the well-telegraphed amalgamation of its constituent parts. The orchestral section is resoundingly American jazz and the vocal passage South African, and the distinctive nature of one highlights the other, especially as the singers, whose harmonies are a considerable embellishment, make just the one appearance in the arrangement, thus weighting the work culturally towards America.

Generally speaking this pattern defines the whole-cast recording. The compositions featuring English lyrics – "Marvellous Muscles"; "The Earth Turns Over"; "Quickly In Love" – are shaped by both the rhythmic vocabulary of the big band swing of Ellington, Fletcher Henderson and Basie and the melodic sensibility of the classic Broadway musical by Rodgers and Hammerstein or Jerome Kern.

However, the Black South African elements in the score are by no means insignificant. The pounding beats, crisp handclaps and chants on "Gumboot Dance", a popular step developed by Black miners, are striking because the performance is galvanized by a raw energy and raucousness that contrasts with the much smoother, polished sounds that are heard elsewhere. As for the ecstatic harmonies of "Tshotsholosa", these are punctuated by occasional flurries of sharp ululations that are alien to western theatrical conventions.

Another piece that is vividly South African is "Crazy Kid", where the charmingly rustling, whirring timbre of a penny-whistle ensemble rings out over a walking bass and chugging acoustic guitar. It is a joyous sound that jumps sweetly into life.

The musicians who performed this rollicking kwela for London audiences had made history in their country of origin. Lemmy 'Special' Mabaso and the Alexander Junior Bright Boys became the first black South Africans featured on a vinyl recording in 1958 (*Something New In Africa*) and were enormously popular. Kwela, as an acoustic music, could be performed on street corners as well as shebeens. The great heartbeat of the genre was the penny whistle, the little instrument that was cheap and transportable, not unlike the harmonica in American blues.

Mabaso's appearance in *King Kong* was important because he and the Alexander Boys presented a form of music that was emblematic not just of township creativity but of township adversity. Mabaso's character was a street urchin who went by the name of Penny Whistler. His poverty chimed with the song "Gumboot Dance", whose title evoked the plastic Wellingtons, the inadequate protective gear for those who had to dig coal. The sound of the boots stamping in unison became part of a musical culture as a vigorous rhythmic accompaniment to the songs sung by the miners. They had dust in their lungs, loose rocks falling about their heads, but they did not have diamonds on the soles of their feet.

These realities were absent from the sleeves notes of the 1961 release of *King Kong* that was issued on Decca, one of the major labels of the era. The text summarises both the play and the life story of its subject, the boxer Ezekiel Dhlamini, but there is no mention of the malicious racism of post-Sharpeville South Africa. There was no mention of apartheid.

Perhaps the lyrics of the song "Sad Times, Bad Times" were written in Xhosa precisely because any reference to the Treason Trial had to be implicit rather than explicit, but nowhere in the packaging of the album is there an indication of the backdrop of oppression against which the story was set. This is clear in the following statement: "This musical has come as a revelation to many South Africans that art does not recognise racial barriers... the first export of indigenous South African theatre will reveal to the rest of the world the peculiar flavour of township life as well as the unrecognised artistic talents of its people." If only the ruling National Party had actually recognised that Blacks were *worthy* of equal rights.

Produced by Jack Hylton, the bandleader and impresario who had brought Duke Ellington to Britain in the 1930s, the cast recording of *King Kong* is an invaluable document of South African culture presented on a international stage that was contemporary to the success of one of its original cast members, Miriam Makeba, as a solo artist in America. Sadly, the London recording does not provide comprehensive information about all of those who took part, and although the singers – Nathan Mdledle, Peggy Phango, Joseph Mogotsi, Patience Gowabe, Sophie Mgcina, Stephen Moloi, Ben Masinga – are listed, there is little information on the orchestra that accompanies them throughout the show.

The consensus among music historians is that members of The Jazz Epistles, the founding fathers of South African jazz who came together in the mid 1950s, who were part of the orchestra of the original *King Kong* production, also travelled to Britain with the show. It is known, for instance, that the alto saxophonist Kippie Moeketsi played in some if not all of the 201 British performances. Moeketsi was also credited as an arranger on the *King Kong* recording, along with the tenor saxophonist Mackay Davashe, who had worked with the Epistles in Johannesburg, and the pianist Sol Klaaste.[10]

With such a wealth of talent, it is not surprising that the musical has a number of highlights, particularly Mabaso's penny-whistle playing and several of the lead vocals, notably by Phango and Mogotsi. But *King Kong* as a show with disparate elements lacks cohesion. This is primarily because of the structural constraints of the Broadway model, which lead to the precedence of songs sung in English over those in indigenous languages, and a preference for short compositions, of which there are nineteen, that leave little room for the improvisation for which Moeketsi was renowned. The beautiful clarinet on the overture "Sad Times, Bad Times" is actually one of the few instances where a soloist is really given a chance to blow and the melodic content on several of the vocal pieces leans to the saccharine side of the western show-tune tradition. The description of *King Kong* as an "All African Jazz Opera" does not ring entirely true, and if there is a conceptual problem from a musical point of view, then this is paralleled by the mediated, if not sanitized depiction of township life, which though replete with stories of poverty, romance and gang-related violence, makes no mention of the iniquity of minority white rule that framed the existence of its denizens, though it goes without saying that the production would have been banned had it done so.

Having said that, "Kwela Kong" is a brilliant piece that recasts the richness of the American big band tradition within a rhythmic and melodic context that is resoundingly South African. The pulse is set by the distinctive stomping and hissing chants of the "Gumboot dance" and the bass, piano and drums swing, or rather sway with the kind of leisurely nonchalance that defines penny whistle bands. As for the brass and reeds, they are deployed in a series of busy, chattering, interlocking riffs that make the most of the tonal contrast between the sharp, high brass and the throatier drawl of the baritone saxophones, whose phrases have the kind of curling, glowing vibrato that fully enhances the boisterous, joyous atmosphere created by the very audible hollers of the gumboot dancers. Indeed "Kwela Kong" is very much dance music, or, more to the point, shebeen dance music.

One of the many melodic figures heard in the arrangement has particular cultural significance. The baritones play a fleeting but irresistibly catchy, drumming-like phrase, almost like the gentle tapping of palms on a conga, which is achingly familiar. The four-note riff is a variation on the chorus of "Wimoweh" or "Mbube", the song written by Solomon Linda also known under the title "The Lion Sleeps Tonight". It remains an iconic composition which, through versions by Miriam Makeba, Hugh Masekela and the American doo-wop group, The Tokens, showed that South African music that drew on the rich choral and rhythmic traditions of its oppressed black population, could have international appeal. Quotation of standards is also an integral part of the jazz aesthetic because it flows from the desire of the improvising musician to transform and personalise existing source materials, to make us hear what we do know in ways we don't, and the use of this local song imbues South African jazz with a sense of self, something beholden to the sons and daughters of the soil.

As a dynamic force, South African music in general was evolving at the time that *King Kong* was in Britain, and the arrival of mbaquanga, a genre that grew from the elision of marabi and jazz sensibilities, attested to a restless creative energy among township musicians.

It is not unreasonable to think that the South African musicians who came to Britain with the musical would have ventured into some of the jazz clubs in London to sit in with local musicians, but there is no documentation that proves this happened. Todd Matshikiza, the composer, did appear at venues in London, but he did not keep a regular band together or make a recording. Whether this was because his strengths were more as a composer than improviser, or whether the focus of his life was the media rather than music, is a matter of speculation. Matshikiza maintained strong links with South Africa, chronicling arts, culture and politics both in his homeland and in Britain, and, most significantly, took part in events organized by the anti-apartheid movement in London.

Successive waves of West Indians, such as Dizzy Reece and Joe Harriott, who arrived in the 1950s, had shown that to survive in the highly competitive London jazz scene, a musician had not only to be talented but resourceful, in making contacts and holding down regular gigs. A South African who did just that was the white double bassist, Harry Miller.[11] He was the first of a wave of expatriate South Africans who have had a lasting impact on British jazz and Black British music.

A tremendously gifted player and composer who was born in Cape Town in 1941, Miller arrived in London in 1961, the year of *King Kong*, and secured work as a member of "Geraldo's Navy", the musician's term for the transatlantic cruise-ship bands that were booked by a New Bond street agency run by the conductor-bandleader Gerald Bright. Although aspiring British jazz musicians cared little for the commercial dance music they had to play on board, they did not turn their noses up at the gig because it provided the opportunity to visit the epicentre of the jazz world, New York, and attend concerts by the musicians they admired. Miller was able to see legends such as pianist Thelonious Monk, the "high priest of bebop".

In London, Miller gigged around and in 1963 formed a band with the West Indian drummer Don Brown that, following Brown's departure, was renamed Ground Sounds Five. This band was notable for the presence of other young musicians who made their mark on the London scene in the years to come, above all the excellent trumpeter Henry Lowther.

Miller continued to work with a variety of up-and-coming musicians, but the really important aspect of his career was the timing of his arrival in Britain. He came at a moment of decisive shift in the character of the UK jazz scene that reflected the emergence of talented young players who were original composers, brimming with new ideas and energy. While the bebop icons such as Ronnie Scott and John Dankworth were still going strong, Mike Westbrook had emerged as a composer with an identity that drew on all areas of American jazz, from the swing of Duke Ellington to the avant-garde of Sun Ra via the gospel-fired grooves of Charles Mingus. Westbrook realised that there was a creative space formed by this holy trinity, and he melded it with a different sensibility to that of any previous British jazz albums.

Raised in Torquay, Westbrook formed his first band in Plymouth in the late 1950s, before moving to London in 1962 where he led several groups and appeared regularly at venues such as Ronnie Scott's club in Gerrard Street, Soho and The Little Theatre in St. Martin-in-the-Fields just behind Trafalgar Square. These sessions hothoused a sextet whose backbone was

Westbrook on piano, Alan Jackson on drums and Harry Miller on double bass. Other talented soloists, multi-reedist John Surman, alto saxophonist Mike Osborne and trombonist Malcolm Griffiths were part of this group that subsequently evolved into the 10-12-piece Concert Band, augmented by more brass instruments such as French horn and tuba.

Released between 1967 and 1968, Westbrook's first two albums *Celebration* and *Release* were orchestral works where the writing was fearlessly eclectic, veering from the pastoral to the turbulent, the arrangements often episodic and densely layered. Miller's performance on these recordings is superb. His tonal strength and faultless timekeeping support the elaborate architecture of the compositions, making the foundation rich and firm amid swirling themes and harmonies. The thought-provoking artwork of Westbrook's third album, *Marching Song* (1969), resonated with changing currents in both creative music and the political landscape, as the anti-Vietnam war movement, the formation of militant Black groups and the ongoing momentum of CND made the second half of the 1960s a period of social upheaval. The emergence of another strain of jazz in America in which the spirit of experimentation was taken to new levels of radicalism chimed with the thinking of some young players in Europe and Britain. Saxophonists John Coltrane, Albert Ayler and pianist Cecil Taylor were among the torchbearers of the "New thing" or "free jazz", and there was an intensity, if not violence in their playing and a daring approach to tonality, which largely eschewed the long and winding steeplechase of chord changes that characterised bebop. There was also saxophonist Ornette Coleman who had walked down not dissimilar pathways to those of Ayler in the late 1950s, as had Jamaican saxophonist Joe Harriott (discussed in Chapter 21). But the very striking sound of Ayler, the raw, primeval, dawn-of-time quality of his 'cry', its sheer ecstatic, deeply human fervour, had a strength of character that resonated with the outlook of young British players such as the saxophonists Evan Parker and Trevor Watts, flautist Bob Downes, pianist Keith Tippett and drummer John Stevens, who created an active musical community in London venues like The Little Theatre, the Sun in Drury Lane and Ronnie Scott's first ever address in Gerrard street, which was now dubbed The Old Place.

Miller would play with all of these musicians in a wide variety of contexts that reflected the exciting state of flux of British jazz, where lines between composition and improvisation were blurring. Though the principle of the bandleader still had currency, many of the new groups were predicated on the notion of greater collective thinking, the exchange of ideas between all members on an equal footing. For this to work, the players had to listen closely to one another and develop great empathy, so that there was a sense of a common language emerging from the array of individual sounds, a musical Esperanto from a potential Babel.

Greatly valued as a double bassist, Harry Miller created a special musical chemistry with a drummer, a compatriot who arrived from South Africa, and with whom, in the words of Trevor Watts, he would go on to form "the bedrock of many a group." The man in question was Louis Moholo-Moholo, a Cape Towner who was part of The Blue Notes, a highly talented group which, after setting out for Europe in 1964, playing in France, Denmark, and Switzerland, arrived in London in spring, 1965, and made a lasting impression on British jazz.

Along with Moholo were double bassist Johnny Dyani, trumpeter Mongezi Feza, alto saxophonist Dudu Pukwana, who were all black, and a white pianist, Chris McGregor. The band established its reputation with a residency at The Old Place as well as regular gigs at the Institute for Contemporary Art, which was then located in Dover Street, where they shared the bill with Mike Westbrook's band, featuring their compatriot, Harry Miller.

For a multi-racial band such as the Blue Notes there was no alternative but exile from South Africa, given the humiliations they had to endure, a truly grotesque spin on the phenomenon of the American minstrel. As Louis Moholo-Moholo, today the only surviving member of the group, recalled in 2016: "We're playing a gig with Chris McGregor. And Chris wants to hang out with us; you know what Chris would do? He'd polish himself with black polish and wear a cap, and we'd drag him in [to a nightclub]. Then there was a state of emergency so if black and white were seen together... it was *total* segregation. So we decided let's go; so we went. Thank god we went, because we preserved the music." [12]

Relieved as they were to escape apartheid, the Blue Notes had to grapple with the complex realities of exile, the fact that uprooting from one's homeland entails economic and above all cultural, emotional and psychological challenges. Indeed, the band arrived in London a man short because their tenor saxophonist, Nick Moyake, part of the original line-up, had a nervous breakdown. "Nick, he freaked out, man," Moholo-Moholo explained. "When we left South Africa he was a star, then he finds himself in the cold in December in Switzerland, with snow and he just got homesick, he was unknown. He was the eldest of us all, he was about 51, and he wanted to go home now, he wouldn't die here." [13]

According to Moholo-Moholo life in London was infinitely better than what the Blue Notes had experienced in Europe, and, certainly, compared to the repression endured by Blacks in South Africa, the much more liberal atmosphere that enabled them to play with white English as well as black West Indian musicians represented a morale booster, because local players offered genuine warmth and enthusiasm. "The English musicians, they opened up their hearts to us, " Moholo-Moholo says with a broad smile.

Recordings of the Blue Notes in concert in Durban, South Africa just prior to their departure for Europe provide a vivid illustration of what must have endeared them to the London jazz fraternity. There is an enormous energy generated by the ensemble by way of the fiery improvisations of the horns, particularly Pukwana, and the relentless propulsion of the rhythm section. Roughly speaking, the band were skilled practitioners of the hard bop school patented by the likes of Horace Silver and Art Blakey, but Moholo-Moholo's endless stream of percussive ideas, his continually inventive accenting off the central beat of a song, imparts to the music a febrile dynamism and sense of agitation, of restlessness, that connected to the work of the avant-garde, where rigidly set time and harmony were being stripped away.

Over the next few years, members of the Blue Notes, through their work both in Britain and abroad, moved deeper into the realm of free jazz by way of collaborations with a wide range of musicians. As a symbol of this spirit of musical adventure and internationalism, the rhythm section of the Blue Notes became part of a band with two renowned foreign musicians who were visiting London in 1965, the American soprano saxophonist Steve Lacy and Italian trumpeter Enrico Rava, who had been impressed by the Blue Notes when he saw them in concert at the Antibes jazz festival in France the previous year. Lacy felt that the drums and bass of that group, Moholo-Moholo and Johnny Dyani, were particularly important. They played in Europe and South America, notably Argentina, and a recording of a concert at the Centro De Experimentation at the Instituto Di Tella in Buenos Aires was released under Lacy's name with the title *The Forest and The Zoo* in 1966.

The lack of conventional signposts in the songs, namely a stated "head" and chord-based improvisations, may have proved a challenge for some listeners, but the embrace of this conceptual daring, the uncertainty of the premise, accounts for its excitement. There is one long 21 minute piece per side on the album, "Forest", and "Zoo", and in each case the musicians create a stream of ideas, converging and diverging on a tonal area to create a feeling of flux and flutter. While Rava's brash, fractured statements and Lacy's animal-like trills are striking, there is great timbral colour and rhythmic fluidity provided by Dyani's bass and Moholo-Moholo's drums. The former's lines are a kind of punk flamenco while the latter fashions a march that twists in and out of time, with the tom toms throbbing away to create the insistent rumble usually heard on balaphones, marimbas or logs. In any four bars of music you can hear the snare lash whimsically on and off the central pulse of the music, bouncing through varying patterns of two, three or five beats, but the more you listen the more you come to realise that Moholo-Moholo is really not thinking in terms of four bars.

Despite an original intention to stay just a few months in Buenos Aires, the band was stuck there for more than a year, and it took the efforts of Chris McGregor to raise the funds to bring Dyani and Moholo-Moholo back to London at the same time as Lacy and Rava went to New York. According to Rava, the South Africans were the only two black guys in the Argentine capital at the time, "so people had a tendency to look at them in a very insistent way, with the obvious consequences, so my father-in-law, who signed as Johnny's tutor to let him in Argentina, since he was under age for Argentinian law, had to go to the police station several times to get them out."[13] The return to Britain thus came after a picaresque sojourn.

Consider the political and sociological magnitude of these events. Black South African jazz musicians who were beginning to impact on the European scene took a detour via South America with white Italians and Americans, an adventure that would have seemed absolutely improbable in South Africa.

On the evidence of their next recording, it seems that the bond between Dyani, Moholo-Moholo, McGregor and the other members of the Blue Notes was strengthened by the separation. As the Chris McGregor Group, rather than the Blue Notes, the band recorded an album in London in 1967, *Very Urgent* that saw the quintet augmented by another white South African, the tenor saxophonist, Ronnie Beer. It is an outstanding set for its idiomatic breadth, the cohesion of disparate elements, and the deeply expressive nature of both the soloists and the ensemble. Much of the spontaneity heard on the Lacy album is flowing into the older Blue Notes' sound.

With a title such as *Very Urgent*, the music must be seen as a comment on the need for an immediate end to apartheid and sweeping change in South Africa. The Blue Notes were in exile in Britain, severed from a homeland that, as Moholo-Moholo states, they all loved and missed. What the band achieved on the album was a thorough alliance of deep emotion and creative exertion, bringing together passion, grace and fire. The pieces are like winding roads without obvious staging posts and destinations because the players have a large pool of cultural and stylistic references to draw on, an ability to move from jazz to folk to pop, as they had *lived* it, either in the raucous atmosphere of shebeens or in the decidedly more sedate mood of a jazz club.

Seeing no great divide between the danceable and the intellectual, McGregor, Pukwana, Feza, Dyani, Beer and Moholo-Moholo made music in which form was malleable, stretching themes and improvisations into passages that were not organized in conventional multiples of 4 bars or tied to a time signature of 4/4. The band brought sunny, rousing riffs (which a listener could sing with relative ease) into direct contact with harmonies and solos that were much more incendiary in character. It's as if *Very Urgent* is a series of songs being pulled apart and skilfully re-stitched, more or less on the fly. The music is rhapsody and rupture.

The set comprises just four tracks, the shortest, "Heart's Vibrations" being 7:51, while the longest "Marie My Dear/Travelling Somewhere" is

16:51, a length of track that gave the musicians extended creative scope to develop their ideas, producing a narrative that is epic and eventful. As a manifesto for the band, the segue of Pukwana's "Marie My Dear" and McGregor's 'Travelling Somewhere', could not be a stronger opener, not so much a journey from tenderness to turbulence as a demonstration of how to frame melodic lyricism with subtle shifts in pulse and fairly dissonant harmony that becomes cumulatively more intense, picking away at the tonal centre as the second piece reaches its conclusion. The initial theme is airy and relaxed and bears a strong echo of the wry, crinkled lament of Thelonious Monk's "Ruby, My Dear", with ribbons of sound created by the horns wafting into chord changes in leisurely, almost lazy fashion. After five minutes, the ballad pace wheels into a slightly higher tempo set by Moholo's gently patted rimshots. But just as the players appear to be settling into the new section it comes to an abrupt end after 14 bars, a relatively uncommon duration, and the left turn is underlined by a striking unaccompanied solo passage from Pukwana's alto saxophone in which he produces tight, clenched phrases and energetic rasps that ease into an upward dancing line that heralds the entry of the other horns and rhythm section. A jumpy, jaunty groove frames this more celebratory mood and suggests that the arrangement will henceforth head towards the rhythmic bustle of kwela. The statements are reiterated before giving way to a raking Feza trumpet solo and the rhythm section really starts to swing. However, Moholo lashes out stark offbeats on his kick drum and McGregor's upper register chords grow loud and eerie, as Pukwana's alto wails now create a similarly fraught energy.

Tension builds relentlessly as harsher sounds come into play, and at the 12 minute mark McGregor's right-hand runs become more skittish and Beer's tenor solo sustains the overall intensity. However, the other horns intermittently play a sweet, skipping contrapuntal riff that brings back the kwela flavour before the brass and reeds withdraw and McGregor's solo becomes Cecil Taylor-like in a twisting, tumbling attack as the power of the group as a trio is heard. Then Pukwana's first horn line returns. The contrast of its relative simplicity, especially the last catchy triplet, and the hyperactivity of the piano, is enormously satisfying. Dyani takes a short bass solo marked by broken lines and aggressive chording before one more extended lyrical theme from the horn section brings the piece to a grandstand climax.

It is an engrossing performance and symbolic of an ecumenical approach to jazz which treads a middle path between accessibility and abstraction, presenting the listeners with riffs that, born of township shebeen culture, were inherently South African, as well as spiky chords and barbed improvisations in line with the ways of the American avant-garde movement. Yet there were also echoes of swing and bebop. This musical saga is challenging and is not devoid of an element that was integral to the origins of jazz but was often subsumed by its elevation to a form of high art: dance.

Exactly why "Marie My Dear/Travelling Somewhere" materialised as it did, with its guile and grind, sweetness and sting, is not easy to pinpoint, but it suggests the sum total of all of the experiences that the players had had in South Africa, Europe and South America; the culture shocks of London, Copenhagen and Buenos Aires seem to permeate the atmosphere. Moholo-Moholo, in any case, was keen to point out that the emergence of free jazz was something that felt familiar rather than foreign to him. "We didn't have a problem when we heard Coltrane in South Africa. We thought 'yeah, man right on!' [So called] 'Free music' to me… is *natural*, it just came. In South Africa we don't count, we don't have one, two, three, four, like the west does… We just sing, everybody starts to sing, but there would be a leader and the time would be correct. That's the magic of it."[14] As Moholo-Moholo remembers, the session for *Very Urgent* had a spontaneity in the way the bulk of the arrangements came together, above all in the use of township riffs. "The kwela that was Dudu – Dudu would do that, he killed that, man, and immediately Johnny would turn it on. We were young… we were really hungry."

By the time *Very Urgent* was recorded the individual members of The Blue Notes were doing all kinds of projects. They worked with many of the mostly avant-garde musicians on the London scene and Moholo-Moholo went on to create a formidable partnership with his compatriot, the double bassist Harry Miller. However, there were several other South African expatriates in the city and inevitably they came into contact with one another.

As we have seen in previous chapters, the phenomenon of the cast members of a musical or singers who backed a major Black American name settling in Britain was well established (examples being Precious Wilson and Madeleine Bell). The South African equivalents were the *King Kong* vocalists Patience Gowabe, Hazel Futa and Eunice Mthombeni. In the early 1960s, having stayed on in London, they formed their own soul-influenced group, The Velvettes and began to work with the popular and respected blues singer, Cyril Davies.

Another singer who also stayed on was Peggy Phango, who had replaced Miriam Makeba in the original production of *King Kong*. She worked with Moholo-Moholo many times in London. The drummer considers the show to be a landmark in the history of South African music and recalls the major effect that it had on him as a teenager. "*King Kong*… it knocked me out, the songs. We had a band called The Cordettes in South Africa and I played some of the songs from *King Kong*, (like "Kwela Kong"), we played it with my band when we were like 18. We were so proud of *King Kong* and then we came to England and we were all together (with Peggy

and other cast members) and it put the icing on the cake."[15] Further proof
of the legacy of the show included the career of alto saxophonist Gwigwi
Mrwebi, part of the orchestra for the London production, who formed a
group comprising some of the Blue Notes (McGregor, Pukwana and Beer),
Jamaican double bassist Coleridge Goode and English drummer Laurie
Allen, and although together for only a short time the band recorded an
album *Kwela* in 1967, the year of *Very Urgent*. There was a fascinating connection and contrast between the two records insofar as the snappy riffs of
Mrwebi's album were not dissimilar to those that dotted McGregor's, but
in the case of the former they were set to a constant rhythm for 3 minutes
rather than frequent structural change for 16. Mrwebi played something
called kwela, McGregor and co turned it into something else.

Gwigwi's band may have been notable for its multi-racial character,
but it was also a multi-generational ensemble. Goode was the doyen at 53
years old, Mrwebi and McGregor both 31, Pukwana 29, Beer 26 and Allen
the youngest at 24. In other words there was a range of life experience as
well as musical knowledge that could have made the group dynamics very
interesting. As a rhythm section, Goode and Allen cohered nicely, supplying
a steady, swaying groove for the piano and saxophones that played themes
that were as joyous as they were catchy.

What was part of the flow and dynamic between musicians was sometimes geographic proximity. Often in the areas of migrant settlement such
as Moss Side or Notting Hill, musicians – across musical genres, ethnicity
and age – quite often found themselves as neighbours. For example, South
African double bassist Johnny Dyani, upon his return from Buenos Aires
with Moholo-Moholo, lived in a house in Kilburn, North West London,
that was full of tenants who all made a mark on different areas of British
music. On the ground floor was Graham Simpson, bass guitarist with
the influential "glam rock" band, Roxy Music, while on the top were free
jazz saxophonist Evan Parker and experimental composer-double bassist
Gavin Bryars. Whether or not they ever played together is perhaps not as
important as the fact that they found themselves in a shared living space.
Players who have open minds and an inquisitive nature know that there is
great deal to be learned from those who have a concept of time, texture or
tonality that is not the same as their own. For adventurous thinkers, talking
about music is a valuable complement to playing music.

Don't Stop the Carnival

Sometimes stylistic cross-fertilization occurred because of this
neighbourliness, as the case of John Surman shows. The Plymouth-born
multi-reeds player, who excelled on baritone and soprano saxophones

and bass clarinet, moved to London in 1962, became an important member of Mike Westbrook's Concert Band and also gigged with electric blues rocker Alexis Korner. Surman came into the orbit of West Indian musicians in the street where he lived. One of these was pianist/steel drummer Russ Henderson, who was 44 to Surman's 24. Both men were based in Notting Hill.

"I was living in Bassett Road (just off Ladbroke Grove), and next door to me was John Surman," Henderson told me in 2013. "I was having a little session one day with the [Trinidadian] guitarist Fitzroy Coleman and he [John] knocked on the door. He said he was a musician and he just stayed and listened. After that we became good friends."[16]

As they spent more time together, the two men played regularly, blending calypso and jazz, and then widened their circle of collaborators in a manner that straddled the divide between the trad and modern schools, which meant there were sessions with the senior, well-established trumpeter Humphrey Lyttleton and junior, double bassist Dave Holland, who would soon make his name by joining Miles Davis's band. The Henderson-Surman collaboration would further develop at the Colhearne, a pub in Earls Court. "On Sunday lunchtimes, they got together," Surman recalled in 2011. "Russ was in the house band with Sterling Betancourt, and me and [alto saxophonist] Mike Osborne, after the all-nighters [in Soho] had finished, we'd just go straight there and jam."[17]

Word reached Ronnie Scott's and they were invited to play. It was the popularity of those appearances that in turn attracted the attention of Peter Eden, a producer at Deram, the division of Decca records that issued Mike Westbrook's albums. Given the fact that the music would be for an orchestra as well as a small group it made sense for Surman to call on several other Westbrook alumni: the trombonists Malcolm Griffiths and Paul Rutherford, and South African Mike Osborne. Alan Jackson and Harry Miller were on drums and bass, respectively, for some tracks. The young Dave Holland replaced the latter on others.

"He [Eden] said we'd like to do an album with some of the calypso jazz. So I said fine; it was very popular,"[18] Surman explained. The result was the 1969 recording *John Surman* that remains a great landmark in British jazz for its wide stylistic range and alignment of different schools of thought. The second side is an audacious 21-minute suite comprising three movements, "Incantation", "Episode" and "Dance", written for an 11-piece ensemble featuring two brilliant trumpeters, the Bajan Harry Beckett and the Canadian Kenny Wheeler, the jewels in a formidable crown of horns. Here the music moves stealthily between scored parts and free, collective improvisation in which the players explore and create in the moment.

Side one has four cuts of calypso jazz for a sextet consisting of Surman and Mike Osborne on baritone and alto saxophone respectively, Henderson

JOHN SURMAN

on piano, Miller on bass, Sterling Betancourt on drums and Errol Philip on congas. Henderson wrote an original, "Good Times Will Come Again", and brought three other well known calypsos to the table: The Mighty Sparrow's "Obeah Wedding", Lord Kitchener's "My Pussin'" and the traditional "Don't Stop The Carnival". So if the album ended in avant-garde jazz mode, it started in the vein of West Indian folk. Stylistically speaking, Surman and his band covered a lot of ground.

Yet it would be wrong to assume that there is a division between the accessible and the less accessible. The calypso tunes side has some quite fierce improvising from Surman, whose baritone has a wonderfully throaty, rugged tone that contrasts effectively with Osborne's piping alto. On the "avant-garde" side there is much more abstraction and the melodic content is not as pronounced, but the suite ends with "Dance", a piece that wears its title well. It is built on a busy, conga-led groove that launches boisterous riffing from the brass. Henderson had written "West Indian Drums" a few years prior. Here was Surman with West Indian Horns.

John Surman is thus a beguiling album that has an enormous cultural sweep. The arrangements recognize the influence of 'in' and 'out' schools of jazz, but also make the point that West Indian music, with all of its percussive cut and thrust, has its place in a suite where both melody and rhythm are creatively deployed. Although the album is very different to the Chris McGregor Group's masterful *Very Urgent*, I see them as part of a continuum in British jazz, namely music that places non-western folk and popular music within a context of free improvisation. In McGregor's case South African kwela and jazz coalesce; in Surman's, West Indian calypso and jazz. Although the elements in question are woven together in different ways by each artist, there are common denominators, above all the beautiful themes and swaying riffs, to which it is hard not to dance. Kwela and calypso were the creation of the disenfranchised "natives" of Africa and its diaspora, but they sound entirely relevant to this context of abstract arrangements executed by a set of highly skilled musicians, black and white, who hailed from several different corners of the globe.

Even though it is an album of instrumental pieces, *John Surman* also serves as a reminder of the political content of calypso. "Don't Stop The Carnival" is more than an incitement to party. As Russ Henderson explained the lyrics are borne of anti-colonial sentiment: "That's singing about the police inspectors who tried to stop carnival in the olden days. It was only after independence that we had our own police; before, the inspector was always English. It's *against* him. It's a political song. Definitely, it was a political song."[19]

In the light of the future struggles of the Black community in Notting Hill to hold carnival amid institutional belligerence and a hostile police presence, the song is prophetic. It is a call for resistance, a fist raised against power.

"Don't Stop The Carnival" also expresses a sentiment that resonates powerfully with a number of key tropes in other genres of music. It aligns with R&B's incitement to "Dancin' in the Streets", with funk's unifying subversion of "One Nation Under a Groove", with reggae's irrepressible urge for "Jammin'", and with hip-hop's lucid resignation that "You gotta fight for your right to party." In each case there is an anti-authoritarian stance, a desire to overturn social regulations that curtail the freedom of the individual for whom the act of revelry, the celebration of self and community, is freighted with political significance. The common man knows full well that "every day we pay the price with a living sacrifice." To start a movement against this oppression is to "Don't Stop The Carnival."

In any case it was not an obscure tune in Britain, and had been covered by Alan Price. He was already known as the keyboardist and a founder member of The Animals, the rugged Newcastle R&B group whose bass player Chas Chandler had launched Jimi Hendrix in London. The Animals did engaging covers of classic folk-blues numbers such as "House of The Rising Sun" and "Don't Let Me Be Misunderstood" as well as good, punchy originals like "I'm Crying". Price left the band in 1965 to embark on a solo career, with a string of hit singles that included his original "The House That Jack Built" and a cover of "I Put A Spell On You". His version of "Don't Stop The Carnival" reached number 13 in the national chart in 1968, the year before the release of John Surman's interpretation. It is tempting to see it as a piece of pop-calypso fluff to be dismissed as a pale imitation of "authentic" Black music, such as Russ Henderson's *Caribbean Carnival*. The somewhat leaden rhythm, absence of swing and the faux West Indian accents on the chorus might lend credence to the argument that this is calypso that has been watered down by English musicians on the make. I think that what Price did was more interesting than that. The use of a horn section with a chugging, oompah quality taps into a brass band tradition associated as much with the colliery as the Salvation Army. The new sounds that they bring to the table are as English as a bottle of brown ale or a nice cup of tea.

Then the joyous, street-party atmosphere of the chorus is tempered by the reality-check lyric of a new B section – "Sunshine, I'm only dreaming"– which is further cast into a lugubrious shadow by the next phase of the arrangement. The song slows to ballad pace and Price's delivery becomes wistful rather than hopeful. His new lyrics blow away the hitherto breezy escapism with a gust of gritty social realism.

> This is England on a winter's afternoon,
> There is no sun, there's just a pale and tired moon,
> The shivering sparrows on the smoking chimney tops,
> And all the children suffer from colds and flu and raindrops.

It is easy to overlook the poetic grace and political charge of these lyrics. The image of "shivering sparrows on the smoking chimney tops" is one of the most accomplished lines in British pop song-writing for its juxtaposition of innocence and industrialization, the frailty of nature and the danger of man-made construction. This is then compounded by the references to ill health among the young. The vulnerable in society are not cared for. This song foreshadows the dissent expressed in Price's "Jarrow Song" of 1974, a moving account of the famous hunger march of 1936 to protest the 70% unemployment rate and high incidence of childhood diseases such as rickets. The brilliant opening line – "My name is Geordie McIntyre an' the bairns don't even have a fire"– makes a clear link back to the social concerns that Price voices on "Carnival".

While both songs have a distinct Britishness, the sentiments were ones to which West Indians could emphatically relate. Rain, cold and the conspicuous absence of the sun were among the most common complaints made by the Windrush arrivals, as well as the harsh realities of discrimination in employment and housing. If they had listened to Price's lyrics, West Indians living in Birmingham, Cardiff, Leeds, Liverpool, London, Manchester or Glasgow, would have heard unsettling echoes of their own experience. It is about real life in Blighty.

All of which makes the point that calypso can be reshaped and recycled, like the sequence of chords on which a jazz artist composes new melodies. The two versions of "Don't Stop The Carnival" neatly show the way music from the Caribbean became part of a British music that was in all kinds of ways becoming "blacker". West Indian rhythms and folklore were permeating the mainstream of contemporary pop.

Russ Henderson brings a final twist to the tale of "Don't Stop The Carnival" and makes a point about the unpredictability and intensity of carnival culture and the calypso aesthetic by mentioning a lyric that is less well known and startlingly strange. "A chap in Trinidad blow off he head with a dynamite… so somebody [write] 'Blow, blow, blow… the dynamite' with the same tune as "No, don't stop…. the Carnival". So "Blow The Dynamite" and "Don't Stop The Carnival" is the same tune. This was suicide. Any major incident becomes a calypso for the carnival!"[20]

Recalling his childhood in Trinidad, Henderson points out that any aspiring calypso singers had to be able to create lyrics "extempo" on any given subject once they had named a key signature in the presence of musicians. Despite the growth of calypso as a recorded medium, the ability to pass comment spontaneously, both insightful and humorous, on topical issues remains a highly prized skill. The players who back them also have to be both alert and open-minded. This was something that attracted English musicians like John Surman. "Calypso and Caribbean musicians – those cats were great fun to hang out with," Surman noted. "The music was happening. I liked the people, I liked the lifestyle of the Caribbean guys. It was what jazz musicians wanted to be but were too British to be able to be."[21] Between them, Surman and Alan Price's versions of "Don't Stop The Carnival" encapsulate the unpredictable, shape-shifting nature of Black music in Britain, underlining the way that a song could exist in two entirely different contexts that bridge the gap between high art and popular culture. Surman's music was calypso jazz, Price's calypso pop. Each retained integrity in its own way, the former through an original arrangement bolstered by the input of superb band and an important expatriate Trinidadian musician, Russ Henderson, the latter by an original lyric that was relevant to the lives of the downtrodden working classes in Britain, Black and White – ordinary folk who could but dream of warmer climes.

Notes

1. *Tropic* magazine, March 1960.
2. *Tropic* magazine, March 1960
3. The Group Areas Amendment Act was among the most repressive laws of apartheid.
4. See Tom Lodge, *Black Politics in South Africa Since 1945* (Longman, 1983).
5. See BBC, On This Day/21/1960: Scores die in Sharpeville shoot-out (on-line).
6. *Tropic* magazine, June 1960.
7. See *The New Dictionary of South African Biography*, vol 2 (Vista University, 1999.
8. See Gwen Ansell, *Soweto Blues, Jazz, Politics and Popular Music in South Africa* (Continuum, 2004).
9. The details of the progress of *King Kong* are drawn from the sleeve notes of the cast recording.
10. See John Wickes, *Innovations in British Jazz* (Soundworld, 1999), pp. 32-48.
11. Interview with the author, Ronnie Scott's, London, 2016.
12. Enrico Rava quoted in the booklet of Blue Notes, *The Ogun Collection*, Ogun, 2008.
13. Interview with the author, Ronnie Scott's, London, 2016.
14. Interview with the author, Ronnie Scott's, London, 2016.
15. Interview with the author, Kensal Rise, London, 2013.
16. Interview with the author, Bore Place, Sevenoaks, 2011.
17. Interview with the author, Bore Place, Sevenoaks, 2011.
18. Interview with the author, Kensal Rise, London, 2013.
19. Interview with the author, Kensal Rise, London, 2013.
20. Interview with the author, Bore Place, Sevenoaks, 2011.

EPILOGUE: ...WITH THAT GUN IN YOUR HAND?

Several months after its UK release, the album *John Surman* was issued in America under the title of *Anglo Sax*. Whilst the directly implied Englishness of this debut album is given as its unique selling point, both in terms of the repertoire and the international identities of the band, the reality was much broader. The notion of a multi-cultural Englishness was yet to emerge. As a joyous musical Commonwealth summit, *Anglo-Afro-Caribbean Sax* may have been a more truthful reflection of Surman's music, but it would have left many confused. *Anglo Sax* was a clear pun on Anglo Saxon, a historical ethnic reference that would have chimed with western sensibilities.

Canadian Kenny Wheeler, who played on Anglo-Sax, was an important link to another band with a multi-cultural identity, the 1967 Joe Harriott-John Mayer double quintet, discussed in Chapter 21, whose players were drawn from Jamaica, India, St. Vincent, Scotland, Ireland and England. All of this music is a seminal part of the history of Britain as a nation whose culture has been as shaped by the world, as it has sought to shape the world politically. Sounds, rhythms and melodies, as well as people, were crossing borders. Nothing could have been more logical. Black music in Britain was fashioned by the many peoples with whom the Crown had engaged, through the successive agencies of the slave trade, colonialism, world wars, and mass migration, as well as by the UK's existing white population.

As significant as the formation of multi-racial, multi-nationality groups was the journey of musical raw materials. A beat, a riff, a tune, could be passed from one musician to another as freely as colloquial expressions heard in casual conversation. We don't know who was the composer of "Don't Stop The Carnival" (it is "traditional"), but we do know that Russ Henderson first heard the calypso in Port of Spain, Trinidad, after which he taught it to John Surman in London. But in 1968, the year they made a recording of it together, the piece ended up in the hands of the Newcastle-born, organist-vocalist, Alan Price, who may have possibly first heard the melody performed by Sonny Rollins, the American saxophonist of West Indian parentage. At each juncture the song underwent conceptual change.

The creative chain, in which Russ Henderson, Alan Price and John

Surman were links, signalled an enlightening blend of cultural energies. There was a great spirit of adventure in British improvised music at the heart of which were exchanges of creative ideas between English, West Indians, Indians and Africans, and partnerships willing to experiment with a wide range of idioms. As well as Henderson and Surman there was John Mayer and Joe Harriott; Mulatu Astatke and Frank Holder. In the case of the latter, a present day record label marketing department and festival programmers would classify the Astake-Holder anthem "Asiyo Bellema" as "World Music", which tends to mean non-European. Nothing demonstrates the shortcomings of the term more than this song, because it is really as "made in Britain" as a chicken tikka, a saltfish pattie or a Cornish pasty. The Astake-Holder meeting *had* to happen in London, precisely because of the geographical, administrative and cultural relationships that Britain had with other parts of the world. Astatke's Ethiopian parents sent him to the UK because of the prestige of its educational institutions, whereas Holder made his way here because his native Guyana was a British colony. There was a substantial class divide between the two men, but they were bound by both their ethnic minority status and an overwhelming desire to give vent to their creativity to make music that was new.

While the West Indies and Africa are integral parts of the story of Black music in Britain, America is, of course, the other pivotal element. All three territories were connected by the horrors of the Middle Passage and they have remained bound by an ongoing transit through economic, political and artistic channels.

Since New York was the focal point of the entertainment world and, subsequently, the record industry at the dawn of the 20th century, it was inevitable that West Indian musicians would set their sights on Broadway as well as the "black Mecca" of Harlem. Yet the creative wealth of the African-American community, flowering in forms of music such as gospel, ragtime, swing, modern jazz and blues was such that a wide range of venues in Britain, from aristocratic drawing rooms to theatres, dance halls and clubs were obliged, for the sake of commercial gain rather than political correctness, to provide a platform for Stateside Blacks in search of dignity as well as remuneration. In the 1960s, Jimi Hendrix was but the latest in a long line of African-Americans who brought creative wealth to Britain: Paul Robeson, Sidney Bechet, Will Marion Cook, the Bohee Brothers, Pete George Hampton, the Fisk Jubilee Singers.

Because of the geographically segregated nature of the majority of historical chronicles, this flow of African-Americans to Europe is rarely connected to that of African-Caribbeans, but there was indeed a parallel movement of West Indians that included the Kingston Choral Union, Leslie Hutchinson, Lord Kitchener, Joe Harriott, Millie Small and Ernest

Ranglin. Sam Manning mapped his career between the Americas and Europe, leaving his native Trinidad for New York before moving on to London. And whilst the English capital may have been a great magnet for musicians, regional venues were no less important, because the demand for Black music in Britain was always national rather than just metropolitan.

The several Black communities spread throughout the United Kingdom themselves produced musicians who made an invaluable cultural contribution. If the story of Shirley Bassey's rise from the humble setting of Tiger Bay in Cardiff to international stardom is well known, then the lives of countless others – Andy Hamilton in Birmingham, Lord Woodbine in Liverpool, Ossie Roberts in Manchester – are no less worthy of celebration. The black provincial musician is absolutely crucial to our national cultural identity.

This book has been an attempt to highlight the existence of these geographically diverse exponents of Black music in Britain, and to unveil the extent to which they, and many others, have played a role in disseminating artforms not always within the national consciousness. The practitioners of black music who did not 'make it', so to speak, also played the invaluable role of maintaining and extending a rich repertoire, and certainly in Woodbine's case, generously sharing their knowledge with others.

No musical event is more important in this respect than Carnival, simply because its essential voice, the steel band, has been a great democratizing force both in the West Indies and Britain. Pan is open to all and stands as a form of collective expression that parallels the sense of liberation and togetherness that people can achieve through their participation in the transformative and energizing ritual of "mas".

The carnival histories of Notting Hill, London, Chapeltown, Leeds and St. Paul's, Bristol are roughly contemporary and they achieved the common goal of fostering community solidarity and raising the spirits of Black people who had suffered debilitating indignities in their daily lives in Britain. Large-scale cultural activity required stout hearts and resolute minds in the face of resistance from within and without Britain's Black communities. It took courage to start the carnival. The song rightly says "Don't stop" it.

If it is appropriate to describe those early activists as warriors, then the military metaphor extends in the literal sense to other areas. In Notting Hill, scene of the most high profile of Britain's carnivals, West Indians, women as well as men, had to take up arms in the face of rampaging thugs during the race riots of 1958 that formed a sombre prelude and indeed catalyst to the event, for it became clear that one of the most effective means of lifting the gloom on the Black community was precisely through a cultural celebration.

Moreover, some of those who fought in the pitched battles of West

London, and also in the civil disturbances that preceded them in Nottingham, were individuals who had seen action in altogether more horrific circumstances. They were West Indian ex-servicemen – soldiers, sailors and airmen – who had enthusiastically answered the call of the "motherland" and signed up to defend Britain and the Allies in the Second World War. They were actually following in the footsteps of their compatriots who had done the same in the First World War. Colonial regiments were integral to the defence of the realm, even though they were in the invidious position of serving the Empire that was a source of oppression at home.

Hence a black man in uniform carrying a rifle, a pistol or a bayonet is an essential part of the military history of the United Kingdom, and it should be prominent in the national psyche, given the lofty status assigned to the successive generations of leaders who have either conquered in the name of Britannia, the super power that once ruled the waves, or defended its borders against the threat of invasion, stiffening the spine of the common man with a pledge to fight the enemy on the beaches, on the landing grounds, in the fields and in the streets. There was something of a parting of the ways after the Second World War. Churchill made it clear that he was determined to retain control over the Empire; for those who supported the war effort from the West Indies and India, the war was about a wider commitment to freedom, which meant taking control of their own affairs. It was a contested argument. The Jamaican novelist Roger Mais was, for instance, sent to prison in colonial Jamaica for sedition because he dared to write a newspaper article criticising Churchill's stance on holding onto imperial control.

But to the image of the black soldier with a weapon one must add that of a black soldier with a musical instrument, the black soldier who can play as well as fight. The black soldier whose idea of rhythm is more complex than that of the routines learned in "square-bashing". One of the key themes of *Don't Stop The Carnival* is the presence of black musicians who have emerged from the British, West Indian and American Armed Services. Throughout the ages, people of colour have joined up, and militarization has not precluded artistic endeavour, indeed in some cases it has provided a springboard to a future career as an artist. Entertaining the troops has sometimes preceded entertaining the British public.

The key names in this lineage include Sam Manning, Leslie Thompson, Leslie 'Jiver' Hutchinson, Joe Appleton, Frank Holder, Robbie Robinson, Geno Washington and Jimi Hendrix. Their experiences and length of tenure in the army or air force may have been different, yet these musicians, who were active between the 1920s and 1960s, all learned what it meant to subsume one's personality and follow orders. Although they are categorised in different genres, from calypso and jazz to soul and rock, the aforementioned endured the mental and physical constraints of the armed services. This is no doubt why an iridescent individual like Hendrix did not stay too long in khaki fatigues. But others, like Thompson and Holder, acknowledge that the services provided musicians from the West Indies with an opportunity to expand their horizons and discover the mother country, and the extent to which the military helped shape the arc of cultural history from the colonies to Britain is symbolised by the fact that the early bandmasters at the legendary Alpha School for Boys in Jamaica, whence came scores of influential players, were from the West India regiment.

All these musicians loom large in this subsection of the history of the Black artist (as serviceman) in Britain because they were active during the war and the immediate post-war period when jazz, in the form of big band swing, was much more rooted in the mainstream than it is today. The phenomenon of the "coloured orchestra", several of whose members may have been former army or air force recruits, was recognized as sufficiently important for it to be documented in the popular press and live broadcasts on BBC radio.

If West Indian and African-American musicians were to be found in the armed services, a significant number of African musicians came to Britain via the merchant navy. As sailors – Nigerians and Somalis as well as South Asians, Chinese and West Indians – they made a vital contribution to Britain during the war, by keeping open lines of communication and transporting fuel and food to the United Kingdom.

Yet, however they came, they were "the other". They did not, so the wisdom held, behave like whites. Whilst sexual stereotyping was hugely destructive, there was also a continuing curiosity over the general cultural oddity of Blacks, which reached back to the Victorian era when theories were advanced on their musical gifts in proportion to their relative distance from civilization. "Natural rhythm" supposedly sustained Blacks alongside other acts of creative spontaneity. The Black tambourinists in the Coldstream Guards in the 18th century were noted for the flamboyance of their rhythmic skills, while English war correspondents wrote of the Sudanese who joined the Queen's infantry in the 1890s:

> The first thing that these black troops do when they get into camp is strike up some of their unearthly tunes, and in the absence of normal appliances they have been known to fashion old tin biscuit boxes into a species of wind instrument.

Therein lies a further example of the richness of the Black musical military heritage, but note that the war correspondent spoke of black troops, not officers. They are conspicuous by their absence and the lack of graded military personnel of colour is a stain on our conscience that is hard to ignore. The failure to see black troops as leaders has a long record in British culture, as shown by Thomas Rymer's attack in 1693 on Shakespeare's imagining of Othello's leadership when he wrote: "Shall a Poet thence fancy that they will set a Negro to be their

General or trust a Moor to defend them against the Turk?"

In 2011, an educational programme, *Speaking Out and Standing Firm*, was launched in Haringey to bring together young people and African-Caribbean veterans "whose experiences span from World War II to modern day peace-keeping and international conflicts." The two parties engaged in discussion and in the course of their interaction a number of significant statements were made. Firstly, the young people said that "At school, we learn more about American Black History than British", while former soldiers, such as Vince McBean, chair of the West Indian Ex-Servicemen and Women Association, evoked the significant barriers to career progression: "An uphill struggle and a slippery slope… we didn't get very far regardless of our qualifications." His was not a lone voice. Many others concurred.

Finally, and perhaps most ruefully, the point was made that "On this Remembrance Sunday, you didn't see a black face at all." This comment is pertinent to the history of Black music in Britain; some of the singers and players who have enriched our culture were not spared such a lack of respect when they were doing their duty. Cy Grant, the Guyanese vocalist who found fame when he sang calypso news items on the *Tonight* show in the 1950s, had been a navigator in Bomber Command during World War II. But that was not what he was supposed to be. He recalled:

> I was one of the first four people who joined the RAF from the colonies. They had just changed their policy towards recruiting black people, so that's how I got in. I trained as a pilot, but then halfway through my training I was switched to navigator. I didn't make anything of this at the time because I did not realize that this was not above board. But much later, I discovered through a friend that there were problems with the English aircrew not wanting to fly with black pilots.[1]

Discrimination of this kind was further reinforced by segregation in the American army stationed in Britain. The requests made by white officers that Negroes not be allowed to take lunch in the same restaurants as them were duly upheld by their British counterparts. Some made light of this. "If he takes a banjo with him, they'll think he's one of the band,"[2] was the revealing comment passed on the plight of one "coloured colonial" who was barred from sitting at the table with other Allies. These were the words of Winston Churchill.

Whether you were a guitarist in a bus crew, a horn player in a factory or a calypso singer in the RAF, you could feel the hand of exclusion drop on your shoulder at any time. Brilliant Black entertainers who found favour with royalty were by no means immune to racial discrimination before they set foot on stage, and once they had left it and found themselves staring at the forbidding face of a hotel doorman or slum landlord. For black people to have power over an audience did not mean power in society.

Lord Kitchener, the calypsonian, speared this kind of discrimination with the sharpness of his satire on a military establishment that was riddled with gross social inequalities. He is a different kind of conquering hero to the one who sailed up the Nile to dispose of Dervishes in the name of the Empire. Aldwyn Roberts may have styled himself as Kitchener in recognition of a military hero, but the very idea of a young black man from Trinidad appropriating a white peer's name was a truly subversive act.

It was in a second-hand clothing store that Jimi Hendrix echoed Kitch's mockery when he found a hussar's jacket that became an iconic part of his apparel. The shop was in Portobello Road, West London, home of the Notting Hill Carnival. It was called "I Was Lord Kitchener's Valet". It is easy to overlook the politics of the image of Hendrix in the ornately braided tunic. Here was a black man mocking the battledress that was the privilege of elite white cavalrymen – and none of them ever had hair like Hendrix's, or the imagination to promise that they would *chop the mountain down with the edge of my hand*. Jimi became a general on his own terms. His music was volcanic, but it stood against violence.

So turbulent were the 1960s there is no telling what would have happened to Hendrix had he not come to Britain. If he had stayed in the U.S. Air Force it is entirely possible that he might have been packed off to Vietnam, and that somebody else might have had to compose and perform "Machine Gun" for him, or rather in his memory. He *had* to dedicate the song to the grunts at the famous Fillmore East gig of 1970.

So let us push the pacifist sentiment of one of the greatest musical talents of the 20th century into a chorus for the unknown soldiers who would make war on war. Let us see and hear music as a weapon of peace. Let us jam the barrel of a rifle with an arsenal full of plectrums and break the bayonet with an amp. Let us imagine what Jimi might have whistled to himself if he had rolled his unwelcome draft papers into a reefer the size of a tank turret. Let us take the liberty of making the ballad prevail over the bullet.

Hey Joe, where you going with that gun in your hand?
Why you gonna shoot your old lady when you can sing her calypsos from another land?
Hey Joe, don't be no soldier, stay alive, brotherman.
Take that gun and make it a guitar with your own sweet hands.

Notes

1. See Cy Grant, *Blackness and the Dreaming Soul*, p. 15.
2. Andrew Roberts, *Eminent Churchillians* (Phoenix, 1995), p. 214.

26 INDEX